T0355185

THE CAUSES OF WAR AND THE SPREAD OF PEACE

THE CAUSES
OF WAR AND
THE SPREAD
OF PEACE

BUT WILL WAR REBOUND?

AZAR GAT

OXFORD
UNIVERSITY PRESS

OXFORD
UNIVERSITY PRESS

Great Clarendon Street, Oxford, OX2 6DP,
United Kingdom

Oxford University Press is a department of the University of Oxford.
It furthers the University's objective of excellence in research, scholarship,
and education by publishing worldwide. Oxford is a registered trade mark of
Oxford University Press in the UK and in certain other countries

Published in the United States of America by Oxford University Press
198 Madison Avenue, New York, NY 10016, United States of America

British Library Cataloguing in Publication Data

Data available

Library of Congress Control Number: 2016956899

ISBN 978-0-19-879502-5

Printed in Great Britain by
Clays Ltd, St Ives plc

Links to third party websites are provided by Oxford in good faith and
for information only. Oxford disclaims any responsibility for the materials
contained in any third party website referenced in this work.

Preface

Why War? The Unsolved Mystery

The causes of war—why people fight—is one of the big questions of human existence. The subject of much speculation and consternation throughout the ages, it remains a puzzle. Two contrasting views of war have always manifested themselves. On the one hand, war is perceived in utilitarian terms as a rational means for the attainment of desired ends—a continuation of state policy by other means, as theorist of war Carl von Clausewitz (1780–1831) famously put it. At the emotional level, people throughout history have celebrated war and sung the praises of its heroes and heroism. On the other hand, and with the same intensity, people have lamented war as a scourge from heaven wreaked upon a hapless humanity, along and often in conjunction with pestilence and famine. According to this view, war is a wholly senseless activity whose lethality, destructiveness, and resulting misery outweigh any potential benefit to either of the sides involved. War as an absurdity, a mistake, or 'prisoner's dilemma' tragedy has become a widespread notion in today's modern developed world. Which of these two contrasting views is correct, and can they be reconciled? In explaining why people fight one needs to account for both.

Another salient difficulty with the question of why people fight is that it is widely regarded as inherently unanswerable, because the causes of war are assumed to be too varied or context-/culture-dependent. Although we tend to have a generally good intuitive idea of the aims that motivate collectives to go to war, an attempt at forming a stricter definition of them is believed to be futile. Historians, in particular, whose job it is to bring out the unique specifics and rich diversity of the particular societies they happen to study, are inclined to hold this view. By contrast, students of international relations are oriented towards the general; and yet the discipline's yield on the causes of war is poor.[1] Furthermore, what are regarded as the grand theories of international relations have either addressed the causes of war only obliquely or, as we shall see, have espoused manifestly incomplete or incoherent explanations for them. As a review of the literature on the causes of war has concluded: 'a clear answer is yet to be found'.[2] Finally, while Steven Pinker's study of the decrease of violence in history, *The Better Angels of Our Nature: Why Violence Has Declined* (2011), is superb, some of the few reservations I have about it concern its treatment of the causes of violence and war. And the questions of why war occurs and why it has declined—if it has—are intimately connected.

In my *War in Human Civilization* (2006) I advanced a comprehensive answer to the question of why people fight. However, that book was an 800-page, multifaceted treatment of the phenomenon of war, in which the causes of war were only one among many topics.[3] Given the subject's great significance, there seems to be a need for a shorter book dedicated entirely to the causes of war and explaining why peace has become the norm in the most developed parts of today's world. Proceeding from what I wrote in *War in Human Civilization*, this book brings the subject into sharper focus, condensing some of my arguments there, while developing, updating, and expanding on some of the major themes. Like its predecessor, the book cheerfully breaks through disciplinary boundaries. Instead of the disparate, closed-onto-themselves and, as suggested here, often contrived discourses on the causes of war found in disciplines such as anthropology and international relations, the book combines the wealth of evidence and many valid insights from these disciplines, as well as from other social sciences, history, and evolutionary theory, to offer a general answer to a lingering mystery. At the same time, I have striven to keep the book as free as possible from academic jargon and make it accessible to the general public, no less than to scholars and students.

The book progresses as follows. Chapter 1 sets out to resolve a centuries-old puzzle: when did human fighting begin—have people always fought among themselves, or did warfare emerge only later in human history? The chapter refutes the last-ditch attempts—made over the past fifteen years—to salvage the latter position, known as Rousseauism. Chapters 2 and 3 summarize my evolutionary scheme of the human web of desires in relation to the causes of war. Chapter 2 explains the root causes of war during the human evolutionary state of nature, the more than 90 per cent of our species' history that took place before the adoption of agriculture and the emergence of states. It was during this immensely long time period, when people lived in small kin groups as hunter-gatherers, that our natural propensities and system of desires were shaped, with violent conflict as one of the means for achieving them, alongside cooperation and peaceful competition. Chapter 3 traces the multifarious ways in which our deep evolutionary core inter-acted with the rich and diverse human cultural evolution built around it in shaping the causes of war since the adoption of agriculture and the rise of state societies.

Chapters 4 and 5 pause to offer a critical panoramic review of the historical development of, state of research in, and problems that beset the disciplines of anthropology and international relations (which study the pre-state and state era, respectively) with regards to conflict, war, and their causes. This part opens a prism, and provides a sobering lesson, on how dominant dis-ciplinary discourses are formed, often become overbearing, and may lead the members of scholarly communities astray.

Returning to the real world, Chapters 6 and 7, together constituting nearly half of the book, greatly expand my analysis of the forces and counter-forces behind the decline of war during the past two centuries, and probe more extensively into the future. Chapter 6 analyses how developments since the onset of the industrial age from 1815 onwards have radically shifted the cal-culus of war and peace as means for fulfilling desired human ends, sharply decreasing belligerency in the parts of the world affected by the process of modernization. Rather than war becoming more costly in terms of life and resources, as many believe to be the case (not so), the real change is that peace has become more rewarding. Scholars who have suggested that there has been a decline in belligerency differ on the causes, scope, and time frame of this decline. The Modernization Peace concept presented here scrutin-izes, contextualizes, and encompasses within a comprehensive framework the various peace theories advanced over the past few decades, such as the 'democratic' or 'liberal peace' and the 'interdependence/capitalist peace'. Finally, Chapter 7 accounts for the divergences from the Modernization Peace, most conspicuously the two world wars. It shows that although the Modernization Peace is a very real development, it has been disrupted in the past—and may still be challenged in the future—by projections of 'alternative modernity', by anti-modernists, and by failed modernizers, all of which are still active in today's world. While the world has become more peaceful than ever before, with war unprecedentedly disappearing in its most developed parts, there is still much to worry about in terms of security and there is no place for complacency.

Acknowledgements

A s always, I owe a debt to friends and colleagues who read parts of the manuscript and offered much valuable advice. They include: Uriel Abulof, Peter Berkowitz, Nizan Feldman, Amir Lupovici, Yotam Margalit, Gil Merom, Benjamin Miller, Yossi Shain, and Alexander Yakobson. Anonymous article reviewers have driven me to expand and deepen. The following journals published early versions of some themes from the book: *Anthropological Quarterly*, *World Politics*, *Foreign Affairs*, *European Journal of International Relations*, *Journal of Peace Studies*, and *Evolutionary Anthropology*. The research and writing of the book have been generously supported by the Axel and Margaret Axson Johnson Foundation, by the Israel Science Foundation (grant 1258/13), and by Tel Aviv University. I thank them all.

Contents

Illustrations, Diagrams, Maps, and Tables

Maps

Tables

Past Imperfect
Prehistory and History

I

When Did It All Begin?

Before addressing the question of why people fight, there is a no less fundamental and stubborn riddle to solve. Was human fighting always there: is it as old as our species? Or is it a late cultural invention, emerging after the adoption of agriculture and the rise of the state? These later developments began only around 10,000 and 5,000 years ago, respectively, and took a long time to spread across the globe. In the now advanced societies of northern Europe and Japan, for example, states emerged only about 1,500 years ago. Viewed against the lifespan of our species *Homo sapiens*, stretching back 150,000–200,000 years, let alone the roughly two million years of our genus *Homo*, this is just the tip of the iceberg.

The two conflicting answers to the question of the genesis of war were formulated by Thomas Hobbes in the seventeenth century and by Jean-Jacques Rousseau in the eighteenth. For Hobbes in his *Leviathan* (1651), the pre-state condition was characterized by a 'warre' of every man against every man, when in the absence of a peace-enforcing authority life was 'poore, nasty, brutish, and short'. By contrast, according to Rousseau's *Discourse on the Origins and Foundation of Inequality among Mankind* (1755), the aboriginal condition of humans was fundamentally peaceful and innocent. In the absence of private property before agriculture, there was little to fight about. War, according to Rousseau, is a late development, one of the ills of civilization. So persuasive have each of these two positions appeared to be that they have continued to reverberate throughout the centuries, with their popularity changing with the *Zeitgeist*: the nineteenth century was dominated by the Hobbesian image of the savage and the brute, whereas the twentieth century, with its critique of civilization, was predominantly Rousseauian.

Still, who was right, Hobbes or Rousseau? For political philosophers the question barely exists at all. They usually claim that Hobbes and Rousseau postulated the state of nature as a hypothetical thought experiment, and leave it at that. However, this is not an entirely accurate description of the two thinkers' view—and, in any case, irrespective of how they saw it, the question of aboriginal fighting, or its absence, is unquestionably historical and empirical.

We now have a temporal frame and plenty of empirical evidence for the state of nature that Hobbes and Rousseau discussed in the abstract. All human populations until about 10,000 years ago were hunter-gatherers— also known as foragers. Just before and after that date there was a transition in some places to more sedentary and denser populations of foragers-fishers and foragers-horticulturalists that later led to full-scale agriculture. Excavating prehistory, archaeology is thus the first discipline to look to for answers to the question of aboriginal human fighting (or lack thereof), and yet the light it can shed is limited. There are several reasons for this. Weapons for fighting before the introduction of metals from about 5,000 years ago are practically indistinguishable from hunting implements: stone axes, spears, and arrows. Whether these were used for hunting only or were dual-purposed and employed also for fighting is difficult to determine. Specialized fighting equipment such as shields are made of perishable material—wood and leather—and do not survive. The difficulties increase enormously as we go further back in time, to the Old Stone Age, or Palaeolithic, before sedentism and agriculture—the more than 90 per cent of *Homo sapiens*' history when the world was inhabited solely by hunter-gatherers. Apart from a few exceptionally lush environments, hunter-gatherers needed to move around to subsist and lived in shifting campsites. Therefore, evidence of fortifications or violent destruction, as often found in sedentary settlements after the transition to agriculture, scarcely exists for earlier times. The same applies to marks of violent death on human skeletons. Skeleton remains only become plentiful during the past 10,000 years, after people began to live in sedentary settlements and buried their dead in permanent cemeteries, a treasure trove for archaeologists. Human skeleton remains from earlier times are remarkably scarce and often consist of only a few badly preserved bones. In addition, violent death is often caused by injuries to soft tissues that are undetectable to archaeology. Notably, we have no direct archaeological evidence for human copulation either during the Palaeolithic, though logic suggests that it was there. But humour aside, the archaeological evidence alone makes an unambiguous verdict regarding man-inflicted violent death during the vast majority of humans' time on earth very hard to reach.

Biology has played a significant role in shaping perspectives about human fighting. During the 1960s, the pioneering student of animal behaviour, Nobel laureate Konrad Lorenz, claimed that fighting between animals of the same species is mostly 'ritualistic' and mainly involves display. The loser retreats or submits, while the victor refrains from pressing its advantage to the finish. According to Lorenz, the reason for this pattern of behaviour was the need to preserve the species.[1] It thus appeared that humans, who fight to kill their own kind, are a horrific deviation from the normal pattern in nature. Two distinct notions emerged to account for this alleged human abnormality. There was the notion of the 'killer ape', a murderous perversion that occurred during the early evolution of mankind and distinguished us from the rest of the animal kingdom, where species supposedly 'do not kill their own kind'. This notion was popularized in bestselling books of the 1960s and in Hollywood's *Planet of the Apes* and *2001: A Space Odyssey* (both released in 1968). Conversely, there was the view that fighting, rather than aboriginal to man, was a late 'cultural invention' that emerged only during the last few millennia. This view sat well with the Rousseauian doctrines of the 1960s regarding nature's purity and the corruption of civilization.

As it happens, biological science has made a complete turnaround since the 1970s. Innumerable field studies have revealed that lethal violent competition within species in nature is endemic and widespread. This also includes our closest cousins, the chimpanzees, studied in their natural habitats and documented to engage in intra-group killing, as well as in inter-group fighting and killing to the point of group extermination.[2] It is true that adult male animals usually avoid a fight to the finish among themselves for reasons of self-preservation—any serious injury might render an animal incapable of getting food and result in starvation. There is no social security in nature. Yet when deterrence by the display and demonstration of force fails, serious fighting, injuries, and death often follow. Furthermore, most killing within species is carried out against the young and the weak, including eggs, chicks, and cubs. Additionally, among social animals (like the chimpanzees), killing mostly takes place when the attackers are able to isolate individuals or small groups from a neighbouring band and so enjoy overwhelming numerical superiority. Either way, killing is performed with relative safety for the killer(s)—is carried out asymmetrically. No benevolence towards one's kind exists.

Indeed, since the 1960s it has been widely recognized that natural selection mostly takes place within species, rather than between them. As

Darwin himself argued, the struggle among individuals from the same species is the most intense, because they compete for the same sorts of food and for the same mates, in the very same ecological niches. As scenes of deadly violence within species have become one of the highlights of television nature documentaries, I am sure most readers are quite familiar with the evidence: lions killing the cubs of the former monarch of the pride; chicks in a nest pecking their siblings to death when there is a food shortage; birds throwing the eggs of other birds of their kind from nests; and so on. Thus, the 1960s' commonplace and troubling puzzle has all but evaporated. Humans are no longer held to be unique in nature in extensively killing their own kind and so do not call for some special explanation. Widespread killing within the species is very much the norm in nature.[3]

This complete turnabout in biological science has not entirely resolved the issue of human violence, as the scale and form of killing in nature is not uniform among all species. These depend on each species' particular mode of adaptation, especially its forms of subsistence and mating. Most pertinent with respect to human violence, while the common chimpanzee (*Pan troglodytes*) has been found to be very violent, the pygmy chimpanzee or bonobo (*Pan paniscus*) exhibits a semi-idyllic life of free sex and far less violence, much as in the 1960s perceptions of the common chimpanzee.[4] Physical aggression, mostly by groups of females against males, exists among the bonobo, and can be fierce and end in serious injury, but no actual killing has been recorded. Noticeably, the common chimpanzees, with their dominant aggressive male coalitions, resemble the known patterns of aboriginal human social life far more than the bonobos, who are dominated by female alliances. Nonetheless, the bonobo has kept alive the question of what our human ancestors in the state of nature were like.

The discipline that is richest in relevant information for answering this question is anthropology, which studies pre-state and pre-agricultural societies that survived until recently or still survive in remote corners of the world. And yet access to, and interpretation of, that information has been intrinsically problematic. The main problem has been the so-called 'contact paradox'. Hunter-gatherers have no written records of their own, and therefore documenting them requires contact with literate state societies—and this contact necessarily affects the former. As in quantum mechanics, the very activity of observation changes the object under observation. Agricultural and state societies have goods—such as farm products, livestock, and manufactured tools—which hunter-gatherers might want to steal, for example. How can it be determined that a warlike behaviour on their part did not originate only with contact but had existed before? How can one observe pure hunter-gatherer societies that are free from contact with agriculturalists and states? This is like the light in a refrigerator: how can we establish if it really turns off when the door is closed?

As hunter-gatherer societies had been fast disappearing into the fold of civilization by the middle of the twentieth century, research since the 1950s has mainly focused on sparse surviving populations such as those in the savannahs and deserts of East and Southern Africa, and some other particularly isolated and marginal populations. Only a few within the discipline have called attention to the resulting distortion of perspective.[5] The hunter-gatherers of East Africa and the Kalahari were unrepresentative in the sense that before the advent and spread of agriculture, hunter-gatherers did not only inhabit arid marginal land that agricultural and pastoralist societies were unable to use and did not want, as today; rather, they also—in fact mainly—lived in the world's most fertile environments. In such environments hunter-gatherers had denser populations, which resulted in greater contact and more intense competition among their groups. In addition, the hunter-gatherers of East and Southern Africa interacted for more than a thousand years with their agricultural and pastoralist neighbours. Furthermore, during the twentieth century they were increasingly subjected to the pacifying intrusions of state authorities and police.

Classical Rousseauism and Extended Rousseauism: Their Rise and Fall

The focus on the hunter-gatherers of East and Southern Africa coincided with the rise of Rousseauism in both anthropology and popular culture by the 1960s. The Kalahari Bushmen, for example, were celebrated as the 'harmless people'.[6] Their chief researcher, anthropologist Richard Lee, propagated this view, which conformed to his Marxist concept of 'primitive communism' and to the new catchphrase in reference to the foragers, 'the original affluent society'. However, after the initial spate of enthusiasm for the peaceful children of the earth, Lee himself discovered that before the imposition of state authority, these people had more than four times the 1990 US homicide rate, which was itself by far the highest in the developed world.[7] Similarly, the Inuit of mid-Arctic Canada, one of the sparsest populations on earth, were celebrated as peaceful in titles such as *Never in Anger*. Yet it was later revealed that their violent mortality was ten times higher than the United States' 1990 rate.[8]

These finds constituted a potentially fatal challenge to what we shall call Classical Rousseauism, the view that human existence was fundamentally non-violent before the adoption of sedentary and denser habitation, transition to agriculture, and development of more complex social and political structures. However, before the full significance of the challenge to Classical Rousseauism had sunk in, a more radical Rousseauian view, which we shall term Extended Rousseauism, came into vogue in the 1980s and early 1990s. According to this view, serious fighting began at an even later stage, really taking off only with the emergence of states.

Extended Rousseauism was associated with the so-called 'tribal zone' theory.[9] Proponents of the theory claimed that it was only after contact with and in response to intrusive states—their goods, military forces, and settlers—that tribal structures sprang up and competition and warfare between them rocketed, most notably in parts of the world affected by European exploration and expansion, but also earlier in history.[10] This argument was applied to the great microcosms of pre-state hunter-gatherers and horticulturalists that survived until the nineteenth and twentieth centuries, or still survive, in the American Northwest, Central America, Amazonia, and Highland New Guinea. Each of these areas extended over a huge territory and comprised hundreds of tribes and separate languages. In all of them people fought ferociously among themselves during and after contact. The proponents of the 'tribal zone' theory remained vague on whether contact with state societies actually introduced—'invented'— warfare among previously peaceful indigenous peoples, or merely intensified long existing patterns of warfare. The former was strongly implied, and was the undertone or subtext of their whole argument. At the same time, however, the majority of these scholars, in agreement with all other research, in fact recognized that warfare in all these areas was very old and long predated contact with states.[11]

Fortified settlements were known to have been archaeologically recorded in the American Northwest, for example, from at least four thousand years ago.[12] Body armour made of hide or wood, an unmistakably specialized fighting device, was known to have been extensively used by the indigenous people in many places before the European arrival, and its usage actually *declined* after contact as it was rendered useless by musket fire.[13] Similarly, the

European Neolithic, the millennia of prehistoric, pre-state agricultural-tribal settlement, offers abundant archaeological evidence of warfare.[14] All in all, although tribal bonds tightened and tribal conglomerations grew in size in response to outside pressures and challenges, most notably from states, inter-*tribal* conflict had been widespread, galvanizing tribal identity and solidarity.[15] Given that most of the 'tribal zone' proponents were well aware of the evidence for extensive and vicious warfare before contact with state societies, their point, or what remains of it, is very difficult to rationalize.

The 'tribal zone' theory's brief moment ended with the publication of Lawrence Keeley's *War before Civilization: The Myth of the Peaceful Savage* (1996), which was a game changer in many ways. Calling attention to the Rousseauian bias in the research, Keeley amassed a great deal of archaeological and ethnographic evidence for deadly violence, warfare, and very high killing rates among pre-state societies. Other wide-ranging studies, largely reviewing different cases from those covered by Keeley, arrived at remarkably similar conclusions.[16] They all found widespread violence and warfare among both hunter-gatherers and pre-state horticulturalists, which resulted in exceedingly high rates of violent deaths. Readers interested in the wealth of anthropological evidence on the subject from across the world are invited to consult these studies. As with Lorenz's 'ritualistic' fighting among animals, anthropologists were long misled by what they termed the 'ritualistic battle' into believing that pre-state fighting was not serious. Indeed, in battle the sides normally kept their distance from each other, hurling missiles, and casualties were few. However, as students of 'primitive warfare' have shown, it is not the open pitched battle but the raid and ambush—asymmetrical fighting—that universally constituted the principal and by far the most lethal form of warfare among pre-state societies. The surprise attack was the main form of fighting among prehistorical people because humans are quintessential 'first strike' creatures. Whereas animals have their 'weapons' on them, and are therefore difficult to surprise unarmed, people use tools as weapons and are almost defenceless if caught without them (Illustrations 1.1 and 1.2).[17]

The following are some examples of the high rates of killing recorded in such societies. We start with Amazonia (and the Orinoco basin). Among the Hiwi hunter-gatherers, 36 per cent of all pre-contact adult deaths were due to warfare and homicide. Among the Aché hunter-gatherers, about 55 per cent of all deaths were violent.[18] The Waorani (Auca) hunter-gatherers hold the registered world record: more than 60 per cent of adult deaths were caused

Illustration 1.1. A battle in Highland New Guinea

by feuding and warfare. Among the Yanomamo hunter-horticulturalists, about 15 per cent of the adults died as a result of inter- and intra-group violence: 24 per cent of the males and 7 per cent of the females. In Highland New Guinea violent mortality among the native hunter-horticulturalists was very similar: among the Dani, 28.5 per cent of the men and 2.4 per cent of the women; among the Enga, 34.8 per cent of the adult males; among the Goilala, whose total population was barely over 150, there were 29 killed (predominantly men) during a period of thirty-five years; among the Lowland Gebusi, 35.2 per cent of the adult males and 29.3 per cent of the adult females met violent deaths. The Plains Indians showed a deficit of 50 per cent for the adult males in the Blackfoot tribe in 1805 and a 33 per cent deficit in 1858, while during the reservation period, when warfare ceased, the sex ratio rapidly approached 50–50.[19] The societies of multi-island Polynesia—long the object of Rousseauian fantasies of social harmony, free love, and peace—have been revealed to have been rife with violence and warfare. According to a major study of eighteen of these societies, from the largest to the smallest, not one lacked endemic warfare: 'Warfare . . . was ubiquitous in Polynesia.'[20]

Finds might be inaccurate or otherwise questionable in any individual case, but as they are consistently repeated in one independent anthropological

Illustration 1.2. The Yanomamo of Amazonia: a raiding party assembling

case study after another, they form an unmistakable pattern. Indeed, the cited cases do not represent the peaks (or picks) in term of lethality, but are fairly representative of the norm. Around 25 per cent of the adult males in pre-state societies—about 15 per cent of the adult population as a whole—suffered a violent death, while all the rest of the men were covered with scars. This extremely high violent death rate encompassed all forms of killing, both within and between groups. Revealingly, it is on the same range as that registered within and between chimpanzee communities in the wild. Three separate studies of different chimpanzee communities have found their overall violent mortality rate to be: 20 per cent (24 per cent among the males); 36 per cent; 16 per cent.[21] Another comprehensive study of six chimpanzee populations sets the median number of violent deaths among them at 271 per 100,000 individuals per year, as compared with 164 per 100,000 per year which the authors calculate as the average among human hunter-gatherers.[22] Recall that the equivalent number for the United States during the peak violent decades of the 1970s and 1980s was ten violent deaths per 100,000 per year. Thus, average killing rates among hunter-gatherers have been revealed to be many, many times higher than those incurred in historical state societies, with only the pinnacles reached by the most lethal state wars coming anything close to the pre-state average. Steven Pinker's *The Better Angels of Our Nature: Why Violence has Declined* (2011) has drawn wider public attention to these finds.

Keeley, an archaeologist, called on other archaeologists to turn their attention to and refine their methods in approaching the hitherto neglected signs of prehistoric warfare. During the following two decades archaeological studies of warfare, particularly among the more sedentary communities of pre-state foragers and horticulturalists that proliferated during the past 10,000 years, have increased substantially. These studies have extensively documented unmistakable indications of violence and warfare, such as the prevalence of palisades around settlements; other defensive indications in settlements' nucleation, protected location, and spacing out with 'no-man's-land' between them; and widespread traces of violent trauma to crania and forearms, known as 'parrying fractures'.

The skeletal evidence that has accumulated since I researched *War in Human Civilization* is particularly striking. Broad surveys of the North American evidence reveal that while rates of violent trauma varied considerably from place to place, they were exceedingly high in some areas and very high on average.[23] Among the prehistoric hunter-gatherers of coastal Southern California, for example, traces of healed cranial vault fractures range from 15 to nearly 40 per cent among males and around 10 to 20 per cent among females. These rates are even higher when children of both sexes are factored out. The percentage for males from the earliest period in the sample (6630–4050 BC) is close to 20 per cent (again higher if only adults are counted). Traces of projectile injuries in the skeleton range from around 3 per cent to over 20 per cent of the males and up to 10 per cent among females.[24] Other studies of California and the West have found that cranial injuries, including marks of scalp trophies, were highest during the earliest periods they surveyed, from 3050 BC on, and actually decreased during later periods, when sedentism grew.[25] Similarly, in British Columbia, as in some other sites of the American Northwest (a prime case of the 'tribal zone' theory), in the period 3500–1500 BC violent skeletal trauma is evident in

21 per cent of fifty-seven observable individuals.[26] This is as high as the rate of violent trauma recorded for the subsequent period, between 1500 BC and 500 CE, when the region's population became denser and clustered into large villages.[27] All this suggests that increasing density and social complexity were not the factors that initiated human fighting.

Indeed, the earliest human settlement in the New World comprised of mobile, non-sedentary hunter-gatherers and was very thinly dispersed. Still, as archaeologist Philip Walker writes: 'Bones bearing cutmarks inflicted by other humans are surprisingly common considering the paucity of early hominid remains.' The 'earliest immigrants to the New World...lived at low densities and had ample opportunity to avoid violence by moving away from it but apparently were unable to do so'.[28] Walker summarizes the evidence from a number of studies:

> The 9000-year-old Kennewick find, one of the earliest Native American skeletons, has a large leaf-shaped projectile point, probably propelled by a spear thrower, healed into the bone of his pelvis as well as a small, well-healed cranial fracture...Similar injuries, including embedded points and cranial injuries, have been found in other early Native American remains.[29]

Walker concludes: 'The search for an earlier, less-violent way to organize our social affairs has been fruitless. All the evidence suggests that peaceful periods have always been punctuated by episodes of warfare and violence.'[30]

Another recent study of the skeleton remains of the sparse populations of Paleoamericans, between the earliest identifiable arrivals and approximately 9,000 years before the present (calibrated), identifies violent injuries in 58 per cent of the males and 18 per cent of the females. This is about double the rates cited earlier for many parts of later and more densely populated periods of prehistoric North America.[31]

The evidence from a comprehensive study of the Andes reveals a similar picture and similarly high rates of injuries from the earliest settlement. The cranial trauma frequencies studied varied significantly during the millennia from early human habitation to the rise of states and of the Inca Empire. Nonetheless, the average rate for the Archaic period, well before the coming of states, is around the average for the entire period and just under 15 per cent for cranial trauma alone, and it is skewed towards the adult male population.[32] A study of the Natufians of the southern Levant, in today's Israel, the world's first known semi-sedentary/sedentary hunters and collectors of wild wheat (fourteenth to tenth millennia BC), has found that 16.7 per cent of the adult males and 20 per cent of adult women had healed cranial injuries.[33] All these very high rates of injury are all the more remarkable when considering that signs of skeletal trauma remain undetected in many cases; injuries to soft tissues, including fatal injuries, are not preserved; and that men killed in raids and battles away from home often do not find their way back to village cemeteries that are archaeologists' main source of information.*

The emerging archaeological evidence of extensive violence and belligerency among pre-state hunter-gatherers and horticulturalists over the past ten millennia (earlier with respect to the Natufians) has been particularly devastating for the Extended Rousseauian 'tribal zone' theory. As Brian Ferguson, the theory's most active exponent, conceded in his contribution to the edited volume that incorporated the initial finds in this wave of research: 'If there are *people out there* [sic! my emphasis] who believe that violence and war did not exist until after the advent of Western colonialism, or of the state, or of agriculture, this volume proves them wrong.' Ferguson attempted to redress the balance in his next sentence: 'Equally, if there are people who believe that all human societies have been plagued by violence and war, that they were always present in human evolutionary history, this volume proves *them* wrong.'[34] However, the various claims in the second proposition were anything but 'proved'. At best, they remained *unproved* and open to further investigation.

In time, Ferguson would attempt to salvage parts of his 'tribal zone' theory, an attempt which, as I have shown elsewhere, remains deeply flawed.[35] He also foreshadowed a new stance in the Rousseauian position, which I shall call Quasi-Rousseauism.[36] Indeed, the focus of the debate has shifted markedly. The very high killing rates that were documented—originally by Rousseauian anthropologists—among even the most thinly dispersed hunter-gatherers, who possessed little if any property, have debunked what we have called Classical Rousseauism which postulated a non-violent primordial past. Archaeology has then helped to refute the Extended Rousseauian

---

* A recent study, José María Gómez, Miguel Verdú, and Adela González-Megías, 'The Phylogenetic Roots of Human Lethal Violence', *Nature*, 538 (Oct. 2016), 233–7, surveying hundreds of mammalian species, has confirmed that intraspecific killing is part of our prehistorical, and indeed genetic, inheritance. However, the study estimates the human killing rate at about 2 per cent. Given the evidence we have seen and are yet to see in this chapter, I believe this is a gross underestimation, mostly attributed to the factors mentioned in the paragraph above. Indeed, in the article the authors admit that the evidence on the distant past of our species, derived from archaeology, reveals less killing than that shown by anthropology for historically known hunter-gatherers. They seem to agree that there may be a serious bias here also in my communication with them.

claim that deadly violence and warfare were non-existent, rare, or at least very infrequent among the denser and more stratified populations of settled foragers, horticulturalists, and agriculturalists that proliferated from around 10,000 years ago onward. It made untenable the claim that violence and warfare only flared up after contact with states. However, in response to these developments, the Rousseauian position has been adjusted and reformulated, taking a form that I have labelled Quasi-Rousseauism. At variance with Classical Rousseauism, Quasi-Rousseauians explicitly or implicitly acknowledged the high violent death rates ethnographically documented among simple, mobile hunter-gatherers. Yet they claim that these high rates of killings resulted from individual and private conflicts. They argue that such killings should be categorized as 'homicide' and 'feuds' rather than 'warfare', which is collective inter-group fighting. By this definition, the simple, mobile hunter-gatherers that populated the vast time span of our ancestral past, during the Palaeolithic—more than 90 per cent of human existence on earth—allegedly lacked warfare, which only emerged much more recently in human development. Taking centre stage since the turn of the twenty-first century, and constituting the most recent—perhaps the last—Rousseauian line of defence, Quasi-Rousseauism requires close examination.

Quasi-Rousseauism: Claims and Concepts

In his *Warless Societies and the Origin of War* (2000) anthropologist Raymond Kelly fully accepts that, as the ethnographic record reveals, hunter-gatherers experienced exceedingly high rates of killings, far higher than those incurred in later state societies. In this he effectively breaks with the standard Rousseauian tradition, which, as he writes, has tended to have a naïve view of a serene and violence-free aboriginal human past.[37] At the same time, analysing the evidence, Kelly argues that the less organized, less clustered around clan and tribe, less 'segmented' in anthropological parlance, a hunter-gatherer community was, the less it experienced collective, inter-group 'warfare', as distinguished from 'homicide' and 'feuds' that did not involve the entire community on either side. Kelly's analysis suggests that the absence of 'segmentism' correlates with, among other things, the mobility and low population density of simple hunter-gatherers. As our Palaeolithic ancestors overwhelmingly were such simple hunter-gatherers, Kelly concludes that although homicide and feuds were probably rife among them, warfare as such seems to have developed only after that time. More or less the same view has been adopted by anthropologist Douglas Fry.[38] A champion for the cause of world peace, Fry, unlike Kelly, systematically avoids any specific mention of the fact that killing rates among hunter-gatherers were on average very high. However, he tacitly accepts this, while claiming that these killings fell under the categories of homicide and feuds rather than warfare.

Note that the framing of aboriginal human violence by the Quasi-Rousseauians is very different from either Hobbes's or Rousseau's. Hobbes's 'warre' encompasses *all* forms of human deadly violence, including 'homicide' and 'feuds', which made the human state of nature so insecure and lethal. Similarly, Rousseau's peaceful aboriginal condition, presupposing minimal human sociability and interaction, was ostensibly free from *all* forms of human violence. Thus, both Hobbes's and Rousseau's understanding of belligerence and peacefulness are very close to that employed in the anthropological surveys and statistics of aboriginal human deadly violence that Kelly and Fry criticize for conceptual fuzziness.[39] Both Hobbes and Rousseau referred to all human-caused lethality, which Hobbes thought was very common whereas Rousseau believed that it scarcely existed. This is why I refer to claims such as those made by Ferguson, Kelly, and Fry as Quasi-Rousseauism. These claims *sound* very significant with respect to aboriginal human violence. But they actually hang on a thin thread of definitions (whose empirical basis, as we shall see, is itself unfounded),[40] while turning the spotlights away from the question of hunter-gatherers' violent mortality rates—which is the most significant question in the debate regarding the aboriginal human condition, whether it was violent or not. Quasi-Rousseauism is incompatible with Classical Rousseauism and portrays a very different picture of deadly human violence in our aboriginal past. It represents a major—unacknowledged and unrecognized—change in the Rousseauian position. The centuries-old debate appears to have been discarded at a stroke, without anybody admitting or even realizing it.

The distinction between homicide, feuds, and warfare involves both semantic and substantive questions. On the semantic side, one should avoid reification: the fallacy of treating a particular historically shaped reality as an abstract and universal concept. The difference between homicide, feuds, and warfare sounds fundamental, natural, and significant to us as citizens of orderly state societies. However, it is largely a product of the later reality constructed by states, with the sharp, historically embedded contrast they have created between internal peace, sporadically interrupted by homicide and feuds, and external, large-scale war. A huge conceptual and practical gap now separates homicide and feuds, on the one hand, and warfare on the other. Yet this was not the case in pre-state societies.

Indeed, native linguistic usage was different from the state-era dichotomy between 'homicide' or 'feud' and 'war'. For example, the root of the English word war, *werra*, is Old Frankish-German, going back to their tribal, pre-state past and meaning confusion, discord, or strife—in effect Hobbes's 'warre'.[41] Similarly, as the founding father of American academic anthropology at the beginning of the twentieth century, Franz Boas, wrote: among the eastern, Great Plains, and Northwest American Indians (whom he studied first-hand), 'the term "war" includes not only fights between tribes or clans but also deeds of individuals who set out to kill a member or members of another group'.[42] Note that in addition to the native terminology which he describes, Boas accepts the reality of large-scale inter-tribal fighting as a matter of course.

This brings us to the residual *substantive* question that Quasi-Rousseauians raise: whether or not, in addition to extensive and highly lethal 'homicides' and 'feuds', *group* 'warfare' existed among simple, mobile hunter-gatherers and, by extension, throughout the vast expanses of human prehistory. But before turning to the reality, one more semantic obstacle has to be set aside. Any definition of warfare that postulates the existence of large-scale, politically organized communities, let alone regular armies, command structure etc., *ipso facto* excludes simple hunter-gatherers and is in this respect tautological. Simple hunter-gatherers lived in small-scale and relatively egalitarian groups that numbered around fifty people of several generations or perhaps a dozen man-warriors in the local family groups, and about 500 people or several scores of man-warriors in the regional group or tribe. The only question that is relevant to the debate is whether or not the people in these groups cooperated in communal inter-group fighting. The definition of warfare that Marilyn Roper adopted in a pioneering study of prehistoric warfare: 'sanctioned violence, including killing, of one group against another',[43] agrees in this respect with that of a Rousseauian like Jonathan Haas: 'inter-group armed conflict, often with lethal force'.[44] It is the existence of warfare defined in this way—a definition that Quasi-Rousseauians accept[45]—that is the issue at stake.

We begin with some general comments. The idea—first suggested by celebrity anthropologist Margaret Mead[46]—that individual killing was a primordial feature of human societies, while group fighting was not, makes no sense. People are a social species, and habitually practise many forms of cooperation among group members. A recent model has demonstrated how conditions of small group solidarity and inter-group fighting were likely to bring a strong evolutionary advantage during the Palaeolithic era.[47] Moreover, Fry refers to hunter-gatherer groups as bands, which is a common anthropological term. This term gives the impression of a random collection of people. In actuality, the hunter-gatherer band was a kin group, criss-crossed by kin ties and marriage alliances.[48] The people in these groups exhibited family devotion and solidarity among themselves and against outsiders. In acts of aggression, a man, while sometimes acting alone, just as often called for help from his father, sons, brothers, uncles, cousins, and in-laws, as well as from close friends. Occasionally, fighting took a wider form, engulfing much of the tribal manhood. Inter-group fighting occurred at *all* levels—that of the individual, small group of closely related men, and larger tribal groupings.

Kin solidarity in relatively small, kin-based societies undermines the logic of another widespread Rousseauian claim: that while intra-group killing may have occurred among hunter-gatherers, inter-group fighting and killing were unknown or scarcely took place.[49] As Christopher Boehm's extensive survey of simple, mobile hunter-gatherer societies concludes, deadly fighting was more common, and conflict resolution less deeply embedded and less effective, between than within groups.[50] The simple and pretty obvious reality was that violence within communities was more constrained and more regulated, whereas different communities were both alien to each other and less well equipped with mechanisms of mediation and conflict resolution. To be sure, such mechanisms were often also employed between groups to resolve individual or inter-communal grievances, including the agreed punishment of a member of one community who had committed an offence against a member or members of the other community. In many cases, however, group members defended their own people, or they fought other groups over issues in dispute that were more collective in nature and unresolved. Notably, most killing among chimpanzees is also documented to take place between rather than within groups.[51]

This finally brings us back to the empirical ethnographic evidence. Keeley, dissecting the Extended Rousseauian claim, mainly concentrated on horticulturalists as well as on the more sedentary and economically and socially more complex hunter-gatherers that proliferated during the past ten millennia. He has been so effective in this that the battleground has shifted to the earlier, temporally much longer, and more fundamental domain of simple, mobile hunter-gatherers. As mentioned previously, archaeology is at present unable to settle the question of human fighting in the more distant past that encompasses more than 90 per cent of human history. There is evidence of violent skeletal trauma, including cannibalism, among both Neanderthals and *Homo sapiens* during the Palaeolithic. However, the paucity and poor condition of that evidence make the scope and exact nature of the violence difficult to determine.[52] Our most promising resource for unlocking the mystery is anthropological observations of extant and recently extinct simple, mobile hunter-gatherers. Kelly ostensibly grounds his argument about them in a carefully crafted analysis of the ethnographic record. However, by far the best and clearest evidence we have, that from Aboriginal Australia, reveals communal as well as individual and inter-familial violent conflicts, documented across the whole range of group densities and organization, and in every ecological niche, from the lushest to the most barren. Exchange and other forms of peaceful interaction were also very common in Australia, as elsewhere. Both hostile and peaceful relations existed and interchanged. All the same, the Aboriginal tribal groups generally suspected and feared their neighbours, because violence was always a distinct possibility and occasionally erupted. Trespassing territorial group boundaries risked death.

In earlier works I have singled out Australia as the indispensable key to overcoming the contact paradox and as particularly significant for the study of simple, mobile hunter-gatherers.[53] A recently published edited book, *Violence and Warfare among Hunter-Gatherers* (2014), focuses on simple, mobile hunter-gatherers as the ultimate subject of contention. It draws on a rich variety of ethnographic and archaeological studies of simple hunter-gatherer populations, most of them documented to have engaged in group fighting. Critics may argue that the majority of these populations were 'contaminated' by contact, as they neighboured for centuries or even millennia on horticultural/agricultural societies. However, the book also includes two chapters on Australia, whose conclusions are similar to mine. What is still missing in the scholarly discourse is a full realization of how crucial Australia is to our subject and how qualitatively incomparable it is to any other ethnographic 'case'.

Australia was an entire continent of Aboriginal hunter-gatherers—with no agriculturalists, pastoralists, or states—whose isolation came to an end only as late as 1788, with the arrival of the British. People reached Australia some 50,000 years ago, shortly after our species first left Africa, and the Australian Aborigines remained practically out of touch with other human populations and cultural developments elsewhere around the world. They did not even have the bow, invented some 20,000 years ago and assumed by some scholars to have enhanced, or even inaugurated, warfare. Thus, isolated both genetically and culturally and home to about 300 tribal groups when the Europeans arrived, Aboriginal Australia is the closest to a pure, uncontaminated laboratory of hunter-gatherer communities on a continental scale that we are ever going to get. There is nothing else even remotely equivalent in the whole world. I came across the Australian dream laboratory in my search for evidence, and found in every decent university library shelf upon shelf containing numerous volumes of field research carried out by early explorers and anthropologists among the Aboriginal tribes during the nineteenth and early twentieth centuries. And yet, although the rich Australian evidence was widely familiar at the time to anthropologists throughout the world, it has been strangely forgotten in, and has largely disappeared from, anthropological discourse from the 1960s onwards, as more recent fieldwork, particularly in East and Southern Africa, drew the discipline's attention away.

Anthropology's indispensable emphasis on field research, which, of course, is the only means for generating genuine empirical evidence on pre-state societies, turned out to have had some unfortunate consequences. It resulted in a kind of collective amnesia, a loss of disciplinary memory. Only the hot new stuff from recent field studies now counted in shaping perceptions of hunter-gatherer societies. Neither disputed nor rejected, it was as if the evidence from Australia never existed or was not the most vital and irreplaceable information we are ever likely to get. Unreflectively, the discipline moved on.

Fry is quite exceptional in devoting an entire chapter in his book *The Human Potential for Peace* (2006) to Australia and in recognizing its unique significance for the study of hunter-gatherers. However, with the chapter titled 'Aboriginal Australia: A Continent of Unwarlike Hunter-Gatherers', both the picture he portrays and his conclusions are the opposite to mine and to those presented by other recent studies.[54] Thus, a re-examination of the evidence from Aboriginal Australia is called for. I went back to the sources, further expanding on my survey of Australia. The following focuses on the evidence for large-scale inter-communal fighting, or 'warfare', the kind of human violence that simple, mobile, thinly dispersed, and unorganized, unsegmented, 'egalitarian' hunter-gatherers are alleged not to have engaged in.

Back to Australia: The Evidence for Aboriginal Inter-Group Fighting

In 1803, only fifteen years after the Europeans first arrived in Australia, a 23-year-old Englishman named William Buckley (1780–1856) was brought to the new continent with the first convict ship, arriving at the penalty settlement at Port Philip (now Melbourne). He escaped shortly afterwards, and for thirty-two years, until 1835, he lived with an Aboriginal tribe. During that time, he learned to speak their language and participated in their daily activities. No other anthropologist has ever achieved such familiarity, and at such an early date. After returning to civilization, Buckley related his experiences on several occasions. His account is extremely inconvenient for Rousseauians, who either ignore it or insinuate that it is unreliable. And yet it appears to be remarkably authentic with respect to everything that can be verified concerning the Aborigines' lives. Indeed, it also tallies with everything we shall see regarding Aboriginal violence and warfare from other sources throughout Australia.

Among other things, Buckley recounts some dozen battle scenes, as well as many lethal feuds, raids, and ambushes, comprising a central element of the Aborigines' traditional way of life. He describes their weapons of war in great detail: clubs, spears, 'war boomerangs', throwing sticks, and shields.[55] Tribes typically consisted of between twenty and sixty families, and were egalitarian, without chiefs.[56] There was fighting at all levels: individual, familial, and tribal. Some of the inter-tribal encounters that Buckley recorded involved large numbers: five different tribes collected for battle;[57] a battle and raid against an intruding enemy tribe, 300 strong;[58] several full-scale inter-tribal encounters, the last one a raid with many dead;[59] two other encounters, the second of those against a war party of sixty men.[60] Ceremonial cannibalism of the vanquished was customary.[61] Buckley reports that the large-scale raid was the deadliest form of violence and often involved indiscriminate massacre: 'The contests between the Watouronga, of Geelong, and the Warrorongs, of the Yarra, were fierce and bloody. I have accompanied the former in their attacks on the latter. When coming suddenly upon them in the night, they have destroyed without mercy men, women and children.'[62]

In the 1870s, Lorimer Fison and A. Howitt studied the Kurnai tribe in southern Australia (Gippsland, Victoria). In their section entitled 'War', they described both feuds and whole groups fighting. In one episode, fresh tracks indicating trespassing into the tribal territories were revealed, and a spy was sent to reconnoitre. He found the intruders, with 'lots of women and children'. The Kurnai men 'got their spears ready'. After securing enough hunted food for the womenfolk they left behind, and more reconnoitring, 'in the middle of the night they *all* marched off well armed [my emphasis].' After several marches, 'when near morning... they got close to them... The spies whistled like bird, to tell when all was ready. Then all ran in; they speared away, and speared away! They only speared the men, and perhaps some children. Whoever caught a women kept her himself. Then they eat the skin of the Brajeraks [the trespassing tribe]'.[63] The native inform-ants told of other episodes that ended in ceremonial cannibalism of the vanquished.[64]

Fison and Howitt went on to describe how the members of the families, divisions, and clans were connected by descent and kinship and 'depended on each other for mutual aid and protection'.[65] In addition to raids, many feuds also took place, as well as formal battles, which were often agreed upon and were stopped after the first injuries. According to the inform-ants, 'the last great battles of the Gippsland clans' took place around 1856-7. Escalating from a feud, much of the tribal group assembled on the strength of kin ties: 'There could not have been less than two hundred of us—at least the white men counted and told us so.'[66] There followed a protracted spate of hostilities against the rival tribe, with several encounters.[67] Police intervention was the factor that put an end to the fighting. Fison and Howitt conclude that whereas feuding within the tribe did not necessarily entail killing, killing was inseparable from the settling of accounts between tribes. Further, 'the feud attaches not only to the individual, but also to the whole group of which he is a member', and they were prosecuted not only by relatives, 'but also by the whole division, or even by the whole clan'.[68]

Gerald Wheeler is no less clear. He describes at length the regulated fights used to fulfil demands for justice between individuals and whole local groups throughout Australia. In such fights, which mainly involved spear throwing at a distance, little blood was shed.[69] However, in his following chapter, entitled 'War', Wheeler writes: 'Such is regulated war, by far the commonest form in Australia; but by its side exists what may be called war in the true meaning—that is, revenge or justice carried out by one group on another, under few, if any, restrictions or conditions, and carried out *indiscriminately* on the individuals of the group to which the offender belongs by that to which the injured person belongs.'[70] Wheeler cites different observers' reports from all over Australia. According to one such report, after 'march by night in the most stealthy manner . . . then follows a night attack and a *wholesale extermination*'.[71] According to another report: 'A common procedure in such warfare is to steal up to the enemy's camp in the dead of night, and encircle it in the earliest dawn. With a shout, the carnage then begins.'[72] Wheeler concludes that tribal solidarity generally prevented internal warfare. 'What seems clear is that war proper is marked off from other forms of justice by the fact that the vengeance is carried out *indiscriminately* on the members of another tribe.'[73]

Australia's subtropical Northern Territory was reached by Europeans much later than the temperate south, but the picture revealed is barely distinguishable. Lloyd Warner, studying the Murngin hunter-gatherers of Arnhem Land during the 1920s, wrote: 'Warfare is one of the most important social activities of the Murngin people and surrounding tribes.'[74] Warner described a whole spectrum of violent conflicts, ranging from individual feuds to small group, clan, and tribal conflicts. Such conflicts could lead to face-to-face confrontations, right up to the scale of battles. However, as with all pre-state societies, the most lethal and common form of warfare among the Murngin was the surprise night raid. This could be carried out by individuals or small groups intending to kill a specific enemy, or members of a specific family. But raids were also conducted on a large scale by raiding parties coming from whole clans or tribes. In such cases, the camp of the attacked party was surrounded, and its unprepared, sleeping occupants were massacred. It is in these larger raids that by far the most killings were registered: thirty-five people were killed in large-scale raids, twenty-seven in small-scale raids, twenty-nine in large battles in which ambushes were used, three in ordinary battles, and two in individual face-to-face encounters.[75] Thus, the largest number of casualties was incurred in large-scale, tribal clashes.

Arnold Pilling writes about armed conflict among the Tiwi of northern Australia: 'The night raids were effectively terminated, about 1912, when Sir Baldwin Spencer was inadvertently injured by a Tiwi during a spear-throwing demonstration.'[76]

> This Spencer incident was correlated with the end of night raiding and sneak attacks and it *appeared* to have stopped pitched battles producing death. But, in fact, as late as 1948 death-causing battles with clubs were occurring... Under the old pattern, sneak attack was sufficiently common that informants spoke of special ecological adjustments to it... the threatened group A was likely to move to the mangroves, a very specialized and unpleas-ant ecological niche with, among other things, crocodiles and a sloshy mud floor.

Demographically,

> It is important to note the incidence of fatalities associated with the old pattern of attacks and the way of life with which it was correlated. In one decade (1893–1903), at least sixteen males in the 25-to-45 age group were killed in feuding; either during sneak attacks or in arranged pitch battles. Those killed represented over 10 per cent of all males in that age category, which was the age group of the young fathers.

One major action in Arnhem Land is described by T. G. H. Strehlow:

> To punish Ltjabakuka and his men meant the wiping out of the whole camp of people normally resident at Irbmankara, so that no witness should be left alive who could have revealed the names of the attackers. A large party of avengers drawn from the Matuntara area along the Palmer River, and from some Southern Aranda local groups, was accordingly assembled and led to Irbmankara by Tjinawariti, who was described to me as having been a Matuntara 'ceremonial chief' from the Palmer River whose prowess as a war-rior had given him a great reputation... Tjinawariti and his men fell upon Irbmankara one evening, after all the local folk, as they believed, had returned to their camps from their day's quests for food. Men, women and children were massacred indiscriminately.[77]

In a chapter titled 'Hordes at Home and at War', Wilbur Chaseling, too, mentions the whole spectrum of violence, from frequent individual fights, to regulated battles between clans, to raids. 'Raids are common, and as the men are killed the vendetta passes from one generation to another. *Entire hordes have been exterminated.*'[78] If no such decisive result is reached, peace-making may eventually end the conflict.

R. G. Kimber, drawing on a variety of studies and sources, summarizes as follows:

> One can infer from archaeological evidence that conflict has been an ancient problem, and many mythological accounts also suggest this. Small-scale conflict, with very occasional deaths, was no doubt the norm, but the 'payback law' could result in lengthy feuds. On other occasions major conflicts had dramatic demographic implications.

Kimber cites evidence of some major conflicts, including the one described by Strehlow:

> In about 1840, at a locality called Nariwalpa, in response to insults, the 'Jandruwontas and Piliatapas killed so many Diari men, that the ground was covered with their dead bodies'... Strehlow gives the most dramatic account of a major arid-country conflict. He estimates that 80–100 men, women and children were killed in one attack in 1875 at Running Waters, on the Finke River. In retaliation, all but one of the attacking party of 'perhaps fifty to sixty warriors' were killed over the next three years, as were some of their family members. This indicates that some 20% of two identifiable 'tribes' were killed in this exchange.

Kimber adds:

> The red ochre gathering expeditions... involved travel from the eastern portion of the study area to the Flinders Ranges... These expeditions took place on a regular basis, were normally all-male parties, and although cordial relationships between groups were sought, fighting appears to have been a common hazard faced by travelling parties. One entire party, with the exception of one man, is recorded as having been ambushed and killed in about 1870, whilst in about 1874 all but one of a group of 30 men were 'entombed in the excavations'.

Kimber concludes:

> The evidence suggests that major conflict could be expected in the well-watered areas, where population density was at its greatest, or during regular 'trespasser travel' for high-prized products. Although exact figures will never be known, a low death rate of possibly 5% every generation can be suggested for the regions of least conflict, and a high death-rate of perhaps 20% every three generations elsewhere.[79]

Warfare was not confined to water-rich northern and southern Australia, but was evident in every climatic zone throughout the continent. M. J. Meggitt studied the Walbiri tribe of the Central Australian Desert, one of the most forbidding environments on earth, whose population density was as low as one person per 35 square miles. Walbiri relations with some of their neighbours were friendly, but were hostile with others. In the latter case, raids and counter-raids were common:

> The men's descriptions made it clear that the Warramunga (and Waringari) trespasses were not merely hunting forays impelled by food shortages in the invaders' own territory but rather were raids undertaken to combine hunting for sport and the abduction of women. Often, too, the raiders were simply spoiling for a fight. They were met with force, and deaths occurred on both sides. Walbiri war parties would then invade the Warramunga country in retaliation. If they were able to surprise the enemy camps and kill or drive off the men, they carried away any women they found.[80]

On one recorded occasion around the beginning of the twentieth century, things came to a head on a wider scale and with a different motive:

> Until then, the Waringari had claimed the ownership of the few native wells at Tanami and the country surrounding them, but in a pitched battle for the possession of the water the Walbiri drove the Waringari from the area, which they incorporated into their own territory. By desert standards the engagement was spectacular, the dead on either side numbering a score or more.[81]

Finally, with its human population isolated from mainland Australia for more than 10,000 years, Tasmania, an island double the size of Taiwan and nearly the size of Ireland, was the backwater of backwaters. There were an estimated 4,000 Tasmanians when the Europeans arrived (and ultimately annihilated them). Their technology and social organization were the most primitive ever recorded. They did not even possess the boomerang. Their population density was among the lowest there is. Still, lethal raiding and counter-raiding took place among their groups. Territorial boundaries were kept, and mutual apprehension was the rule.[82]

Thus, the range of evidence from across Aboriginal Australia, the *only* continent of hunter-gatherers, strikingly demonstrates that deadly human violence—including group fighting—existed at all social levels, in all population densities, in the simplest of social organization, and in all types of environments.[83] Contrary to Classical Rousseauism, Aboriginal fighting was highly lethal, with violent death rates far higher than those normally incurred by historical state societies. Contra Quasi-Rousseauism, fighting comprised inter-communal 'warfare' as well as 'homicide' and 'feuds', with the evidence consistently suggesting that most casualties were incurred in large-scale raids and battles. Recall the anthropological reports: Pilling's 10 per cent of all males in the 25 to 45 age group killed in one decade; Kimber's 20 per cent of two identifiable tribes in a single three-year conflict, a general death rate estimate of 5 per cent every generation for the regions of least conflict, and a high death rate of perhaps 20 per cent every three generations elsewhere. Obviously, such estimates are highly tentative. Nonetheless, they are remarkably similar, and are also in general agreement with those suggested by Warner. Of a population of 3,000 in the tribes in his study area, he recorded and calculated about 200 deaths 'caused by war' in the last twenty years.[84] All of these are precisely the very high death rates that Fry (and Ferguson[85]) tend to dismiss with scorn. Furthermore, as we have seen, most of them were incurred in large-scale, inter-tribal encounters.

The evidence of pre-contact violent skeletal trauma among the Aborigines is just as indicative. According to Graham Knuckey, 57.3 per cent out of the sample of 366 adult crania from all over Australia reveal human-inflicted injuries.[86] Stephen Webb shows somewhat lower figures and considerable variation between places, but the range is still high and very similar to that we have seen elsewhere in the world.[87] Moreover, unlike in most other places, the Australian figures can be compared with the ethnographic evidence of Aboriginal killing rates. They reinforce the conclusion that these were very high, and also suggest that two main adjustments are required in such comparisons: injuries to the crania were mostly suffered in non-lethal, mainly internal, and regulated disputes, including a particularly high percentage of blows to the head registered among the Aboriginal women;[88] killings in inter-tribal night raids are largely unrecorded in the skeletal evidence because the spearing of those taken by surprise and unable to defend themselves mostly resulted in fatal injuries to soft tissues.

Such insights from the correlation of the archaeological and ethnographic record provide an indispensable clue for other places. An example is the rich archaeological finds of violence that we have seen to have been revealed in early North America and the question of whether they were caused in 'homicide' and 'feuds' only or are also indicative of collective inter-group 'warfare'.[89] The ethnographic record from the sparse populations of simple hunter-gatherers on the Great Plains offers the closest analogy to early populations in North America, and elsewhere. Bison herds' migration routes on the Great Plains were changing and difficult to predict.

Hunting in other tribes' territories thus became necessary from time to time, often resulting in warfare.[90] Indeed, early Paleo-Indians may have exhibited similar patterns of behaviour as Upper Palaeolithic hunters of large game in Europe, from France to the Ukraine. Fighting patterns on the Plains, both before and after the adoption of the horse, are extensively documented and reveal a familiar picture.

According to Marian Smith: 'Whether a war party consisted of one warrior or a man and one or two of his most intimate friends, or of one to four hundred warriors, or even of the whole tribe the purpose and general form of its procedure did not change.' The night raid and dawn attack was the norm. 'The mortality in Plains fighting was highest when attack took the enemy unprepared... In such cases the weaker groups were often completely annihilated.'[91] John Ewers, specifically documenting the historical and archaeological evidence for Plains Indian warfare before contact, writes: 'The greatest damage was done when a large war party surprised, attacked, and wiped out a small hunting camp.'[92] Frank Secoy describes the same pattern of pre-horse, pre-gun fighting. According to the testimony of the old Blackfoot Saukamappee: 'The great mischief of war then, was as now, by attacking and destroying small camps of ten to thirty tents.'[93] The similarity with Aboriginal Australia (and other pre-state societies) is striking.

The references in Fry's book chapter, 'Aboriginal Australia: A Continent of Unwarlike Hunter-Gatherers', show that he is familiar with a great deal of the Australian evidence cited above (though perhaps not with some of the earliest sources, or at least he does not cite them even though they are cited by his sources). Nonetheless, while he does not deny that aggression and violent death were common among the Aborigines, he carefully avoids any mention of their overall prevalence and very high lethality rates as attested to in the records. Furthermore, he assigns all killings to the categories of murder and feuds, again contrary to the above evidence. Finally, in Fry's Australian chapter, as throughout his book, one encounters only photos of smiling faces and peaceful activities. Pictures and photos of Aboriginal groups of warriors carrying shields—an unmistakable fighting device—as recorded throughout Australia in the nineteenth and early twentieth centuries are nowhere to be seen, nor mentioned. However, for what other possible purpose would the Aborigines carry a cumbersome shield, so out of step with their nomadic light gear and alleged 'unwarlike' life (Illustrations 1.3 to 1.10)?

No. 4 —Native Warriors.

Drawing by " Yertabrida Solomon," an Aboriginal of the Coorong, in 1876. [*From original in possession of Rev. Geo. Taplin.*]

SURVEYOR GENERAL'S OFFICE, ADELAIDE. *Frazer S.Cranford. Photo-lithographer.*

Illustration 1.3. Australian Aboriginal warriors

No. 9.—Group of Warriors.

Drawing by an Aboriginal Woman. [*From original in possession of Capt. C. H. Bagot.*]

SURVEYOR GENERAL'S OFFICE, ADELAIDE. *Frazer S.Cranford. Photo-lithographer.*

Illustration 1.4. Group of Australian Aboriginal warriors

Throwing the Boomerang (p. 77)

Illustration 1.5. War boomerang

Illustration 1.6. Arunta warriors

Illustration 1.7. Welcome ceremony—beginning of a quarrel, Arunta tribe

Elsewhere I subjected Fry's handling of the evidence to a detailed scrutiny.[94] It is a sad story. But as Fry has been the most active and polemical representative of the Quasi-Rousseauian position, and in view of the major issues involved, this was inescapable. A more fundamental question is: what is the cause of such one-sided tactics in approaching the subject of aboriginal warfare?

War and Peace: Biologically Embedded, Alternative, and Complementary Behavioural Strategies

Rousseauism is a legitimate—indeed, ostensibly plausible and persuasive—position on the human past, whose test is empirical. True, the evidence regarding violence and fighting among aboriginal people is not easy to isolate and interpret. And yet, more than objective difficulties are involved. Many of those inclined towards a Rousseauian view are scholars with no axe to grind, who are genuinely grappling with the elusiveness and intricacies

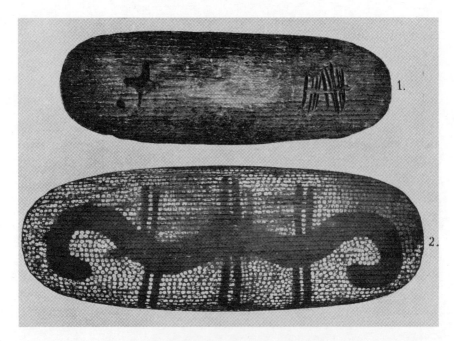

Illustration 1.8. Aboriginal shields (1)

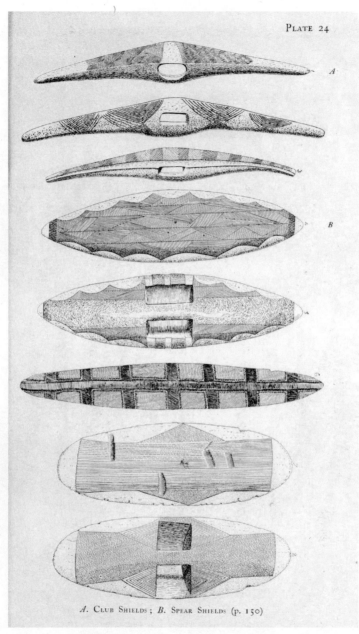

PLATE 24

A. CLUB SHIELDS ; *B.* SPEAR SHIELDS (p. 150)

Illustration 1.9. Aboriginal shields (2)

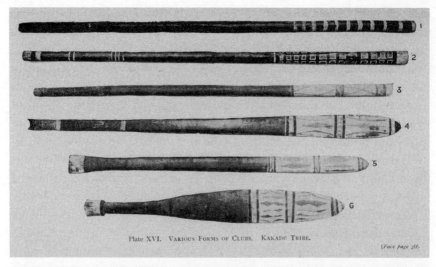

Plate XVI. Various Forms of Clubs. Kakadu Tribe.

[Face page 366.

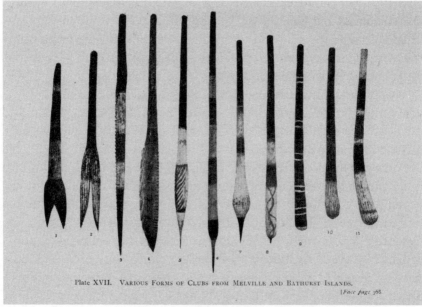

Plate XVII. Various Forms of Clubs from Melville and Bathurst Islands.

[Face page 368.

Illustration 1.10. Aboriginal clubs

of the evidence. For others, however, Rousseauism often functions not merely as a scholarly position, but as an ideological creed.

During much of the twentieth century (as with Rousseau himself) Rousseauism served as a statement about modern society, an expression of attitude towards its supposed ills. Nowadays, it mostly serves two extra-scientific goals. First, it is a creed commonly adopted by those who work to protect the rights, cultural inheritance, and well-being of aboriginal populations still scattered here and there in remote corners of the world. This, however, may be a very worthy cause even if they are not presented as virtuous and innocent creatures living in a lost paradise. Second, Rousseauism is often adopted by those who are concerned that the antiquity of human fighting may suggest that it is inseparable from human reality, and seek to dispel this notion in support of the effort to reduce or eliminate war in today's world. This is Fry's openly and repeatedly stated mission. However, the antiquity of human fighting and the question of the future of war are not at all connected in the direct way that people tend to assume. My *War in Human Civilization* (2006) and this book, Steven Pinker's *The Better Angels of Our Nature: Why War Has Declined* (2011), Joshua Goldstein's *Winning the War on War: The Decline of Armed Conflict Worldwide* (2011), and Ian Morris's *War: What is it Good For?* (2014) have all argued that while human fighting was ubiquitous and highly lethal in prehistory, its mortality rates actually decreased under the state, and war in general has declined sharply during modern and recent times. Thus, there is no simple connection between the bloody human past and potentially better present and future.

Fry has an important contribution to make. He has stressed the point—not coming out sufficiently in the debate on human violence—that violence and war are not invariably all-pervasive. He elucidates the other side of the human behavioural repertoire, which makes up what he rightly calls our potential for peace. This side consists of basic interpersonal and social techniques that in Fry's list include avoidance, toleration, negotiation, and settlement, all enhanced by social norms, group pressure, and communal ceremonies intended to dissipate, deflect, and suppress the outbreak of violence.[95] Fry is correct in arguing that these most common practices of daily life have always been with us, and are widely attested to in hunter-gatherer societies, as later. However, in pursuit of the cause of a future peaceful world, Fry errs in the other direction, underplaying the role of violence and suppressing the evidence for communal fighting in the aboriginal human past. They too, like the various forms of conflict resolution and aversion, have always been with us. Indeed, the ever-present prospect of violent conflict is precisely the reason why conflict resolution has always been such a central social practice, proving more or less successful in both intra- and inter-group settings. Furthermore, although the vast majority of hunter-gatherer life is spent in peace, as Fry argues, the imminent *potential*

of violence is a social fact that hangs over their lives even when violence is
not activated.[†]

Fry argues correctly that levels of violence and killing among hunter-
gatherer societies are not uniformly very high, and that some of these
societies are even quite pacific. Clearly, there was some range of variation
in the violence among hunter-gatherer groups, including at the end of
a bell curve a few groups that exhibited little violence, withdrawing to
isolated environments, often, reportedly, in response to earlier experiences
of violence. Historical state societies are an apt analogy. In an 'anarchic'
international system some states fought more than others, the large majority
fought some of the time, and a few—such as Sweden and Switzerland—
have remained largely outside the circle of war during the past two centuries,
although both countries had an exceptionally violent, warlike, and bloody
earlier history. Clearly, while the human past was generally rife with warfare, particular and changing circumstances mattered.

The root of the confusion is this: people habitually assume that if
widespread deadly violence has always been with us, it must be a primary,
'irresistible' drive which is nearly impossible to suppress. Many find in this
conclusion reason enough to object to the idea that human fighting is primordial, while others regard it as compelling evidence that war is inevitable.[96]
Both sides are wrong. Contrary to fashionable 1960s notions, traced back to
Freud's latter-day theorizing about a death drive or instinct, violence is not
a primary drive that requires release, like hunger or sex. The Swiss or Swedes,
for example, who have not fought for two centuries, show no special signs
of deprivation on this account. But try to deny them food for more than a
few hours, or sex for more than a few days, and their reaction would be
quite predictable.

On the other hand, the fact that violence is not a primary drive does not
mean that we are not hardwired for it. Studies on 'warless' pre-state societies
usually intend to prove that, neither primordial nor natural to humankind,

---

† In his seminal study, *Yanomamo: The Fierce People*, 162–3, Napoleon Chagnon has long emphasized both sides of the coin while putting them in a proper perspective:

First of all, the Yanomamo do not spend all or even a major fraction of their waking hours
making wars on neighbors...Second, warfare among the Yanomamo varies from region to
region and from time to time: it is extremely intense in some areas at particular times, and
almost non-existent in other areas. Even the most 'warlike' villages have long periods of relative peace during which time daily life is tranquil and happy...On the other hand, even the
least warlike villages suddenly find themselves embroiled in an active war, or the peace of the
temporary tranquil is shattered by an unexpected raid.

warfare was probably a late, and in any case wholly contingent, cultural phenomenon. Margaret Mead's framing of the problem, 'Warfare is Only an Invention—Not a Biological Necessity', is the mother of all mistakes.[97] It expresses the widespread assumption that violence must be either a primary drive or entirely learned, whereas in reality its potential is deeply ingrained in us as a means or tool, ever ready to be employed. People can cooperate, compete peacefully, or use violence to achieve their objectives, depending on what they believe will serve them best in any given circumstance. In cooperation the parties combine efforts, in principle because the synergic outcome of their efforts divided among them promises greater benefit to each of them than their independent efforts might. In a competition, each party strives to outdo the other in order to achieve a desired good by employing whatever means they have at their disposal except direct action against the other. Competition runs parallel. By contrast, in a conflict, direct action against the competitor is taken in order to eliminate them or lessen their ability to engage in the competition.[98] If physical injury is inflicted, a conflict becomes a violent one.

Cooperation, competition, and violent conflict are the three fundamental forms of social interaction (in addition to isolation or avoidance—that is, zero interaction). People have always had all three options to choose from, and they have always assessed the situation to decide which option, or combination of them, seemed the most promising. Violent conflict as a behavioural strategy did not suddenly emerge sometime in later human history. People are well equipped biologically for pursuing any of the above social strategies, with conflict being only one tool, albeit a major one—the hammer—in our diverse behavioural toolkit. Furthermore, *Homo sapiens* is a social species, whose local and regional groups—universally and uniquely bound together by ties of both kinship and shared cultural codes, including language and customs—cooperate within themselves in a variety of group activities, including fighting. To be sure, extreme conditions of sparsity, as in the central and eastern Canadian Arctic, may make large group action less common. But as the evidence from the Central Australian Desert demonstrates, even the most forbidding environments, with extremely low population densities, could see intense group fighting, sometimes for collective goods such as hunting territories and water sources.

Neither a late invention nor a compulsive inevitability independent of conditions, group fighting is part of our evolution-shaped behavioural menu. It is in this sense that *both* war and peace are 'in our genes', which accounts for their widely fluctuating prevalence in different socio-historical contexts. As the 'Seville Statement on Violence' (1986), issued by an international group of scientists under the auspices of UNESCO, rightly put it in rejection of the view that human biology made violence and war inescapable: 'There is nothing in our neurophysiology that compels us to react violently... We conclude that biology does not condemn humanity to war.' However, the Statement fell into the opposite fallacy, stating that warfare 'is a product of culture', and solemnly prescribing that 'IT IS SCIENTIFICALLY INCORRECT to say that war or any other violent behaviour is genetically programmed into our human nature... Violence is neither in our evolutionary legacy nor in our genes.'[99]

A number of scholars who have dealt with the question in fact express the view that human societies have always been Janus-faced, interchangeably resorting to both peace and violent conflict. According to Walker: 'Everywhere we probe into the history of our species we find evidence of a similar pattern of behavior: People have always been capable of both kindness and extreme cruelty.'[100] Ernest Burch, documenting the Alaskan Eskimos' highly belligerent record, also devotes one part of his book to their peaceful interactions.[101] Robert Kelly (not to be confused with Raymond Kelly) writes: 'To summarize so far, it is not useful to ask whether hunter-gatherers (inclusive of egalitarian and nonegalitarian types) are peaceful or warlike: we find evidence for both among them.'[102] He adds: 'Aggression appears in many species, suggesting that it has a long evolutionary history... It is part of our behavioral repertoire, and at times served us well.'[103] Boehm similarly rejects the view 'that there should be an either-or choice between setting up friendly, cooperative relations with neighbors, as opposed to fighting with them'.[104] Both took place, interchangeably, with the same and with different neighbours. Based on his survey of forty-nine simple hunter-gatherer societies, Boehm writes: 'The finding here is that intergroup conflict and external peacekeeping would both seem to have been prominent in human political life, back to at least 45,000 BP and probably earlier.'[105]

Indeed, Boehm puts both sides of simple hunter-gatherer societies' behavioural repertoire in a proper—and striking—perspective: '59 percent of the... forager sample has enough lethal intergroup conflict for this to be reported in an ethnography'.[106] He adds: 'With human foragers, negotiations of some type (including truces and peacemaking) are found in more than half of the... societies surveyed (59 percent). However... formal and effective peacemaking is reported only for a few of the 29 societies'.[107] This agrees remarkably well with an earlier survey of hunter-gatherers across the world: '64 percent had warfare occurring at least once every two years, 26 percent had warfare somewhat less often, and only 10 percent . . . were rated as having no or rare warfare'.[108] In the same study, by stricter definitions, 'warfare is rare for only 12 percent of . . . hunter-gatherers. In sum, hunter-gatherers could hardly be described as peaceful.' Hunter-gatherers suffered far greater violent mortality rates than state societies not because they lacked well-established and partly successful patterns of conflict resolution. It is just that hunter-gatherers' anarchic condition, the absence of effective coercive authority, limited the effectiveness of these patterns as compared to state societies.

We began this chapter with the classical philosophers who had outlined two conflicting concepts of our aboriginal past. It may be appropriate at this point to get back to and comment on these concepts in the light of the rich ethnographic and archaeological knowledge we now possess. Clearly, Hobbes was much closer to the truth than Rousseau with respect to the pervasive insecurity and very high levels of violence and killing in the state of nature. Rousseau was also wrong in projecting aboriginal people as solitary rather than social creatures. On the other hand, Hobbes's image of the state of nature left no room for the brighter aspects of hunter-gatherers' life, such as their quite abundant leisure, relatively 'egalitarian' social structure, strong familial envelope, and strong relationship with nature. Indeed, a third philosopher of the same era, John Locke, in his *Two Treatises of Government* (1689), suggested that the human state of nature was not so bad, with people and communities finding ways to live together. At the same time, he held that the transition to state societies was nonetheless a considerable improvement, among other things in terms of security. Locke, like Hobbes and Rousseau, was not a researcher of the past but a political philosopher defending a particular political creed. His interest was the present. All the same, his more balanced depiction of pre-state as compared to state societies was suggestive. From the other direction, and closing the circle, Rousseau offered very striking insights concerning the mass deprivation, social exploitation, and political oppression that were the norm in the majority of premodern state societies. We shall see more about this later in the book. But now, after establishing the prevalence of deadly fighting—including, most prominently, group fighting—throughout the human past, we proceed to examine more closely the question of *why* people fight, or their motives for doing so.

2

Why People Fought in the Evolutionary State of Nature

The age-old philosophical and psychological inquiry into the nature of the basic human system of motivation is fundamental to the question of why people fight. Numerous lists of basic needs and desires have been put together over the centuries, more or less casually or convincingly. The most recent ones show little if any marked progress over the older, such as Hobbes's insightful propositions in *Leviathan*, chapter 6.[1] Such lists have always had something arbitrary and often trivial about them. They lack a unifying regulatory rationale that would suggest why the various needs and desires came into being or how they relate to one another. Indeed, when various unitary 'principles' of human behaviour have been put forward, it is mostly in this respect that they were deficient. The splits in the psychoanalytic movement are a good example of this. While Sigmund Freud claimed that the basic human drive was sexuality, Alfred Adler argued that it was in fact the striving for superiority, and Karl Jung emphasized the quest for creativity and whole-being. There was no way of deciding, other than faith within what indeed became semi-religious orthodox sects, why it was this drive rather than the other that was the 'truly' basic one, or why in fact there should be a unitary basic drive at all.

The past decades have seen an explosion in the application of the evolutionary logic to explaining human physiological features and behaviour traits. Charles Darwin's theory of evolution was revolutionary because for the first time it made it possible to explain how life's immensely complex functional design came into being without assuming conscious design or a designer. The mechanism involved is piecemeal adaptation through natural selection for the qualities that have proved most successful in organisms' continuous struggle for survival and reproduction under conditions of fundamental scarcity. Having overcome massive initial resistance since its revival in the 1970s, the evolutionary understanding of basic human traits and propensities has become commonplace in both the scientific and popular discourse, except among extreme cultural relativists and zealot religious creationists.

What, then, were the evolutionary rewards that could make the highly dangerous activity of fighting worthwhile for our hunter-gatherer ancestors in the human state of nature, who lacked accumulated property and were thinly dispersed over wide territories? Although I shall now go through the reasons for warfare among hunter-gatherers one by one, it is not the intention here to provide yet another 'laundry list' of separate causes. Instead, I seek to show how the various 'causes' come together in an integrated motivational complex. This was shaped by the logic of evolution and natural selection for billions of years, including the roughly 2 million years of our genus *Homo* and the estimated 200,000–150,000 years of our species *Homo sapiens*. In the previous chapter we have extensively covered Aboriginal Australia, uniquely preserved out of touch with both agriculturalists and states. The evidence for the causal web leading to fighting presented below is drawn from a large number of pre-agricultural and pre-state societies around the globe. The anthropological case studies themselves will be cited here very scarcely, and readers interested in the rich and fascinating detail on the real peoples concerned can consult Part One of my *War in Human Civilization*. For the causes of human fighting per se, what follows is a concentrated distillation.

Subsistence Resources

Competition over resources is a primary cause of aggression and deadly violence in nature. The reason for this is that food, water, and, to a lesser degree, shelter against the elements are tremendous selection forces. As Darwin, following Malthus, explained, living organisms, including humans, tend to propagate rapidly. Their numbers are constrained and checked only by the limited resources of their particular ecological habitats and by all sorts of competitors, such as members of the same species, animals of other species which have similar consumption patterns, predators, parasites, and pathogens. Contrary to the Rousseauian imagination, humans, and animals, did not live in a state of primordial plenty. Even in lush environments plenty

is a misleading notion, for it is relative, first, to the number of mouths that
have to be fed. The more resource-rich a region is, the more people it
attracts from outside, and the greater the internal population growth that
takes place. As Malthus pointed out, a new equilibrium between resource
volume and population size would eventually be reached, recreating the
same tenuous ratio of subsistence that was the fate of pre-industrial societies
throughout history. The concept of 'territoriality' that became popular in
the 1960s should be more subtly defined in this light.[2] Among hunter-
gatherers, territories varied dramatically in size, and territorial behaviour
itself gained or lost in significance, in direct relation to the availability of
resources and resource competition. The same applies to population density,
another popular explanation for violence in the 1960s. Except in the most
extreme cases, it is mainly in relation to resource scarcity, and hence as a
factor in resource competition, that population density functions as a trigger
for fighting. Otherwise, Tokyo and the Netherlands would have been among
the most violent places on earth.[3]

In a fundamental state of scarcity, human competition—like that of
animals—was rife. In arid environments, like that of the Central Australian
Desert, where human population density was extremely low, water holes
were often the main cause of resource competition and conflict, as we have
seen. They were critical in times of drought, when whole groups of
Aborigines are recorded to have perished. For this reason, however, there
was a tendency to control them even when stress was less pressing.[4] In the
majority of other cases, competition over resources was mainly about food
acquisition, the basic and most critical somatic activity of all living creatures,
which often caused dramatic fluctuations in their numbers. The nature of
the food in question varied with the environment. Still, it was predominantly meat of all sorts that was hotly contested among hunter-gatherers.
This fact, which is simply a consequence of nutritional value, is discernible
throughout nature. Herbivores rarely fight over food, for the nutritious
value of grass is too low for effective monopolization. Fruit, roots, seeds, and
some plants that are considerably more nutritious than grass are often the
object of competition and fighting, both among animals and humans. Meat,
however, represents the most concentrated nutritional value in nature and is
the object of the most intense competition. Meat eaters violently defend
their hunting territories against competitors from their own and other species, because hunting territories are quickly depleted. Hence the inherent
state of competition and conflict among Stone Age people.

We have seen how the Australian Aborigines staunchly defended their hunting territories. Trespassers were killed. With the Great Plains Indians, the issue of hunting territory was more complicated, but no less explosive, as the migration of bison herds made hunting in other tribes' territories a necessity. The Eskimo of Alaska offer another example:

> Previous to the arrival of the Russians on the Alaskan shore of Bering sea the Eskimo waged an almost constant intertribal warfare; at the same time, along the line of contact with the Tinné tribes of the interior, a bitter feud was always in existence... Several Tinné were killed by Malemut while hunting reindeer on the strip of uninhabited tundra lying between the districts occupied by the two peoples.[5]

Let us understand more closely the evolutionary calculus that can make the highly dangerous activity of fighting over resources, most notably prime food such as meat, worthwhile. In our affluent societies it might be difficult to comprehend how precarious people's subsistence was (and still is) in pre-modern societies. The spectre of hunger and starvation was ever-present. Affecting both mortality and reproduction, they constantly trimmed down population numbers. Thus, struggle over resources was very often evolutionarily cost-effective. The benefits of fighting also had to be matched against possible alternatives (other than starvation). One alternative was to move elsewhere. This, of course, often happened, especially if one's enemy was much stronger, but this strategy had clear limitations. By and large, there were no empty spaces for people to move to. In the first place, space is not even, and the best, most productive habitats were normally already taken. One could be forced out to less hospitable environments, which may also be already populated by other less fortunate people. Indeed, finding empty niches required exploration, which again might involve violent encounters with other human groups. Furthermore, a move meant leaving a habitat with whose resources and dangers the group's members were intimately familiar, and travelling into uncharted environments. Such a change could involve heavy penalties. Hunter-gatherers were indeed nomadic, but only within a well-defined ancestral territory, rather than freely roaming across the land. Finally, giving in to pressure from outside might establish a pattern of victimization. Encouraged by its success, the alien group might repeat and even increase its pressure. A strategy of conflict concerns not only the object presently in dispute but also the whole pattern of future relations. Standing up for one's own might in fact mean lessening the occurrence of conflict in the future. Conflict is about deterrence no less than it is about actual fighting.

Having discussed fighting's possible benefits and alternatives, deterrence brings us to its costs side. Conflict would become an evolutionarily more attractive strategy for those who resort to it, the lower their risk of serious bodily harm and death. Consequently, displays of strength and threats of aggressive behaviour are the most widely used weapons in conflict, both among animals and humans. As Hobbes noted, it is the state of mutual apprehension and armed surveillance—more than the spates of active fighting which, of course, establish this pattern of relations—that is the norm among human groups. Furthermore, when humans, and animals, resorted to deadly violence, they mostly did so under conditions in which the odds were greatly tilted in their favour. As mentioned before, it is not the open battle but the raid and ambush—asymmetrical fighting—that constituted the principal and by far the most lethal form of 'primitive warfare'.

Reproduction

The struggle for reproduction is about access to sexual partners of reproductive potential. There is a fundamental asymmetry between males and females in this respect, that runs throughout nature. At any point in time, a female can be fertilized only once. Consequently, evolutionarily speaking, she must take care to make the best choice. It is quality rather than quantity that she seeks. She must select the male who looks the best equipped for survival and reproduction, so that he will impart those genes, and qualities, to the offspring. In those species, like humans, where the male also contributes to the raising of the offspring, his skills as a provider and his loyalty are other crucial considerations. In contrast to the female, there is theoretically almost no limit to the number of offspring a male can produce. He can fertilize an indefinite number of females, thereby multiplying his own genes in the next generations. The main constraint on male sexual success is competition from other males.

Around this rationale, sexual strategies in nature are highly diverse and most nuanced, ranging from extreme polygamy to monogamy, or pair-bonding.[6] The need to take care of very slowly maturing offspring, which required sustained investment by both parents, turned humans towards pair-bonding. However, although pair-bonding reduces male competition, it by no means eliminates it. If the male is restricted to one partner, it becomes highly important also for him to choose the partner with the best reproductive qualities he can get: young, healthy, and optimally built for bearing offspring; that is, in sexual parlance, the most attractive female. Furthermore, humans, and men in particular, are not strictly monogamous. In most historical human societies polygamy was legitimate, though only a select few well-to-do men were able to support, and thus have, the extra wives and children. Second, in addition to official or unofficial wives, men often have extra-marital sexual liaisons.

How does all this affect human violent conflict and fighting? The evidence across the range of hunter-gatherer peoples tells the same story. Within the tribal groupings, quarrels, violence, so-called blood feuds, and homicide related to women were rife, often constituting the principal category of violence. Between groups, the picture was not very different, and was equally uniform. Warfare regularly involved stealing women, who were then subjected to multiple rapes, taken for marriage, or both. According to William Buckley, the escaped convict who lived with the Australian Aborigines from 1803 to 1835, most of the frequent fights and killings among them 'were occasioned by the women having been taken away from one tribe to another; which was of frequent occurrence. At other times they were caused by the women willingly leaving their husbands, and joining other men'; 'these dear creatures were at the bottom of every mischief'.[7] In isolated Tasmania, the Aborigines reported similar reasons for the endemic fighting, territorial segregation, and mutual apprehension that prevailed among their groups. Food could become scarce in the winters, but women were the main cause of feuding and fighting.[8]

In the extremely harsh conditions of the mid-Canadian arctic, where sparse human population and highly diffused resources made fighting over resources very rare, wife-stealing was widespread and the main cause of the high killing rate and 'blood feuds' among the Inuit. 'A stranger in the camp, particularly if he was travelling with his wife, could become easy prey to the local people. He might be killed by any camp fellow in need of a woman.' Among the Eskimo of the more densely populated Alaskan Coast, abduction of women was a principal cause of warfare. Polygyny, too, was more common among them, although restricted to the few.[9] Strong *Ingalik* ('big men') often had a second wife, and 'there was a fellow who had five wives at one time and seven at another. This man was a great fighter and had obtained his women by raiding'.[10]

Some anthropologists remained sceptical. Despite Freud's tremendous cultural impact and our great awareness of the significance of sex to people—indeed, most importantly, despite the uniform testimonies in anthropological studies of pre-state societies—they found it difficult to accept sex as a major, 'serious' cause of fighting and warfare. They felt that while sex was a major human activity and obviously great fun, it must have been external rather than central to warfare. Even if hunter-gatherer fighting commonly involved stealing and raping women, they queried whether this was the cause or a side effect of their fighting for other coveted prizes, such as resources.[11] The source of some controversy, this question was in fact point-less and only led anthropologists astray. It artificially isolates one element from the whole of the human motivational complex that may lead to war-fare, and loses sight of the overall rationale that underpins these elements. It is as if one were to ask what people are *really* after when they go to the supermarket: meat, bread, or milk? Both somatic and reproductive elements are present in humans. Moreover, both these elements are intimately inter-connected, for people must feed, find shelter, and protect themselves in order to reproduce successfully. Conflict over resources was at least partly conflict over the ability to acquire and support women and children, and to demonstrate that ability in advance, in order to rank worthy of the extra wives. Thus, competition over women can lead to warfare indirectly as well as directly. As with mass and energy in Einstein's equations, resources, repro-duction, and, as we shall see, status, are interconnected and interchangeable in the evolution-shaped complex that motivates people.

Indeed, a positive feedback loop existed between these various elements. Anthropological studies have shown that the largest clans in a tribe moved on to increase their advantage by controlling leadership positions, resources, and marriage opportunities at the expense of the others. As a result, large clans tended to dominate a tribe, politically and demographically, over time.[12] The notion that there is a self- and mutually-reinforcing tendency which works in favour of the rich, mighty, and successful, facilitating their access to the 'good things of life', goes back a long way.

Successful men in hunter-gatherer societies had several wives, in rare cases as many as a dozen, with a record of two dozen in the most productive environments, such as Australia's Arnhem Land. Many wives naturally meant a large number of children for a man, sometimes scores, who often com-prised a large part of the next generation in the tribe. Among the Xavante horticulturalists of Brazil, for example, sixteen of the thirty-seven adult males in one village (74 out of 184 according to a larger survey) had more than one wife. The chief had five wives, more than any other man.

He fathered twenty-three surviving offspring, who constituted 25 per cent of the surviving offspring in that generation. Shinbone, a most successful Yanomamo man, also in Amazonia, had forty-three children. His brothers were also highly successful, so Shinbone's father had fourteen children, 143 grandchildren, 335 great grandchildren, and 401 great great grandchildren.[13]

Again, women are such a prominent motive for competition and conflict because reproductive opportunities are a very strong selective force indeed. This does not mean that people always want to maximize the number of their children. Although there is some human desire for children per se and a great attachment to them once they exist, it is mainly the desire for sex—Malthus's 'passion'—which functions in nature as the powerful biological proximate mechanism for maximizing reproduction. As humans, and other living creatures, normally engage in sex throughout their fertile lives, they have a vast reproductive potential, which, before the introduction of effective contraception, mainly depended on resource availability for its realization.

Polygamy (and female infanticide) created a scarcity of women and increased men's competition for and conflict over them.[14] Young men have been the main victims of this scarcity throughout human evolution—hence their marked restlessness, risk-taking behaviour, and belligerency. Young men are 'programmed' for greater risk-taking, as their matrimonial status quo is highly unsatisfactory. They still have to conquer their place in life. Thus, they have always been the most natural recruits for violent action and war. Male murder rates peak in both London and Detroit—although forty times higher in the latter—at the age of 25.[15] Similarly, over 90 per cent of all homicides in every society surveyed—hunter-gatherer, agricultural, or industrial—are committed by men.[16] Again, this remarkable consistency holds even though the homicide rates themselves vary widely between societies. The two sides of the above statistics—the constancy and the variation—are a striking demonstration of both the deeply ingrained innate element and highly context-sensitive triggers of violent behaviour.

Dominance: Rank, Honour, Status, Prestige

The interconnected competition over resources and reproduction is the *root* cause of conflict and fighting in humans as in all other animal species. Other causes and expressions of fighting in nature, and the motivational and emotional mechanisms associated with them, are derivative of, and subordinate to, these primary causes, and originally evolved this way in humans as well. This does not make them any less real, but only explains their function in the evolution-shaped motivational complex, and thus how they came into being. It is to these 'second level' causes and motivational mechanisms, directly linked to the first, that we now turn.

Among social animals, possessing higher rank in the group promises a greater share in the communal resources, such as hunting spoils, and better access to females. For this reason, rank in the group is hotly contested. It is the strong, fierce, and among our sophisticated cousins, the chimpanzees, also the 'politically' astute that win status by the actual or implied use of force. Rivalry for rank and domination in nature is, then, a proximate means in the competition over resources and reproduction. In traditional societies in particular, people were predisposed to go to great lengths in defence of their honour. The slightest offence could provoke violence. Where no strong centralized authority existed, one's honour was a social commodity of vital significance.

To avoid a common misunderstanding, the argument is not that these behaviour patterns are a matter of conscious decision and complex calculation conducted by flies, mice, lions, or even humans. It is simply that those who failed to behave adaptively were decreasingly represented in the next generations, and their maladaptive genes, responsible for their maladaptive behaviour, were consequently selected against. The most complex structural engineering and behaviour patterns have thus evolved in, and programme, even the simplest organisms, including those lacking any consciousness.

As with competition over women, competition over rank and esteem could lead to violent conflict indirectly as well as directly. For instance, even in the simplest societies people desired ornamental, ostentatious, and prestige goods. Although these goods are sometimes lumped together with subsistence goods, their social function and significance are entirely different. Body ornamentation and decorative clothing are designed to enhance physically desirable features that function everywhere in nature as cues for health, vigour, youth, and fertility.[17] For example, artificial colouring is used to enhance eye, lip, hair, and skin colour; natural—and by extension, added—symmetrical, orderly, and refined features signal good genes, good nourishment, and high-quality physical design; tall and magnificent headgear enhances one's apparent size. It is precisely on these products of the 'illusions industry'—cosmetics, fashion, and jewellery—that people everywhere spend so much money. Furthermore, where some ornaments are scarce and therefore precious, the very fact that one is able to afford them indicates wealth and success. Hence the source of what economist Thorstein Veblen, referring to early twentieth-century American society, called 'conspicuous consumption'. In Stone Age societies, too, luxury goods, as well as the ostentatious consumption of ordinary ones, became objects of desire in themselves as symbols of social status. For this reason, people may fight over them.

Indeed, plenty and scarcity are relative not only to the number of mouths to be fed but also to the potentially ever-expanding and insatiable range of human needs and desires. Human competition increases with abundance—as well as with deficiency—taking more complex forms and expressions, widening social gaps, and enhancing stratification. While the consumption capacity of simple, subsistence products is inherently limited, that of more refined, lucrative ones is practically open-ended. One can simply move up the market.

Revenge: Retaliation to Eliminate and Deter

Revenge is one of the major causes of fighting repeatedly cited in anthropological accounts of pre-state societies. Violence was resorted to in order to avenge injuries to honour, property, women, and kin. If life was taken, revenge reached its peak, often leading to a vicious circle of death and counter-death.

How is this most prevalent risky, and often bloody behaviour pattern to be explained? From the evolutionary perspective, revenge is retaliation that is intended either to destroy an enemy or to foster deterrence against him as well as against other potential rivals. This applies to non-physical and non-violent, as well as to physical and violent action. If one does not pay back for an injury, one may signal weakness and expose oneself to further injuries not only from the original offender but also from others. A process of victimization might be created. Of course one's reaction depends on one's overall assessment of the stakes and relative balance of power, and if the challenger is much stronger than oneself, it is equally common to accept an injury in silence along with the consequences of reduced status. All this applies wherever there is no higher authority that can be relied on for protection, that is, in so-called anarchic systems. In modern societies it therefore applies to the wide spheres of social relations in which the state or other authoritative bodies do not intervene. In pre-state societies, however, it applied far more widely to the basic protection of life, family, and property.

But is this explanation for revenge not too clinical? Are people not moved to revenge by blind rage rather than by calculation? Also, is revenge not simply a primitive method of administering justice, and thus ought to be considered within the realm of morality rather than that of security and deterrence theory? I raise these typical questions only in order to once more reiterate the point which is all too often misunderstood with respect to the evolutionary logic. Basic emotions evolved, and are tuned the way they are, in response to very long periods of adaptive selective pressures. They are proximate mechanisms in the service of somatic and reproductive purposes. To work, they do not need to be conscious, and the vast majority of them indeed are not, in humans, let alone in animals. Thus, the instinctive desire to hit back is a basic emotional response which evolved precisely because those who hit back—within the limits mentioned above—were generally more successful in protecting their own.

A famous computer game in game theory demonstrated 'tit-for-tat' to be the most effective strategy a player can adopt. You should reciprocate positive actions in the interest of mutually beneficial cooperation and retaliate when your partner fails you in order to persuade this partner that he or she cannot get away with it.[18] However, tit-for-tat poses a problem. Your offender cannot always be eliminated. Furthermore, the offender has kin who will avenge him or her, and it is even more difficult to eliminate them as well. Thus, in many cases tit-for-tat becomes a negative loop of retaliation and counter-retaliation from which it is very hard to exit. One original offence may produce a pattern of prolonged hostility. Indeed, retaliation might produce escalation rather than annihilation or deterrence. In such cases, fighting seems to feed on, and perpetuate, itself, bearing a wholly disproportional relation to its 'original' cause. Like a Moloch, it seems to take on a life of its own. People become locked into conflict against their wishes and best interests. It is this factor that has always given warfare an irrational appearance that seems to defy a purely utilitarian explanation.

How can this puzzle be explained? In the first place, it must again be stressed that both the original offence and the act of retaliation arise from a fundamental state of inter-human competition that carries the potential of conflict and is consequently fraught with suspicion and insecurity. Without this basic state of somatic and reproductive competition and potential conflict, retaliation as a behaviour pattern would not have evolved. However, while explaining the root cause of retaliation, this does not in itself account for retaliation's escalation into what often seems to be a self-defeating cycle.

Again, game theory proves helpful. The most famous game in this branch of rationality research is known as the 'prisoner's dilemma'. It demonstrates how under certain conditions people are rationally pushed to adopt strategies which are not in their best interest. The story goes as follows. Two prisoners are separately interrogated on a crime they jointly committed. If one throws the blame on the other, the former goes free while his friend, who keeps silent, gets a heavy sentence. If both tell on each other, both get heavy sentences, though somewhat moderated by their willingness to cooperate with the authorities. If both keep silent, the authorities would have little evidence against them, and both of them would get a light sentence. Under these conditions, the rational strategy for each of the isolated prisoners is to 'defect' and tell on the other, because, unable to secure cooperation with the other, this option is best *regardless* of the option the other takes independently. However, since both prisoners are rationally driven to betray each other, both get a heavy sentence. Their rational choice under conditions of isolation is thus inferior to their optimal choice had they been able to secure cooperation between them.

Like any game, the prisoner's dilemma is predicated on its assumptions. It has proven so fruitful because it has been found that many situations in real life have elements of the prisoner's dilemma. It explains, for example, why people are rational in trying to evade paying taxes if they believe they can get away with it, even though the existence of the tax system as a whole benefits them; or why they would bring their livestock onto an unregulated, over-grazed common land, even though over-grazing would deplete it completely, to everybody's loss. Similarly, in the absence of an authority that can enforce mutually beneficial cooperation on people, or at least minimize their damages, retaliation is often their only rational option, although, if it deteriorates into a vicious circle, not their best option.

The prisoner's dilemma is of great relevance for explaining the war complex as a whole and not only revenge and retribution. Among other things, it draws our attention to the difference between the *motives* for war and the *causes* of war. Whereas human motives, the pursuit or defence of objects of desire, in this context by violent means, are the fundamental causes of war, the situations generated by this pursuit may lead to war—may be its cause—via prisoner's dilemmas, even when the sides do not actively covet any object of desire. On the other hand, it must be emphasized that not all violent conflicts or acts of revenge fall under the special terms of the prisoner's dilemma. In the context of a fundamental resource scarcity, if one is able to eliminate, decisively weaken, or subdue the enemy, and consequently reap most of the benefits, then this strategy is better for one's interests than a compromise.

Power and the Security Dilemma

Revenge or retaliation is an active reaction to an injury, emanating from a competitive, and hence potentially conflictual, basic state of relations. However, as Hobbes saw (*Leviathan*, chap. 13), the basic condition of competition and potential conflict, which gives rise to endemic suspicion and insecurity, invites not only reactive but also pre-emptive action, which further magnifies mutual suspicion and insecurity. It should be stressed that the source of the potential conflict here is again of a 'second level'. It does not necessarily arise directly from an actual conflict over the somatic and reproductive resources themselves, but from the fear, suspicion, and insecurity that the potential of those 'first level' causes for conflict creates. Thus, yet again, potential conflict can breed conflict. When the other must be regarded as a potential enemy, his very existence poses a threat, for he might suddenly attack one day. For this reason, one must take precautions and increase one's strength as much as possible. The other side faces a similar security problem and takes similar precautions.

Things do not stop with precautionary and defensive measures, because such measures often inherently possess some offensive potential, either indirectly or directly. Indirectly, defences may have the effect of freeing one for offensive action with less fear of a counter-strike—they reduce mutual deterrence. Directly, most weapon systems are dual-purposed, and a defensive alliance may similarly be transformed into an offensive one. Thus, measures that one takes to increase one's security in an insecure world often decrease the other's security and vice versa. One's strength is the other's weakness.

What are the consequences of this so-called 'security dilemma'?[19] In the first place, it tends to escalate arms races. Arms races between competitors take place throughout nature.[20] Through natural selection, they produce faster cheetahs and gazelles; deer with longer antlers to fight one another; more devious parasites and viruses, and more immune 'hosts'. Many of these arms races involve very heavy costs to the organisms, which would not have been necessary if it were not for the competition. This, for example, is the reason why trees have trunks. Trees incur the enormous cost involved in growing trunks only because of their life-and-death struggle to outgrow other trees in order to get sunlight. As with humans, competition is most intense in environments of plenty, where more competitors are involved and more resources can be accumulated. This is why trees grow highest in the dense forests of the water-rich tropical and temperate climates.

Arms races also often have paradoxical results. The continuous and escalating effort to surpass one's rival may prove successful, in which case the rival is destroyed or severely weakened. However, in many cases, every step on one side is matched by a counter-step on the other. Consequently, even though each side invests increasing resources in the conflict, neither gains an advantage. This is called, after one of Alice's puzzles in Lewis Carroll's *Through the Looking-Glass*, the 'Red Queen' effect: both sides run faster and faster only to find themselves remaining in the same place. Arms races may become a prisoner's dilemma.

Thus, arms races are in general the natural outcome of competition. The special feature of arms races created by the security dilemma is that their basic motivation on both sides is defensive. One way to stop this paradoxical spiral is to find a means to reduce mutual suspicion. But suspicion and insecurity are difficult to overcome because it is difficult to verify that the other side does not harbour offensive intentions. There is, however, another way to reduce the insecurity. Although both sides in the security dilemma may be motivated by defensive concerns, they may choose to actively pre-empt—that is, take not only defensive precautions, but attack in order to eliminate or severely weaken the other side. Indeed, this option in itself makes the other side even more insecure, making the security dilemma more acute. Warfare can thus become a self-fulfilling prophecy. Since full security is difficult to achieve, history demonstrates that constant warfare can be waged, conquest carried out afar, and power accumulated, all truly motivated by security concerns, 'for defence'. Of course, in reality motives are often mixed, with the security motive coexisting with a quest for gain.

Thus, as we have seen with respect to honour and revenge, the basic condition of inter-human competition and potential conflict creates 'second level' causes for warfare, arising from the first level causes. This does not mean that actual competition over somatic and reproductive resources has to exist on every particular occasion for the security dilemma to flare up. It is the prospect of such competition that stands behind the mutual insecurity, and the stronger the competition and potential conflict, the more intense the security dilemma will grow. As we shall see in Chapter 5, the roots of the security dilemma in actual or potential competition over objects of desire have been largely misunderstood by so-called structural realists in international relations theory, who have made this dilemma the centrepiece of their explanation of international insecurity and conflict.

World-View and the Supernatural

But what about the world of culture that after all is our most distinctive feature as humans? Do people not kill and get killed for lofty ideas and ideals? In the Stone Age, as later, the spiritual life of human communities was permeated with supernatural beliefs, sacred cults and rituals, and the practice of magic.

The evolutionary status of religion is beyond our scope here. The human quest for ordering the cosmos appears to be a product of *Homo sapiens'* vastly expanded intellectual and imaginative faculties. Humans must have answers as to the reasons and direction of the world around them. They need a cognitive map of and a manipulative manual for the universe, which by lessening the realm of the unknown would give them a sense of security and control, allay their fears, and alleviate their pain and distress. Where answers are beyond their scope, or beyond experience, they fill up the gaps by 'mythologizing'. Some scholars, believing religion to be detrimental for survival because it consumes time and resources with no apparent gain, suggest that religion emerged as a 'bug', 'parasite', or 'virus' on *Homo sapiens'* advanced intellectual 'software' and its search for ultimate causes.[21] Conversely, religion may have had in it, evolutionarily speaking, more than a worthless expenditure. From Emile Durkheim, whose *The Elementary Forms of the Religious Life* (1915) concentrated on the Australian Aborigines, functionalist theorists have argued that religion's main role was in fostering social cohesion. Machiavelli, Rousseau, and the nineteenth-century French positivists had held more or less the same view. This means that in those groups in which common ritual and cult ceremonies were more intensive, social cooperation became more habitual and more strongly legitimized, which probably translated into an advantage in warfare.[22] Indeed, ritual ties among hunter-gatherers—in Australia as elsewhere—formed the principal basis for larger tribal alliances and confederations, the so-called (after the ancient Greek example) amphictyonic alliances. And one of the primary roles of such alliances was cooperation in war.

Thus, communal cults and rituals may have constituted an adaptive advantage, which would help to explain their survival and widespread prevalence. But how did hunter-gatherers' supernatural beliefs and practices affect not only communities' conduct and success in war but also the reasons for conflict and fighting, our subject here? On the whole, they seem to have added to, and sometimes accentuated, the reasons we have already discussed. The all-familiar glory of the gods, let alone missionary quests, never figure as reasons for hunter-gatherers' warfare. These will appear later in human cultural evolution. The most regular supernatural reasons cited by anthropologists for fighting and killing among hunter-gatherers are fear and accusations of sorcery. It should be noted, however, that such fears and accusations did not appear randomly, but were directed against people whom the victim of the alleged sorcery felt had reasons to want to harm him. This, of course, does not necessarily mean that they really did. What it does mean is that competition, potential conflict, animosity, and suspicion were conducive to fears and accusations of sorcery. In societies that invariably believed in the efficacy of such forces, every ill was attributed to a dark spell cast by someone with whom one's relations were tense. To a greater degree than with the security dilemma, the paranoia here reflected the running amok of real, or potentially real, fears and insecurity, thus further exacerbating and escalating the war complex. Of course, in some cases accusations of sorcery were made as a pretext for other reasons, again adding an extra dimension in the realm of the spiritual, sanctified, and legitimate to motives we have already seen.

Pugnacity: Playfulness, Sadism, Ecstasy

Do people not sometimes fight for no particular purpose, as a game, an outlet, arising from sheer pugnacity? Playing and sports have often been regarded—even defined—as a purposeless, expressive, pure fun activity.[23] What is its evolutionary logic? After all, it is an activity that consumes a great deal of energy for no apparent gain. In reality, though, the purpose of games and sport is physical exercise and behavioural training for the tasks of life, such as hunting, escaping predators and natural dangers, fighting, nurturing, and social cooperation in all of these. For this reason, in all mammalian species, distinctive for both their learning ability and playing activity, it is the young who exhibit the most active and enthusiastic play behaviour.[24] Since adaptive behaviours are normally stimulated by emotional gratifications, play and sport are generally enjoyable.

Games and sports thus serve, among other things, as preparation for fighting. However, is fighting not sometimes perpetrated not for any purpose other than producing the sort of emotional gratifications associated with play or sport behaviour? It certainly is, but as an extension rather than a negation of the evolutionary logic. In the first place, as with respect to accusations of sorcery, it should be noted that even seemingly purposeless violence is not purely random. It is much more often unleashed either against alien groups or in pursuit of superiority within the group. In this form, it is a potentially adaptive outgrowth from a fundamental state of competition and potential conflict. However, there are also cases of purely purposeless violence, triggered or 'mis-activated' outside its evolutionarily 'designed' context. Since it is often maladaptive, how does such behaviour survive? In reality, maladaptive traits *are* constantly selected against. For this reason, their prevalence remains marginal. Still, they do exist. It is not only that natural selection is perpetual because of mutations, the unique gene recombination that occurs with every new individual, and changing environmental conditions. The main reason is that no mechanism, whether designed purposefully by humans or blindly by natural selection, is ever perfect, 100 per cent efficient, or fully tuned. Like any other design, the products of natural selection, for all their marvels, vary in their level of sophistication, have limitations, flaws, and 'bugs', and can only operate in a proximate manner. The emotional mechanisms controlling violence have all of these limitations. Thus, they can be triggered or 'mis-activated' into 'purposeless', 'expressive', 'spontaneous', or 'misdirected' violence. Like overeating or sleeplessness, to give more familiar examples, such behaviour should be understood as a range of deviation from an evolutionarily-shaped norm.

Consider sadism. It can produce all sorts of behaviour—including fighting—which have no purpose other than emotional gratification from others' pain. In this form, however, sadism is relatively rare and originates as a deviation from evolution-based emotions. Above all, it derives and deviates from 'normal' cruelty, whose evolutionary rationale is clear: cruelty is the urge to hurt one's adversary, an urge which is often tempered by, and takes a back seat to, other behaviour patterns within the overall behavioural calculus. There should be no misunderstanding—'normal' cruelty expresses itself horrendously. The point is only that it is an evolution-shaped and potentially adaptive behaviour. In addition to cruelty, sadism may also derive and deviate from the evolution-shaped desire for superiority over others.

Ecstatic behaviour is another case in point. Ecstasy is a feeling of elation and transcendence produced by an increasing flow of hormones such as adrenaline, serotonin, and dopamine. It reduces the body's sensitivity to pain and fatigue, raises its energy to a high pitch, and lowers normal inhibitions. In nature, ecstatic behaviour can be produced during extreme bodily exertion, often associated with struggle and fighting. However, humans very early on found ways to arouse it artificially for the feel-good effect itself, for instance through rhythmic dance and singing or by the use of narcotic substances. In some cases, narcotic substances were consumed before fighting and in preparation for it—a few shots of alcohol before an assault was ordinary practice in most armies until not very long ago.[25] However, in other cases, the ecstatic condition itself can breed violence. Drunkenness greatly contributes to the occurrence of violence in many societies. Furthermore, in some cases, the sequence is reversed, with fighting entered into in order to produce ecstatic sensations. For example, in addition to 'ordinary' reasons, such as money, females, and social esteem, this motive plays a prominent role—often in conjunction with alcohol consumption—in perpetrating 'purposeless' youth gangs' violence. Again, what we have here is an often maladaptive outgrowth and deviation from evolution-shaped stimuli and behavioural patterns.

Fighting in and for a Group

Fighting for all the reasons mentioned so far was carried out in the human state of nature at both the individual and group levels. Group cooperation in fighting took place among family, clan, and tribe members. In principle, there are strong advantages to cooperation. In warfare there is, for example, a strong advantage to group size. However, the problem with cooperation is that one has a clear incentive to 'free ride'—reap the benefits of cooperation while avoiding one's share in the costs.[26] A number of overlapping mechanisms established a measure of cooperation and enhanced internal solidarity in hunter-gatherer groups.

First, people risk their lives in support of close kin, with whom they share more genes.[27] Needless to say, hunter-gatherers knew nothing about genes. Like any natural propensity, kin solidarity evolved because those who acted on it increased their genes' representation in the population and, consequently, also that propensity itself. Siblings share, on average, 50 per cent of their genes, the same percentage as parents and offspring. Half-siblings share, on average, 25 per cent of their genes, as do uncles/aunts with nephews/nieces. Cousins share, on average, 12.5 per cent of their genes.* This is the basis of the age-old notion that 'blood is thicker than water', now explained scientifically by the awkwardly sounding term 'inclusive fitness'. Thus, family members tended to support one another in disputes and clashes with members of other families. In inter-clan rivalry, clans which were intermarried were likely to support one another against other clans. Tribe members, numbering in the hundreds and more, were not as closely related as family and clan members, and yet (weaker) cooperation among them took place, particularly in conflict against alien tribes. The same logic that, in the formulation of one of the pioneers of modern evolutionary theory J. B. S. Haldane, makes it evolutionarily beneficial to sacrifice one's own life in order to save more than two siblings or eight cousins, and take risks at even lower ratios, holds true for 32 second cousins, 128 third cousins, or 512 fourth cousins. This, in fact, is pretty much what a tribal group was. Moreover, although not every member of the tribal group was a close relative of all the others, the tribe was a dense network of close kinship through marriage ties. Marriage links criss-crossed the tribe, making families and clans ready to take risks in support of one another, as they had a shared genetic investment in the offspring. Since most marriages took place within the tribe, there was a wide gap between the 'us' of the tribe and the 'them' of outsiders.[28] Throughout history, political treaties and alliances were cemented by marriage.

Certainly, competition and even conflict among kin were also ubiquitous. Evolutionary logic explains why this is so: the closer the kin, the greater the reward for caring for them, but only as long as they do not threaten the prospects of even closer kin. For example, one is genetically doubly closer to one's self than to a sibling. Therefore, in case of severe competition between them, sibling rivalry can become intense and even deadly. The

---

* There should be no confusion here. More than 99 per cent of the genes are identical in all people. All the variations among individuals are due to the remaining less than 1 per cent, and it is to this variation in the genome that the shared genes above refer. It should not be thought that this less than 1 per cent difference in genes is so small as to be insignificant. Humans share more than 98 per cent of their genes with chimpanzees, yet crucial changes in a small number of genes can trigger huge differences.

biblical story of Cain and Abel demonstrates both the intense competition and strong inhibitions against the killing of kin. Similarly, while uncles/aunts are evolutionarily inclined to favour their nephews/nieces, they doubly favour their own offspring. Hence the all -too familiar jealousy, tensions, and antagonism between relatives.[29] In extreme cases this may even result in cooperation with outsiders against kin, which sometimes happens but which has always carried the strong stigma of betrayal. An Arab proverb expresses the evolutionary rationale of kin solidarity, still very much alive in contemporary family-, clan-, and tribal-based Arab society: 'I against my brother; I and my brother against my cousin; I and my brother and my cousin against the world.' This is somewhat more complex, and realistic, than the simple in-group-cooperation/out-group-rivalry suggested by Herbert Spencer and William Graham Sumner.

Second, social cooperation—in fighting, as in all other activities—can be sustained in groups that are intimate enough to allow mutual surveillance and social accountability. If detected, a 'free rider' faces the danger of being excluded, or 'ostracized', from the system of cooperation which is on the whole beneficial to him. He might also be punished by the group. People keep a very watchful eye for 'cheaters' and 'defectors'. They would help other people on the assumption that they would get similar help in return, but if the expected return fails to arrive they are likely to cease cooperating and/or actively retaliate against those who breach faith. The term 'reciprocal altruism' has been coined to describe this logic of 'you scratch my back and I'll scratch yours'.[30] The tribal group is small enough to have dense kinship networks, as well as for all its members to know one another, to be in contact with them, and to hold them to account. Furthermore, we watch people's behaviour towards other people to establish how trustworthy they might be towards us or the common good. A 'positive character' is rewarded. 'Reciprocal altruism' is thus extended into 'generalized' or 'indirect reciprocal altruism', which lies at the root of morality.[31]

Third, apart from biology, humans have culture, and are differentiated by their cultures. As culture, particularly among hunter-gatherers, was local and thus closely correlated with kinship, cultural identity became a strong predictor of kinship. Moreover, sharing a culture is also crucial for human social cooperation. Cooperation is dramatically more effective when cultural codes, above all language, are shared. Tribal groupings, differing from their neighbours in their language and customs, were thus the most effective frameworks of social cooperation for their members. Outside them, people would find themselves at a great disadvantage. Therefore, shared culture in a world of cultural diversity further increases the stake of a tribe's members in their group's survival.[†] This unique human quality makes group connection and solidarity more vital among humans than they are with any other social species. The regional group (tribe) is bound together by the mutually reinforcing and overlapping ties of kinship, social cooperation, and cultural distinctiveness. Hence the phenomenon of 'ethnocentrism', a human universal that already very much existed at the level of the hunter-gatherer tribal group and would be expanded onto larger ethnic groupings later in history.[32]

Fourth, 'reciprocal altruism' and cultural distinctiveness within groups bring us to the contentious issue of (inter-)group selection. Modern evolutionary theory has shown that genes for individual self-sacrifice on behalf of the group could not have been selected if they had the effect of annihilating those who possessed them faster than it aided them through improved group survival. There is a fine balancing act here between individual egoism and altruism for the group. Still, under conditions of intense competition and conflict among small-scale groups, as prevailed during the vast time span of the Stone Age, a group that evolved greater solidarity and individual willingness to sacrifice for the group would defeat less cohesive groups. Already suggested by Darwin, this calculus is now supported by mathematical modelling.[33]

To conclude, in pursuing the objectives that contributed to survival and reproduction in the human evolutionary state of nature, people are inclined to help kin who share the same genes with them, as well as those, often from their broader kin-culture group, on whose cooperation and survival they depend for achieving these objectives.

[†] Even between relatively close culture groups, people are acutely attuned to the subtlest of differences in dialect, accent, dressing style, and behaviour that separate their own group from others, and they tend to give preference to those most like them. The perplexed Freud called this the 'narcissism of minor differences': Sigmund Freud, 'Group Psychology and the Analysis of the Ego' (1921) and 'Civilization and its Discontents' (1930), in *The Complete Psychological Works*, vol. 18, 101–4, and vol. 21, 108–16. Again, Freud tried to explain this 'narcissism' as a bottled-up expression of an elementary aggressive drive, thus turning the matter on its head and denying it of any logic, evolutionary or otherwise. Why aggression should express itself in this particular domain remained wholly obscure. Indeed, Freud confessed his puzzlement over the reasons for group ties in general. In actuality, it is ethnic differences, even minor ones, that create the boundaries between kin-culture communities of identity, solidarity, and cooperation and may spark competition and aggression between them, rather than the other way around.

The Causes of Fighting in the Evolutionary State of Nature

The prehistoric human state of nature is neither a philosophical fiction nor an exotic curiosity. More than 90 per cent of the history of our species *Homo sapiens*, people who are like us, was spent in a hunter-gatherer existence. History's short span is illuminated by the bright light of written records. But beyond that very limited area under the lamp post, with no known names or any concrete record of events, people of our species had lived for thousands of generations. And it was during this geological time span that our natural propensities and behavioural strategies, including warfare, were shaped.

Conflict and fighting in the human state of nature, as in the state of nature in general, was fundamentally caused by competition. While violence is evoked, and suppressed, by powerful emotional stimuli, it is not a primary 'irresistible' drive. Rather, it is a highly tuned, both innate and optional, evolution-shaped tactic, turned on and off in response to changes in the calculus of survival and reproduction. In this sense, *both* war and peace are in our genes. In pursuit of their aims people may employ any of the following strategies: cooperation, peaceful competition, and violent conflict. In reality, they did employ all of them interchangeably (and often conjointly), as aboriginal people engaged in exchange and other forms of peaceful cooperation, competed, and also fought each other, depending on the particular circumstances and prospects of success. We are very adept in using each of these behavioural strategies because we are evolutionarily well-equipped with the heavy biological machinery necessary for carrying them out. The reason why we are so well equipped is that each of these strategies has been widely employed by humans throughout our long evolutionary history. Violence is the hammer in our behavioural toolkit, which has always been readily available and handy. Indeed, it often proved necessary and advantageous, while also carrying tremendous risks.

At the root of human fighting is the pursuit of the very same objects of desire that constitute the human motivational system in general—only by violent means. Violence was habitually activated by competition over scarce resources, as scarcity and competition are the norm in nature because of organisms' tendency to propagate rapidly when resources are abundant, thereby increasing the pressure on the resources. Deadly violence was also regularly activated in competition over women, directly as well as indirectly, when men competed over resources in order to be able to afford more women and children. From these primary somatic and reproductive aims, other proximate and derivative 'second level' aims arise. The social arbiters within the group can use their position to reap somatic and reproductive advantages. Hence the competition for—and conflict over—esteem, prestige, power, and leadership, as proximate goods. An offence or injury will often prompt retaliation, lest it persists and turns into a pattern of victimization. Tit-for-tat may end in victory or a compromise, but it may also escalate, developing into a self-perpetuating cycle of strikes and counter-strikes, with the antagonists locked in conflict in a sort of prisoner's dilemma situation.

Similarly, in a state of potential conflict, security precautions are called for, which may take on defensive but also offensive or pre-emptive charac-ters. The security dilemma variant of the prisoner's dilemma breeds arms races that may give an advantage to one side but often merely produces a 'Red Queen' effect, by which both sides escalate their resource investment only to find themselves in the same position vis-à-vis one another. A con-flictual condition may thus, at least partly, feed and grow on itself, leading through prisoner's dilemmas to clashes that seem to be forced on the antag-onists against their wishes and best interests, to costs that can be heavier than the rewards for which the sides are ostensibly fighting. This paradoxical state of affairs is possible because natural selection operates on the principle of individual competition. There is no higher authority ('Nature') that regulates the competition and prevents prisoner's dilemmas or market fail-ures. Sometimes, fighting is the most promising choice for at least one of the sides. At other times, however, fighting, while being their rational choice, is not their best one. In such cases, conflict seems to take on a life of its own. Like a Moloch, it consumes the warring parties caught up in its fire, irrespective of their true wishes or interests.

Competition and conflict are thus 'real' in the sense that they arise from genuine scarcities and desires among evolution-shaped self-propagating organisms and can end in vital gains for one and losses for the other. At the same time, they are often also 'inflated', self-perpetuated, and mutually dam-aging, because of the logic imposed on the antagonists by the conflict itself in an anarchic, unregulated environment. This duality creates a distinction between the motives for war and the causes of war. The violent pursuit or defence of objects of desire, the fundamental cause of war, produces situations that may lead to war even on occasions when the sides do not actually seek to win coveted objects of desire by force, but, on the contrary, may all lose. In a way, this justifies both of the diametrically opposed attitudes to war: the one that sees it as a serious business for serious aims and the other that is shocked by its absurdity.

Steven Pinker well understands the cost-effectiveness rationale that tilts people's choices between violent and non-violent behavioural options. Still, some of the few significant reservations I have about his superb book, *The Better Angels of Our Nature: Why Violence Has Declined*, concern the causes of violence. Surprisingly, the evolutionary parts of the book are, in my opinion, not up to its otherwise very high standard. 'Angels' versus 'Demons' in the human behavioural system is an allusion to Lincoln's first inaugural address and this is largely invoked metaphorically. And yet not entirely, because to reduce central aspects of human behaviour, including those Pinker labels predation, dominance, and ideology, to 'demons' is to flatten human aims and motivations, and the means for achieving them. Furthermore, the distinctions that Pinker draws between different categories of violence respectively related to the above 'demons' are questionable. He cites studies showing that separate parts of the brain may trigger violent behaviour, and this is of course true of nearly all behaviours. But it does not mean that all violent behaviours are not subject to, regulated, and shaped by a unified evolutionary calculus of survival and reproduction, the very definition of the evolutionary rationale, which Pinker as an evolutionist would surely be the first to accept. Thus, the wide category he calls predation violence and describes as a means to achieve an end in fact also covers most of the other motives for violence that he cites. As we have seen, the quest for dominance among all social animals is an evolutionary means to achieve preferential access to resources and superior sexual opportunities. Another problem with Pinker's conception is that dominance can be pursued non-violently as well as violently, which makes the 'demon' label all the more awkward. The same applies to ideology, also labelled a 'demon': it can be both pursued non-violently and can be a force for good. Revenge, yet another 'demon', is similarly, as Pinker recognizes, a means to an end: it is intended to establish fragile security in an unruly society by demonstrating that one is not a pushover. Finally, Pinker on occasion gives the impression that overcoming war is a matter of escaping a prisoner's dilemma. While there are all sorts of prisoner's dilemmas in conflict situations, not all conflicts fall under this category. Throughout human history there have been many winners and losers in war.

The main cause of resistance to the application of evolutionary theory to human affairs is the belief that it upholds biological determinism in a subject which is distinctively determined by human culture. This, however, is a false dichotomy—a misplaced either/or distinction—as both nature and culture, and the interaction between them, are crucial.[34] Once humans developed agriculture some 10,000 years ago, which led to the growth of the first states about 5,000 years ago, they set in motion a continuous chain of developments that have taken them far away from their evolutionary natural way of life. Original, evolution-shaped, innate human wants, desires, and proximate behavioural and emotional mechanisms now expressed themselves in radically altered, 'artificial' conditions. In the process, they were greatly modified, assuming novel and diverse manifestations. At the same time, however, cultural evolution did not operate on a 'clean slate', nor was it capable of producing simply 'anything'. Its multifarious and diverse forms have been built on a clearly recognizable deep core of innate human propensities. Cultural take-off took place much too recently to affect human biology in any significant way. Except for some specific traits associated with life in dense agricultural settlements, such as the ability to digest lactose (in milk) and disease resistance, we are biologically virtually the same people as our pre-agriculture kin and are endowed with the same propensities. With cultural evolution all bets are not off; they are merely hedged. Gene–culture interactions are the stuff from which human history is made, including the history of fighting.

We now turn to examine these gene–culture interactions to see how they shaped the causes of human fighting in historical state societies.

3
The Clash of the
State-Leviathans

Violence and War under the Leviathan

Although humankind's transition to farming and animal husbandry from about ten thousand years ago onwards did not inaugurate human fighting, it greatly transformed it, as it did human life in general. Productivity and population grew steadily, increasing about a hundredfold by the eve of modernity. Because the rise in productivity was more or less offset by population growth, surpluses did not increase much, and the vast majority of people continued to live as food producers precariously close to subsistence levels. However, increasingly dense and sedentary populations, stationary means of production, and accumulated property now made possible a differential concentration and appropriation of surpluses. In a process first outlined by Rousseau, existing natural differences between people were enormously magnified and objectified by accumulated resources. Rousseau was much closer to the truth here than in his portrayal of the human state of nature.

As power and the accumulation of resources reinforced each other in a positive loop mechanism, massive social power structures emerged. Relying on concentrated wealth and the power that emanated from wealth, the rich and powerful dominated social life. The emergence of states was the culmination of this process, as a single power nucleus won against all others in often violent intra-social competition. It established command over a population, institutionalizing power, driving other social power nuclei into subordination, and introducing hitherto unprecedented levels of hierarchic organization, coercion, systematic resource extraction, and manpower mobilization, while competing with neighbouring state structures.

This violent process was the main driving force for the growth of states and civilizations. We tend to forget how recent in our species' history these developments have been. The first states emerged—in Mesopotamia and Egypt—only some five thousand years ago, and the emergence and spread of the state system in other parts of the globe took many millennia more. As already noted, in both northern Europe and Japan, for example, states only emerged during the second half of the first millennium AD, and in some other parts of the world they are younger still. Nonetheless, the superiority of power that scale and coercive structuring accorded in competition and conflict unleashed an evolutionary race that, despite occasional collapses and regressions, spiralled continuously upwards. This self-reinforcing process was responsible for both the spread of the state system and the increase in states' size. Individual state populations swelled from a few thousand to tens and hundreds of thousands, to millions. States created economies of scale, aggregated and purposefully directed resources and human activity, and gave rise to monumental building, literacy, and high culture. Neither long-distance trade nor religious authority were even remotely as significant as the accumulation of force in bringing about this process in overwhelmingly agrarian and thus fundamentally local and self-sufficient societies. Indeed, both trade and religious authority constituted at least as much a consequence as a cause of political unification.[1] Readers interested in the rich texture of these processes in states and civilizations around the globe and throughout history are again referred to my *War in Human Civilization*.

The struggle for power and for the benefits that power entailed took place simultaneously and inextricably both within and between states. The state has all too often been perceived as the elementary and coherent unit of war. Yet the state did not entirely eliminate violent domestic power competition but, rather, more or less bounded and suppressed it. In Max Weber's definition, the state successfully holds claim to monopoly over legitimate force.[2] However, a *claim* to monopoly over legitimate force, even a successful one, never actually amounted to a monopoly, not even over legitimate force. Existing around and inside the Leviathan were not only countless sardines but also many sharks and barracudas: powerful aristocrats, provincial governors, generals, bandits, and pirates. All of them limited, challenged, or strove to usurp state power.

The state's internal and external power politics thus mutually affected each other. While raising troops to confront foreign rivals, the state had to consider that these troops—aristocratic, professional, or popular—might each become an agent of domestic power politics. Furthermore, the state's success or failure to master the domestic arena affected its ability to deal with foreign rivals, while its record abroad greatly affected its political standing at home. Despite all the ink spilled on this subject, it is no more possible to generalize which of these spheres—foreign or domestic politics—holds the primacy than to determine which hand is responsible for clapping. Moreover, this interdependency could be deliberately manipulated, as action in one sphere could actually be intended for its effect in the other. For example, state rulers might instigate war in order to create a galvanizing 'rallying around the flag' effect that would consolidate their domestic position, while generals might do the same to win the resources and prestige necessary for a successful usurpation. This so-called two-level game often involved violence on both levels.[3]

Indeed, in the domestic arena, too, open violence sometimes ruptured the state's crust. Mass popular uprisings often resulted in horrendous blood-baths. Even intra-elite violent struggles could exact a huge toll on society as a whole in terms of economic disruption, devastation, and mass killing. Although such 'civil wars' did not result in a complete return to the 'state of nature', their closeness to home and the spread of anarchy which could result from them sometimes degenerated into a Hobbesian 'warre', whose destructiveness and lethality dwarfed foreign war.

However, in 'normal' times the state's imposition of relative internal peace created a gulf between in-group and out-group violence, which had been far less distinct from one another in both scale and methods in pre-state societies. A sharp difference opened up between small-scale deadly violence, labelled 'murder' and 'feud' and now outlawed, on the one hand, and large-scale organized violence, construed as 'war', on the other. As noted before, this distinction, which people tend to conceptualize as fundamental, is as recent a historical development as the state itself. War is customarily identified with the state and with politics—it is regarded as 'a continuation of state policy', as Carl von Clausewitz, the Prussian philosopher of war, famously defined it in his *On War* (1832), during the apogee of the European state system and of state-run warfare.[4] However, these formal concepts might be misleading if understood as representing distinct 'essences', rather than historically framed forms of human deadly violence. Indeed, what many regard as the mystery of the differences between human wars and intraspecific animal violence dissolves once the historical trajectory of human violence is recognized. Among social animals, as with small-scale pre-state human societies, group fighting and killing are prevalent. It is just that group fighting grew in scale with the growth in size of the human groups themselves.

Some readers of *War in Human Civilization* have suggested that I conflate violence and war. They have implied that the two phenomena should be kept conceptually apart, as the latter represents something else in terms of both scale and social organization and derives from different and 'elevated' political reasons of state. Indeed, not only do I explain war as one, histori-cally-shaped form of human deadly violence rather than as a reified cat-egory; I argue that war is caused by the very same objects of desire that underlie human behaviour in general. War, to adjust Clausewitz, is intended to achieve these objects at the collective level of state politics and by violent means.

Certainly, states' wars differed considerably from pre-state fighting, as well as from intra-state deadly violence. The main differences were the much larger absolute size of the armed forces and the scale of coercive structuring, regimentation of manpower, and organizational efforts generated by the state. Participation in war became obligatory rather than voluntary; armed forces grew from scores of men-warriors into thousands, tens of thousands, and hundreds of thousands; warriors became soldiers; unorgan-ized kin-based war parties gave way to orderly fighting formations; stricter hierarchic command replaced leadership by example. Fortifications, much denser sedentary settlement, and greater distances spelled a decline in the significance of the raid—the predominant and most lethal form of warfare in pre-state societies—because wholesale surprise of the enemy community became more difficult to achieve. The siege and the battle became almost synonymous with war. Large-scale and long-distance campaigning required complex logistics, and the state's bureaucracy was called upon to support and sustain larger and more permanent armies, to secure finance and supervise the acquisition and requisition of provisions. The state apparatus also made possible permanent conquest and direct rule over foreign people—that crucial upgrade in the activity of war which was responsible for the state's continuous increase in size.

Still, the main feature widely responsible in many people's eyes for the close association of the state with war—the level of violent mortality—actually *decreased* under the state. The greatest decline occurred in in-group deadly violence, and resulted from the state's success in enforcing internal peace. Hobbes was right in claiming that anarchy is the most significant cause of violent mortality, and could in many cases be worse than bad government.[5] However, less recognized, if not wholly in contrast to commonly-held perceptions, the death toll in out-group violence—state wars—also decreased in comparison to pre-state times, despite the lingering anarchy of the international system. The size of states and their armies was larger, often much larger, than that of the tribal groups that had preceded them, creating a spectacular impression of large-scale fighting for state wars. State wars look big, and they are big—in *absolute* terms. However, in terms of lethality the main question is not absolute but *relative* casualties—what percentage of the population died in war? And relative casualties actually decreased under the state, precisely because states were large. Large states—and hence distance and complex logistics—meant lower mobilization rates and less exposure of the civilian population to war than was the case with tribal groups. Thus, whereas armies, wars, and killing in individual engagements all grew conspicuously larger, only particularly catastrophic spates of state warfare resulted in anything near the 25 per cent violent mortality rates among adult males that small-scale segmentary societies are recorded to have incurred as a matter of course.[6]

Take Egypt, for example, one of the earliest states and empires. The size of the Egyptian army with which Pharaoh Ramses II fought the Hittite Empire at the Battle of Kadesh in thirteenth-century BC northern Syria was 20,000–25,000 soldiers. This was a very large army by the standards of the time. Yet the total population of Egypt was about 2–3 million, so the army constituted only 1 per cent of the population at most. This was very much the standard in large states and empires throughout history because of the great financial and logistical problems of maintaining large armies for long periods at great distances from home. Thus, in comparison to the high military participation rates of small-scale tribal societies fighting close to home, participation rates, and hence war casualties, in large states' armies were much lower. Moreover, in contrast to the great vulnerability of women and children in small-scale tribal warfare, the civilian population of Egypt was sheltered by distance from the theatres of military operations and not often exposed to the horrors of war. Such relative security, interrupted only by large-scale invasions, is one of the main reasons why societies experienced great demographic growth after the emergence of the state. It is also the reason why civil war, when the war rages within the country, tends to be the most lethal form of war, as Hobbes very well realized. Thus, the rise of the state meant bigger, more spectacular wars, but, by and large, fewer casualties relative to population. Both internal and external violent death rates declined under the state.

The decline in violent mortality under the Leviathan runs counter to the view that blames fighting on the state. Historical states have been likened to organized crime, in the sense that they monopolized force and compulsorily extracted resources from society for their own profit in return for the promise of protection from both internal and external violence.[7] Indeed, some would further extend the analogy by arguing that the main threat of both types of violence came from the state itself—that it offered a solution to a problem of its own making. However, in view of what we have seen, at least the latter conclusion should be regarded with caution. Pre-state violence— 'ordinary crime', as it were—was more rife and more lethal than state violence would become. Systematic 'extortion' by the state was economically less disruptive than 'warre', while the state offered more protection. Undeniably, however, 'protection money' was channelled upwards, and the larger the span of the coercive organization, the more hierarchic and differential was the distribution of the rewards.

Cui bono?—Who Gains? The Material Element

As argued in Chapter 2, the motivations that lead to fighting are fundamentally derived from the human motivational system in general. How did cultivation, accumulated resources, stratification, coercive political authority, and a growing scale affect the motivational system that led to fighting? Although the changes were very considerable, they were fundamentally less than one might expect.

Materially, territories for cultivation (and for pasture) replaced hunting and foraging territories as an object for competition. However, where both of these involved competition over the right of access to nature, the real novelty brought about by cultivation was the exploitation of human labour. With cultivation it became possible to live off other people's work. Accumulated foodstuffs and livestock could be appropriated by looting. Other somatic-utility objects, such as fabrics, tools, and metal were also desirable targets. In addition to their utility, objects possessed decorative, status, and prestige value. Precious objects that acquired the role of money, most notably precious metals, became the most highly prized booty. Control over both natural sources of raw materials and trade intensified as a source of competition. Furthermore, not only products but also the producers themselves could be captured and carried back home as slaves, to labour under direct control. Finally, looting could be further upgraded to tribute extraction, a more systematic and more efficient appropriation of labour and resources through political subjugation that did not involve great destruction, waste, or disruption of productive activity. Looting made the loss of the vanquished far more extensive than the victor's gain, which in effect meant that the victor extracted far less than it was potentially able to. Like any profitable venture, efficient exploitation required careful husbanding of the resources for exploitation, so as not to kill the goose that laid the golden eggs. Despite their administrative and military overheads, the richest empires by far were those based on regulated tribute extraction. Thus, the often made claim that empires experienced declining profits as they ceased to expand is fundamentally untrue.

The balance of costs and gains in war is the most intricate, and intriguing, subject. Cultivation greatly increased the material costs of fighting. Hunter-gatherers' fighting harmed mainly the antagonists and their productive activity, but barely the resources themselves. Cultivation, however, added to this the ability to inflict direct damage on the resources and on other somatic and labour-intensive hardware. Antagonists regularly ravaged crops, livestock, production implements, and settlements in order to weaken and/or increase the cost of war incurred by the opponent. Furthermore, growing political units and technological advancement meant that fighting no longer took place close to home, during lulls in productive activity, and with simple arms and improvised logistics. Metal weapons, fortifications, horses, ships, long-term paid soldiers, and provisions consumed huge resources. Military expenditure regularly constituted by far the largest item of states' expenditure, in most cases the great majority of it. States' tax revenues may have reached as much as 10 per cent of the domestic product, and rose to even higher levels during military emergencies.[8] In pre-modern subsistence economies, where malnutrition was the rule and starvation an ever-looming prospect, such a burden literally took bread out of people's mouths.

Resources ravaged by and invested in war thus constituted a new, massive addition to the costs of fighting. Whereas among hunter-gatherers the struggle for resources approximated a zero-sum game, in which resource quantity remained generally unaffected, fighting now invariably *decreased* the *sum total* of resources. Only the relative *distribution* of these decreased resources and, moreover, the re-channelling of their *future yield* might result in net gains for one at the expense of the other.

Who was that 'one'? Neither humanity nor even individual societies counted as real agents or units of calculation in the competition. Unequal distribution was the rule not only between but also within rival sides. The state itself was largely the outgrowth of such processes: power gave wealth, which, in a self-reinforcing spiral, accentuated intra-social power relations in a way that obliged people down a progressively more hierarchic social pyramid to follow their superiors while receiving a smaller and smaller share of the benefits. People could be made to fight not only for the expected benefits (including the defence of their own), but also, and even solely, through coercion; that is, for fear of punishment from their superiors that outweighed the loss that they might incur from the fighting itself. Contrary to Clausewitz's idealist view that politics is the 'representative of all interests of the community', it rather represented the *ruling* interests in society, which could be more or less inclusive.[9] Thus, cultivation, resource accumulation, and the state made predatory, 'parasitical' existence on the fruits of other people's labour possible for the first time. Whereas productivity-related competition generally increases productive efficiency, predatory-parasitical competition increases predatory-parasitic efficiency while decreasing productive efficiency. All the same, by being efficient in predatory competition, one was able to secure the benefits of production. Indeed, once anyone in an anarchic system resorts to the option of predatory competition, he *ipso facto* imposes on anyone else a choice between resource surrender and entering the violent competition themselves, at least for defensive purposes.

Despite the general overall loss of resources in war, there were also spin-off and long-term net productive gains resulting from the power race. How substantial an independent spin-off effect military innovation in metallurgy, engineering, horse breeding, naval architecture, and supply had on society is difficult to establish. But the most significant spin-off effects appear to have come from the state itself. There is a long-standing debate on whether states were created from above by an exploitative elite that imposed itself on society, or, alternatively, emerged in complex societies in response to demands from below for social regulation and other social services.[10] Rather than being mutually exclusive, it would seem that both processes were combined in varying ways. It was through violence that one power established authority over a territory or society, thereby securing increased internal peace and imposing coordinated collective efforts, some of which, at least, were in the common good, decreasing 'free riding'. Large states introduced economies of scale, and, as long as they did not become monopolistically big and overburdened by overheads, they generated and accelerated innovation.[11] Ian Morris has brilliantly developed this point in his *War: What is it Good For?* (2014), demonstrating the seemingly paradoxical huge gains in terms of longevity, development, and well-being progressively achieved by the born-out-of-war and war-making state.

The warriors and the population at large might share the benefits of successful war-making. Furthermore, successful military expansion that was consolidated into relatively stable large states—as, for example, in Egypt, Rome, and China—considerably increased security, contributing to rising prosperity and demographic growth, for which heavy military expenditures might be considered a worthwhile premium. However, while the populace increased in number as a result of growing security, stability, and economic development made possible by state power, its prosperity per capita normally remained little improved, whereas the elite accumulated great wealth (differentially again, down the hierarchic pyramid). Indeed, the larger the conquered realm, the greater the command span and resource base from which the elite was able to draw benefits. Thus, heavy investment in the armed forces once the realm had been consolidated did not necessarily pay off directly, that is, through the benefits of foreign war; rather, it paid off indirectly, as a defensive-security premium for a huge tax-paying internal domain. Again, war was a 'two-level game', in which both external and internal power relations and external and internal benefit extraction were linked.

Although in the great majority of historical states the benefits of war were unevenly distributed down the social hierarchy, this does not mean—as it is popularly suggested—that selfish elites' interests enforced on peace-loving and war-averse peoples were the underlying rationale of war. Some of the most successful war-making states in history were those in which the people ruled or at least were co-opted into the state and therefore had a far greater motivation to enlist for war. In premodern times, democratic Athens and republican Rome, where the people directly profited from war, conquest, and empire—and repeatedly voted for it—are particularly striking examples. Asymmetric benefit allocation did not mean that those below the top of the social ladder did not stand to gain at all. Much depended on the actual

distribution of benefits (both offensive and defensive), where a whole range
of variations existed among historical state societies.

Sex and Harems

The same logic applies to that other principal source of human competition—the sexual—considered from the perspective of male fighting.
Students of war scarcely think of sexuality as a motive for fighting. It obviously did not occur to Clausewitz that sexual benefits might be included
among the 'serious ends' of 'politics', for which the 'serious means' of war
were employed (*On War*, i.1.23). The underlying links that connect the
various elements of the human motivational system have largely been lost
sight of.[12]

Silence is one reason for this blind spot. While some aspects of sexuality
are among the most celebrated in human discourse, others are among the
least advertised and most concealed by all the sides involved. Nonetheless,
the evidence is overwhelming and has recently returned to the headlines,
shocking Western public opinion with extensive documentation of mass
rape from the wars in Bosnia, Rwanda, Sudan, equatorial Africa, Syria, and
Iraq. There is a view that has gained much currency in recent discourse,
according to which rape is an act of violence, humiliation, and domination,
rather than of sex. However, this false dichotomy is greatly misleading, for
rape is precisely violently forced sex. To the extent that the perpetrator also
gives vent to a desire to dominate and humiliate his victim, there is a combination rather than a contradiction of motives here.[13] Throughout history,
widespread rape by soldiers went hand in hand with looting as an inseparable part of military operations. Indeed, like looting, the prospect of sexual
adventure was one of the main attractions of warlike operations, which
motivated men to join in. Young and beautiful captured women were a
valued prize, in the choice of which—as with all other booty—the leaders
enjoyed a right of priority.

In Chapter 2 we have seen the great reproductive advantage enjoyed by
distinguished individuals and large clans in hunter-gatherer and horticul-
tural societies. Rapidly advancing genetic studies have yielded astounding
finds regarding the reproductive success of leaders during the early rise of
polities. For example, analyses of the Y (male) chromosome of modern
Europeans reveal that more than half of them are descended from a handful

of men who lived between c.5000 and 1500 BC.[14] Archaeology tells us that Europe in this period was dominated by powerful chiefs, who controlled the technologies of the war chariot and, later, bronze weapons. They and their dynastic descendants over generations and centuries enjoyed massive reproductive opportunities by virtue of their social supremacy and military exploits. This reality is still reflected in the heroic sagas of protohistoric societies, such as the *Iliad*, in which the sexual prizes of war are barely veiled.

No less remarkable with respect to more recent historical times is a study of the Y chromosome in Central and Eastern Asia. It reveals that some 8 per cent of the population in the region (0.5 per cent of the world's population) carry the same Y chromosome, which can only mean that they are the descendants of a single man. The biochemical patterns indicate that this man lived in Mongolia about a thousand years ago. It was not difficult to identify the only likely candidate, Chinggis Khan, an identification confirmed by an examination of the Y chromosome of his known surviving descendants.[15] This, of course, does not mean that Chinggis Khan alone sired so many children from a huge number of women, an obvious impossibility even if he had ceased his military conquests altogether. As with the prehistoric chiefs in Europe, the tremendous spread of his Y chromosome is due to the fact that his sons succeeded him at the head of ruling houses throughout Central and East Asia for centuries, all enjoying staggering sexual opportunities.

Another major reason for the oversight of sexuality as one of the potential benefits of fighting, apart from the silence of both victors and victims, was the exponential rise in large-scale civilized societies of accumulated wealth, which functioned as a universal currency that could be exchanged for most of the other good things in life. Even more than before, fighting advanced reproductive success not only directly, as women were raped and kidnapped, but also indirectly, as the resources and status won by fighting advanced one in the intra-social competition for the acquisition and upkeep of women domestically. By and large, power, wealth, and sexual opportunity comprised overlapping and interlinked hierarchic pyramids. While mass rape, like looting, was considered the troops' inviolate right when storming a city—in compensation for their risk—those at the top drew most of the benefits.

Where polygyny was permitted, as in most historical societies, the rich and powerful acquired a greater number of wives and enjoyed a marked advantage in choosing young, beautiful, and otherwise worthy ones. In addition to wives, many societies sanctioned official concubines, and there were, of course, unofficial concubines or mistresses.[16] Yet another avenue of sexual opportunity was females in the household, some of whom were slave girls captured in war and raiding. Finally, there was the sex trade per se, where again the most consummate and graceful exponents of the trade could be highly expensive.

The manner in which power, wealth, and sexual opportunity were linked is strikingly demonstrated at the apex of the hierarchic pyramid, most notably in the figure of the so-called Oriental despot, who had his counterpart in the empires of pre-Columbian America. Rulers possessed large harems. According to the Greek authors, Alexander the Great captured 329 of King Darius III's concubines after the Battle of Issus (333 BC). As the later Achaemenid rulers found it difficult to extract themselves from the pleasures of life even when on campaign, the women accompanied them into the field, travelling in closed wagons, guarded by their eunuchs.[17] From a slightly later period, Kautilya's *Arthasastra* (i.20 and i.27), that classic inside account of statecraft apparently written by an Indian high official, provides a detailed description of the organization and procedures of the harem, as well as an account of the bureaucratic apparatus that supervised the march of prostitutes who were invited to the court.

Bureaucratic records, where they survive, constitute the most solid source from which verified numbers can be derived. After all, the women and their children had to be maintained by the treasury. The most bureaucratic and most magnificent of empires was China. According to the state's records, the imperial harem of the Early Han (second and first centuries BC) comprised some 2,000–3,000 women, whereas that of the Later Han (first and second centuries AD) reached 5,000–6,000.[18] But affluence for some, derived from a finite resource, meant deprivation for others. Although even thousands of women in the imperial harem did not affect the ratio between eligible men and women in China, polygyny by the rich throughout society did, especially as it was compounded by widespread female infanticide that was the norm in pre-industrial societies, including China. Inevitably, poor males were most likely to suffer from the deficiency in the number of women. During the nineteenth and early twentieth centuries, for which there is recorded evidence, some one-fifth of the males in Chinese provinces are reckoned to have remained unmarried. Thus, a skewed sex ratio is not unique to twenty-first-century China. Groups of young, poor, and unmarried men, the 'bare sticks' (in Chinese *guang gun*: slang for the male sexual organ), were greatly feared by the imperial authorities, constituting the mainstay of bandit bands, which inter alia perpetrated violent sexual offences.[19]

Imperial China seems to represent the ultimate in terms of harem size. A comparison can be made with the harem of the Ottoman sultans, the *grand seigniors*, tales and fantasies about which preoccupied Europe for centuries. The records of the Ottoman Privy Purse indicate that at its zenith, during the first half of the seventeenth century, the harem comprised some 400 women, with another 400 kept in a separate harem on a 'retired list'.[20]

Gardens of Pleasure and Cherubs with a Flaming Sword at their Gates

All this should not be regarded as a piece of exotic piquancy, something peripheral to the real business of government. Quite the contrary. As with the other elements in the human motivational system, it was for the supreme commanding position over the garden of pleasures that people reached out or fought in defence, killed and were killed. As Ibn Khaldun (1332–1406), the classic Arab philosopher of history and statehood, wrote:

> royal authority is a noble and enjoyable position. It comprises all the good things of the world, the pleasures of the body, and the joys of the soul. Therefore, there is, as a rule, great competition for it. It rarely is handed over (voluntarily), but may be taken away. Thus discord ensues. It leads to war and fighting.[21]

The same reality had been vividly captured by the ancient Greek tale of wisdom regarding the sword of Damocles. The ruler, according to this tale, was seated at a table packed full with all the world's delights and objects of desire, while a sword hung on a horsehair above his head, liable to fall down and kill him at any moment.[22] Ruling was a high-stakes—high-risk-high-gain—affair. Modern fables are no less suggestive. The hugely popular television drama *Game of Thrones* (based on a series of novels by George Martin) displays scenes of brutal violence, sex, and unscrupulous pursuit of power and wealth that many viewers found shocking. But although such scenes have obviously been screened for effect and enhanced viewer ratings, much of the strength of the fiction drama derives from the fact that with respect to all the above it is in essence profoundly realistic.

A rigorous study of royal violent mortality rates has yet to be undertaken. All the same, some data may illustrate the point. According to the biblical record, only nine out the nineteen kings of the northern kingdom of Israel died naturally. Of the others, seven were killed by rebels, one committed suicide to escape the same fate, one fell in battle, and one was exiled by the Assyrians. Four or five out of Achaemenid Persia's thirteen kings were assassinated and one was apparently killed in war.[23] During the last century (162–163 BC) of the reign of the Hellenistic Seleucids practically all of the nineteen reigning monarchs became victims (after having been perpetrators) of usurpation and violent death. During the 500 years of the Roman Empire, roughly 70 per cent of its rulers died violently, not to mention the countless contenders who were killed without ever making it to the imperial crown.[24] During the lifespan of the Eastern Roman Empire or Byzantium (395–1453 AD), sixty-four out of its one hundred and seven emperors, more than 60 per cent, were deposed and/or killed.[25] Six out of eight kings of Northumbria in seventh-century AD Britain died in war.[26] It is estimated that during the later Viking period more than a third of the Norwegian kings died in battle, and another third were banished.[27]

The Ottoman Empire provides the most grisly tale. At its height (fifteenth to sixteenth centuries AD), the empire lacked a clear rule of succession to choose from among the hundreds of children the sultans fathered from the many women in their harem. The son who succeeded in winning power after his father's death proceeded to kill all his brothers and brothers' sons, or at least severely mutilate (blind) them, in order to disqualify them for the throne. Father–son killings for power also took place. Only the establishment of seniority succession to the crown within the family in the early seventeenth century put an end to these terrifying battles for power, whose ever-present effect on court and family daily life as everybody anticipated and prepared for the final showdown can only be imagined. For every son of the sultan the struggle for power simply meant a struggle for survival. If for no other motive, the 'security dilemma' in itself—pure self-defence—forced *all* of them to struggle as viciously as they could.[28]

All of these are merely examples taken from countless similar tales of insecurity, violent struggle, and bloodbaths at the apex of political power. When we think about the glory of kings, we rarely contemplate these aspects. Violent usurpations spelled doom not only for the ruler or contender, but also for their families and followers, and, if the struggle turned into a fully fledged civil war, for masses of soldiers and civilians. Still, there was no shortage of candidates to take up this high-risk-high-gain game.

Was it 'worth it' and in what sense? Did people who engaged in the high-gain-high-cost, intra- and inter-social 'two-level' game of power politics improve their ultimate reproductive success, which was the original, evolution-shaped source of their desires and pursuits? Have our evolution-shaped behaviours remained adaptive in much altered, 'artificial' cultural conditions? The answer to this question seems very difficult to compute. On the one hand, rulers enjoyed much greater reproductive opportunities, most strikingly represented in the autocratic harem. On the other hand, contenders to the throne, and even incumbent rulers, played a highly risky game for both themselves and their families. Whereas Chinggis Khan was among the greatest warlords ever, and his dynasty among the most successful, countless unsuccessful contenders for power, whose lines ceased because of their failures, have to be figured into the other side of the equation. Still, the apex of the social pyramid held such a powerful attraction for people because it was there that evolution-shaped human desires could be set loose and indulged in on a gigantic scale. What was adaptive in small aboriginal groups has not necessarily remained so as human conditions changed radically through history. And yet in this, as in so much else, our natural propensities, shaped during our species' long aboriginal existence by tremendous forces of selection, remain extremely potent. Where new conditions sever the original link between a proximate mechanism, human desire, and its original evolutionary end, it is the proximate mechanism that people are tied to by powerful emotional stimuli and the allure of sensual gratification.[29]

People's desire for sweetness serves to illustrate originally adaptive propensities that have gone astray in altered cultural conditions. Indicative of ripeness and high nutritious value in fruits, sweetness is now artificially produced and has become harmful. Obesity, when appetite that was adaptive in an environment of food scarcity is indulged in a society of plenty, is another illustration. On a happier note, people continue to intensely pursue sexual gratification, even though effective contraception has made most of this obsessive activity irrelevant in terms of the reproductive success it originally evolved to achieve. This does not make sexual gratification any less enjoyable, valued, or for that matter rational. All of this does not mean that humans are the slaves of our genes and unaffected by culture. But nor should our biological inheritance be dismissed as irrelevant to social realities, as generations of scholars from the social sciences and humanities have been schooled to believe.

In terms of rationality, many contenders for the ultimate prize of supreme rule might be likened to heavy gamblers for the jackpot in lottery games. Clearly, the odds for winning in any such game are against the gamblers, and for heavy gamblers the losses might be very substantial indeed. Yet there is no shortage of such gamblers, either because, as cognitive psychology reveals, errors in the evaluation of probabilities are among the most common of human cognitive distortions; or because the allure of the prize can generate compulsive-addictive gambling behaviour that disrupts the functioning of our mental mechanisms that assess cost-effectiveness. This, of course, does not mean that *all* the contenders in lethal power struggles at the top played against 'expected utility', the concept in game theory that measures the prize against the probability of gaining it. While many of them, probably the majority, patently did, others made tremendous gains. On a more modest scale, the same considerations held true further down the social hierarchy and between political collectives. It was sufficient that some players judged that they could profit from war to impose the game on all the others, if those others were not willing to surrender everything either right away or in the long run.

The Quest for Power and Glory

Status, leadership, and power were sought out in the evolutionary state of nature because of the advantages they granted in access to somatic and reproductive resources. With resource accumulation and hierarchic organization, the scope and significance of coercive social power rocketed. Furthermore, since both resources and power could now be accumulated and expanded on a hitherto unimaginable scale, while being closely intertwined and interchangeable, power, like money, grew into a universal currency by which most objects of desire could be secured. Power became the medium through which all else was channelled, and the quest for power thus represented all else. For this reason, the quest for power seemingly acquired a life of its own and was also pursued for its own sake. To be sure, power was desired not just for positive gains. The security dilemma itself drove people and political communities to expand their power as a defensive measure, for in a competitive race one would rather swallow than be swallowed. Strong security pressures were associated with the formation, militarization, and expansion of some of the mightiest of empires, such as the Assyrian, Roman, and many others. Although historians tend to be scep-tical regarding professions of defensive motives, citing the expected benefits that drove states into expansion, security considerations intermixed rather than contrasted with the expected gains.

Like status and power and closely linked to them, the quest for honour and prestige was originally 'designed' to facilitate access to somatic and reproductive resources. As such, it too is stimulated by powerful emotional gratifications that give it a seemingly independent life of its own. Again, the potential for the fulfilment of this quest increased exponentially in large-scale societies. Indeed, this indulgence in itself constitutes one of the main attractions of power. Glory—something which could only come into being in large-scale societies—was pursued by rulers (and others, of course) as a means of strengthening their hold on power and everything it entailed, but also as an independent and most powerful source of emotional gratification. The stelae on which autocrats celebrated their achievements in superhuman images are interpreted by scholars as instruments of royal propaganda. Equally, however, they express the quest for the ultimate fulfilment of the craving for boundless glory and absolute domination, which could now be extended to the 'four corners of the world' and 'everything under the sun', as the mightiest of imperial rulers boasted. Satisfaction, and hence motiv-ation for action, were derived from extending one's dominance over—indeed, bringing under one's heel—as many and as much as possible, both at home and abroad, in connection with, but also independent of, the more tangible gains involved.

If the last few pages have concentrated more on the lavish potential for indulgence enjoyed by autocratic rulers, it should be stressed that all of this also applied to individuals in general and to political communities as a whole. Community members bathed in their collective glory and were willing to pay for its advancement and protection. This again was derived from the conversion value of honour and glory in terms of power, deterrence, and inter-state bargaining. Individuals and political communities jealously guarded their honour and responded forcefully even to slight infringements, not because of the trifling matters involved, but because of the much more serious ones that might follow if they demonstrated weakness.[30] To paraphrase Winston Churchill: choosing shame rather than war might very likely beget shame and then war.

Chinggis Khan revealingly bound together the above-mentioned elem-ents of the human motivational system when he allegedly said: 'The greatest joy a man can know is to conquer his enemies and drive them before him. To ride their horses and take away their possessions. To see the faces of those who were dear to them bedewed with tears, and to clasp their wives and daughters in his arms.'[31] As we have shown earlier, we now have remarkable statistical evidence of what he meant by the last clause.

Kinship, Culture, Ideas, Ideals

All the factors considered so far ring true enough, but is this all there is? Are people only interested in these crude materialistic objectives that even after humankind's dramatic cultural take-off can ultimately be shown to derive from evolution-shaped sources? Do people not also live and die for more lofty ideas and ideals than those expressed by a Chinggis Khan? They undoubtedly do, but, as argued in the previous chapter, as a continuation rather than a negation of the above. A highly intricate interface links the natural with the cultural.

Let us start with the factor of identity. We have already seen that people exhibit a marked, innate, evolution-shaped predisposition to favour kin over 'strangers'—that is, to favour those with whom they share more genes. Roughly, this means that people in any kin circle struggle among themselves for the interests of their yet closer kin, while at the same time tending to cooperate against more distant circles. In this incessant multi-level game, internal cooperation tends to stiffen when the community is faced with an external threat, while internal rivalries diminish to varying extents, though never disappear. It should, of course, be added that non-kin cooperation and alliances for mutual gain are commonplace, becoming all the more so with the growth of large-scale organized society.

The range of kin affinities and kin bonds expanded dramatically with the adoption of agriculture and the rise of large-scale state societies. Agricultural expansions created *ethne* that often encompassed hundreds of thousands but were divided into separate, competing, and often hostile tribes, tribal con-federations, and petty states. It is not sufficiently recognized that above all it is within such ethnic spaces that larger states tended to emerge and expand, because people of a similar ethnicity could be more easily united and kept united, relying on shared ethnocentric traits and bonds. Indeed, it was pri-marily on their loyal native ethnic core that states and empires relied when they expanded beyond that core to rule over other ethnicities. Thus, contrary to a widely held view, ethnicity mattered a great deal in determining political boundaries and affinities from the very start, rather than only achieving that effect with modernity.

Over the past decades it has become fashionable to claim that ethnicity and nationalism are 'invented' and that the deep sentiment held by most peoples that they each share a common descent or a common stock is a pure myth. Nobly reacting against the explosive and horrendous manifestations of both nationalism and racism, this view of ethnicity as 'constructed', manipulated, and mythologized by states and elites has some truth in it, yet a partial truth nevertheless. The proponents of this view insist that ethnicity is a cultural rather than a genetic phenomenon. However, this is a false dichotomy that misses a far more intricate reality. In the first place, genetic studies show that in general the world's broader cultural (linguistic) and genetic boundaries do coincide remarkably.[32] Most ethnicities far predate modern nationalism, forming the nucleus around which peoples and nations have been built ever since the earliest emergence of states millennia ago and throughout history.[33] Indeed, even where an ethnic formation originally brought together disparate groups, as was often the case, widespread intermarriage over sufficient time created the reality and perception of kinship in the new collective.

To be sure, it is overwhelmingly cultural features rather than genetic gradations that separate ethnicities and peoples from one another. To avoid any misunderstanding, one must hasten to add that most of the genetic differences are negligible and irrelevant to human culture. The point is entirely different, as we have already seen. Since in small hunter-gatherer groups kinship and culture overlapped, not only phenotypic resemblance (similarity in physical appearance) but also shared cultural traits functioned as cues for kinship, as well as proving vital for effective cooperation. Thus, whether or not national communities are genetically related (and most of them are), they feel and function *as if* they were, on account of their shared cultural traits. To be blind to the sources and workings of these intricate mental mechanisms of collective identity formation inevitably means to misconceive some of the most powerful bonds that shape human history. Indeed, this is what explains ethnocentrism—the deep human identification with, devotion to, and willingness to sacrifice for, one's people—whose patently atavistic nature has repeatedly perplexed and shocked modern social thinkers, historians, and commentators, proving transparent to their accepted categories of analysis.

The expansion of kin solidarity beyond its original boundaries in the hunter-gatherer regional group of hundreds to embrace peoples of many thousands and millions overstretched the evolutionary rationale that had shaped this predisposition in the first place. The far larger grouping, which because of its shared physical and cultural phenotype one identifies as one's people, is not as closely related to one's self as the tribal group was. Furthermore, although one's fate is closely linked to that of one's people, the ability of an individual to influence the fate of his/her people by self-sacrifice is negligible. All the same, it is again the deeply ingrained propensity, or proximate mechanism, that dominates people's behaviour, despite the changes that have taken place in the original conditions that shaped this mechanism. Although they balance the interests of their people against their own and those of their close kin, individuals are emotionally deeply invested in the prosperity of their people. While state and communal coercion are obviously major enforcers of collective action, individuals are *willingly* susceptible to recruitment on these grounds.

Independence from foreign domination has been perceived as crucial to a people's prosperity, often evoking most desperate expressions of communal devotion in its defence. Furthermore, people are highly tuned to and predisposed to cherish the infinite, subtle, and distinct manifestations of behaviour, outlook, and appearance that mark them as a community of kinship and mutual cooperation. Once acquired in youth by a long process of socialization, cultural forms become extremely difficult to replace. Brain structure consolidates in adults, losing most of its earlier elastic ability to rearrange itself through learning. Sticking to the things that one knows best and are unlikely to supplant successfully—language, patterns of behaviour and belief, social codes—is thus largely imposed on people as their superior option. Similarly, the intimately familiar landscapes of one's native land, engraved in one's consciousness for the very same reasons, evoke great attachment and devotion, and will not be forfeited carelessly. Needless to repeat, rather than 'blind instincts', these are all deep-seated but highly modulated predispositions, whose particular expressions are largely circumstantial. Obviously, people regularly adopt foreign cultural forms, sometimes eagerly, and they might also migrate from their native land (where conditions might be harsh), provided they consider these acts beneficial to them and that they can pull them through.

The power of ideas is even more far-reaching. People everywhere kill and get killed over ideas, irrespective of kinship and nationality. How is this lofty sphere—the most abstract of metaphysical ideas, indeed, all too often seemingly absurd notions—connected to the practicalities of life? The key for understanding this query is our species' strong propensity for interpreting its surroundings as deeply and as far as the mind can probe, so as to decipher their secrets and form a mental map that would best help us cope with their hazards and opportunities. *Homo sapiens* possesses an innate, omnipresent, evolution-shaped predisposition for ordering its world, which inter alia forms the foundation of mythology, metaphysics, and science. We are compulsive meaning-seekers. It is this propensity that is responsible for our species' remarkable career.

Thus, the array of ideas regarding the fundamental structure and workings of the cosmos and the means and practices required for securing its benevolent functioning have been largely perceived as *practical* questions of the utmost significance, evoking as powerful emotions and motivation for action—including violence—as any other major practical question might.[34] Indeed, they might evoke *more* powerful reactions than any ordinary practical question, for the supreme forces concerned might be perceived as more potent than anything else and are surrounded by 'sacred horror'. They hold the key to individual, communal, and cosmic salvation in this and/or other worlds, worthy of the greatest dedication and even of dying for.

With the growth of social complexity and the rise of polities, large-scale institutionalized religions were formed.[35] As a matter of course, rulers moved to consolidate their hold on the spiritual realm as a major element of social power. The world of belief and ritual constituted an arena of power politics, because control over minds formed an aspect of power; because, as such, it was inextricably linked to the attainment of all the other benefits in the human motivational system; and because, like other major cultural differences, differences of faith between communities, sects, and denominations might lead to divisions and conflict, whereas unity of faith fostered political unity. Consequently, questions of faith and ritual were themselves political issues. It should be noted that, contrary to the view espoused by Enlightenment thinkers since the eighteenth century, manipulative power holders were not simply cynical crooks, but more customarily were themselves emotionally and intellectually deeply invested in the world of belief. To adopt a manner of expression in the tradition of the Enlightenment, they were 'superstitious crooks', themselves addicted to the 'opium of the masses'.

The supernatural sphere thus constituted as potent an instrument of and motivation for war as did other, more 'real' factors. Notably, though, the supernatural scarcely stood alone as an independent source of warfare, as is sometimes claimed, for example with respect to the Aztec war complex.[36] The Aztec elite in fact acted as quintessential 'superstitious manipulators', whose drive to conquer, subjugate, and extract tribute became inextricably linked with the gods' thirst for human blood. Massive killing and ruthless exploitation rather than the taking of prisoners for ritual sacrifice were the rule in Aztec warfare.[37] Moreover, it should be noted that *only* the sort of metaphysical and ethical doctrines that appealed to large numbers of people with the promise of personal and communal salvation were capable of mobilization for action. No purely academic metaphysical or scientific doctrine that failed to touch on these deep sources was ever capable of generating such an intense response.

Although religious, and later secular, salvation-and-justice ideologies regularly emerged and sometimes remained grounded within a particular people, they increasingly carried a universal message that transcended national boundaries. Furthermore, the relationship of the universal religious, and later secular, ideologies with war was complex. The obligation of a 'just war' was already evident in many of the older national religions. With the new universal ideologies, this obligation was reinforced, as was the ban on belligerency among the faithful. On the other hand, some of the salvation ideologies incorporated a strong missionary zeal that could be translated into a holy belligerency against non-believers. Furthermore, militant salvation ideologies generated a tremendous galvanizing effect on the holy warrior host, because the world's salvation was dependent on the triumph of the true faith; because these ideologies universally preached cooperation and altruism within the community of believers; and, indeed, because they were often able to foster such cooperation and altruism by the promise of great worldly and non-worldly rewards, possibly imagined in the eyes of external observers but often more real than anything else in the eyes of the believers.[38] In conjunction with the other motives for fighting in the human motivational system—always in conjunction with them—the real and the imagined-but-perceived-and-functioning-as-real rewards offered by such salvation ideologies thus explain Richard Dawkins's proclamation: 'What a weapon! Religious faith deserves a chapter to itself in the annals of war technology.'[39]

Christianity, starting as a religion of love, compassion, and non-violence, later developed a brutal militant streak towards non-believers and heretics that coexisted awkwardly with its opposite in both doctrine and practice.

With regard to the relations among the faithful, its position was more consistently pacifist. Islam incorporated the holy war against non-believers as an integral part of its doctrine from its inception, while preaching unity and non-belligerency within its own house. The blatant fact that within both Christianity and Islam fighting went on incessantly despite religious condemnation merely indicates that, while being a very potent force, religious ideology was practically powerless to eradicate the motivations and realities that generated war. Much the same applies to eastern Eurasia, where spiritual ideologies such as Buddhism and Confucianism were more tolerant than the monotheistic faiths and even more conflict-averse. Although war of opinion in the transcendental sense—involving systems of belief and conduct with respect to life and afterlife—was markedly less noticeable in eastern than in western Eurasia, warfare in general was more or less as prevalent. Thus, monotheism's supposedly special belligerency is largely exaggerated.[40]

War: A Serious Matter for Serious Ends or a Senseless Affair?

Chinggis Khan's alleged pronouncement, quoted above, regarding the fruits of war as the greatest of joys undoubtedly represented a genuine human sentiment. Yet, as already mentioned, he was among the most successful warlords ever, and when one wins on such a grand scale one naturally tends to be enthusiastic about the game. While many individuals and collectives gained from war, sometimes tremendously, few were even remotely as successful as Chinggis Khan. If only for this reason, misgivings about war were as prevalent as its praises.

The potential dangers and costs of fighting deterred people (as all animals) from it as much as its potential gains attracted them, making fighting one of the most polarized of human activities in terms of the conflicting emotional mechanisms that switched it on and off. The death, mutilation, material loss, and hardship that individuals and collectives were likely to suffer caused massive pain, fear, misery, anguish, weariness, and despair. Quick and decisive victories have been the exception rather than the rule in history. Armed rivalries often endured from generation to generation, many times with little apparent gain to one side or the other. Massive costs of life, invested resources, and ravaged wealth were seemingly swallowed into that black hole to no avail. Even when success was achieved, the pendulum often swung back as the vanquished reasserted themselves to restore the balance. Although people did not conceptualize theoretical tools such as the prisoner's dilemma, the paradoxes of the Red Queen in arms races, the traps of tit-for-tat, and the cycles of escalation—in all of which antagonists in unregulated competitive systems were locked—they acutely sensed them. The notion that war was a curse from heaven, devouring people against their true wishes, one of those catastrophic and alien, nature-like forces—together with famine and pestilence—that bedevilled humankind, gained wide currency.

Indeed, ever since the advent of farming and accumulated property, war almost invariably meant an overall net loss of resources—which might still result in a net gain, sometimes even a huge one, to one of the sides. The shorter and jollier a war could be kept, the easier the victory, and the more obvious the benefits, the more easily enthusiasm for it could be sparked from sources very close to the surface of people's psyche. Defence of self, kin, property, and communal identity was similarly capable of generating tremendous feats of emotional mobilization—often more desperate than enthusiastic. In other cases, even when war seemed to promise nothing good, people often chose to cling to it with a mixture of grimness, desperation, and bewilderment, because all other options seemed to harbour still worse consequences, imminently or in the longer run.

The ancient Greeks put a sceptical and paradoxical view of the benefits of war in the mouth of the philosopher Cineas, a companion of King Pyrrhus of Epirus, the celebrated but ultimately unsuccessful general and adventurer who fought Rome and Carthage in an effort to carve for himself a Hellenistic Empire in the West (281–274 BC). Pyrrhus has been viewed as an embodiment of the compulsive gambler for the jackpot, mentioned earlier in the chapter. The ancients acutely felt so:

> what he won by his exploits he lost by indulging in vain hopes, since through passionate desire for what he had not he always failed to establish securely what he had. For this reason Antigonus used to liken him to a player with dice who makes many fine throws but does not understand how to use them when they are made.[41]

The notion of a 'Pyrrhic victory'—a victory on the battlefield that, because of the losses incurred, amounts to defeat—applied to Pyrrhus not only militarily but also politically.

It was this point but also another one that Cineas sought to make in a conversation with the king. He asked Pyrrhus how he would use his victory over the Romans, if such a victory were won. Pyrrhus replied by describing the size, richness, and importance of Italy. Cineas pressed him to describe what they would do next. Pyrrhus replied that they would then be able to seize Sicily, with all its wealth and people. In response to further probing by the philosopher, the king said that these initial victories would make it possible for him to conquer Carthage and North Africa, and that with the strength thus accumulated he would proceed to take Macedonia and Greece. Cineas continued to ask what they would do then, to which Pyrrhus smiled and said: 'We shall be much at ease, and we'll drink bumpers, my good man, every day, and we'll gladden one another's hearts with confidential talks.' The philosopher, who had anticipated that conclusion all along, retorted that, since they already possessed all that was necessary for enjoying the leisurely activities mentioned by the king, what prevented them from the privilege of pursuing these activities right then, rather than go through all the perils, pain, and bloodshed of protracted wars.[42]

Notably, it was the philosopher rather than the king-general who expressed this view, and apart from the differences in inclinations and occupational perspectives between the two, it was obviously the latter rather than the former who was positioned to indulge in the fruits of success, if they came. But, indeed, in view of the costs and risks of war, when did indulgence reach the point of diminishing returns? Although people's drive to attain greater access to material benefits is in many ways insatiable and infinite, above a certain level people tend to become more risk-averse and pursue more conservative strategies, preferring to preserve what they already have. Furthermore, as Cineas suggested, one might aspire to achieve more and more, but above a certain level how much more can one consume, even of the most ostentatious luxuries? It is for this reason that it is mainly the lean and hungry upstarts who are willing to take the greatest risks. Much the same applies to sexual gratification. Males' sexual appetite in particular is in many ways open-ended. At the same time, above a certain (high) level it is nonetheless practically constrained. Could the Han emperors of China really avail themselves of all the 2,000–6,000 female beauties in their harem? Here, too, at some point a further increase becomes less important than preservation. The same applies to honour and the other elements in the human motivational system.

A yet more radical attitude revealed itself in the literate civilizations and large-scale societies of Eurasia. Our system of desires has been 'imposed' on us by evolution. However, in contrast to other animals, our vastly enlarged intellectual and imaginative faculties and shared inter-generational wisdom detect the insatiable, largely Sisyphic, and intrinsically frustrating aspects of our worldly pursuits, the pain and suffering involved, and our ultimate death. This is particularly true of large-scale and complex societies, where (a) the range of temptation but also of frustration is far greater; (b) communities are less intimate and less supportive; and (c) the realm of texts both expresses this and creates worlds of the imagination—fictional and non-fictional—where one can concern, hide, and console one's self: 'sublimate' worldly desires. The most extreme expression of the reaction against the pains and frustrations inherent in our evolution-shaped system of motivation is the ascetic quest to cut loose from and transcend sensual desires and all activities relating to them, and find peace of mind in sensual denial, eschewing the restless race for fulfilment. Among the many manifestations of asceticism, Buddhism is the most famous and widespread creed. Asceticism also permeated Christianity. However, although great masses of people identified with these creeds, only a small minority took up their example in practice as hermits and monks. Indeed, asceticism has remained marginal in human society, as it has gone against our most deeply rooted, innate predispositions.

Rather than the rigours of asceticism, it was both the relative internal peace instituted by the state and the amenities of civilization that eroded belligerency. In comparison to tribal and other less orderly societies, people were socialized into far less violent daily behaviour—they were 'domesti-cated', which necessarily reflected on their warlike inclinations. Documenting this process with respect to the modern West, Norbert Elias termed it the 'civilizing process'.[43] As the ancient philosophers and moralists were agreed, people, elites, and rulers alike grew 'soft' with spreading peace and increasing affluence. After all, what should have motivated rulers of rich empires and elites steeped in luxury to engage in dangerous and tedious military exploits when they already possessed all the pleasures of life to indulge in? For this reason, large, rich, and populous states and empires throughout history regularly fell prey to relatively small armed groups led by ambitious upstarts from their poor and warlike barbarian marches.

Indeed, as long as both at home and abroad there existed a direct link between the covert and overt use of armed force and benefit acquisition, armed force remained as essential as—more essential than—productivity for reaping benefits. Even though, because of destruction and lost productivity, fighting among agrarian and pastoralist societies generally resulted in an overall net loss to those involved, it could still lead to a substantial redistribution of benefits in favour of the victor, which meant that there were great benefits to be won by force. Let it be clear: great benefits *were* sometimes won by force. Consequently, there were always those who were willing to take up the game of violence—espouse the conflictual option of competition—in the hope of making gains, and thereby forcing the game on those who may have been more reluctant to engage in it. For this reason, at the very least, one had to prepare for conflict. Very often— but not always—this meant that all sides found themselves locked in a prisoner's dilemma and experienced a 'Red Queen' effect, where they continuously spent resources on war and on preparation for it without gaining an advantage over their rivals or making any gain; that is, they could all lose in comparison with what they might have had in the absence of conflict. Thus, rather than being mutually exclusive, *both* of the common attitudes to war have touched on deep truths: violent conflict has been *both* a 'serious means to a serious end' and sometimes shockingly absurd; *both* highly beneficial to some and terribly wasteful overall, sometimes even for all; *both* an indispensability which could not be eliminated by idealist visions and often imposed on all the protagonists 'against their will', as if it were an alien force.

It was only during modernity that the tie between force and wealth acquisition would begin to unravel. But before we turn our attention to this development and its revolutionary effects on the balance of costs and benefits between war and peace, we pause in the next part for a critical examination of anthropological and international relations grand theories regarding the causes of war.

Flaws and Misconceptions in Disciplinary Grand Theories

This part deals with the intricacies of grand theory in relation to the causes of war in two well-established academic disciplines: anthropology and international relations. The former addresses warfare in pre-state societies, while the latter is concerned with state wars. Although the grand theories are different and practically unrelated between the two disciplines, they play a similar role in each of them. They dominate the disciplinary discourse and are paramount in the education of students and the socialization of young scholars. This, of course, is only to be expected, as these are precisely the roles disciplinary grand theories are supposed to perform. And yet, as suggested here, what are regarded as grand theories in the social sciences are often scarcely more than crude and highly contrived intellectual constructs. While they may offer more or less valid insights and stimulate study and debate, their heuristic value can sometimes be lesser than the closure or tunnelling effect they have on the mind. Arising somewhat haphazardly in response to specific debates in the particular historical development of the discipline in question, grand theories might ossify into orthodox traditions in the minds of their protagonists and attract vastly disproportionate attention.

In fields that are both fundamentally close to ordinary human experience and commonsensical—neither rocket science nor nuclear physics—the result is all too often ponderous concepts, arcane jargon, and mountains of scholastic debate. These, indeed, are sometimes reminiscent of medieval schoolmen and comprehensible only to the initiated. Leaving outsiders bemused and perplexed, they constitute the world for participant members of the professional community. Furthermore, ideas relevant to the subject might be virtually incomprehensible to members of the discipline unless expressed in the familiar grooves and moulds of the prevailing discourse. This is how the sociology of scholarly communities works.

This may sound condescending, perhaps even arrogant. Moreover, counter-arguments are strong: the above is an exaggerated caricature; professional scholarly communities with shared terms of reference and a common research agenda are a necessity, and their internal debates are the way knowledge is advanced through the dialectics of trial and error, argument and counter-argument, in these as in all other disciplines; no better way to knowledge exists or can exist; for all their shortcomings, most if not all of what we know on the subjects in question comes from the scholarly work done in these disciplines; many illuminating theories, important insights, and invaluable empirical data have been generated in them. Indeed, this book itself relies heavily on such data and theories. Nonetheless, I keep to the stark formulation already set out in order to stress the point: overbearing grand theories in both disciplines of anthropology and international relations, rather than explaining the causes of war, have all too often distorted perspectives on the subject. As suggested here, evolutionary theory can help to untie the contradictions and fill in the gaps that pervade grand theories in both disciplines.

Because of the self-contained character of each of the disciplinary discourses, each of the two chapters in this part can be read independently by those concerned with the discipline in question. The general reader may find a brief panoramic tour of the two disciplines over the past century rewarding. Alternatively, he or she can safely choose to skip this part, or either of its chapters, and proceed directly to the next part which deals with the causes and apparent decline of war in the modern world.

4

Anthropology
Why People Fought (if They Did)

A Rousseauian bias—coupled, as we have seen, with a focus on the hunter-gatherers of East and Southern Africa, who were initially proclaimed non-violent—has led anthropological research astray on the subject of pre-state and pre-agricultural human fighting from the 1960s onwards. Furthermore, disciplinary interpretative traditions and grand theories have greatly affected anthropologists' approaches not only to the question of whether aboriginal people fought, but also as to *why* they fought. These interpretative traditions and grand theories have been largely shaped by anthropology's response to the impact of evolutionary theory—both biological and cultural—since the late nineteenth century.

Anthropology's Reaction against Cultural and Biological Evolution

Cultural evolution is an even older concept than biological evolution. It became prominent with the eighteenth century's idea of Progress and with nineteenth-century Hegelian, Marxist, and positivist philosophies. It was influentially championed by founding fathers of sociology and anthropology such as Herbert Spencer, Edward Tylor, and Lewis Henry Morgan. At its base is the telling observation that the general trend of human societies throughout history has been towards increasing technological sophistication and social complexity, with earlier steps in this development constituting a precondition for further development. However, a reaction against the nineteenth century's great evolutionary systems soon set in. They were criticized for being abstract and dogmatic, insensitive to the actual untidiness of historical reality, speculative, metaphysical, and teleological, postulating History as the unilineal advance of Progress. Furthermore, by the late nineteenth century evolutionary theories were increasingly marred by racialism and social Darwinism. Franz Boas, who founded the modern discipline of anthropology in American academia during the first decades of the twentieth century, changed the direction of anthropological research. While embracing Darwin's revolution in biology, he rejected sweeping speculations about then unknown early stages of human cultural evolution and concentrated instead on the empirical study of extant societies, their diverse cultures, and particular cultural adaptations to their specific environments.

Major schools of anthropological research during the twentieth century continued various aspects of Boas's legacy. In the main, anthropology retained—indeed radicalized—his strong empiricist emphasis and culture-specific sensitivity. In a sharp reaction against racialism and its horrendous manifestations, the post-1945 period saw the triumph of the *tabula rasa* view of the human mind: the view that people were born a clean slate, and entirely shaped by cultural experience and social learning. This encouraged a view of human fighting as a wholly acquired phenomenon, a mere cultural artefact. Boas himself, a pioneering student of the American Northwest, took the ferocious warfare that had prevailed among the indigenous people there as a matter of course.[1] His student, anthropologist Margaret Mead, became a celebrity with the publication of her best-selling book *Coming of Age in Samoa* (1928). The book presented to an eager American public an idealized primordial society of easy-going social relations and relaxed sexual mores. Half a century later the book became the centre of a much publicized controversy, as it was found that Mead had imposed her own expectations on her subject matter.[2] However, by remarking briefly that 'war and cannibalism are long since passed' in Samoa, Mead revealed that she was actually aware that things had been very different, and far more violent, before the arrival of Europeans.[3] In contrast to the general drift of her argument, pre-contact Samoa presented the all too familiar picture of intense social competition and widespread violence and warfare, whose blood toll was many times greater than that of any modern society.[4] Indeed, as we have already seen, in all the supposedly idyllic Polynesian island societies, small and large—the object of European fantasy since their discovery in the eighteenth century—warfare before contact was ubiquitous and very bloody. In later years, well aware of the evidence of extensive warfare among the Australian Aboriginal hunter-gatherers, which she never denied,

Mead suggested that rather than primordial, warfare—deadly group fighting—was an addictive cultural invention that spread and was picked up by human populations throughout the world.[5] Why such an invention should suddenly pop up among aboriginal people whose way of life underwent very little change, and why it should prove so addictive, remained unclear. As already mentioned, and quite inexplicably, Mead did not think 'homicide'—individual killing—was similarly a 'cultural invention'.

The causes of 'primitive warfare' remained no less of a puzzle in anthropology, with explanations ranging from the materialist to cultural and psychological ('sheer pugnacity').[6] In an almost comical reversal of the evolutionary rationale, some anthropologists have failed to see any adaptive logic behind 'primitive warfare'. One representative of this tradition, C. R. Hallpike, writes:

> Why, then, is primitive warfare so common if it is not adaptive? The answer is clearly that there are a number of very widespread factors that lead to it: the aggressive propensities of young males, lack of effective social control in acephalous societies, mutual suspicions between different groups, revenge, the self-maintaining properties of social system, problems in developing mediatory institutions, religious associations between success in warfare and vitality in general, and so on.[7]

But *why* is it that young males have such aggressive propensities? *Why* does a lack of social control and mediatory institutions lead to warfare if no underlying conflict exists? *Why* should there be any mutual suspicion at all under these circumstances? *What* triggers revenge in the first place? *Why* are religion and vitality associated with success in war? Finally, is the widespread occurrence of intraspecific fighting among animals also to be regarded as non-adaptive?

These questions remained unasked, let alone answered. The untenable notion that in the highly competitive evolutionary state of nature, fighting occurred 'just so', as a 'ritualistic' and 'expressive' purposeless activity, to satisfy 'psychological' needs that had no basis in the practical conditions of life, has gained much currency. It is still widely found in anthropological literature. As one anthropologist writes: 'The violence that can erupt in foraging communities often has no particular objectives other than expressing anger...a product of rage, not calculated risk, and even be a form of temporary mental illness.'[8] Another anthropologist, documenting the patterns of violence among the indigenous people of eastern North America, rightly highlights the revenge motive, a highly distinctive cause of lethal fighting across the anthropological record. He adds: 'there is no necessary political objective beyond the maintenance of personal or group honor'.[9] The deeper rationale that permeates and connects human somatic and reproductive competition, the defence and advancement of honour, revenge to eliminate and deter rivals, and anger or rage as one of the emotional mechanisms that underpins all of these, has been lost sight of.

Cultural Evolution vs Biological Evolution?

In an anthropological discipline that became very culture-specific and suspicious of sweeping generalizations, an important strand kept the tradition of cultural evolution alive during the twentieth century. While striving to avoid the non-empirical aspects that had marred their predecessors' work, proponents of cultural evolution called attention to the highly conspicuous sequence and trajectory of human prehistory and history, multi-lineal and diverse as it surely was. Furthermore, in accounting for these developmental trends, they emphasized human cultural adaptations to the environment. However, like their peers, most cultural evolutionists tended to draw a sharp divide between biological and cultural evolution. Beyond the most trivial sense, they regarded human biological propensities as scarcely relevant to the study of human social behaviour, which was supposed to be almost infinitely malleable by culture.[10]

What then is the relationship between biological and cultural evolution? To begin with, both deal with the continuous, recursive reproduction of replicating forms—biological or cultural—whose occasional variations are at least to some degree subject to all sorts of selective pressures. In biology, the replicators are the genes, stored and transmitted between generations in the cellular nuclei. In culture, the replicators are behaviours and ideas—'memes' in Richard Dawkins's phrase—accumulated during life in brains and transmitted between them through learning. Hence one of the chief differences between biological and cultural evolution: the former involves 'inborn' replicators that can only be passed on to offspring; the latter is concerned with acquired traits that can be replicated 'horizontally', in principle to any brain. This 'Lamarckian' inheritance of acquired traits makes the pace of cultural evolution infinitely faster. Still, in cultural evolution too, the replicators are highly durable. Systems of symbols and practices, such as languages and customs, passed on and reproduced generation after generation, are particularly slow to change. But even they do—by random 'drift' and 'mutation', by purposeful adaptation, or by the influence of foreign 'memes'.[11]

Furthermore, fuelled by selection in a never-ending evolutionary competition, both biological and cultural evolution tend to produce ever more complex designs over time.[12] Complexity is defined by the number and diversity of different, specialized, and mutually dependent parts, integrated in functional hierarchical structures. The process described is not 'Progressive' in any value sense, necessarily leading to growing happiness, well-being, or any other goal. Nor does the tendency in evolution towards greater complexity confer inevitability on the process. Evolutionary forms can remain little changed for a very long time. They can also regress or go extinct when evolving into a dead end or when encountering a drastic—self-generated or extraneous—adverse change in their environment. The process is not preordained. Where there is a strong element of inner propensity involved, and there is, it is only to be understood in terms of the non-transcendent, immanent tendency of recursively reproducing and propagating replicators to evolve—through competition and selection—more sophisticated and complex designs for dealing with a competitive environment. (To be sure, greater efficiency sometimes involves simplification rather than growing complexity, but in most cases the opposite is true.) The way in which ordered complexity, or self-organization, evolves spontaneously from simple elements engaged in simple interactions is one of the hottest topics on the edge of current scientific research.[13]

Finally, and most importantly for our subject, biological and cultural evolution represent a continuum. In the first place, one originated from the other. Underlying the take-off of cultural evolution was the perfection of one of the latest tricks of biological evolution: a greatly enhanced ability to teach and learn. A bigger and more flexible, open brain design, capable of being partly shaped during life by interaction with the environment through experience and learning, had been a device increasingly developed in later products of the evolutionary arms race, such as birds, big mammals, primates, apes, and archaic humans. With *Homo sapiens* this growing capacity crossed a threshold. In response to outside stimuli, our genetically constructed 'hardware' is capable of considerable restructuring throughout life (especially at early ages) and of taking on an unprecedented diversity of 'software'. Consequently, it can generate a yet more staggering range of 'applications'. Cultural evolution proved to have an explosive potential. The engine of human development since the adoption of agriculture has been overwhelmingly cultural rather than biological.

Cultural evolution has not worked on a clean slate, however. Not only did it originate, as a capacity, from biological evolution, it has also been working on a human physiological and psychological landscape deeply grooved by long-evolved inborn predispositions. The staggering diversity of human cultural forms and the amazing trajectory of human cultural evolution have given rise to the view that humankind's peculiar quality is precisely that it lacks such a thing as nature. Humans have been proclaimed to be wholly determined by culture or history. Given the right socialization, they have been supposed to be capable of embracing practically *any* behaviour. However, since the 1950s, Noam Chomsky's revolution in linguistics has presented the humanities and social sciences with an illuminating old–new model that heralded the eclipse of the *tabula rasa* view of the human mind that had dominated the middle of the twentieth century. Chomsky and his disciples have argued that although thousands of human languages are recognized today, and an unknown, far larger number were spoken in the past, all human languages share a common 'deep' set of syntax patterns. These patterns reflect our innate language handling mechanisms that make language use so easy and natural to us. Thus, humans are in principle capable of generating any hypothetical language, but only as long as its meta-structure complies with these deep common patterns.[14] This would give an infinite but at the same time also highly constrained variety.

As the quintessential form of culture, language has proven to be an illuminating model for human mind structures in general. Social scientists and historians have stressed cultural diversity in human societies for excellent reasons, but all too often to the point of losing sight of our easily observed large core of species specificity.[15] Most cultural evolutionists have erred in embracing one side of a false nature–nurture dichotomy. There is indeed a staggering diversity of cultural forms and great cultural elasticity, but not quite any form goes. Cultural choices and preferences did not simply take over from biology. Instead, the rich diversity of cultural forms has been built on and around a fairly recognizable deep core of evolution-shaped innate propensities, needs, and desires—ultimate ends, proximate mechanisms, and derivative by-products. Biology and culture constitute an amalgamated compound that co-evolves in mutual interaction. The whole thing is better viewed as a marvellously complex but far from arbitrary edifice. The evolutionary perspective on human social life and historical trajectory, rather than promoting biological determinism, as the standard anthropological response has had it, is about the intricate array of gene–culture interactions. Our biological predispositions heavily bias our cultural choices; in turn, as studies have demonstrated, our cultural choices can select for some biological traits.[16]

Cultural traits, too, are subject to selective pressures. They do not necessarily have to have a better adaptive value. Some cultural traits are simply more 'addictive' in more or less specific biocultural settings, and may spread in the same way that a virus or a parasite spreads in a biological population. They may even be harmful to the survival and reproductive success of the population they 'infect', but because they spread fast enough to other populations, they avoid extinction. There is a leash connecting the elements of the biocultural compounds—in some aspects of behaviour a short one, in others long, and overall variably stretching. Although a number of anthropologists have played a leading role in advancing this emerging perspective, and the evolutionary logic in general has been making great strides in the disciplinary discourse since the 1980s, it still remains somewhat alien to mainstream anthropology.

Cultural Materialism and the Causes of War

The most ambitious anthropological theory of cultural evolution, which has also been the most influential in the anthropological study of the causes of war, is 'cultural materialism', put forward by Marvin Harris and his disciples. 'Cultural materialism' has some important features in common with the evolutionary rationale. Influenced by Marx, Harris sensibly postulated people's struggle to make a living, which he labelled 'production', as the driving force of human cultural evolution. Next to production, Harris, citing Malthus, stressed reproduction, child-bearing, and the efforts to balance population against limited resources in any given environment. He further suggested that the 'superstructure' of higher cultural forms was built on these fundamentals.[17] Clearly, this conceptual framework appears to be barely distinguishable from the somatic and reproductive struggle which we have described as the root cause of the other elements in the human motivational system. The main difference was Harris's sharp distinction between biological and cultural evolution and denial that the former was significant for understanding human social behaviour.[18] And it was precisely this point—the failure to grasp the intimate connection and interaction between the two forms of evolution—that left 'cultural materialism' without a deeper rationale that would explain *why* all the above elements mattered to people and how they were interconnected. Thus, Harris discusses reproduction, sexuality, the family, and kinship separately from one another, without even a hint as to how they might be connected. Among the most glaring lacunae: he considers reproduction mainly from the point of view of population pressure; he describes but never explains the widespread practice of polygamy and the universal phenomenon of kin solidarity; and in line with a long anthropological tradition, he favours a purely socio-cultural explanation for the incest taboo, overlooking the fact that its strong biological base—the product of evolutionary selection against harmful inbreeding—is evident not only in humans but among social animals in general, where either the males or the females usually leave the group and join another on reaching puberty.[19] The proponents of 'cultural materialism' never connected the dots. Indeed, 'cultural materialism' incorporated many valid points precisely where it happened to reflect bits and pieces of the evolutionary rationale in its application to human gene–culture interactions. In the same way, it fell short where it failed to comprehend the entirety of that rationale.

I would not have dwelt on all this at such length had Harris and his disciples not played a central role in the anthropological study of the causes of war and the controversies surrounding it. The Yanomamo of the Orinoco basin and the Highlanders of New Guinea stood at the centre of the debate during the 1970s. It was not clear why these horticulturalists fought among themselves, for there was no real sign that they experienced agricultural land shortage. The proponents of the materialist school suggested that they fought over highly valued animal protein. With the Yanomamo, this supposedly took the form of competition over hunting resources in the forests around their villages. In New Guinea, the competition was allegedly over grazing grounds in the forests for domesticated pigs. While this interpretation was plausible, it did not sit quite comfortably with all the evidence. Indeed, the cultural materialists themselves began to look for complementary explanations.[20]

From the mid-1970s, modern evolutionary theory slowly began to win attention among a small number of anthropologists. One of the first anthropologists influenced by it was Napoleon Chagnon, who had already become the best-known student of the Yanomamo. Chagnon argued that Yanomamo warfare, as well as their internal conflict, was predominantly about reproductive opportunities. In inter-village warfare, women were regularly raped or kid-napped for marriage, or both. Village headmen and distinguished warriors had many wives and children, many times more than ordinary men did. Violent feuds within the village were chiefly caused by adultery.[21] As we have seen, most of these claims were true. Unfortunately, Chagnon, who in the 'protein controversy' wholly opposed the idea that Yanomamo warfare involved competition over hunting territories, gave the impression that evolutionary theory was about reproduction in the narrow rather than the broadest sense, encompassing also the somatic elements that made successful reproduction possible. His arguments have thus opened themselves to all sorts of criticisms.

Anthropologists have in any case exhibited considerable resistance to the intrusion of evolutionary theory, which called for a thorough re-evaluation of accepted anthropological interpretative traditions.[22] Many of the criti-cisms levelled against Chagnon's position have been poorly informed about the fundamentals of the evolutionary rationale. For instance, one critic queried why, if fighting was beneficial for inclusive fitness, was it not con-tinuous and ubiquitous.[23] He failed to realize that fighting, like any other behaviour, could be only one possible tactic for inclusive fitness, depending for its success, and activation, on the presence of specific conditions. Another cluster of often-voiced criticisms claimed that it was not true that people were motivated by the desire to maximize the number of their offspring; that the widespread occurrence of infanticide among primitive people was one example that belied this idea; and that women were sought for economic as well as sexual purposes, as a labour force.[24]

The flaws in these criticisms will be pointed out only briefly. As we saw in Chapter 2, more than a conscious wish to maximize the number of chil-dren, it is mainly the desire for sex that functions in nature as the biological proximate mechanism for maximizing reproduction. Before effective contraception, people's vast reproductive potential was mainly constrained by limited resources and resource competition. Infanticide typically takes place when the birth of a new baby in conditions of resource scarcity threatens the survival chances of his or her elder siblings, for example of an older nursing infant; for inclusive fitness is not about maximizing offspring number but about maximizing the number of *surviving* offspring. The fact that women and children may in some fortunate circumstances generate more resources than they consume, and be valued economically as well as for sexual-reproductive reasons, is strictly in line with evolutionary theory, as successful subsistence is essential for successful reproduction. Rather than pointing in opposite directions, the two activities can sometimes happily intertwine.

A failure to grasp the two interrelated sides of the survival and reproduction equation led both sides in the controversy astray. While Chagnon was right that there were other, and perhaps even more important (reproductive) reasons for Yanomamo warfare, he was wrong in claiming that game competition was not a factor. Indeed, before and during the 'protein controversy', game resources have been consistently shown in a series of studies to play a similar role across a whole range of primitive human societies examined. As Chagnon's adversaries reminded him, he himself had noted that 'game animals are not abundant, and an area is rapidly hunted out'. His adversaries accepted that the Yanomamo suffered from no 'protein deficiency'. Yet they pointed out that the minimum levels of consumption achieved were only secured by a static population level, kept static inter alia by the high mortality rates in fighting recorded among the Yanomamo, as well as among other primitive peoples. A rise in human population level easily translated into game depletion.[25]

Thus, having initially emphasized only the reproductive aspects of warfare, giving rise to the misguided notion among his critics that this was all that evolutionary theory was about, Chagnon correctly began to stress the complementary nature of the somatic and reproductive efforts in this theory.[26] Curiously, however, he largely undermined his own position, and left the whole debate on the wrong track, by suggesting that in doing so he was 'synthesizing' the insights of evolutionary theory with those of cultural materialism. There seemed to be a similar need for a synthesis from the other side. Chagnon's main rival in the debate, anthropologist Brian Ferguson, whom we have already encountered in Chapter 1, advanced a highly elaborate and increasingly one-dimensional materialistic interpretation of the causes of primitive warfare. However, after exhausting all options for explaining away and playing down any non-material motive, he had to admit that some such motives did in fact exist.[27] Offering as he did an increasingly narrow interpretation, he too called for a broadening of approach to the study of the causes of war.[28]

The false dichotomy of the reproductive versus materialist debate is demonstrated by some of the debate's strange twists and turns. Looking for a complement to the game shortage hypothesis, Harris advanced a reproductive interpretation. He suggested that widespread female infanticide in primitive societies was largely caused by a preference for men-warriors in an insecure world; in turn, in a vicious circle, the shortage of women only made the struggle for them all the more severe.[29] Harris had always posited reproduction in relation to population pressure as one of the pillars of his theory, while also stating emphatically that people were highly sexed. Curiously, however, cultural materialists have been loath to recognize the all too obvious connection between the two. Ferguson in particular ignored reproduction in his materialist interpretation of the causes of war. As mentioned in Chapter 2, he raised the question of whether the stealing and raping of women was the cause or a side effect of hunter-gatherer fighting— which is tantamount to asking what people are *really* after when they go to the supermarket: meat, bread, or milk.[30] On the other side, even though Chagnon acknowledged both the somatic and reproductive elements of evolutionary theory, he continued to claim that with primitive people—in general, not only with the Yanomamo—it was the reproductive rather than somatic reasons that were chiefly responsible for warfare.[31]

In reality, the human state of nature was not that different from the general state of nature. Both somatic and reproductive struggles were an integral part of it. The real meaning of Chagnon's call for a synthesis was that evolutionary theory in fact *encompassed* the materialist interpretation, not to mention its ecological counterpart; indeed, that it offered the broad explanatory rationale for principal materialist/ecological insights. What required a synthesis were the somatic and reproductive elements in explaining war rather than the materialist and evolutionary theories, for evolutionary theory had *always* consisted of both elements and explained how they were woven together.

Evolution as Life's Immanent Regulating Principle

Things are not very different with respect to 'functionalism', another formerly popular approach in the social sciences that has more recently come under criticism. It is motivated by much the same questions and comes up with much the same answers as evolutionary theory. However, functionalism evokes function for social phenomena without making clear who gave them this function; does it arise from a transcendent harmony supposedly existing in Nature and even in Society? Functionalism turns things on their head or approaches them from the wrong direction. Rather than explaining general social phenomena and relationships from the bottom up, by contextual interactions of living agents it purports to explain individual action by social abstracts, particularly that of 'stability'.

Thus, in our subject, renowned anthropologist Andrew Vayda suggested in a functionalist vein that fighting was a demographic mechanism triggered by pressure on resources.[32] Indeed, it is the functionalist reasoning rather than its answers that is misconstrued. Fighting is not one of Nature's or of Society's regulating mechanisms for contending with overpopulation; rather, it is one of the strategies that *people*, and other organisms, employ to gain the upper hand in response to increased competition that may arise from demographic growth. The same applies to Malthus's other positive checks on overpopulation: famine and pestilence. These are not 'regulating mechanisms' embedded in Nature's design. Instead, famine is actually what happens to a population that has outgrown its means of subsistence. Similarly, a denser population is simply more vulnerable to the propagation of parasites and pathogens. Obviously, if functionalist reasoning was merely *façon de parler* or accepted shorthand, in the same way that we speak of organisms 'wanting' to increase their numbers, there would have been no problem. However, for functionalists, function is regarded as a genuine explanation rather than *façon de parler* or shorthand.

Some readers may fail to see the advantage of the evolutionary over the cultural materialist or functionalist interpretations of demographic pressure, or, indeed, wonder why evolutionary theory should be presented here as different from and superior to any other scholarly approach to the study of humans in the state of nature. It is because evolutionary theory is nature's *immanent* principle rather than an artificial analytical construct. As already mentioned, it is the only non-transcendent mechanism for explaining life's complex design. This mechanism is blind natural selection, by which those who in every stage were endowed with the most suitable qualities for surviving and reproducing remained. There is no reason why they remained other than that they proved successful in the struggle for survival. Success is not defined by any transcendent measurement but by the immanent logic of the evolutionary process. It should be emphasized that the evolutionary logic in itself has no normative implications. It can inform us about human natural predispositions, whose often ignored effects we would be wise to take into account but which are often variable and even conflicting. There is nothing sacred or morally compelling about maximizing survival for the fittest. Late nineteenth- and early twentieth-century Social Darwinists, on the one hand, and *tabula rasa* liberals and Marxists, on the other, erred here in two opposite directions.

The legacy of Rousseauism, coupled with the great disciplinary investment in the rejection of the evolutionary perspective in the study of man during the twentieth century, still heavily burdens mainstream anthropology and afflicts it with 'false consciousness'. At the same time, anthropology deserves huge credit for being the main source and repository of indispensable data on aboriginal societies, from which a more genuine picture can be reconstructed. Moreover, outside and in conflict with mainstream anthropology, some anthropologists have been among the pioneers in the application of evolutionary theory to the understanding of human motivation and practices in prehistorical, and indeed historical, societies. As our only grand scientific theory for understanding life in general, evolutionary theory does not compete with scholarly constructs such as psychoanalytic theories, 'materialism', or 'functionalism' in explaining the deep roots and underlying rationale of the human motivational system and its behavioural offshoots. Rather, it may encompass some of their main insights within a comprehensive interpretative framework. Thus, Freud's sex drive, Jung's creativity and quest for meaning, and Adler's craving for superiority, each posited by their proponents as the primary regulating principle for understanding human behaviour, come together and interact within the framework of evolutionary theory, which also provides an explanation for their otherwise mysterious origins. The same applies to other long-cited motives for human action—including fighting—such as William Graham Sumner's hunger, love, vanity, and fear of superior powers.[33] It is the intricate interactions and manifold refraction of these motives in humans, exponentially multiplied by cultural development, that are responsible for the staggering wealth and complexity of our species' behaviour patterns, including that of fighting.

To be sure, in the same way that evolutionary theory builds on, obeys, and *adds to* the elementary laws of physics in the realm of living, self-replicating systems, more specific conceptual frameworks may become useful in illuminating different aspects and branches of human social activity as it grows enormously in scope and structural complexity. The study of each such aspect or branch thus becomes a discipline or 'social science', and the various conceptual frameworks within them may be more or less deserving of their designation as 'theories', depending on their validity, comprehensiveness, and rigour. While such theories are obviously not derived from, or reduced to, evolutionary theory—or, for that matter, the laws of physics—they should still be compatible with its broader principles and insights, especially as extended to the human gene–culture interactions that make us what we are. This applies to anthropology as well as to the so-called grand theories in the discipline of international relations and their treatment of the causes of war, to which we now turn.

5

The Causes of War (or Their Absence) In International Relations Theory

The discipline most concerned with the phenomena of conflict and war at the state level is that of international relations. Since its inception in the first half of the twentieth century, it has been dominated by a continuous debate between the competing schools known as 'realism' and 'idealism'/'liberalism'. At the root of the debate has been the fundamental puzzle that has increasingly preoccupied people since the eighteenth century and is the subject of this book: why does war happen? Is war not so harmful as to render it irrational and facilitate its elimination once people devise ways to peacefully resolve their differences, as 'idealists' or liberals have suggested? Or, as those called 'realists' have contended, are conflict and war—and therefore the cultivation of military means and pursuit of power—far more deeply grounded in reality? Are they, for one reason or another, an intrinsic element of international relations that cannot be eradicated by the methods suggested by well-meaning visionaries? Clearly, much of this hinges on what causes conflict and war, and thus a fully fledged theory addressing this question has been very much required. However, as already stated in the Preface, theorists from both schools have either treated the causes of war only obliquely or have advanced manifestly incomplete or incoherent explanations for them.

Realism: Power, Human Motives, and the Causes of War

Realists have had a very important role to play in countering naïve aspirations and high hopes of eschewing power politics and directing foreign policy towards the shaping of a just world order based on utopian visions, moral imperatives, and common goodwill. They have maintained that in an anarchic international arena, in which a multiplicity of states exist with no compelling higher authority, states' behaviour is dominated by self-interest and self-help. Realists have further argued that under these conditions, state action is driven by a fierce competition for power and security that is highly conducive to war. However, on the question of *why* states seek power realists have differed among themselves. Buckets of ink have been spilled on these differences and on those between realists and their critics in the discipline of international relations. One suspects, however, that the argument is largely misconstrued.

Hans Morgenthau established realism in American academia, and his *Politics among Nations* (1948) became the dominant textbook in the field for several decades. In the tradition of Friedrich Nietzsche and Alfred Adler, he claimed that states seek power and act to gain it even by force because the quest for power and dominance is in human nature. Critics have long suggested that realists tend to confuse ends and means. Inter alia their generally correct emphasis on the quest for power has made them lose sight of the underlying reality that explains why the struggle for power takes place. Morgenthau was famously obscure about the relationship between power and other aims of foreign policy that he mentioned, such as 'freedom, security, prosperity', or an ideal of some sort. Sometimes he suggested that power was so central because it was a universal means for attaining any aim. However, more often he claimed that all other aims were largely a disguise for the quest for power and dominance. Most strikingly, he discussed resources purely as a means for power (which some of them obviously are) but not at all as coveted objects in themselves.[1] He boldly asserted that 'what the precapitalist imperialist, the capitalist imperialist, and the "imperialist" capitalist want is power, *not economic gain*...Personal gain and the solution of economic problems through imperialist expansion are for them a pleasant afterthought, a welcome by-product, but not the goal by which the imperialist urge is attracted'.[2] This claim would have surprised the Athenians, Venetians, Spanish *conquistadors* in America ('Gold, God and Glory'), or the British in eighteenth-century India, to mention but a few examples. Supreme monopolistic domination has been hotly desired by many empire builders, variably and conjointly as a means for wealth, for security, as well as for other ends—with all these motives being mutually connected and mutually affecting. In the final analysis, Morgenthau explains neither why the quest for power and dominance is rooted in human nature, nor why its significance is so overwhelming, to the extent that it is.

Morgenthau postulated 'the concept of interest defined in terms of power' as the hallmark of politics, both domestic and international.[3] He justified this restrictive identification of political interest with power not only on substance but also on methodological grounds. He claimed that power was to politics what wealth was to economics ('interest defined as wealth'): an underlying rationale that set politics apart as an autonomous sphere of investigation, separate from others and studied on its own terms by a distinct discipline. This claim sounds analytically neat and has been persuasive to many, but in reality people do not act in separate spheres in pursuit of distinct interests. They pursue their desires and the means necessary to achieve them intermeshed wherever they can be found. Historically, wealth and power flowed into each other, as power served to gain wealth and wealth was translated into power.[4] In addition, the analogy with economics is misleading. Both wealth and power are regarded as universal means for achieving other human ends—hence the analogy's superficial attraction. However, modern economics has been predicated on the actual historical process whereby the use of force has been excluded from the economy in developed societies, first domestically and increasingly also internationally. By contrast, politics—domestic or international—certainly does not exclude the pursuit of economic gain. There is no symmetry in this respect between the two 'autonomous spheres'.

Indeed, other pioneers of the 'realist' school were more cautious than Morgenthau about equating the national interest with power. Writing before Morgenthau, Reinhold Niebuhr searched deeper and more broadly. He mentioned human 'impulses of envy, jealousy, pride, bigotry and greed, which make for conflict between communities' under conditions of anarchy.[5] 'Ambition and vanity' easily turn from defensive to offensive, from the 'will-to-live' to the 'will-to-power',[6] because 'means of defense may be quickly transmuted into means of aggression' (the security dilemma).[7] 'Nature endows him [man] with a sex impulse which seeks the perpetuation of his kind with the same degree of energy with which he seeks the preservation of his own life.' Libido translates into a will-to-power.[8] The struggle for social eminence is intense.[9] Here, more or less, is the entire causal array that leads to conflict and war, with some understandable weaknesses: Niebuhr did not specify a rationale that would explain why all these elements were there and how exactly they related to one another; this partly accounts for the fact that his work understates the quest for material rewards, although he is not oblivious to them, as in 'greed for greater treasures';[10] finally, Niebuhr regarded these human desires negatively as weaknesses or faults, as his realism drew closely on his religious view of man's defective nature.

Arnold Wolfers has been the most broad-minded, sensible, pluralistic, and least doctrinaire of realists. He firmly placed human motives at the centre of his analysis. He began by rejecting the widely held notion that individual human needs and the interests of states form two distinct categories: 'state interests are indeed human interests—in fact the chief source of political motivation today', when popular sovereignty prevails.[11] People 'share a strong inclination to profit from opportunities for acquisition or reacquisition of cherished national possessions, with national power as the chief means of preserving or acquiring national values'.[12] 'Attachment to possessions, fear, and ambition—although they vary in degree from man to man and from people to people—can properly be called "general traits of human nature".'[13] 'Danger as well as opportunity for gain, and fear as well as appetite' constantly vie with each other in people's minds,[14] and the desired values themselves change with individual and collective preferences. Tactfully criticizing Morgenthau,[15] Wolfers wrote: 'Normally, power is a means to other ends and not an end in itself... To treat the quest for power, positively or negatively, outside the context of ends and purpose which it is expected to serve, therefore, robs it of any intelligible meaning.'[16] Furthermore, Wolfers pointed out that the view that power was a universal means for the attainment of all other ends was simplistic: power is itself very costly and thus there are always pressures to reduce investment in it as much as it is felt safe to do in order to free resources for the attainment of other human aims.[17] Wolfers rejected the view that security is paramount because survival is the most vital human aim: 'A quick glance at history is enough... to show that survival has only exceptionally been at stake, particularly for the major powers.'[18] Wolfers saw confusion also with respect to the role of anarchy. Like power, he wrote, anarchy is one prerequisite but not the substantive cause of violent conflict. This cause is the actual goals that the sides pursue.[19]

The desire for economic benefits—being a most earthly and tangible (as opposed to 'idealistic') factor—should have been a natural element of the realist world view, and it was in fact accorded a major role by some leading realists. Prominent among them was Robert Gilpin, who posited power and wealth (as well as other goals) as the two pillars of international relations. States' interests, he wrote, might be 'security, economic gain, or ideological goals'. Changes in the international system involved changes in the 'distribution of benefits'.[20] 'During different eras the mix of objectives has varied in terms of the proportions of various sets of objectives. The ratio of security objectives to economic objectives, for example, may vary depending on internal and external factors.'[21] Like Wolfers, Gilpin pointed out that there were sometimes both trade-offs and a mutual reinforcement between 'guns and butter', as the former could be either a diversion from, or an investment in, the latter.[22]

Another leading realist, Stephen Krasner, wrote that 'the notion of national interest has been subject to much abuse in recent years'. A basic assumption was made in constructing a logical-deductive model centring on the role of power.[23] However, the problem with Morgenthau is that 'power for what is always the puzzling question'.[24] Krasner suggested a different approach, whereby 'the national interest is defined inductively as the preferences of American central decision-makers... These range from satisfying psychological needs to increasing wealth, weakening opponents, capturing territory, and establishing justice.'[25] In his book titled *Defending the National Interest: Raw Materials Investments and US Foreign Policy*, Krasner pointed out that raw materials were sought variably for economic prosperity as well as security.[26]

The above discussion of the respective roles of, and interrelationships between, wealth, power, and other goals that states pursue in the international arena may seem to be pretty much stating the obvious, unnecessary labouring of the point. However, the parameters of the subject have remained deeply confused among international relations scholars, and have become all the more so with the major shift that has occurred in the discipline with the publication of Kenneth Waltz's *Theory of International Politics* (1979). The book introduced new basic assumptions and a new claim for a logical-deductive model (to repeat Krasner's terms), whose influence on realists and resonance in the discipline of international relations in general has been astounding. As a result, the disciplinary discourse on the root causes of conflict and war has been thrown further away from reality. We are now entering a thick forest of concepts and arguments that may seem ponderous and artificial to many readers, and yet they have meant the world for their exponents and have been regarded as the cutting edge of realist theorizing for a generation.

The Waltzian *perpetuum mobile*: Where do the Causes of War Come From?

Like Morgenthau, Waltz claims that a theory in any disciplinary field should be 'domain specific', that is, derived from the particular features of that field itself, as distinct from other, even related fields. Whereas Morgenthau regards politics as the field in question, Waltz holds that with respect to international relations this field is, *ipso facto*, international relations, as distinct from politics in general. The questions he poses, then, are: what are the distinctive and fundamental features of that field or domain, and how do they prescribe its underlying patterns? He argues that in contrast to domestic politics, the defining feature of the international system is anarchy, the lack of an enforcing authority above the states, which results in endemic insecurity between them. In such an environment every state worries about its survival, is apprehensive of every other state because it may attack it, can only rely on itself, and needs to arm and take other measures to protect itself. Waltz well recognizes that different states have different and diverse objectives. Yet he claims that no matter what their other goals may be—irrespective of the actual wishes of their leaders or peoples—states are pressured by the anarchic nature of the international system to seek security as their prime objective. Unlike Morgenthau, he regards power primarily not as an end in itself but as a means for security.[27] Although, curiously, Waltz never wrote this in so many words, perhaps did not fully realize this, his whole intellectual edifice is in effect based on the logic of the security dilemma.[28]

Central to Waltz's argument is the distinction he draws between a 'reductionist' approach, like Morgenthau's, that seeks to explain a system through the qualities of the system's component units, and a 'systemic' approach, like his own. The systemic approach focuses on the emergent features that arise between the component units by virtue of the interaction that the nature of the system imposes on them—features that cannot be traced to the units taken separately.[29] According to Waltz, the structure and intrinsic dynamics of the anarchic system of states form the linchpin of a proper explanation of why conflict and war exist. For this reason, his brand of realism has been labelled 'structural' or 'systemic neo-realism', as opposed to Morgenthau's unit-level analysis that was supposedly driven by a natural human craving for power and dominance and has now been named 'classical realism'.

Waltz's book was a model of deductive reasoning. He carefully and systematically developed what seemed like a tight, parsimonious, and impregnable analytical edifice. His systemic or structural realism stood at the centre of a hectic disciplinary debate for two decades, and it remains prominent. The theory's huge seductive power drew realists in its direction, while its critics struggled to find where and why its schoolman-like logic failed and its claims for internal coherence and external validity were not met. The most significant criticisms, striking at the heart of Waltz's reasoning, concerned his pivotal claims regarding the role and consequences of anarchy, and indeed its very nature.

The crucial problem is this: although Waltz recognized that other causes for war—from the 'state level'—exist, his exclusive focus on the security dilemma at the 'system level' has obscured the intimate connection between state objectives and the *emergence* of the security dilemma. He thus accorded to the latter a seemingly separate and independent life, and in any case has directed all attention to it alone. Certainly, the availability of the violent option makes the very real prospect that any number of the actors involved would find that option the most profitable one sufficient to make the system inherently insecure. However, for this prospect to exist, for insecurity to prevail, and for the security dilemma to flare up, there has to be a state of actual or potential competition over *something*. No real insecurity arises between, say, deer and squirrels, even though they might inhabit the same unregulated, anarchic environment, because they do not compete over the same somatic or reproductive resources (or, for that matter, feed on each other). This is what Waltz and his disciples have missed in their causal schema. The anarchic nature of the international system is not sufficient to explain the recurrence of war. It requires the extra assumption, from the 'unit' rather than 'systemic' level, that states have motives other than security that they may opt to pursue violently—which is, moreover, the *reason* why the system is infused with insecurity.

As mentioned before, Wolfers saw this clearly as far back as 1962:

> It might seem that the mere existence of a multitude of nation-states, each capable of independent decision and action, would suffice to explain the peaceless state of the world and the power struggles that fill the international arena. Undoubtedly, the anarchical condition inherent in any system of multiple sovereignty constitutes one of the prerequisites of international conflict; without it, there could be no international relations, peaceful or non-peaceful. *Yet, in the last analysis, it is the goals pursued by the actors and the way*

*they go about pursuing them that determine whether and to what extent the potential-
ities for power struggle and war are realized.*[30]

This crucial and, indeed, pretty obvious point has failed to be noticed by Waltz
and his disciples, and has needed resurrection by a number of scholars.[31] Among
realists it has been developed by Randall Schweller. In an article aptly titled
'Neorealism's Status-Quo Bias: What Security Dilemma?' (1996), he wrote:

> If states are assumed to seek nothing more than their own survival, why should
> they feel threatened?...Waltz's statements make sense if, and only if, we
> assume the prior existence of a threat. Otherwise, the need for security never
> arises in the first place. What triggers security dilemmas under anarchy is the
> possibility of predatory states existing among the ranks of the units the system
> comprises...contemporary realists ignore the very states that activate the sys-
> tems and behaviors they seek to explain...structure alone, defined as the
> number of great powers and the anarchic order, cannot account for the out-
> comes and behaviors Waltz claims to explain.[32]

As Schweller has pointed out, one fundamental error has reinforced and
has been reinforced by another in structural realist theorizing: because the
quest for security has been posited as the self-sufficient driving force of the
anarchic international system (which could not logically be the case), other
goals, although habitually acknowledged, have been pushed to the sideline.
Moreover, structural realists have cultivated a 'status quo bias'. Waltz and
so-called 'defensive realists' have in any case held that—*inherently and
universally*—no real profit could be made from aggressive action in the
international arena because of the balancing effect of the coalition that
would form to oppose an expansionist state.[33] This, however, is simply
untrue. Although balancing against a threatening dominant state has been a
most common and powerful mechanism in international relations, to posit
it as all-powerful is sheer dogma. While balancing was particularly effective
in the traditional European great power system—from which, indeed, the
doctrine has been abstracted and universalized—it has been far less effective
in other state systems throughout history and around the world. It did not
prevent quite a number of such systems from becoming hegemonic, with
immense wealth and splendour won by the dominant power in each case.
A study has documented this fact, quite familiar to any student of world
history, in systems such as those of ancient Rome, China, Mughal India, the
Aztecs, and Inca, to mention only some of the most prominent cases.★[34]

★ These were not merely 'regional' systems, as realists are predisposed to claim, but often constituted the contemporary *acumen* that was sometimes entirely separated from the rest of the world.

Thus, structural realism's defensive bias is both internally incoherent and in violation of historical experience.

Grasping only parts of the above criticisms, realist John Mearsheimer has in any event recognized that in Waltz's 'defensive realism' there are actually no reasons for war.[35] Purporting to correct the theory and add the missing engine to the system, he has put forward an 'offensive' variant of structural realism, arguing that the security pressures of the anarchic state system, in and of themselves, force states that seek to survive not merely to defend their power but ever to try to increase it actively by dominating and subduing others. Note that Mearsheimer's position is structural. In this framework, other motives for war, which may variably exist, need not be assumed for insecurity, conflict, and war to arise in an anarchic state system. The anarchic system in itself is posited as the cause of war, because it pushes states to act offensively when they can, in sheer self-defence, regardless of the true wishes of their leaders and peoples, and whatever their other aims might be. Mearsheimer has labelled this 'the tragedy of the great powers'.[36] However, he has failed to see that his 'offensive structural realism' resolves nothing, suffering as it does from the same fatal problem as structural realism in general. Clearly, both defensive and offensive reactions to the security dilemma have variably existed. However, any concept based on the quest for security and the security dilemma alone, including Mearsheimer's 'offensive' one, leaves unanswered, indeed unasked, the question of why the quest for security—expressed defensively or offensively—should arise at all if no positive motives for aggression exist on any side, at least potentially.

Indeed, Mearsheimer's offensive structural realism is at one with the defensive variant in its 'status quo bias', the assumption that bids for domination are likely to be of limited value because of the balancing action of the other states in the system against the aspiring hegemon. The offensive action and bid for domination he claims are forced on the powers by their quest for security are therefore both inescapable and largely Sisyphean. This is another aspect of the 'tragedy of the great powers'. In fact, although priding themselves on their hard-nosed realism, realists have increasingly tended to share the view of their 'idealist' antagonists that war does not pay, while differing from them only on the question of whether or not it can be eliminated or is 'tragically' enforced on all sides.

In reality, and in contrast to structural realist assumptions, many aggressive states throughout history have reaped huge rewards, whether or not they won hegemony in the system (as quite a few did). The 'tragedy' was mostly that of the vanquished. As if to justify the old quip that the realist school is actually the most unrealistic, realists have lost touch with the purpose of the whole exercise. Above all, they have grossly misconstrued the pivotal subject of human motives in generating conflict and war. Morgenthau concentrated on the craving for power and dominance in a way that obscured all other motives for human action and conflict. Structural realists have focused on the security imperative to a degree that practically pushed these motives out of sight. Their celebrated system has remained with no engine, is a true *perpetuum mobile*, supposedly fuelled by the internal logic of the anarchic system alone. Everything else has been posited as extraneous circumstances and exogenous to the system. Hence the utterly paradoxical result that the quest for coveted objects of desire, such as economic gain and much else, should be viewed by mainstream realists as being out of step with the tenets of realism, a deviation from its doctrine. In fact, realists should have been the first to highlight such motives or self-interests as the powerful engine of the real world of competition and conflict. Rather than being the limited but distilled and parsimonious logic of the international system, as Waltz modestly framed his theory, structural realism actually reflects the truly limited logic of the security dilemma alone. It has turned attention away from the crucial component that explains what brings the dilemma into being and actually drives the whole conflictual situation.

It is a measure of the huge gravitational pull of structural realism during the last generation that it has bent the disciplinary discourse its way even with respect to its critics. In his otherwise penetrating review of Mearsheimer's book, Glenn Snyder has underlined the prominence of objectives other than security, such as national glory, honour, advancing an ideology, seeking national unification, and, as the only qualified proposition: 'perhaps economic enrichment'.[37] What an uncertain motive indeed.

The Neoclassical Critique and Misstep

Schweller has been among those who (like Wolfers a generation earlier) have pulled the carpet from under the structural realists' fundamental premise that the anarchic nature of the international system is sufficient to account for conflict and war, irrespective of the actors' motives. Schweller has pointed out that states regularly go to war in order to achieve 'coveted values', and are motivated by goals as diverse as, 'for example, greed, divine right, manifest destiny and revenge.'[38] Moreover, all these 'unit-level' motives are the actual *causes* of the insecurity that all the other states in the system feel. Schweller and others have launched a 'neoclassical' revival, centring on the idea that a coherent understanding of the international system requires a combination of *both* individual states' behaviour *and* the system effect, which cannot be separated from one another.

Unfortunately, the full significance of states' goals as the actual driving force of the international system has not been fully grasped even by the so-called neoclassical realists. Rather than on state ambitions, they concentrate on interferences with the primacy of power caused by state '(mis)percep-tions' of the balance of power and on domestic 'constraints' on the state's quest to maximize its power.[39] Surprisingly, Schweller himself has fallen into this trap. In his initial exposure of the fatal flaw in the structural logic, he specified 'greed', the 'opportunity for gain', 'profit', 'rewards', and 'spoils' among the goals that states pursue.[40] For this reason, his approach has been dubbed 'motivational realism'.[41] Increasingly, however, Schweller has restricted himself to *power*-seeking states as the main driving force of international relations. He now treats resources purely as means for gaining power rather than as the coveted ends in themselves that fuel the quest for power, while also often underpinning power. Gone are the broad concepts of 'possessions' and 'coveted values' that he named as the motives for state action in his early work. His 'revisionist state' now appears to seek only power, and other states are supposed to be inhibited in their pursuit of power solely by 'domestic constraints', rather than, say, by other goals, such as economic prosperity.[42] He presents this focus on power as a realist prin-ciple, and this is indeed how mainstream realism has developed. But is the wholesale concentration on power/security—as opposed to a due emphasis on its key role—realistic? As we have seen, some leading realists—from Niebuhr to Wolfers, Gilpin, and Krasner, recently joined by Charles Glaser—thought otherwise.[43]

The term 'offensive realism' is indiscriminately applied to both Mearsheimer's offensive *structural* realism, predicated solely on the quest for security, and truly offensive forms of realism. These are two very different things.[44] The latter recognize the ambition, often fulfilled, to win something in this world, including by force. Such ambition is central to the world we know, and yet it has strangely disappeared from international relations theory over recent decades, most notably from so-called realism.

Evolution-Shaped Human Motives, and a 3D, Truly Systemic Explanation for War

In his early work Schweller quotes Machiavelli, widely regarded as one of the forefathers of realism, concerning the role of *ambizione*: 'The desire to acquire possessions is a very natural and ordinary thing'.[45] Wolfers similarly grasped the role of elementary human desires, writing that 'state interests are indeed human interests', rather than something distinct and elevated.[46] Charles Glaser makes more or less the same point: 'The decision-making state is characterized in terms of its *motives*. Motives embody what a state values, capturing its fundamental interests or goals.'[47] Indeed, state interests are quite simply what people who exercise influence on political decisions—at the top or more widely—are interested in. Without an understanding of human motivation there is neither a real account of state goals, nor a driving force to the international state system.[48] As this book suggests, wars have been fought for the attainment of the same objects of human desire that underlie the human motivational system in general—*only by violent means*, through the use of force. Politics—internal and external—of which war is, famously, a continuation, is the activity intended to achieve at the intra- and inter-state 'levels' the very same evolution-shaped human aims we have already seen.

Some writers have felt that 'politics' does not fully encompass the causes of war.[49] Even Bradley Thayer, an international relations scholar who has argued that evolutionary theory explains ultimate human aims, has nonetheless gone on to say, inconsistently, that Clausewitz needs extension because war is caused not only by political reasons but also by the evolutionarily-rooted search for resources.[50] This would imply that political objectives, lofty 'reasons of state', are somehow different and apart from ordinary human objectives, and fall outside of the evolutionary logic. More surprisingly, it implies that the search for resources is not among the aims of politics.[†]

Thayer deserves great credit for pioneering the evolutionary perspective in the discipline of international relations. In this discipline evolutionary theory was and still remains unfamiliar and alien, while realist theory has

---

[†] There is some similarity here to Chagnon's misstep in suggesting that the evolutionary and materialist perspectives should be reconciled in the anthropological theory of the causes of human fighting, whereas in fact the former incorporates and explains the latter.

been dominant and prestigious. Thus, Thayer has striven to demonstrate to his peers the usefulness of the evolutionary perspective in validating major realist propositions and in sorting out which of the realist approaches is closer to the truth. However, quite apart from the fact that the logic of the major realist strands regarding the causes of war is seriously muddled, evolutionary theory and realism do not stand on the same level. Like the anthropological schools in the study of pre-state societies, realist 'theory' is a more or less useful analytical construct, whereas evolutionary theory is life's immanent principle.[51] Again, what is required is to show how naturally evolved human desires work in the domain of 'politics'—through the structures of society, state, and the international system—all of which have to some extent affected the cost–benefit calculus and prevalence of the violent option for achieving the desired aims.

Stressing human motives as indispensable for understanding states' goals and international relations, Jack Donnelly and Richard Ned Lebow have both cited human nature and have looked for it in the writings of classical philosophers. Donnelly has found a close similarity between the natural motives specified by the forerunners of realist thought: Thucydides's 'fear, honor, and interest' (I.76); Hobbes's competition, diffidence, and glory (Leviathan, chap. 13.6); and Machiavelli's 'glories and riches', 'honors and ... prosperity' (The Prince, 25.2; Discourses, I.37.2).[52] Lebow has gone as far back as Plato and Aristotle, citing human appetite (most notably for wealth), spirit (self-esteem, honour, standing, and the resulting urge to avenge injuries), reason, and fear as the four basic causes of war.[53] ‡ The classical philosophers are great authorities, to be sure, and their thoughts on the human motivational system remain far fresher than their teachings in biology or physics. Still, all traditional lists of motives such as these, representing as they do the insight and wisdom of the ages, have no explanation for the source of each of these motives, their interrelationship, and internal hierarchy. Only the advent of the evolutionary perspective has thrown light on the deeper rationale that underpins and explains all the above motives. Similarly, the evolutionary perspective places rational choice calculations in their broader context. It clarifies why they to a large degree underlie people's actual behaviour, and offers much more substance on the coveted 'values' themselves, which are not quite simply anything.[54]

‡ Unlike Lebow and the Greek philosophers, and in agreement with David Hume, I see reason as a device for assessing the benefits, costs, and risks involved in the pursuit of various human desires, rather than as an independent drive or goal.

Waltz's original three levels of analysis—man, the state, and the international system—suggested in his early book, *Man, the State and War* (1959), are *all* interconnected, inseparable, and necessary for explaining war. It is not only, as Waltz readily admits, that the causes of war may involve a combination of factors from all three 'levels' (which he later collapsed to only two: the states and the system). It is that in all of these 'levels' there are necessary but not sufficient causes for war, and the whole cannot be broken into pieces, as the three 'levels' are inextricably linked. A three-, not one-dimensional explanation of war is necessary. Waltz defined the distinction between a 'systemic' and 'reductionist' approach in a very specific way, which the discipline has come to habitually parrot. Students feel that they have been initiated into the discipline when they have internalized and can speak such disciplinary linguistic peculiarities with ease. However, to concentrate as Waltz did on one 'level' alone—which he wrongly believed to have an autonomous and irreducible effect—rather than on the interrelationship and interconnectivity between all 'levels', is anything but a systematic, 'structural' grasp of how a system works. It is in fact the truly reductionist approach.

Relying on developments in the philosophy of science spawned by Thomas Kuhn and Imre Lakatos, Waltz insisted that a theory—an abstract model of a connection between variables—could not be empirically disproven. Instead, he claimed that those wishing to dethrone it needed to present a superior theory.[55] A superior theory both logically and empirically adopts a truly integrative approach, combining human natural motivations, the state, and the international system, in their mutual interaction, in a 3D edifice. Thus, people's needs and desires, which may be pursued violently, as well as the resulting quest for power and state of mutual apprehension which fuel the security dilemma, are all moulded in human nature (some of them existing only as options, potentials, and skills in a behavioural 'tool-kit'). They are so moulded because of strong evolutionary pressures that have shaped humans in their struggle for survival over a geological timespan, when all the above literally constituted matters of life and death. The violent option of human competition has been largely curbed within the state-Leviathans, yet it is occasionally taken up on a large scale between them because the anarchic nature of the inter-state system allows it, and at least one of the sides believes that it can profit from it more than from the peaceful options (cooperation and/or peaceful competition). However, returning to step one, international anarchy in and of itself is not an explanation for war were it not for the potential for violence in a fundamental state of competition over scarce resources that is embedded in reality and, consequently, in human nature.

The necessary and sufficient causes of war—that obviously have to be filled with the particulars of the case in any specific war—are therefore as follows: politically organized actors that are capable of harming each other and operate in an environment where no superior authority effectively monopolizes power resort to violence when they assess it to be their most cost-effective option for winning and/or defending human ends, and/or their power in the system that can help them win and/or defend those desired ends. To understand the fundamental causes of war is to grasp how (a) the pursuit of evolution-shaped human objectives (b) by means of the violent behavioural option (c) is an immanent potential in anarchic systems. Again, it is *all* the so-called 'levels'—the individual, the state, and the international system—in their causal interactions, that have to be grasped three-dimensionally, as a whole.§

The great majority of books on international relations whose stated subject is the causes of war actually deal with various conditions that supposedly affect the likelihood and frequency of war. Thus, they are concerned with enabling and promoting conditions rather than with the underlying causes or motives that lead to war, about which they are practically silent.[56]

A Static or Evolving Reality: Enter Historical Transformation (3D+Time)

Alexander Wendt has been among the most notable critics of the structural realists' premise that anarchy, in and of itself, necessarily breeds insecurity and war. He aptly coined the phrase: 'anarchy is what states make of it'. He suggested that in an anarchic condition the other can be an enemy, a rival, or a friend, depending on the circumstances, and has identified these three different postures with the different anarchic orders delineated, respectively, by Thomas Hobbes, John Locke, and Immanuel Kant.[57] This distinction is perhaps even better explained in terms of the three alternative and

§ The three 'dimensions' are conceptualizations of currently salient empirical features rather than reified metaphysical entities. Other 'dimensions' (such as domestic pressure groups, multinationals, supranational confederations), presently 'folded' into these three, may be conceptualized distinctly if they grow in significance, or even if they do not.

complementary behavioural strategies that people employ to achieve their aims or self-interests. As specified earlier, these include: peaceful cooperation, non-violent competition, and violent conflict—activated interchangeably according to people's assessments of their respective cost-effectiveness in any given situation. While people have always made variable use of all three behavioural strategies, the violent option was very prominent indeed in anarchic pre-state societies.[58] Violence was almost as pervasive in the anarchic state system throughout history. However, might the cost–benefit calculations and actual payoffs between the three behavioural strategies in the anarchic international system have significantly changed under modern conditions?

This brings us to another critical flaw in realism that has a major bearing on the question of why wars occur. Realist theory has long been criticized for being formulated as a set of immutable, metaphysical-like principles regarding the nature of the international system.[59] But cannot the patterns of international relations undergo radical change as a result of a far-reaching transformation of historical conditions? Realists' response to this question has been ambivalent. Waltz stated that if the anarchic order of the international system were to change into something else, which he admitted was not beyond the realm of the possible, then international relations would not be the same and his theory would no longer be valid.[60] At the same time, he saw no signs that this was happening. More importantly—writing as he did in the 1970s, during the Cold War—he found no evidence that the anarchic order was becoming either more interconnected or more benign.[61] Gilpin's theory has been praised for allowing for change in the system, as changing technological, economic, and social conditions constantly alter the cost-effectiveness calculations of states and account for some of them growing in power and others declining. But then again, might radical change in historical conditions affect not only the activation of the option to pursue power, but, indeed, the entire choice structure between the three strategies of conflict, peaceful competition, and cooperation? Writing at the same historical moment as Waltz, Gilpin was cautious if not sceptical that such a historic transformation was actually occurring.[62] Other theories of power shifts and conflict have been much narrower than Gilpin's, while being similarly 'cyclical', 'more of the same', in their conception of historical change.[63]

With realists concentrating on the quest for power/security as the closest approximation or most useful abstraction of reality's main features and driving forces, critics have felt that the reality left out was too significant to ignore. Thus, a 'constructivist' school has emerged in international relations theory, emphasizing the major role played by the actors' identities, values, ideas, and perceptions, all largely shaped by the particular historical development of the societies and people involved. Constructivism is best viewed as a limited response to, and sensible correction of, realist excessive reductionism. It is a useful reminder of the quite obvious fact that in the real world a lot more than the pursuit of power/security shapes political attitudes and outcomes.

Liberalism poses a more substantial challenge to realism. While constructivism holds that history matters, liberalism *centres* on historical change. In a sense, liberalism can be regarded as constructivism's most significant case by far of how historical developments alter the actors' choice setup, and therefore also the logic of the international system. Although some liberal strands are couched in a universalistic, ahistorical (and naïve) language, others clearly ground themselves in the most profound historical transformation experienced by humanity since the adoption of agriculture millennia ago: the onset and spread of industrial-commercial-affluent society, modernity, and liberal democracy since the early nineteenth century. Realists have adamantly denied that the world—including the logic and reality of international relations—has been changing in any significant way. The notion of such a change goes against the realists' abstract schema and habit of mind, even though, in a deeper sense, nothing requires that this schema—its preconditions and effects—should remain immutable to historical transformation. With realism emerging as a healthy antidote to idealist flights of fancy, realists have been predisposed to resist the evidence that a very significant change has been occurring, even after this evidence has become overwhelming.

Although the various strands of liberalism have also lacked an expressed, fully fledged theory of what causes war, the wealth of finds and insights generated in some of them with respect to the factors working against war during modern times has been very significant and illuminating. In the following chapters, we shall examine the various explanations proposed for the apparent decline of war throughout the world, most notably in its developed parts. We shall seek to determine how modern developments have changed the cost–benefit calculus of the violent versus the peaceful options for achieving human desires, whose pursuit is the engine of human behaviour. Returning to Waltz's challenge to his critics to offer a superior theory, such a theory of international relations should incorporate, beyond the 3D—human desires, the state, and the state system—also a fourth dimension: time. Social conditions and the international system are evolving.

This is not to say that realist precepts have entirely lost their validity, but only that a very real shift has been occurring in the world arena. As leading proponents of the liberal and constructivist schools have sensibly maintained, these schools should not be seen as contrasting with realism, realistically understood, but as combining with it to create a more comprehensive outlook.[64] The gap between liberalism and realism has in any case narrowed as, since the 1970s, the so-called neoliberals have stressed people's pursuit of their self-interests rather than idealistic harmony and altruism. Constructivist Wendt has also conceded that self-interest is more central than he previously realized: 'Human beings probably never would have survived evolution without such a self-interested bias, and the same is probably true of states'.[65] However, as realist doctrine stiffened, centring on power/security rather than on interest, or tending to conflate the two, and with realists being suspicious of anything that might suggest a lessening of violent conflict in the world arena, realists have failed to appreciate this converging of views. The three 'schools' are not mutually exclusive. The debate between realism and idealism–liberalism touched on some crucial questions in its time, and in some of its aspects it called for additional evidence. However, there is a widespread feeling among international relations scholars that it has been going on for too long, appears to have become ossified, and needs to be transcended.[66] Certainly, arguments—both practical and theoretical— over issues involving power, morality, and the boundaries of the possible, practical, and desirable in the conduct of foreign policy will persist, and necessarily so. A sense of proportion in assessing the efficacy of global developments and the need to guard against millenarian flights of fancy are both crucial. In the real world, power has been pivotal, and it remains so in large parts of the world. At the same time, forms of peaceful competition and cooperation for advancing people's self-interests have been growing momentously, going hand in hand with far-reaching changes in social values and norms.[67] All of the above count, inter alia greatly affecting the occurrence of war.

The Modernization
Peace

6

Has War been Declining— and Why?

The Puzzle

Has the world been changing, becoming less belligerent and more peaceful? This notion first appeared in Europe and the West during the nineteenth century. Yet it seemed to have been brutally shattered by the two world wars, some of the most destructive and lethal wars in history, which cast their long shadow over the first half of the twentieth century. Realist thought, emphasizing human conflict and the struggle for power and security that occasionally and inevitably bursts into war, thus emerged as a reaction against idealistic-liberal premonitions of peace. Indeed, it drew strength from the eruption of the Cold War, a clash of titans which arguably did not turn hot and develop into a third world war only or primarily because of nuclear deterrence. However, even before and increasingly after the end of the Cold War, new claims about the decline of war have been voiced and have commanded attention. From the 1970s onwards, the initially startling finding that democratic/liberal societies do not fight each other has progressively gained credence. An alternative or complementary theory has suggested that the crucial factor lies elsewhere, and that what we are witnessing is a capitalist rather than democratic peace. Others have detected an even broader phenomenon. In his *Retreat from Doomsday: The Obsolescence of Major War* (1989), John Mueller has claimed that the change was general, irrespective of political or economic regimes, and that it preceded and was independent of the nuclear factor. According to Mueller, an 'attitude change' against war was responsible for the decline. My own *War in Human Civilization* (2006), Steven Pinker's *The Better Angels of Our Nature: Why Violence Has Declined* (2011), Joshua Goldstein's *Winning the War on War*

(2011), and Ian Morris's *War: What is It Good For?* (2014) have all argued that violent mortality in general decreased with the rise of states, and that war has greatly diminished during recent times.

Thus, several questions call for answers. First, has war really been declining? This proposition encounters widespread disbelief, not only from theorists in intra-disciplinary wars of ink but also from ordinary people, who are very surprised by the claim that we live in the most peaceful period in history. Are we not flooded with reports and images in the media of conflicts around the world, some of them very active and bloody and others seemingly waiting to happen? Have the United States and its allies not been repeatedly involved in a series of messy wars over the past few decades? Alternatively, is the relative peacefulness of today's world not attributable to a transient American hegemony since the collapse of the Soviet Union, to a fleeting post-Cold War moment? Are we in fact being tempted once more by the old illusions that will yet again be dispelled by the rise of China to a superpower status, by a resurgent Russia, or by vicious wars in south or Central Asia, the Middle East, and Africa?

Second, if war has indeed declined, why is that so? As mentioned earlier, various types and causes of peace have been suggested to explain current realities: a nuclear peace of mutual deterrence; the notion that war, even in conventional forms, had simply become far too lethal, ruinous, and expensive to indulge in, or, when looked at from the other direction, that it no longer promises rewards; the idea that war has *always* been a big mistake, and was finally being got rid of as people became wiser and sick of it; a democratic peace; a capitalist peace; and peace through international institutions. How valid is each of these explanations? How do they relate to, supplant, or complement one another?

Third, what is the time frame of the decline in belligerency, if indeed this has taken place? Did it begin, as various scholars hold, with the end of the Cold War, in 1945, in 1918, or in the nineteenth century? Clearly, the answer to this question may also offer a vital clue as to the causes of the change.

As computerized information processing capacity has increased exponentially over recent decades, quantitative research techniques have been used to test these and other hypotheses. Large data sets, encoding various potentially relevant variables across time and space, have been mined in search of compelling evidence. The result has been richly rewarding. An understandable tension exists between 'quantitative' and 'qualitative' researchers, but in actuality both have a crucial role to play, and they complement each other. Data neither exists in itself nor speaks for itself. It needs to be selected and categorized—processes that necessarily involve choices and judgement. Informed questions need to be posed, and they affect the answers that one gets. Context is vital for the interpretation of finds, and meaningful and valid comprehensive explanations or theories need to be constructed. Broad (large N) statistical studies sometimes disguise little conceptual and empirical discrimination. Whereas international relations scholars tend to deplore the inability of many historians to think more generally beyond the particular society and period they study, historians are often appalled by the crude simplifications and lopsided or contrived propositions in much that passes as theory and explanation in international relations research. This chapter examines the data and various theories relating to the decline of war with the tools of comparative historical analysis in an attempt to put the pieces of the great jigsaw puzzle together. It asks how the causes of war that we have seen throughout this book have been transformed under altered conditions, with human motives and actions increasingly channelled towards peaceful behavioural strategies.

Are Nukes the Answer? The Long Peace—Not One but Three

In the wake of two destructive world wars and during the tense years of the Cold War, the notion of an increasingly peaceful world seemed wholly misguided, and understandably so. The only good thing that could be said about the nuclear balance of terror between the superpowers was its flip side: that the fear of mutual assured destruction (MAD) may have prevented the Cold War from turning into a third world war. As the years without a great power war accumulated after 1945, they were dubbed the Long Peace.[1] As of now, the Long Peace among the great powers has passed its seventieth year and counting, with the only partial exception being the limited war involving the United States and China in Korea (1950–3). As the argument goes, the cautiousness of the superpowers has affected the entire system, because they acted to restrain their allies and clients from getting involved in wars that might have escalated to engulf the nuclear powers themselves.

It has scarcely been noted, however, that the Long Peace among the great powers is not that special.[2] It was preceded by forty-three years of peace among the great powers between 1871 and 1914, with the Russo-Japanese War

(1904–5) as a partial exception. And this Second Longest Peace was preceded by the Third Longest Peace among the great powers, spanning thirty-nine years between 1815 and 1854 (Diagram 6.1). The wars between the great powers are of particular significance, because historically they were always both the most crucial and most destructive inter-state wars, which took place between the most powerful and by far the most belligerent states. Notably, both the Second and Third Longest Peace occurred before the advent of nuclear weapons, and within a highly competitive multi-polar great power system.

However, are these long periods of peace unusual compared to earlier times? Is it not the normal pattern of history to have long lulls of peace, either random or not, between periods of intense war? The most widely used quantitative database on wars and militarized inter-state disputes, the Correlates of War (COW), covers the period from 1816 onwards. Thus, it has given researchers no indication of whether or not the Long Peace phenom- enon is exceptional, or, indeed, no inkling that it exists in and is special to the period COW covers. Our horizons, and the questions that we are conscious of, have been constrained by the time span of the database. Fortunately, a few longer range statistical studies of the trend do exist.[3] A comparison of the European great power system before and after 1815 reveals that years of war among the great powers decreased by roughly two-thirds during the century following Waterloo, to only a *third* of what they had been in the preceding centuries. As Jack Levy has written with respect to the COW data and a few earlier statistical studies that covered a similar time span: 'Their starting point immediately after the Congress of Vienna introduces a serious bias into trend analysis, for this was the most peaceful period in the last five centuries [cov- ered by Levy's study].'[4] Austria and Prussia, for example, neither of them a democracy, registered the sharpest decline in overall belligerency (counting all wars rather than only great power wars). Compared to their record during the eighteenth and seventeenth centuries, they fought about a third to a quarter as much during the century after 1815. Austria had been at war in one out of every two years during the eighteenth century, and in three out of four during the sixteenth and seventeenth centuries. Prussia had been at war in one out of every three years during the eighteenth century, and dur- ing 60 per cent of the time in the seventeenth century.[5]

Similarly, there was no Long Peace between the great powers during the eighteenth century (or earlier). The following survey is restricted to the wars that pitted at least two of the five classical European great powers of the eighteenth and nineteenth centuries against each other: Britain, France,

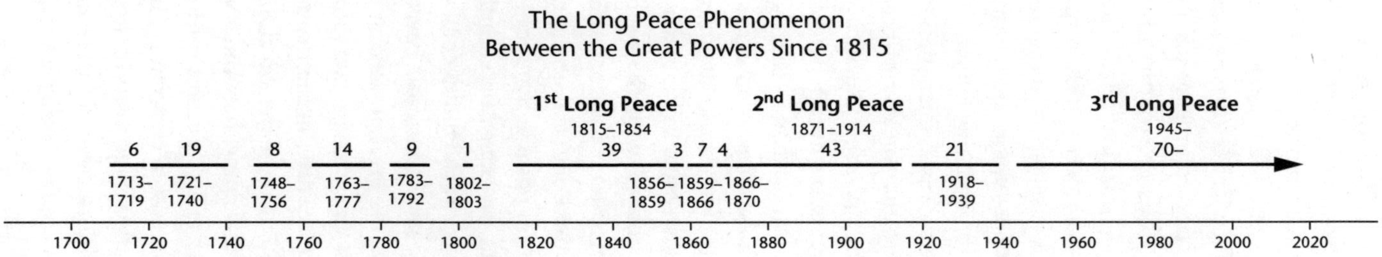

The Long Peace Phenomenon
Between the Great Powers Since 1815

1st Long Peace
1815–1854
39

2nd Long Peace
1871–1914
43

3rd Long Peace
1945–
70–

6
1713–
1719

19
1721–
1740

8
1748–
1756

14
1763–
1777

9
1783–
1792

1
1802–
1803

3
1856–
1859

7
1859–
1866

4
1866–
1870

21
1918–
1939

1700   1720   1740   1760   1780   1800   1820   1840   1860   1880   1900   1920   1940   1960   1980   2000   2020

Diagram 6.1. The Long Peace phenomenon between the great powers since 1815

Prussia/Germany, Austria, and Russia. We thus compare like with like, excluding Sweden, Spain, the Dutch Republic, Poland, and the Ottoman Empire, all of which were still claiming great power status at the beginning of the eighteenth century. Even by this restrictive definition, in the Wars of the Revolution and Napoleon (1792–1815) there was barely a one-year break (1802–3) when all the powers were at peace with France; there were nine years between the end of the American Revolutionary War (which involved France in 1778–83) and the French Revolutionary Wars; fifteen years between the War of the Bavarian Succession (1777–9) and the French Revolutionary Wars; fourteen years between the Seven Years' War (1756–63) and the War of the Bavarian Succession; eight years between the War of the Austrian Succession (1740–8) and the Seven Years' War; nineteen years between the Great Northern War (which included Britain in the anti-Russian coalition in 1719–21) and the War of the Austrian Succession; six years between the War of the Spanish Succession (1701–13) and the Great Northern War. Great power wars during the sixteenth and seventeenth centuries were even more frequent than in the eighteenth century.

Thus, the three Long Periods of Peace among the great powers are in fact highly unusual compared to earlier history. The three longest periods of peace by far in the modern great power system have all occurred since 1815, and in a progressively ascending sequence, with the peace becoming ever longer each time. It would be foolish to argue that the nuclear factor has contributed nothing to the durability of the Longest Peace, after 1945, as the prospect of mutual assured destruction—no possible winners—has acted as the ultimate inhibition to a war that might escalate to a nuclear holocaust. Nuclear weapons have wonderfully concentrated the minds of all involved, as it is said about the hanging rope. And yet, a clear trend had been building long before the nuclear age. As already noted, the great powers are recorded to have engaged in war much more than other states, and the wars among them are the greatest of all wars. But a similar sharp decrease in the frequency of war has also been registered among all the countries of the developed world after 1815. The people of nineteenth-century Europe, between 1815 and 1914, lived in the most pacific century in human history and soon enough noticed that an extraordinary development had been occurring. Clearly, we need to explain the entire trend, throughout the period from 1815 to the present. By the same token, however, we also need to account for the massive divergence from the trend: the two world wars. A comprehensive account of the phenomenon in question must embrace both sides of the coin.

Has War Become Too Lethal and Destructive?

The first, most intuitive and natural response of people when they learn about the decrease in major war is that the change must be due to modern wars becoming prohibitively costly in terms of life and wealth. This is certainly true of nuclear wars, but to a lesser degree the same is believed to apply to conventional wars, most notably the two highly destructive world wars.[6] This line of reasoning would seem to satisfy both of the criteria posited earlier for a comprehensive and valid account: it embraces the pre-nuclear Second and Third Longest Peace, as well as the nuclear era; and it presents the two world wars as milestones in humanity's learning process that modern war had become too ruinous and lethal to indulge in. Statistical studies of the historical record from 1500 onwards suggest that while wars became less frequent over time, particularly in the nineteenth and twentieth centuries, they also became more severe, in the sense that more death and destruction were 'concentrated' in shorter spates of war.[7] Thus, perhaps there is no decrease at all in belligerency. Maybe a trade-off of sorts was created between the intensity and frequency of warfare: fewer and shorter but more cataclysmic wars supplanting a larger number of longer but less intense ones. What took many years in the past, may have taken only a few years or even months under modern conditions. However, even if wars may have become more 'concentrated', they have not become more costly in terms of overall death, destruction, and spent resources. As Levy has found: 'the hypothesized inverse relation between the frequency and seriousness of war is not supported by the empirical evidence'.[8] In fact, for much of the period concerned, war has become *less* costly while its frequency declined.

This is most strikingly the case with respect to the century between 1815 and 1914. Not only did it experience both the First and the Second Long Peace between the great powers; but also, the wars that broke out during the period 1854–71, interposed as they were between these two periods of peace, were far from the upper range in comparative historical terms. They included the limited Crimean War (1854–6), the short Franco-Austrian War (1859), and the short and decisive Prussian–Austrian and Franco-Prussian wars (1866, 1870–1). Nonetheless, following the last two wars, highly advantageous for the winner, Prussia, great power peace returned for another forty-three years. There was no inverse relation between the cost and frequency of war.

That the nineteenth century was by a wide margin the least belligerent in the modern European system between the sixteenth and twentieth centuries, has been established by all the statistical studies that have covered the entire period.[9] But how can this most conspicuous fact be explained? Both Sorokin and Levy, writing during the era of the world wars and the Cold War, tended to bracket their findings with respect to the relative peacefulness of the nineteenth century, and concluded that there was no overall clear trend of either increase or decrease in the amount of war during the past five centuries.[10] Levy has written that 'the nineteenth century should be viewed as an anomaly in an otherwise continuous pattern of warfare over the last five centuries'.[11] Should, then, an entire century be regarded as a statistical fluke? Moreover, the sharp decrease in major war registered during the nineteenth century has returned with even greater effect after the two world wars and in the wake of the Cold War. As this book suggests, this is a continuation of the same trend that began in 1815 but was interrupted by the world wars. However, before we turn to investigating the deep roots of this trend, we first need to examine whether or not the world wars themselves were exceptionally lethal, destructive, and costly. Perhaps, although war did not actually become more lethal and costly in the nineteenth century, thereby accounting for the decrease in warfare, it became so with the world wars, affecting a change of attitude towards war in their aftermath.

The world wars, particularly World War II, were certainly on the upper range in terms of the absolute number of war deaths (more than 16 million in World War I; over 60 million in World War II), and they involved a staggering material outlay. However, absolute numbers are misleading for two reasons. In the first place, modern states are more populous and much wealthier than their premodern predecessors, so the real question is what *percentage* of their people was lost in war and how much economic hardship war involved. Second, as their name suggests, the world wars, particularly World War II, encompassed a large number of states on several continents. This is another reason why the world wars' absolute death toll is so high. Again, one needs to look at *relative* casualties, general human mortality in any number of separate wars that happen to rage around the world, rather than at the aggregate created by the fact that many states participated in the world wars. Absolute numbers, being very impressive, distort our perspective.

In fact, the world wars are far from being exceptional in history. Both Sorokin and Levy have found the twentieth century (practically its first half) in Europe to be the most lethal of the past five centuries, but not exceptionally so. By some indicators 'the seventeenth century was the most warlike'.[12] Levy has concluded that the twentieth century 'is generally comparable to the earlier centuries in most respects. According to the key indicators used here, the similarities between twentieth-century wars involving the Great Powers and sixteenth-to-eighteenth-century warfare are more profound than their differences'.[13] Again, according to all the statistical studies, it is the nineteenth century (as well as the post-1945 period) which is the real exception.

Going beyond the modern European system, the vast expanses of world history tell just as grim a story, and sometimes grimmer. Famously, and as the few statistical studies of war that have ventured that far back note,[14] statistics of any sort, including those of demographics and death, are extremely scarce if not entirely absent in the premodern record; the numbers that do appear in the sources are most often fictitious; and even the most reliable documentation, when it exists, tends to be ambiguous and open to diverging interpretations. So more or less informed estimates must be resorted to. For this reason, the cases outlined below involve imprecise numbers, and are also 'anecdotal' by the standards of quantitative research. Still, taken together, they provide a rough but clear enough gauge, representing, like the world wars, some of the greatest and bloodiest wars in history. Furthermore, they come from some of the best documented civilizations and conflicts of premodern times. No half-mythical or fictitious numbers are cited here.

The Peloponnesian War (431–403 BC) between Athens and its imperial satellites on the one hand, and Sparta and its allies on the other, was ancient Greece's world war. According to Victor Hanson's calculations, the Athenian battle death toll on land and at sea reached about a third of Athens' male population during the three decades of the war. If the famous plague is factored in—and it was directly caused by the war, as the rural population of Attica was evacuated into and was cramped within the city walls—perhaps a third of the entire population perished.[15] Assuming these calculations are true, this death toll is higher than that of any country in World War I and II *combined*. The economic cost of the Peloponnesian War was just as staggering. But none of this stopped the Greek world from continuing to fight within itself and against others later on. Hanson's estimates of population and casualties in the rival coalitions are not beyond dispute.[16] However, even if the actual figures were lower, this does not substantially change the general picture.

Furthermore, we have some of the best of premodern manpower statistics in ancient Rome, which held regular censuses of its citizens. Here too, although the exact interpretation of the data is the subject of some controversy, the overall picture is clear enough and highly revealing. In the first three years of the Second Punic War (218–202 BC), the republic's most severe war, Rome lost some 50,000 citizens of the ages of 17 to 46, out of a total of about 200,000 in that age demographic.[17] This was roughly 25 per cent of the military age cohorts in only three years, in the same range as the Russian, and higher than the German, military death rates in World War II, and in a similar, if not greater, 'intensity' or 'concentration' over time. And the war went on for another fourteen years. Indeed, the war's death toll and the devastation of the Italian countryside and of Rome's free peasantry during the war scarcely reduced Rome's propensity for war after the Second Punic War.

In the thirteenth century the Mongol conquests inflicted death and destruction on the societies of Eurasia that were among the worst ever suffered during historical times. The Mongol wars are also somewhat comparable to the world wars in their geographical extent. Estimates of the sharp decline registered by the populations of China and Russia vary widely. Still, even by the lowest estimates they were at least as great as, and in China almost definitely much greater than, the Soviet Union's horrific death rate in World War II of about 15 per cent.[18] If the Wikipedia List of Wars by Death Toll is any indication, and it is unlikely to be much off the mark, the Mongol conquests rank right after World War II as the most lethal in world history in absolute terms, and are much more lethal in relative terms. Even in absolute terms (again, a poor indicator), World War I comes only sixth, after a number of deadly upheavals in premodern China.[19]

Moving to Europe and the early modern period, during the Thirty Years War (1618–48) population loss in Germany, partly caused by war-related disease and famine, is estimated at between a fifth and a third[20]—again, either way, higher than the German death toll in World War I and II *combined* (Illustration 6.1). All of those mentioned here are some of history's greatest wars in terms of their scope and magnitude. But in countless smaller and less glorious wars between tribes, city-states, and states, relative mortality was often as high.[21]

One reason why this finding sounds counter-intuitive to many is that people tend to assume that more developed military technology during modern times means much greater lethality and destruction. However, with the exception of nuclear weapons, this notion is misguided. Advanced

Illustration 6.1. *Les Grandes Misères de la guerre* (The Great Miseries of War) by Jacques Callot, 1632

military technology also means greater protective power, for example with mechanized armour, mechanized speed and agility, and defensive electronic measures. Offensive and defensive advances generally rise in tandem. In addition, it is all too often forgotten that the vast majority of the many millions of non-combatants killed by Nazi Germany during World War II— Jews, Soviet prisoners of war, Soviet civilians—fell victim to intentional starvation, exposure to the elements, and mass executions, rather than to any sophisticated military technology (Illustration 6.2). Instances of genocide in general during the twentieth century, much like earlier in history, were carried out with the simplest of technologies, as the Rwanda genocide has horrifically reminded us (Illustration 6.3). As we have seen, prehistoric societies registered far higher violent death rates than historical ones, and these were brought about using primitive stone tools. During historical times, long before aerial bombing, conquered cities were sometimes set on fire and razed to the ground, and their populations were massacred. The countryside fared no better. There were many total wars long before industrial mobilization and the massive involvement of the civilian population in production for war gave this designation to the two world wars.

Thus, it is equally wrong to assume that modern wars kill a greater number of civilians.[22] The populations of invaded countries were much more severely affected by war during premodern times, and not only through direct killings and massacres, but mostly due to famine and disease which the ravages of war and moving armies brought with them. As hinted above, a major reason for World War II's high death toll is a *return* to the mass killing

Illustration 6.2. Soviet prisoners of war in World War II

Some 2 million captured Soviet soldiers were made to die by Nazi Germany through deliberate starvation and exposure to the elements within eight months of the start of Barbarossa. Rather than a uniquely modern phenomenon, this was a return to premodern standards.

of civilians that had been increasingly curbed in Europe from roughly the middle of the seventeenth century, after the end of the Thirty Years War. Civilians account for more than half of World War II's death toll, with the Soviet Union and China being the most severely affected, falling victim, respectively, to Nazi Germany's genocidal policies and Imperial Japan's brutality. The extremely high death toll among prisoners of war, again particularly notorious on the Eastern Front (on both sides) and in East Asia, also harks back to the worst premodern standards. It, too, was not associated with any sophisticated military technology. Thus, counting only battle deaths, as some statistical studies do, skews the data of war mortality, diminishing the severity and overall cost of premodern wars. The *overall* death toll of war, rather than merely battlefield death, is more relevant to the calculus of, and decision on, whether or not to go to war.[23]

Nor have wars during the past two centuries been economically more costly than wars were earlier in history, again relative to overall wealth. War has always involved massive economic exertion and has been the single

Illustration 6.3. The Rwanda genocide: the machetes

most expensive item of state spending.[24] Examples are numerous for both the destruction caused by and expenditure on war, and it will suffice to cite only a few instances, beginning with those we have already mentioned. The Mongol conquests wreaked such massive destruction on the highly developed civilizations of north and south China, Central Asia, Iraq, and Russia, that they took generations, sometimes centuries, to recover, and some of them never did. The same applies to the effect of the Thirty Years War on Germany. Both sixteenth- and seventeenth-century Spain and eighteenth-century France were economically ruined by war and staggering war debts, which in the French case brought about the Revolution. Furthermore, as people in pre-industrial societies lived at close to subsistence levels, expenditure on and the devastation of war almost literally took bread out of their mouths. Death by starvation and disease in premodern wars was widespread.

Did We Simply Learn to Kick a Senseless Habit?

If the death toll, destruction from, and expenditure on war have not become greater after 1815, perhaps it is we who have undergone a change of heart? There has been a long tradition of viewing the prevalence of war in ideological and moral terms, and overcoming war as an act of voluntary free will, which we may finally be taking.[25] It should be noted, however, that the most powerful moral doctrines in history, such as Buddhism and Christianity, decried war for millennia without this having any noticeable effect, which begs the question of why the change now. According to John Mueller, the 'attitude change' against war had no particular reason and was not different from a fashion or a fad that suddenly catches on. He believes that the same accounts for the disappearance of other social practices such as duelling and slavery.[26] We have no space here to discuss the many ways in which such a view is historically naïve with respect to all the developments Mueller mentions.[27] But it is worth pointing out that whereas he traces the 'attitude change' against war to the public backlash that followed World War I, the sharp decrease in war had in fact taken off much earlier, after 1815 and during the nineteenth century. From this period, Mueller still cites a succession of statements by philosophers, artists, and statesmen who extolled the noble virtues of war. It would thus seem that the social attitude change trailed more than it prompted the change in reality. An ideological or attitude change has undoubtedly been involved in the modern decrease of war, but one does not need to be a confirmed Marxist to be advised against starting from, or remaining confined to, the sphere of pure, let alone random, ideas.

Returning to the material calculus, perhaps war had *always* been unprofitable and has finally been recognized for the losing game that it is. Alternatively, maybe war has become unprofitable under modern conditions. If there has been no substantial change on the cost side of modern war, perhaps the change has taken place on the gain side. As Carl Kaysen has put it in his critique of Mueller: perhaps war became unprofitable *before* it became unthinkable. We shall first examine the notion that war never paid, and later on consider the proposition that it ceased to pay under modern conditions.

The notion that war is absurd if not crazy has long roots, and it has grown to predominate in modern Western societies. According to this view, war is fundamentally counterproductive and irrational, resulting from the stupidity of some or of the many, or from prisoner's dilemmas of various sorts, which means that everybody loses from war and would be better off without it. As we have seen in Chapter 3, war does mean an overall net loss in life and wealth for as long as it rages. However, this is far from exhausting the logic of the situation. Victors have often secured control over a greater share of the rewards in dispute, from which they might continue to reap the benefits in the long run. While many wars have ended in mutual loss, others have brought huge gains to the victors. As long as at least one side had reason to believe that it stood to gain by war and that this option was superior to any other, war was both its rational and optimal choice. No prisoner's dilemma trap exists in any such case.

Might the rationale of loss and gain have been somewhat different, in that the rulers and elite reaped the benefits of war whereas the common people were coerced into it against their interests and paid the price for it in life, property, and misery? This is another widespread and deeply entrenched view.[28] Such imbalance certainly prevailed in most historical societies, where the people were oppressed and benefits were channelled upwards, towards social superiors. It thus makes sense to think that as the people have become free and sovereign during the past two centuries they have increasingly refused to participate in the old game and shoulder the burden of war. This was in fact anticipated by Enlightenment critics of the Old Regime in the second half of the eighteenth century. Jean-Jacques Rousseau argued that autocratic rulers would never forfeit their hopes of foreign aggrandizement, and that only a popular revolution that would rob them of their power might give hope of peace by mutual agreement between peoples.[29] The Marquis de Condorcet in France and Thomas Paine in the United States also voiced this growing belief. As Paine put it in *The Rights of Man* (1791): 'All the monarchical governments are military. War is their trade, plunder and revenue are their objects.'[30] 'Why are not republics plunged into war', he wrote, 'but because the nature of their Government does not admit of an interest distinct from that of the Nation?'[31] Immanuel Kant expressed very similar ideas in his *Perpetual Peace* (1795). He, too, suggested that as states developed constitutional-republican regimes, people would tend not to vote for war because they themselves would have to shoulder the burden and pay the price for it. Constitutional-republican states should then federate in order to resolve their differences peacefully.[32]

Kant wrote his book amid the general but short-lived enthusiasm among Europe's intellectuals for the French Revolution. At that time, France's revolutionary wars could reasonably be viewed as defensive, a reaction to military intervention by the powers of the *ancien régime* who sought to extinguish the people's newly gained liberties. Soon, however, Revolutionary France took the offensive, and its mass citizen armies swept through Europe, subjugating it under French imperial domination. Moreover, as Alexander Hamilton had argued in the *Federalist Paper* no. 6 in rejection of the pacific view of republicanism, a glance through history would have taught Kant and Paine that some participatory republics were among the most bellicose, aggressive, and militarily successful states ever. This applied not only to direct democracies like ancient Athens, which Kant believed lacked constitutional restraints and exercised a tyranny of the majority; it also applied to other Greek and Renaissance city-state republics, and above all to republican Rome. It was not only the Chinggis Khans of history that profited hugely from war and pursued it eagerly. Nor could war be blamed on a few rotten apples. It was the populace in Athens, not the aristocrats, who pushed for aggressive imperial expansion and war. This was so despite the fact that the people fought in the army, manned the rowing benches of the Athenian navy, and had to endure war's destruction and misery, as in the forced evacuation of Attica during the Peloponnesian War. Similarly, the secret of republican Rome's extraordinary expansion and power was its participatory-inclusive regime which successfully co-opted the populace for the purpose of war and made mass citizen armies possible.

Why, then, did the citizens of Athens and Rome repeatedly vote for war, endure devastating and protracted wars for years and years, and pay for them in blood, property, and misery? It was not because they were stupid or senseless, but because the gain side of war for them was even greater than its cost side, and greater than the expected benefits from purely peaceful conduct. In the first place, there was booty to be had. Furthermore, in Athens the empire levied lavish tributes that financed about half of the Athenian budget, paying for the extensive public construction and huge navy, in both of which the people were employed.[33] Moreover, the empire's might boosted Athenian trade supremacy, which in turn increased its resources and enhanced its might. Finally, poor Athenians were allocated farms in colonies (*cleruchies*) established on territory confiscated from defeated enemies. As Pericles made clear in his speech before the Athenian people, the demos in democratic Athens were the tyrants of an empire which they ruled with merciless ruthlessness.[34] Although Rome did not levy tribute from its satellite 'allies', it confiscated an enormous amount of land from those it defeated throughout Italy, and established on this land colonies of Roman citizens and of Rome's closest allies, the Latins.

Thus, there is little foundation for the view that war has always been a losing game, finally discarded as the mistake has been realized. Nor is it true that the people have always been on the losing side and only coerced into war. Indeed, the more the people held political power and shared in the spoils of war, the more enthusiastically they supported war and imperialism and the more tenaciously they fought. Historically, democracies and republics proved particularly formidable in war precisely because they were socially and politically inclusive.

But wait. Even if Paine, Kant, and countless commentators thereafter were wrong to assume that for the people war did not pay, which should naturally incline them against it, did both thinkers not put their finger on something very real? Both suggested that war could be eliminated in a system of demo-cratic/republican states. Perhaps democracies or republics fought tenaciously against non-democratic states, but not against other democracies or repub-lics. From the 1970s onwards, this was the great discovery of international relations theory with respect to the modern state system.

The Scope and Limits of the Democratic Peace Theory

The idea that democracies are less bellicose and more peaceful than non-democracies has been widespread ever since the Enlightenment. Sceptics suspected that it was just one of those virtues that individuals and collectives are biased to ascribe to themselves. Indeed, when democracy's alleged peacefulness was subjected to a more rigorous quantitative examination there seemed to be no indication that democracies fought less than non-democracies during the nineteenth and twentieth centuries. However, it then occurred to some scholars to pose a slightly different question, and the picture changed dramatically. Rather than ask how much democracies fought, they asked how much they fought *each other* during the above period. The surprising result, corroborated by endless qualitative and quantitative research ever since, was that they did so very rarely or hardly ever.[35] The (inter-)democratic peace proposition has been justly proclaimed the most robust 'law' discovered in the discipline of international relations, with only 'realists', whose tenets it completely undermines, keeping up an increasingly feeble rearguard action against it.

This is not to say that some fundamental questions with respect to the inter-democratic peace do not remain. One puzzling question concerns the application of this peace to premodern times. If modern liberal/democratic states hardly ever fight each other, does the same hold true for earlier dem-ocracies? Again, the democracies and popular republics of classical antiquity are the most important test cases, despite the data problem involved. We do not possess anything even remotely approaching a full record of the ancient systems' wars and regimes, as we do for the nineteenth and twentieth centuries. Still, because the inter-democratic peace theory appears to apply almost universally during modern times, even a few major cases to the contrary in the classical record—if these exist—might indicate that the theory does not work in antiquity.

Research on the subject has been relatively scarce and its results mixed. One study has found little evidence of an inter-democratic peace in classical Greece. If anything, it has found the opposite. The most dramatic case involved the massive and ultimately disastrous campaign by democratic Athens against democratic Syracuse (415–413 BC) during the Peloponnesian War.[36] Some democratic peace theorists have claimed that Athens may not have been aware of Syracuse's turn to democracy. However, Thucydides is quite specific on the subject: 'The Athenians were in utter despondency...For all the cities with which they had gone to war, these alone were at that time similar in character to their own, democratic in constitution like themselves.'[37] Nevertheless, based on a particularly skewed reading of the evidence in this and other cases, one study has argued that ancient republics, too, never fought each other.[38] A few more examples will suffice to falsify this claim.

Many of the known democracies of ancient Greece belonged to the Athenian Empire of the fifth century BC. Indeed, Athens actively fostered democratic regimes among the city-state members of its alliance-turned-empire. The empire was coercive and oppressive, with Athens compelling city-states to join and preventing them from leaving by means of its overwhelming force. Athens also prevented members of the alliance from fighting one another. Rebellions were harshly put down. Sometimes the rebellions involved an oligarchic conspiracy, but in other cases the whole population was involved. Indeed, during the Peloponnesian War, the Athenian demos, usually more extreme than its appointed generals, repeatedly decreed that the entire adult male population of the rebellious city be executed indiscriminately, while the women and children were to be sold to slavery. All the same, after Athenian power had been severely weakened during the later stage of the war, the allies rebelled in great number. Thus, ancient Greece's record during the fifth century BC mostly represents violent democratic imperial coercion rather than inter-democratic peace.[39]

The fourth century BC offers an even more significant test, partly because the number of Greek democracies had increased by this time.

When a second Athenian-led alliance was formed in 377 BC, it was based on voluntary and egalitarian principles. To weaken Sparta, Athens assisted in restoring independence in Thebes. Not only did Thebes become a democracy, but it also re-established the Boeotian League on a democratic basis. In 371 BC, the Boeotian army under the generalship of Epaminondas smashed the invincible Spartans in the Battle of Leuctra. A dramatic change in the Greek balance of power followed. Spartan hegemony and tyrannical imperial rule were broken, while Thebes rose to prominence. Invading the Peloponnese, Epaminondas assisted Sparta's satellites in breaking away and forming democracies and regional democratic leagues. He also freed a large part of Sparta's enslaved subject population, the helots. And yet these noble acts, obviously advantageous to Thebes, were vigorously opposed by none other than democratic Athens. After Leuctra, it was Theban hegemony, rather than Spartan, that Athens feared and balanced against.

In 369 BC, Athens joined the war against Thebes, allying itself against Greek freedom with oligarchic and oppressive Sparta and its oligarchic allies, Greek tyrants such as Dionysius of Syracuse and the bloodthirsty Alexander of Pherae, and foreign, autocratic Persia. For seven years, the two great Greek democracies were engaged in a war that raged all along their imperial peripheries. The war involved numerous encounters, culminating in Athenian participation against Thebes in the Battle of Mantinea (362 BC). It was the greatest battle in Greek history up until then, in which Epaminondas again won a crushing victory, but was killed. Both Theban hegemony and the war thereby came to an end. As Athens attempted to reassert its own hegemony, its conduct towards its allies began to resemble its first empire, prompting a rebellion known as the Social War (357–355 BC) that broke the power of the alliance. Lest Thebes' conduct towards other democracies be considered saintly, remember that Thebes conquered and razed to the ground its old rival, democratic Plataea (373 BC).

Surprisingly, the record of republican Rome's wars in the Italian peninsula has not been examined at all in this context, but it appears to be no less questionable with respect to the democratic peace phenomenon. Classical scholars continue to debate how democratic the Roman Republic was, with recent trends swinging in the more democratic direction.[40] Ancient historian Polybius classified Rome as a mixed regime, in which the people's assemblies and tribunes, the aristocratic senate, and elected officials balanced each other's power.[41] It should be noted, however, that our own modern liberal democracies, too, would have been classified as mixed regimes by the ancients, because unlike ancient republics, they do not include popular assemblies of all citizenry that directly legislate and decide on issues such as war and peace. Knowledge about the internal regimes of the other Italian city-states is meagre. Still, to argue that none of the hundreds of Italic and Greek city-states in Italy that were brought under Roman rule were republics—that Rome was in fact the only republic in Italy—is patently untenable. For example, Capua and Tarentum, the two leading city-states of southern Italy that defected from Rome during the Second Punic War and were harshly crushed by Rome, were both democratic republics at the time.[42] Indeed, it was the democratic factions in both cities that led the revolt against Rome. Furthermore, Polybius, following Aristotle, judged Carthage, Rome's rival during the Second Punic War, to be a mixed regime polity, in which the populace (which supported the Barkaide war party) dominated more than it did in the Roman Republic itself.[43] Not only did this democratic character not prevent the war, but neither in these nor in any other cases does the evidence with respect to public deliberations in Rome on war and peace include even a reference to the enemy's regime as an issue meriting consideration.

But if the inter-democratic peace did not apply before modern times, why did it not apply? Even those theorists of the democratic peace who have been more or less aware of the historical discrepancy between the conduct of democracies in premodern and modern times have not really addressed the question of why this discrepancy exists. This question is important not merely for understanding the past but also for explaining the modern phenomenon. The difference in this respect between premodern and modern democracies may provide a vital clue to the key, indispensable element that makes the inter-democratic peace work.

A Liberal or Capitalist, rather than Democratic, Peace?

Some scholars have held that the peace in question is liberal rather than democratic.[44] Liberalism and democracy have gone together in the form of liberal democracy since the beginning of the twentieth century. For this reason, we tend to regard them as one. However, liberalism and democracy were not as strongly associated before the twentieth century, and the distinction between them may be significant, inter alia for explaining the modern peace, whether democratic or liberal. Those who emphasize liberalism above democracy as the explanation for the modern phenomenon have claimed that the classical democracies can hardly be considered liberal, because they practised slavery and in general did not uphold the liberal rights and other republican preconditions required by Kant, such as a separation of powers.

However, this argument is less compelling than it appears. The existence of slavery is indeed a major and much-cited difference between ancient and modern democracies, but its relevance to the inter-democratic peace is far from clear. Domestically, the difference between freemen and slaves was of course fundamental in the extreme, yet in what way exactly is it supposed to have affected the conduct of the citizens with respect to foreign affairs? The most common answer is that the institution of slavery generally meant less respect for human rights, equality, and dignity, which spilled over to relations between states. This again makes the modern peace a fundamentally ideological phenomenon. Materially, while slaves were certainly one of the main forms of booty of war, it is difficult to make the case that slavery was that crucial among the many spoils of war, ancient or modern. As for liberal rights in general, freedom of opinion and speech, legal safeguards of life and property, due judicial procedure, and the rule of law were all central norms in ancient democracies and republics, even if in somewhat different forms than in their modern counterparts. In Athens of the Peloponnesian War it was possible for Aristophanes to stage a play that called for a sex strike against the war, while in Rome the doctrine of just war was sacrosanct, even if it was interpreted liberally in Rome's favour. Finally, whereas a separation of powers in the sense formulated by Montesquieu did not exist in antiquity, a separation of authority and checks and balances did very much exist. Whereas classical Athens has become proverbial for the perils of direct democracy and tyranny of the majority, in the mixed-regime Roman Republic, for example, institutional constraints were very strong. A popular assembly of the people in arms (*comitia centuriata*), the people who actually served in the legions, was called to vote on war, but only after the senate debated and decided on the question, and a motion for war was introduced in the assembly by a consul who was elected annually in highly competitive elections.

It is evident, however, that liberalism as a distinct concept and major force is a creation of modernity. But if so, why? Again, this fact may harbour a vital clue. So far we have been concerned with the political aspect of liberalism, but political liberalism famously came hand in hand with economic liberalism, both as a doctrine and a reality. It is not a coincidence that political liberalism emerged in the era of commercial capitalism in the seventeenth and eighteenth centuries, first in the Dutch Republic and then in Britain. Liberalism became yet more entrenched in Britain during the nineteenth century, when the country inaugurated industrial capitalism. Political and economic liberalism were intertwined, and they reinforced each other.[45]

The prophets of the democratic–liberal peace during the Enlightenment emphasized the economic dimension of that vision side by side with the political aspect. As Montesquieu wrote in *The Spirit of the Laws*: 'The natural effect of commerce is to lead to peace. Two nations that trade with each other become reciprocally dependent.'[46] According to Paine, commerce 'is a pacific system, operating to cordialize mankind, by rendering nations, as well as institutions useful to each other...If commerce were permitted to act to the universal extent it is capable, it would extirpate the system of war'.[47] Kant similarly mentioned 'mutual self-interest. For the *spirit of commerce* sooner or later takes hold of every people, and it cannot exist side by side with war.'[48]

The notion that mutual trade fosters peace ran through the nineteenth and twentieth centuries, and more recently has been investigated extensively by international relations theorists.[49] Some scholars have gone further, suggesting that what is known as the democratic peace is in reality a 'capitalist peace'. Erik Gartzke, analysing the global data for the period 1950–92, has found that mutual trade and common interest in the global markets is the most significant factor that reduces belligerency between states, whatever their regime. He has claimed that democracy in itself is a far less significant factor, but has conceded that the near absence of war *between* democracies stands out and remains to be explained.[50] Critics have found significant errors in Gartzke's statistical work, which after correction further reinforces the effect of democracy and the inter-democratic peace.[51] Moreover, the limited time frame of his study, confined as it is to the period after World War II, raises broader historical questions.

First, there is the problem of World War I, which pitted developed capitalist great powers closely integrated by mutual trade against each other. This was most conspicuously the case with Britain and Germany, the world's most developed capitalist economies after the United States, and the world's leading traders, which were each other's main trade partner (except for their imports from the United States).[52] The problem has been addressed by Patrick McDonald, another proponent of the capitalist peace, whose work covers a much longer historical time frame than Gartzke's, spanning as it does both the nineteenth and twentieth centuries. McDonald has argued that capitalism was more important than democracy in decreasing war during the nineteenth century, although conceding, like Gartzke for his period of study, that the *inter*-democratic peace was significant even then. He has refined the capitalist peace concept, specifying free trade, competitive domestic markets, and a small government share in the economy as its cornerstones. He has pointed out that although the volume of international trade in relation to GDP was indeed very high in the first global age, before 1914, this was primarily caused by falling transportation costs due to railroads and steamships and came despite growing protectionism and high, rising tariffs from the later part of the nineteenth century. By this analysis, 1914 should not be regarded as a compelling counter-example to the trade–peace connection, because free trade did not exist.[53] A similar conclusion, albeit with somewhat different emphases, was reached by others earlier, and McDonald has been followed by Gartzke.[54] We shall return to this point later on.

A second problem with the capitalist peace theory is that it overlooks the peace that existed among democracies between the two world wars, when international trade reached its modern nadir. In the wake of the 1929 financial crash, all the great powers, including the democratic ones, introduced strict protectionist policies. During that period, the United States' economy, for example, was seriously hurt by the tariff walls built around the British Empire, as Britain abandoned free trade and adopted protectionism from 1932 onwards. The United States itself, which maintained high tariffs during the 1920s, raised them further in 1930. The result was a disastrous free fall in international trade in the early 1930s, to only a third of its pre-crisis levels. Nonetheless, although the Roosevelt administration put diplomatic and economic pressure on other countries to lower their tariffs, the possibility of tearing down trade walls by the threat, let alone the exercise of force, was unthinkable. Indeed, this was despite the fact that American capitalism was constrained not only abroad but also at home, with the New Deal. Thus, *the democratic peace worked during the 1930s, when the capitalist peace should have utterly failed.* Realists have claimed that the lack of war between democracies was due to the coalition effect between them against a greater threat—in the 1930s, that of Germany, Japan, and Italy.[55] This claim, very dubious for the entire twentieth century (why should the democracies flock together, and do so in a status quo camp?), cannot be proved or disproved with respect to the 1930s, and remains a matter of judgement as to what is probable as a counterfactual. However, the proponents of the capitalist peace theory, who reject 'realism', simply do not address the challenge posed by the 1930s. Gartzke's analysis of the period after 1950 excludes the interwar period. McDonald, adopting a broad historical frame, claims that the democratic peace became significant only after World War I. And yet he fails even to mention, let alone explain, the inter-democratic but protectionist peace of the 1930s.[56]

Third, both Gartzke and McDonald fail to specifically address the communist great powers of the twentieth century, the Soviet Union and China. While these countries underwent industrial development, they totally eschewed capitalism, private property, and the markets, and were closed to foreign markets in terms of trade. Nonetheless, they participated in the general decrease in belligerency, compared to these countries' premodern record (particularly Russia's in the highly competitive European and Near Eastern systems). Indeed, this decrease is neither covered by the democratic peace, nor does it fall under the capitalist peace. Finally, what is to be made of social democratic countries? These mostly include the countries of Western Europe and, most conspicuously, the exceptionally peaceful Scandinavian countries, which while capitalist in many ways are characterized by deep state involvement in society and the economy.

Thus, the capitalist peace concepts suggested by Gartzke and McDonald, although touching on something very real, fail to account for the full range of historical experience and cannot tell the whole story. Michael Mousseau has advanced another version of the capitalist peace, positing impersonal contract abiding cultural norms through the market rather than individual free enterprise as the hallmark of that peace. His concept could potentially accommodate social democracy, as well as New Deal America and other protectionist capitalist democracies of the 1930s.[57] However, Mousseau's capitalism as a contract abiding culture hangs everything on a very narrow feature and raises suspicion that it reflects a random statistical correlation or, more likely, an epiphenomenon of something more fundamental.[58] Perhaps Paine and Kant were more accurate in their multi-factor framework that encompassed mutual liberal republicanism, reciprocal trade, and shared international institutions?[59] This framework has proved to be so extraordinarily prophetic that we tend to overlook its shortcomings. Let us take stock of the gaps that we have seen therein: first, premodern democracies and republics actually did fight each other; second, non-democratic great powers shared in the general reduction in belligerency during modern times, from

1815 on, including communist powers that largely opted out of the global trade system; third, until the nineteenth century, states tried to monopolize trade by force and bar all others rather than share with them, a policy known as mercantilism. This was the policy that Alexander Hamilton championed as secretary of the treasury of the new American republic, after having rejected the view of democracy as pacifistic, relying on the historical record, in the *Federalist Papers* (no. 6).

What, then, has changed from the early nineteenth century onwards that can account for all of this? What was it that made states fight less, altered the preferences of democracies to a degree that practically eliminated war among them, and sharply increased international trade while reducing protectionism? What is the missing element that can reconcile these observed phenomena, while encompassing and unifying the general decrease in belligerency, the modern inter-democratic-liberal peace, and the capitalist peace?

The Modernization Peace

The Industrial Revolution constitutes a quantum leap in history. It brought about a sweeping transformation of human society, the most profound since the Neolithic adoption of agriculture. The correlation between the decline of war and the process of modernization—both unfolding since the early nineteenth century but practically overlooked in the discussion in the discipline of international relations—is unlikely to be accidental.[60] But what is the causal relationship between them? Answers to this question were offered very early on, even before the middle of the nineteenth century, as observers began to notice the First Long Peace and how unusual it was. Because quite a number of individual elements within the multifaceted modern transformation appear to correlate with major aspects of the decrease in belligerency—as is the case with the nuclear peace, the democratic peace, the capitalist peace, and more—there is a danger here reminiscent of the tale about the blind men who gather to examine an elephant. Each of them feels a different part of the animal and therefore arrives at a different conclusion about its nature and form. However, as suggested here, we are dealing with a composite effect, whose totality is embraced by the process of modernization. Some elements of this process have affected the general decrease in belligerency from the very beginning of the industrial age, while others have emerged and added their weight later on over the past two centuries, as the process of modernization has unfolded. The combined deepening and accumulation of the factors involved tallies with the progressive decrease in the occurrence of armed confrontation (again, except for the spike during the world wars). Thus, the Modernization Peace should be comprehended in its entirety, as the different forms of peace mentioned earlier would appear to be mutually-interacting and mutually-reinforcing aspects of a broader, more comprehensive phenomenon or development. We now proceed to examine some of the major elements involved, in their mutual interaction.

Industrialization or Economic Development: Escape from Malthus

An exponential increase in wealth has been central to the rise of industrial-technological society. It has been fuelled by a steep and continuous growth in per capita production and marked a sharp break from the Malthusian trap that characterized human history until then. Premodern increases in productivity were largely absorbed by population growth, leaving the vast majority of people in dire poverty, precariously close to subsistence level. With the outbreak of the industrial-technological revolution, however, that changed dramatically. Average growth in the industrial world has become about ten times faster than in pre-industrial times, with production per capita for the first time registering substantial and sustained real growth at an average annual rate of 1.5–2.0 per cent. As these rates compounded, per capita production in the developed countries has increased by a factor of fifteen to thirty since the outbreak of the Industrial Revolution.[61]

Hence the first major change with respect to modernity and its effect on war: the pie has been growing steadily, and this growth has been largely grounded in internal development, in the adoption of machine-based production, the unbound Prometheus. Wealth no longer constitutes a fundamentally finite quantity as it was in premodern times, when the main question about it was how it was to be divided. Thus, the acquisition of wealth has progressively shifted away from a zero-sum game, where one participant's gain could only be achieved at others' expense. The influential social thinker Auguste Comte (echoing his mentor Saint-Simon) expressed the growing feeling in the peaceful decades after 1815 when conceptualizing that warrior society had been giving way to the industrial stage of human development.[62] A similar logic was expressed around the same time by no other than the famous future chief of the Prussian general staff, Helmuth von Moltke. As he wrote in 1841, even before autocratic Prussia had either a parliament or a constitution:

> We candidly confess our belief in the idea, on which so much ridicule has been cast, of a general European peace. Not that long and bloody wars are to cease from henceforth... [however,] wars will become rarer and rarer because they are growing expensive beyond measure; positively because of the actual cost; negatively because of the necessary neglect of work. Has not the population of Prussia, under a good and wise administration, increased by a fourth in twenty-five years of peace? And are not her fifteen millions of inhabitants better fed, clothed and instructed today than her eleven millions used to be? Are not such results equal to a victorious campaign or to the conquest of a province, with that great difference that they are not gained at the expense of other nations, nor with the sacrifice of the enormous number of victims that a war demands?[63]

Moltke was probably wrong about the rise in the 'positive' cost of war, but he very well sensed its 'negative' price, related to the expansion of the economic pie and greater attractiveness of peaceful growth as an alternative to war and conquest. Prussia would remain in a state of peace for forty-nine years, from 1815 until 1864, a staggeringly long period compared to its earlier record.

It is not that conquest has become unprofitable in and of itself in the industrial and information ages as opposed to the agrarian age when territory mattered most, as some scholars have suggested. There are two versions of this argument: that war has become inherently unprofitable, or that it has become less profitable than it was earlier in history. The first proposition does not hold water. It has been shown that the occupation of developed countries or territories could and did pay off.* The other proposition, that

---

* Although Kaysen, 'Is War Obsolete?', suggests that war has become intrinsically unprofitable in the industrial age, he notes Nazi Germany's exploitation of its European empire. This, as well as Japan's exploitation of its own empire and a couple of other cases, is studied by Peter Liberman, in *Does Conquest Pay? The Exploitation of Occupied Industrial Societies*, Princeton: Princeton UP, 1996, which answers in the positive. Stephen Brooks's criticism in his 'The Globalization of Production and the Changing Benefits of Conquest', *Journal of Conflict Resolution*, 43:5 (1999), 646–70, and *Producing Security: Multinational Corporations, Globalization, and the Changing Calculus of Conflict*, Princeton: Princeton UP, 2005, chap, 6, leaves something to be desired. First, his choice of the Soviet Empire as his case study is unfortunate. The empire may have been economically unbeneficial for the Soviet Union, but Brooks fails to note that this was predominantly because the empire, like the Soviet Union itself, was communist, and therefore economically dysfunctional.

war and conquest have become less profitable than before, is difficult to quantify. But, in any case, it distracts attention from the main point. The decisive change in profitability has been not on the war side of the equation but on its peace side. While cost and benefit constitute a continuum, it is important to realize where exactly on that continuum the change has taken place. Rather than war and conquest becoming less profitable or unprofitable in themselves, it is peaceful economic activity that has become a more profitable and promising avenue to wealth, while conquest has remained an uncertain and risky endeavour whose diversion of resources away from economic growth has become less appealing. The question is not whether a system of conquest and military possession pays off, but whether the alternative of an industrial open trade system pays more. The two common propositions—that in an absolute sense modern war has become either more lethal and costly or much less profitable, if not entirely unprofitable, as compared to premodern times—are both untrue. Rather, it is peace that has become more profitable under modern conditions, tilting the relative balance between the two behavioural strategies.[†] Predatory existence, very much the norm during premodern times for social warrior elites, as well as for poor warrior societies on the marches of civilization, all but disappeared. The elites in advanced societies, following the path of greater rewards, turned to productive pursuits, as the British gentry were the first to do during the rise of commercial capitalism during the early modern period. Concurrently, poor societies have become too weak to conquer developed

Second, Brooks's claim that the wealth of countries which constitute part of a global production chain is difficult to retain under alien rule is not entirely persuasive. Consider, for example, the reluctant change of hands in Hong Kong, a major financial and trade hub of the information age. Although sometimes historically crude, Richard Rosecrance, *The Rise of the Trading State: Commerce and Conquest in the Modern World*, New York: Basic Books, 1986, correctly implies that conquest has become less profitable than trade, rather than unprofitable in and of itself. See also his *The Rise of the Virtual State: Wealth and Power in the Coming Century*, New York: Basic Books, 1999.

[†] As an afterthought to his random ideas thesis, Mueller has come to recognize the exponential rise in the levels of affluence since the beginning of the nineteenth century. However, he still espouses a one-directional relationship between ideas and material developments, arguing that changing ideas on prosperity, capitalism, and peace were the *cause* of rocketing affluence. He fails to grasp the deep interconnections between the Industrial Revolution, the growth of prosperity, and the changing attitudes. Mueller further argues that industrialization intensified the militaristic spirit during the nineteenth century, which was in fact the most pacific in history up until then. He also argues that industrialization was responsible for the two world wars, forgetting that he blames at least World War II on Hitler alone, who supposedly dragged the German people into it against their will (John Mueller, *The Remnants of War*, Ithaca: Cornell UP, 2007, 33, 165–6; developed in his 'Capitalism, Peace, and the Historical Movement of Ideas', in G. Schneider and N. Gleditsch (eds.), *Assessing the Capitalist Peace*, London: Routledge, 2013, 64–79.) Similarly, see note 66 later in this chapter.

ones, because, as Adam Smith pointed out, in the modern age of military hardware, unlike earlier in history, greater economic productivity stood in direct relationship to military prowess.[64] The Chinggis Khan option had died out.

Indeed, in the industrial age, belligerency has also decreased among countries that have not yet embarked on the road to modernization, for three main reasons. First, such countries have grown weaker relative to developed countries, and so have their chances of military success. Second, for this reason, as well as for the economic rewards involved, they have been incentivized to spare their resources and invest them in modernization. Third, they have become more susceptible to pressures from the hegemonic developed world, which weighs on them not to disrupt the peace.[65] Thus, economic growth has become more attractive for developed countries in preference to war, while also swaying undeveloped ones, even if they have been ill-prepared or reluctant to embark on the road to modernization for socio-cultural reasons.

This rationale tallies with the observed distribution of the Modernization Peace. First, it is far stronger in the developed world. Whereas in the past the wars among the rich and mighty states were the most frequent and climactic, the great powers and other developed countries have increasingly ceased to fight each other, with the developed parts of the world turning into a 'zone of peace'. The wars that remain take place among less developed countries or between them and developed countries, in the world's less developed 'zone of war'.[66] Thus, Joshua Goldstein's thesis that international peacekeeping forces are responsible for 'the decline of armed conflict worldwide' since 1945 cannot be the main story, as such forces have been mostly deployed in the developing parts of the world, whereas most of the decline of war during that period has occurred in the developed world, where no peacekeeping forces exist.[67] Indeed, given the polarity between the developed and developing parts of the world, aggregating the record of belligerency of both developed and undeveloped countries, as many studies of the trend do, compares apples with pears, as it makes no distinction between modern and largely premodern conditions.[68] The time span from 1815 to the present represents very different conditions in different parts of the world with respect to both modernization and war. Developed and undeveloped countries may belong to the same century, but not quite the same period.

The so-called 'new wars' in the less developed parts of the world supposedly replace increasingly rare old-style, state-centred regular wars.[69]

However, more accurately, they resemble premodern wars in, for example, pre-eighteenth-century Europe. In these old wars, as in the 'new' ones, state authority was weak, non-state players such as local or private militias and enterprising warlords played a major part in the war, civilians were massacred, pillaged, and raped, and sectarian 'identity'—ethnic and religious—dominated. For all that, the Modernization Peace is also noticeable, albeit to a lesser degree, in the developing world, for the reasons explained. This is evident in the marked decline in belligerency in Africa and Asia since 1990, which is somewhat reminiscent of the decrease in war in post-1815 Europe (see Diagram 6.2).

Thus, as we unravel the various threads of modernization and their effects on war, economic growth or development appears to be a fundamental factor that has worked against war since the beginning of the industrial age. Gartzke has cited development as a major factor in his study of the period 1950–92. Håvard Hegre has found that it underlay, and was a prerequisite of the growth of, international trade during the same period. Michael Mousseau, Håvard Hegre, and John Oneal, extending their study as far back as 1885, have shown that it was also essential for the inter-democratic peace to work. Economists Timothy Besley and Torsten Persson have documented what they labelled 'development clusters...the tendency for effective state institutions, the absence of [domestic] political violence, and high income per capita to be positively correlated with one another'.[70] The connection between development and the inter-democratic peace explains why that peace has been stronger in the twentieth as compared to the nineteenth century, and in developed as compared to undeveloped or developing countries. Less often noted, it also explains why the inter-democratic peace was absent *before* modernity.

Indeed, these finds need to be synthesized and placed in full perspective. Whereas much of the recent debate has centred on the question of whether democracy or trade are more fundamental to the decrease in war, both depend on a more fundamental factor: industrialization or economic modernization. Thus, economic development was central to the overall sharp decline in belligerency from the beginning of the industrial age, after 1815, as compared to pre-industrial times, encompassing as it did both democratic and non-democratic, and capitalist and non-capitalist countries, albeit at different rates.[71] This does not mean that economic growth, intensifying trade, and liberal democracy are not mutually connected and mutually reinforcing in many ways (though not fully or

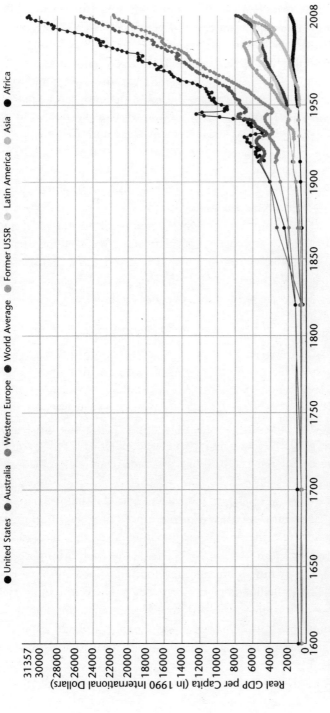

Diagram 6.2. Escape from Malthus: growth in real GDP per capita (PPP)

Note the exponential rise in wealth since the beginning of industrialization, from around 1800 onwards, as compared with premodern times. Also note the still huge gap between the developed and developing countries, which makes the world average unrepresentative in many ways. However, growth in (parts of) Asia, and, less dynamically, Latin America, has taken off, while Africa has yet to demonstrate that it has embarked on the road to modernization.

Legend: United States ● Australia ● Western Europe ● World Average ● Former USSR ● Latin America ● Asia ● Africa

Real GDP per Capita (in 1990 International Dollars)

31357 30000 28000 26000 24000 22000 20000 18000 16000 14000 12000 10000 8000 6000 4000 2000 0

1600 1650 1700 1750 1800 1850 1900 1950 2008

universally so). Nor does it mean that trade and liberal democracy have not each had a very strong and distinct effect in decreasing belligerency. It just means that the development peace is broader and more fundamental than the capitalist or liberal democratic peace, encompassing, for example, non-democratic or communist countries during the industrial age. The legs of Kant's tripod for peace are not only connected, but must also stand on something: they are firmly grounded in the industrial age (Diagram 6.3).

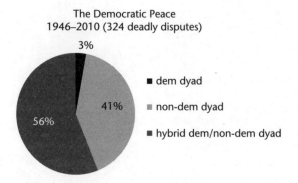

The Democratic Peace
1946–2010 (324 deadly disputes)

On average, democracies (Polity score >3) constituted ~34% of all states during the period 1946–2010. Thus, although ~11% deadly MIDs between democratic dyads should be expected at random probability, the actual number is 3%, which strongly supports the democratic peace proposition.

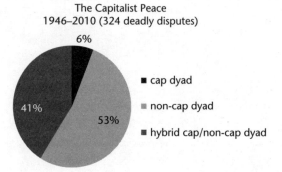

The Capitalist Peace
1946–2010 (324 deadly disputes)

The Modernization Peace
1946–2010 (324 deadly disputes)

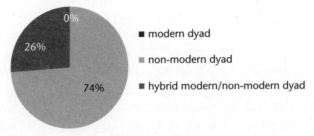

■ modern dyad

■ non-modern dyad

■ hybrid modern/non-modern dyad

While joint democracy, joint capitalism, and joint high level of development/modernization all have a very strong pacifying effect, that of development/modernization is clearly the strongest. Moreover, while there is some overlap between democracy, capitalism, and modernization/development in the period since 1946 (and particular salience of the democratic-capitalist category), the first two are largely a function of modernization. Most strikingly, as the zero occurrence of deadly militarized disputes between modernized states indicates, in *all* the cases of deadly military disputes between two democracies or between two capitalist states in the period concerned, at least one of the states involved—and in the great majority of the cases both states—was not modernized at the time of the conflict.

A word of caution: a review of the widely accepted databases for MID, democracy, capitalism (and modernization), on which the above figures rely, reveal not a few lapses, missing cases, and what sometimes appear as arbitrary categorizations. For the sake of consistency and objectivity, I have not tried to correct, supplement, or otherwise interfere with the data. In any case, the general trend seems well established.[72]

Diagram 6.3. Deadly military inter-state disputes (MID) correlated with democracy, capitalism, and modernization, 1946–2010

(324 dyadic conflicts with fatalities)

The Effects of Commercialism

Together with the democratic peace, peace through commercial interdependence has been the most familiar element of the Modernization Peace. Indeed, it depends on modernization and industrial production for its realization no less than the democratic peace does.

The advantages of free trade were highlighted by Adam Smith and elaborated by David Ricardo. According to the classical economists, protectionism—barring out competitors from markets by political means—and its territorially expansionist and militarized form known as mercantilism, were in the final analysis bad for all the parties involved. This was because protectionism-mercantilism worked against the main engines of economic efficiency: they restricted competition, and they hindered specialization on the largest scale possible, where each part of the system concentrated on what it did best, maximizing its comparative advantage. Still, it was not until the middle of the nineteenth century, three-quarters of a century after Smith, that Britain, the economic hegemon and first industrial nation, abandoned protectionism and adopted free trade, swaying the entire system in the same direction, at least for a while. Why that delay? Was it merely a matter of a good idea taking time to be recognized as such?

Although the logic of free trade, as propounded by Smith and Ricardo, was sound, it was not unlimited or without conditions. First and foremost, its realization depended on each of the major players involved accepting that the discipline of market competition was more promising for *that player* than monopolization by force. Such a reality has been tremendously boosted by the massive shift in the balance and relationship between the significance of the market and military prowess that was brought about by industrializa-tion. Both sides of the equation have changed dramatically. As we have seen, economically weak countries have become militarily impotent and there-fore unable to force the system. On the other hand, the significance of trade in the economy has ballooned to entirely new dimensions, as trade has been the natural corollary of industrial production and its massive division of labour. Lower barriers to the flow of goods enhanced the efficiency of the exploding industrial market economy.[73] Greater freedom of trade has become all the more attractive in the industrial age for the simple reason that the overwhelming share of fast-growing and diversifying production was now intended for sale in the marketplace rather than for direct con-sumption by the family producers themselves, as was the case in the pre-industrial economy. The logic that had emerged and had been identified by Smith in pre-industrial capitalist Britain in the second half of the eighteenth century—the hub of the new global commercial system that connected a still mostly agrarian and self-sufficient world economy—was massively rein-forced with industrialization.

During industrialization, the European powers' foreign trade increased twice as quickly as their fast-growing GDPs, so that by the advent of the twentieth century exports plus imports grew to around half of GDP in Britain and France, more than one-third in Germany, and around one-third in Italy (and Japan).[74] In the same way, the growth of trade also outpaced that of GDP by two to one in the second global age, after the collapse of the communist bloc.[75] To repeat, the advantages of free trade grew steeply with the vast expansion of production for the market in the industrial age. As already noted, rather than war becoming more costly and less profitable in and of itself, the massive change has actually taken place on the peace side of the equation, as the profitability of peaceful interactions increased exponentially. The greater the yields brought by competitive economic cooperation, the more counterproductive and less attractive conflict became.

National economies ceased to be overwhelmingly autarkic and therefore barely affected by one another. They were increasingly connected in an intensifying and spreading network of specialization and exchange, the much-celebrated globalization of markets and the economy. The effects of this development in decreasing the attractiveness of war have been many, and need to be carefully unravelled.

First, there is **mutual dependence**. War between major trade partners breaks the chains of production and trade, creating shortages in the short term and inefficiency overall.

Second, there is **mutual prosperity**. Global markets mean that prosperity abroad becomes interrelated with prosperity at home, whereas foreign devastation potentially depresses the entire system and is detrimental to each country's own well-being. As the others become your customers, their purchasing power makes you rich. Thus, in stark contrast to earlier times, the enemy's economic ruin adversely affects one's own prosperity. Early nineteenth-century thinkers clearly recognized the radical novelty of this situation. As John Stuart Mill put it:

> Commerce first taught nations to see with good will the wealth and prosperity of one another. Before, the patriot, unless sufficiently advanced in culture to feel the world his country, wished all countries weak, poor, and ill-governed, but his own: he now sees in their wealth and progress a direct source of wealth and progress to his own country. It is commerce which is rapidly rendering war obsolete.[76]

What Mill formulated in principle would become an acute reality after World War I. As John Maynard Keynes warned in his *The Economic Consequences of the Peace* (1920), the crippling reparations imposed on Germany prevented its economic recovery, thereby rendering both a recovery of the international economy and the resumption of prosperity among the victorious Entente powers themselves impossible. Indeed, as the economic troubles of the early 1920s appeared to bear out his point, the victors changed course, working to revive Germany's economy and political status, an effort that collapsed with the post-1929 Great Depression. The same logic guided the reconstruction of Germany and Japan with the aid of American money in the wake of World War II.

A third variable that affects belligerency as the economy and the markets globalize is **heightened vulnerability**. As countries get involved in war, markets might be lost to others as buyers go elsewhere to shop, foreign investment flees, and credit on the financial markets might freeze or become expensive. This can be the result of deliberate action by other states in the system or the free operation of market forces. War has always been a very expensive proposition, but much increased interdependence means much greater economic vulnerability.

Fourth, there is **open access**. An open global economic and commercial system has worked against war by disassociating economic access from the confines of political borders and sovereignty. It is not necessary to politically possess a territory in order to profit from it. A strong correlation has been documented between the existence and salience of territorial disputes and the occurrence and severity of war.[77] However, some of the reasons for territorial disputes are removed or diminished when open access prevails, because countries do not need to worry that they will be cut off from vital imports such as food and raw materials or denied the opportunity to export. Again, this enhances the logic of trade as compared to that of war and conquest. As production for the market, and therefore trade, predominates, open access has become more vital, and the threat of war embodied in mercantilism has grown that much more serious and less desirable. Mutual dependence, mutual prosperity, heightened vulnerability, and open access are distinct yet interconnected aspects of the commercial peace, which is, in turn, the natural complement of the industrial or development peace.

It should be stressed, however, that the picture is not entirely rosy or devoid of risks. As noted earlier, the pacifying effects of free trade are not unconditional, as they depend on each of the major players in an anarchic international system accepting the rationale of market competition as more promising than monopolization by force. Yet what happens if some of them do not? As Adam Smith himself put it, considerations of the balance of power might legitimately impose constraints on free trade, for 'defence...is of much more importance than opulence'.[78] For example, if the economic leader allows the free export to and import from a less developed aspiring power in order to increase absolute wealth—including its own—this might enable the challenger to become richer and then use its newly gained power to fight the former leader into ruin.

Britain, the first industrial nation, experienced such a dilemma. During the first half of the nineteenth century, Britain withdrew from mercantilism, opened its markets to foreigners and foreign goods, abolished protectionist tariffs, and lifted restrictions on investment and the sale of technology abroad, eventually becoming a free-trading state. By doing this it boosted its own growth while fuelling that of the rest of the world. However, in relative terms, this open policy made it easier for others—above all the United States and Germany—to catch up and eventually overtake Britain economically, and to challenge its position as the mightiest power. On the other hand, had Britain denied free trade and free access to others, it would not only have stalled the global economic growth from which it profited so much, but may not have been able to prevent others from industrializing, albeit at a slower pace, while increasing their incentive to grab markets and resources by force. This was, and remains, a dilemma, and a gamble. One could argue that Britain's free trade policy was less hazardous politically and militarily with respect to the liberal and democratic United States than in relation to Imperial Germany. However, could Britain have effectively delayed Germany's industrialization, and at what cost to Britain itself and to the prospects of peace?

Similar questions and dilemmas have arisen with China's embrace of the market economy and international trade from 1979 onwards, to which the United States and its liberal democratic allies have responded favourably, opening their markets and fuelling China's meteoric growth. We shall see more about the old and current dilemmas involved in Chapter 7.

Affluence and Comfort

While the connection between commercial interdependence and peace has long been recognized and has been extensively addressed in the scholarly literature, other aspects of the modern economic peace have been largely overlooked. The effect of industrial growth or development and the breaking of the Malthusian trap has been discussed in previous sections. But the industrial-commercialized economy has spawned another new, unprecedented, and distinct factor over time that has contributed to the decrease in belligerency: affluence. Although the concept of affluence has become central to the analysis of contemporary society, its major effect on war has attracted little attention. Throughout history, rising prosperity has been associated with a decreasing willingness to endure the hardship of war. Freedom from manual labour and luxurious living conditions achieved by the rich in prosperous premodern societies conflicted with the physical strain of campaigning and life in the field, which became more alien and unappealing for them. That luxury breeds softness was an age-old philosophical-moralist maxim in all the classical civilizations. As the industrial-commercial age unfolded and wealth per capita rose exponentially, the wealth, comfort, and other amenities once enjoyed only by the privileged elite have spread throughout society. Thus, increasing wealth has worked to decrease war not only through the modern logic of expanding manufacturing and trading interdependence, but also through the traditional logic of the effect of affluence and comfort on society's willingness to endure hardship, now vastly expanded to encompass society as a whole. Affluence—the freedom from scarcity in the elementary, vital needs of life and the ability to afford a great variety of consumer goods—has been achieved throughout the societies of the developed world in the wake of World War II, when the concept itself was coined. And affluence levels have continued to rise ever since. Thus, affluence has been a latter-day add-on to the Modernization Peace, contributing to and much enhancing it in the period since 1945.

It is difficult for people in today's affluent and secure societies to imagine how hard life was for their forefathers only a few generations ago, and how hard it remains today in poor countries. People in premodern societies struggled to survive in the most basic sense. The overwhelming majority of them went through a lifetime of back-breaking physical labour and a constant struggle to escape hunger. The tragedies of being orphaned, of child mortality, of premature death of spouses, and of early death in general were an inescapable part of their lives. People of all ages were afflicted with illness, disability, and physical pain, for which no effective remedies existed. Even where state rule prevailed, violent conflict between neighbours was a regular occurrence and an ever-present possibility, putting a premium on physical strength, toughness, honour, and a reputation for all of these. Misery and tragedy tended to harden people and make them fatalistic. In this context, the suffering and death associated with war were endured as just another natural affliction, along with Malthus's other grim reapers: famine and disease.

Life changed dramatically with the growth of affluent society. In addition to the decline of physical labour, hunger and want have been replaced by abundance, and food has become available practically without limit. In fact, food has become so available that obesity rather than starvation is a major problem, even—and sometimes especially—among the poor, which would have sounded like a baffling paradox throughout history. Infant mortality has fallen to about one-twentieth of its rate during pre-industrial times. Annual general mortality has declined from around thirty to about seven to ten per one thousand people.[79] Infectious disease, the number one killer of the past, has been rendered virtually non-lethal by improved hygiene, vaccinations, and antibiotics. Countless bodily irritations and disabilities— deteriorating eyesight, bad teeth, skin disease, hernias—that used to be an integral part of life, have been alleviated with medication, medical instruments, and surgery. Anaesthetics and other drugs, from painkillers to performance enhancers, have dramatically improved people's quality of life. People in the developed world live in well-heated and air-conditioned dwellings equipped with mechanical/electrical appliances. They have indoor bathrooms and lavatories. They wash daily and change clothes as often. They drive rather than walk. They are flooded with popular entertainment to occupy their spare time. They take vacations in faraway, exotic places. They expect to control and enjoy their lives, rather than merely enduring them, and war scarcely fits into their plans.

Some familiar social science concepts are applicable in elucidating the effects of all these on decreasing belligerency. People embrace 'postmodern', 'post-materialistic', hedonistic values that emphasize individual self-fulfilment. As Ronald Inglehart has documented extensively, people have been moving away from the 'survival values' of old to the 'self-expression values' characteristic of affluent societies.[80] Another relevant concept is Norbert Elias's 'civilizing process', mentioned in Chapter 3, which Steven Pinker has done much to popularize. In an orderly and comfortable society, rough conduct in social dealings decreases, while civility, peaceful argument, and humour become the norm. Psychological sensitivity has risen dramatically. Men are more able to 'connect to their feminine side'. Whereas children and youths used to be physically disciplined by their parents and fought among themselves at school, on the playground, and on the street, they are now surrounded by a general social abhorrence of violence. Yet another familiar and highly relevant concept is 'risk aversion'. Once the vital necessities of life are secured, people tend to adopt more conservative, less desperate, and less risky behavioural strategies. They see far less reason to risk life and limb. On a lighter note, *New York Times* journalist Thomas Friedman gave international relations theorists food for thought when he suggested in the 1990s that a McDonald's Peace prevailed between any two countries that had become rich enough to have the popular restaurant chain.[81] In the meantime, there have been exceptions to his rule, but the basic idea stands.

Indeed, more than the development and commercial elements of the Modernization Peace, it is affluence that is absent in the least developed parts of the world, contributing to the relative weakness of the Modernization Peace there. A transitional, most notable, and intriguing case is today's China.

Urbanism and Urbanity

The 'civilizing process' is intimately associated with one of modernity's major developments: the process of urbanization and the growth of metropolitan service societies. Commercial and metropolitan cities were considered by classical military authorities, such as Vegetius, echoed by Machiavelli, to be the least desirable recruiting grounds, particularly compared to the countryside with its sturdy farmers accustomed to hard physical labour. The residents of large metropolitan centres had typically immigrated from diverse quarters and lacked the traditional communal bonds of solidarity and the social controls of village and small-town communities. Exposed to the cities' quick dealings and temptations, they were regarded as too fickle, rootless, undisciplined, and cynical to be trusted. With modernity, urbanism in large metropolises steadily expanded to encompass the majority of the people. Correspondingly, the number of people living in the countryside declined. Nonetheless, the military continued to regard them as the best 'recruiting material'.

Examples abound. With the coming of the twentieth century, the German army drafted disproportionately from the countryside, and its second choice was people from country towns. It limited recruitment in the large cities, where the masses were regarded as militarily less suitable and—infected with socialism—as politically suspect.[82] Liberal democratic Britain, at the time the world's most urban society, adopted the draft in both world wars. There, too, country folk were regarded as the most fit for military service. Industrial workers were considered less desirable, and office workers were deemed the least suitable for the rigours of military life. The British Empire's best troops during both world wars came from the farms of the still predominantly rural dominions: New Zealand, Australia, and Canada. Similarly, the farmer recruits from Middle America who dominated the United States' armies during World War I were regarded as first-class military material. The American armies of World War II, which included a larger number of city dwellers, still fought well enough, but did not enjoy the same superb reputation as had their predecessors in World War I. And Vietnam War draftees, especially those from urban states, had an even worse reputation for a lack of natural soldierly qualities. An analysis of the home towns of the fallen in the Iraq War reveals that rural and small-town communities contribute nearly twice as many volunteer recruits per head of population as do metropolitan centres.[83] Israel's crack military units during the first decades of its existence were overwhelmingly comprised of young people from a relatively small number of voluntary communal villages (*kibbutzim*) and farm communities (*moshavim*).

Moreover, a far-reaching change in work occupations in society, and especially in the cities, has occurred during the later phases of modernization. City folk during the zenith of the industrial age were mainly factory workers. They were accustomed to physical labour, machines, and the massive, coordinated work regime labelled 'Fordism' or 'Taylorism'. They lived in dense urban communities and were mostly literate. These qualities were major strengths for the military, especially as the military, too, was undergoing mechanization. However, as the industrial-technological era progressed, manufacturing declined and the services sector expanded its share of the workforce in the most advanced economies. In the United States, which led this trend, 70 per cent of the workforce is now employed in services while only 18 per cent work in manufacturing.[84] It can be argued that the military, too, has been moving from mechanized to information-based forces, increasingly relying on computerized data processing and accurate standoff fire to do most of the fighting. All the same, adaptation to military life comes far less naturally to people from contemporary affluent societies who are accustomed to desk work in the office and the seclusion of residential suburbia than it did to their farmhand and factory worker predecessors. Thus, while urbanization transformed society from the very beginning of modernization, the growth of service office employment at the expense of physical industrial labour intensified in the economically most advanced societies after 1945, contributing to the decrease in the people's martial propensity during that period. Again, the world's least developed countries are less affected by this development, whereas China offers a massive transitional laboratory case.

Liberal Democracy

Let us repeat what we know about the (inter-)democratic peace after several decades of intensive debate. It is a very real phenomenon. It sets liberal democracies sharply apart from non-democratic countries, which are involved in wars both with democracies and among themselves. (However, non-democracies too have fought less—and not only recently, as is increasingly recognized, but ever since 1815—as compared to earlier times, a fact concealed by the COW's limited time range.[85]) It has grown stronger over time, becoming more entrenched during the past century than it was during the nineteenth century (and, less well recognized, there is no trace of it earlier in history). And it is stronger among economically developed than among developing countries.

How do all these different features fit together, and how can they be coherently explained? The continuous deepening of the democratic peace has been attributed to the deepening of democracy itself and of liberal values over time.[86] During the past two centuries initially liberal parliamentary societies experienced, successively: an abolition of slavery; a gradual expansion of the franchise to all men and to women; an extension of equal legal and social rights to women and minorities; a rise in social tolerance in general; and an increase in political transparency and accountability. Thus, it has been suggested that the frailness of peace between democracies in the developing world can be explained by lower levels of democracy and liberalism compared to the developed world. In this respect, developing countries are reminiscent of the nineteenth-century West.[87] However, what is the cause of this deepening of democratization and liberalization? Is it a purely cultural-moral-social attitude development that feeds on itself? If so, why do economically less developed societies lag behind in this process?

The connection between socio-economic modernization and the growth of liberalism and democracy has long been noticed.[88] Indeed, it is too often forgotten that democracies on a country scale (as opposed to city-states) never existed anywhere before the nineteenth century. True, the connection between development and democracy is not absolute. There are some poor democracies, at early stages of economic modernization, most notably India since 1947. But there, too, democracy would have been unimaginable without networks of modern communications: railways and automobiles, newspapers, telegraph, radio, and television. On the other hand, there is also the question of developed non-democratic countries, which are examined in Chapter 7. All in all, however, the record suggests that democracy tends to become more entrenched with economic development, and that there is an interconnection between the two factors and the growth of the democratic peace.

Furthermore, although non-democratic countries in the industrial era have also participated in the general decline in belligerency as compared to premodern times, liberal and democratic societies have proven most attuned to modernity's pacifying aspects. Relying on arbitrary coercive force at home, non-liberal and non-democratic countries have found it more natural to use force abroad. By contrast, liberal democratic societies are socialized to peaceful, law-mediated relations at home, and their citizens have grown to expect that the same norms will be applied internationally. Living in increasingly tolerant societies, they have grown more receptive to the other's point of view. Domestically promoting freedom, legal equality, and political participation, liberal democratic powers—though initially in possession of vast empires—have found it increasingly difficult to justify rule over foreign peoples without their consent. And, sanctifying life, liberty, and human rights, they have proven to be failures in forceful repression. Furthermore, with the individual's life and pursuit of happiness elevated above group values, sacrifice of life in war has increasingly lost legitimacy in liberal democratic societies. War retains legitimacy only under narrow, and narrowing, formal and practical conditions, and is generally viewed as extremely abhorrent and undesirable.

As mentioned before, this has been a gradual process. Initially, popular opinion and democratic electorates were scarcely peaceful. In the nineteenth-century West, as the masses moved to the forefront of politics and political systems underwent democratization, it was widely believed that militant popular pressure, rather than the wishes of reluctant governments, drove countries to war. Indeed, popular attitudes were no different from those seen in the classical democratic and republican city-states. Contrary to the cliché, popular agitation should not be attributed primarily to leaders' manipulation of peace-loving peoples. Just as often, leaders were catering to a strong public demand. The word 'jingoism' came into currency in late nineteenth-century Britain, at a time of increasing democratization, and denoted a chauvinistic and bellicose public frenzy. Jingoism was widespread during the Boer War (1899–1902). At the very same time, waves of popular enthusiasm forced the American government's hand and carried the United States into war with Spain (1898). Lest it be thought that the enemy in either of these cases failed to qualify as fully liberal/democratic, it should be noted that it was also public opinion in both Britain and France that proved most bellicose, chauvinistic, and unsympathetic towards the other during the Fashoda Crisis (1898) between the two countries. It was the politicians who backed down from war. Popular opinion was a major driving force behind the burst of the New Imperialism between 1881 and 1920, and it generally supported foreign aggrandizement. Indeed, jingoism today is more alive in developing than in developed countries.

At the same time, the notion that serious war is an unmitigated disaster and constitutes sheer madness, already gaining hold in liberal circles during the nineteenth century, increasingly grew in strength in the newly formed liberal democratic countries at the outset of the twentieth century, as the global industrial, trading, and financial system expanded and interdependence deepened. Norman Angell's famous book, *The Great Illusion* (1910), expressed this view. It was against this background that World War I, despite widespread popular enthusiasm at its outbreak, caused such a crisis in the liberal consciousness and traumatized liberal societies after the event. Mueller has asserted that World War I was a historical turning point in social attitudes towards war, which affected democracies and non-democracies alike.[89] But this is not quite true. The famous 'trauma' of the war was an overwhelmingly liberal phenomenon, which closely correlated with the strength of liberalism in each country rather than with that country's actual losses.

Britain, for example, was Europe's most liberal power, and the retrospective reaction against the war and the mourning for the 'lost generation' were the greatest there, even though Britain's losses were the smallest among European powers. British casualties—three-quarters of a million dead—were terrible, but amounted to no more than 12 per cent of British troops enlisted during the war. They were smaller in absolute terms (and about half relative to population) than France's loss of almost 1.4 million and Germany's nearly 2 million dead. Nonetheless, the reaction against the war in Germany was far more limited than that in Britain.[90] Only liberal (and socialist) opinion, which was less dominant in Germany than in Britain, responded negatively. The most famous anti-war author was Erich Maria Remarque, a German liberal and pacifist. Certainly, there was much war-weariness and a widespread loss of enthusiasm for war in Germany. Moreover, there was the widely shared realization that the country must avoid another general war in which it would again be crushed under the weight of a superior coalition.

Still, Germany had strong nationalist, anti-liberal, right-wing elements that looked for a way around these strategic constraints and vehemently opposed the anti-war sentiments. Ernst Juenger's books, glorifying his experience in the trenches and exalting the qualities of war, competed with Remarque's for popularity in Germany. Most importantly, powerful nostalgic evocation of soldierly trench camaraderie, embodied in voluntary paramilitary organizations such as the Blackshirts and Freikorps, played a major role in the post-war mood that helped bring to power, respectively, the Fascists in Italy and the Nazis in Germany.

Perhaps the two cases that best illustrate the correlation between the post-World War I trauma and the level of liberalism are the United States and Serbia. The mightiest power in the world was not afflicted by heavy losses or crippling economic costs during its brief involvement in the war. Relative to population, the United States suffered the lightest casualties of all the belligerents in the European war, and it gained tremendously from the war materially, replacing Britain as the world's leading banker, creditor, and insurer. Nonetheless, it was in the United States that the onset of disgust with the war and regret over participating in it was the most rapid and sweeping. By comparison, small and backward Serbia suffered, relative to population, the heaviest casualties of all the warring nations, and was totally ravaged by the war and occupation. And yet Serbia hardly experienced the trauma from and disillusionment with the war. Nor, indeed, would other traditional societies that suffered hundreds of thousands or millions of casualties in the wars of the twentieth century (up to and including the Iran–Iraq War and Iraq's later gulf wars) react any more traumatically than had been the norm among pre-industrial societies. By contrast, as the twentieth century ran its course and with the advent of the twenty-first century, the smallest number of casualties has become sufficient to discredit a war in affluent liberal societies, particularly when the threat is not considered existential, imminent, or unsusceptible to alternatives to war, or when the prospects of achieving victory seem dim. Indeed, it is precisely the meeting of these conditions that has become so tricky for advanced liberal democracies.[‡]

[‡] The claim that American casualty sensitivity is overrated has been made by: Eric Larson, *Casualties and Consensus: The Historical Role of Casualties in Domestic Support of US Military Operations*, Santa Monica, CA: Rand, 1996; C. Gelpi, P. Feaver, and J. Reifler, 'Success Matters: Casualty Sensitivity and the War in Iraq', *International Security*, 30:3 (2005/2006), 7–46; and Gelpi, Feaver, and Reifler, 'How Many Casualties Will Americans Tolerate?', *Foreign Affairs*, 85:1 (2006).

Thus, the deep trauma that liberal opinion experienced in the wake of World War I was not a result of the great losses of life and wealth *in themselves*. Again (as Mueller recognizes), these were not greater relative to population and wealth than the losses suffered in massive wars throughout history. The novelty was that liberal opinion now regarded such wars as wholly out of step with the modern world. Most people in post-World War I Britain would probably not have denied that the stakes in that war were high and that it would have mattered if Britain had lost the war to Germany. Yet they felt, even if they were not always able to articulate it precisely, that the war had conflicted with the economic and normative rationale of the modern world—that everybody had more to gain from peace, and everybody had lost from the war, even if some had lost more than others.

Democratic leaders have either shared these values, or have been forced by public pressure to conform to them, or they have been removed from office. The last option, the so-called 'structural' explanation for the democratic peace, makes no sense on its own. It only makes sense *after* a change in the popular preferences, coupled with a 'normative' change in the attitude towards war, its utility, and justification, as compared to premodern times or even the nineteenth century.[91] Unless the perceived utility and justification of war are generally tilted in the negative direction in the eyes of the electorate, voters should be presumed to reward victorious leaders as much as punish defeated ones.

As the aversion to war has grown, wars are now sanctioned in liberal democratic societies only as a last resort—after all other options have failed. However, in practically no situation does it ever become clear that all alternative policies have indeed been exhausted, that war has really become unavoidable. A feeling that there may be another way, that there *must* be another way, always lingers on. Errors of omission or commission are ever suspected as being the cause of undesired belligerency. Moreover, it is never clear that the democracies come to a conflict with entirely clean hands—morally—because of past or more immediate alleged wrongs. Hence the

---

They demonstrate that casualty sensitivity was actually a function of the public's assessment of the prospects of achieving military victory. However, non-democratic and less developed countries are less susceptible to this constraint, and their casualty tolerance in general is much higher. Moreover, liberal democracies' very ability to achieve victory in some types of war, most notably of the counterinsurgency variety, has been severely constrained by their self-imposed restrictions on the use of indiscriminate violence against civilians (see later in this chapter). This takes us back to square one: liberal democracies are far more casualty-sensitive.

inescapable torment of contemporary affluent liberal democratic societies in conflict situations. Strategically, too, they have tended to follow a characteristic pattern of conduct ever since the beginning of the twentieth century, moving cautiously up the scale from appeasement, to containment and cold war, to limited war, and only most reluctantly to fully fledged war.[92]

The consequences of the deepening change in viewing the utility and justification of war, particularly strong in developed liberal democratic societies, have been revolutionary. With growing liberalization, democracy, and economic development, the probability of war between democracies has declined to a vanishing point, where they no longer even fear or see the need to prepare for the possibility of a militarized dispute with one another. A 'positive' peace, based on shared interests, outlook, and ideals, rather than on the balance of power and deterrence, prevails among them. The 'security dilemma' itself, that seemingly intrinsic element of international relations, has entirely disappeared in their relations with each other, a historically entirely unprecedented situation.

Moreover, the inter-democratic peace is only the most conspicuous aspect of a much broader democratic peace. Domestically too, on account of their more strongly consensual nature, plurality, tolerance, and indeed a greater legitimacy for peaceful secession, developed liberal democracies have become practically free of civil wars, the most lethal and destructive type of war. Such wars still plague old-style autocracies and oligarchies, as well as less developed democracies. Consider the American and Russian civil wars, nineteenth-century Europe in general, and today's developing world. Although totalitarian regimes have also avoided civil wars, they have done so by means of ruthless repression, and many of them have killed their own citizens in horrifying numbers.[93] Liberal democracies have been shown to kill their own people far less than other regimes do.[94]

Furthermore, it was widely believed initially that liberal democratic states were peaceful only towards one another, because they fought non-democratic states and appeared to be as prone as those states to initiating wars. However, a more careful reading of the evidence reveals that liberal democratic countries in fact have fought fewer inter-state wars than non-democracies. In addition, their wars have been more reactive than initiated, tending to respond to a war started by others elsewhere, or to an imminent threat of war. That is, liberal democracies typically uphold the status quo against those who seek to change it by force. True, liberal democracies were involved in more 'extra-systemic' wars, mainly colonial, against non-state rivals.[95] Possessing far-flung colonial empires, France and Britain in particular fought far more such wars than non-democratic powers. However, this statistical artefact is somewhat misleading. Having acquired their empires when colonial victories were still winnable on the cheap, these powers later found themselves stuck with them as liberal democracies became increasingly inhibited from engaging in wholesale suppression.

Counterinsurgency warfare has drawn a great deal of attention in recent years, and it constitutes an enigma. Mighty powers that have proved capable of crushing the strongest great power opponents have nonetheless failed to defeat the humblest of military rivals in some of the world's poorest and weakest regions. Various theories, more or less relevant, have been advanced to explain the paradox. It has been barely recognized, however, that, rather than being universal, the difficulty has overwhelmingly been the lot of liberal democratic powers—and encountered precisely because they are liberal and democratic.[96]

Historically, the crushing of an insurgency necessitated ruthless measures that regularly extended to the civilian population on whose support the insurgents depended. Suppression has been the *sine qua non* of imperial rule, as ancient democratic Athens and republican Rome chillingly demonstrate. The British and French empires could sustain themselves at a relatively low cost only so long as the imperial powers felt no scruples about applying ruthless measures. However, as liberalization deepened from the late nineteenth century, the days of formal democratic empires became numbered even while outwardly they were reaching their greatest extent. It has scarcely been noticed that the massive wave of decolonization after 1945 took place *only* vis-à-vis the liberal democratic empires. The non-democratic empires were either crushed in the two world wars, as with Germany and Japan, or dismantled peacefully when the totalitarian system disintegrated, as with the Soviet Union.

The Soviet failure in Afghanistan is widely cited as a counter-example, but Afghanistan, the ideal guerrilla country, was the exception—the outlier—rather than the rule in the Soviet imperial system. Chechnya is more enlightening in this respect, and the sequence is unmistakable: Soviet methods under Stalin—including mass deportation—were the most brutal and most effective in curbing resistance, while the liberal Russia of the 1990s proved to be the least brutal and least effective, with Putin's semi-authoritarian Russia constituting an intermediate case. More generally, as Sherlock Holmes has noted, it is 'the dog that didn't bark'—the Soviet imperial domains within the Soviet Union itself and in Eastern Europe, for decades lying helpless under the totalitarian iron fist—that is the most conspicuous, and most telling. The rise of modern nationalism among the subject peoples is one of the reasons invoked for the failure of imperialism. However, the Soviet Empire included countries such as Poland and Hungary, that are proverbial for their fervent nationalism. This did not help either of them much as long as the totalitarian suppression prevailed. Thus, scholars have failed to count the cases of successful insurgency that *didn't* happen, and note where they didn't happen, and why (in technical terms: there has been a selection bias of a lopsided N). The same logic extends to China, whose continued successful suppression of Tibetan and Uyghur nationalism is likely to persist as long as China retains its non-democratic regime.

All this is clearly at odds with the 'winning of hearts and minds' that has been posited as the key to success in the current liberal democratic discourse and counterinsurgency doctrine. Indeed, the winning of hearts and minds has always been an important component of successful counterinsurgency, as it continues to be. However, it is important to realize that it has only become the liberal democracies' indispensable guideline for the pacification of foreign societies because liberal democracies have practically lost the ability to crush such societies by force if the latter choose to resist. Moreover, this method is both far less effective and far more expensive than ruthless suppression. Thus, despite undeniable brutalities and policy mistakes, the democracies' counterinsurgency war record is very much a testimony to their noblest qualities. All of this does not mean that democracies always fail and non-democracies always win counterinsurgency wars; and yet the stakes are massively skewed against the former.

Foreign intervention by liberal democratic powers has been another thorny question. During the nineteenth and early twentieth centuries, less developed parts of the world were often coerced into connecting to the liberal-centred system, or, more recently, have at least been barred from disrupting it. Neo-Marxist rhetoric against 'informal imperialism' notwithstanding, the *pax Britannica* and *pax Americana* were major catalysts of the modern system of economic development, mutual prosperity, and peace. Needless to say, the process has often been far from pretty, and it has scarcely been driven by purely altruistic motives. But indeed, as with the hidden hand of the market, the egotistical acts of players that work within the liberal-oriented system result in a growing prosperity overall. The democracies' appeasement, containment, and eventual destruction of Nazi Germany and Imperial Japan when the latter set out to wreck the system—as well as the post-war reconstruction of both countries by the victors and their incorporation within a liberal democratic, economically prosperous, and peaceful world order—is the most decisive historical instance of that dual process. The war against Germany and Japan ultimately established peace, however hyperbolic the idea of a pacifying war is made to sound by critics.[97] Such wars are basically collective security ventures, a concept which again is fundamentally fuelled by the modern and liberal logic of protecting the peaceful order of mutual prosperity. Thus, for the purpose of measuring belligerency, it is misleading to simply count the wars in which liberal democracies have been involved without considering the trend that they have steadily advanced. Of course, failed interventions to establish democracy and a liberal order—some of them crushing failures—have also occurred, most notably where the social preconditions for modernization had not yet materialized.

Thus, the forceful democratization of Germany and Japan after World War II, the most successful cases of democratization in the twentieth century, had been made possible not only by the political circumstances of defeat in total war and the communist threat. While considerable cultural resistance to democracy and liberalism had to be overcome in both countries, they both possessed a modern economic and social infrastructure upon which functioning liberal democracies could be built.[98] The Arab Middle East offers a sharp contrast to post-1945 Germany and Japan, and a vital clue as to the close connection between modernization, democracy, and peace. Here is what I wrote in 2005, at the time of the American campaign to bring democracy to the Arab world and long before the locally induced 'Arab Spring' collapsed into bloody mayhem:

> While the attempt to bring democratization to countries—such as those of the Arab word—that lack both a liberal tradition and a modern socio-economic infrastructure, countries that are largely tribal and fraught with ethnic and religious cleavages, should persist, its limitations must be recognized. It will be a gradual process, as it was even in the United States, Britain, and France, and it can backfire under excessive pressure, threatening stability in existing moderately pluralistic state-societies, where the main opposition is not liberal and democratic but Islamist, and often undemocratic and radical.[99]

Finally, when the number of casualties incurred is taken into account—rather than just wars and war years—the evidence shows that during the twentieth century, liberal democracies have suffered far less than non-democracies, or put differently, have engaged in wars that were far less severe. The severity of wars, not just their frequency, should be considered in measuring war avoidance.[100] In part, the liberal democracies suffered fewer casualties because of an accidental reason: they were only briefly involved in major ground warfare during the highly lethal World War II, having been disastrously defeated in 1940 in Western Europe, from which they were thrown out until June 1944. Other than that, they also suffered fewer casualties in their wars because they tended to possess technological superiority over rivals from the world's less developed areas. International relations scholars have ascribed great significance to the data that shows that democracies tend to fight weaker opponents. They have suggested that in this democracies exhibit superior powers of discrimination and judgement, resulting in a better record of victories.[101] However, as practically all the developed countries since 1945 have been democracies, and developed affluent democracies do not fight each other, they fight only weaker states almost by definition. Furthermore, their record against weaker (mainly non-state) rivals is rather poor, because of their self-imposed constraints on violence, as we have seen.

The growth of an extensive web of international institutions for political and economic cooperation, both global and regional, is regarded as another major element of the liberal peace.[102] It is at once a projection and an instrument of political and economic liberalism, which facilitates their implementation in a global system that has become much more attuned to them by the process of modernization.§ Thus, liberal democracy has had a very distinctive effect in reducing war during the past two centuries, but only in connection with the economic development that has revolutionized the world since the advent of the industrial age. While development has tended to tilt the preferences of countries in general towards the peaceful paths to wealth, this tilt has interacted particularly powerfully with liberal values and

---

§ Gary Goertz, Paul Diehl, and Alexandru Balas, in *The Puzzle of Peace: The Evolution of Peace in the International System*, Oxford: Oxford UP, 2016, claim that the evolving international norms that have made the conquest of territory unlawful and territorial integrity inviolable should be regarded as the explanation for the decline of armed conflict since 1945. As territorial disputes have been found to be the most prevalent cause of war (but see Chapter 7, note 2 and the related text), they argue (p. 74) that all other factors proposed as causes of the decline beyond this proposition make the explanation overdetermined and are redundant. However, the question of *why* the norms against territorial conquest have changed—and at this particular historical moment—does not seem to occur to the authors. Nor do they address the democratic/liberal peace and capitalist peace propositions that might have some bearing on the change of norms. That is, they are entirely oblivious to the question of the actual direction of the causal connections. Regrettably, such narrow interpretations are increasingly regarded as standard in much of the international relations literature.

norms, and has been most emphatically expressed in the choices made by modern democratic electorates—all in comparison to premodern times. It is not surprising, then, that the chauvinistic or righteous militancy historically associated with republican foreign policy has greatly diminished in the affluent, consumer-hedonistic, liberal democratic societies that have increasingly come into being since the beginning of the twentieth century.

Sexual Liberalization—Make Love, not War

Side by side with material well-being, reproduction, and therefore sexuality, are at the very core of our evolution-shaped system of desires. Thus, it should not come as a surprise that a revolution in sexual mores and the advent of sexual promiscuity is another factor that has dampened enthusiasm for war in advanced modern societies, especially among unmarried young men. Young single males, who traditionally constituted the most aggressive element in society, now find a variety of outlets for their restlessness. Joining the military for foreign adventure, which once lured many of them away from a conservative and dull countryside or small-town community, has lost much of its attraction, as there is much greater excitement and adventure close to home. At the same time, the authorities in orderly modern societies have curtailed the sexual aspects of military service.

Throughout history, rape, like looting, was one of the major perks of war, and was considered the troops' acquired right after the storming of cities that had failed to surrender. In modern Imperial Japan, the troops still indulged in state-tolerated mass rape while serving abroad, some of it in the form of state-organized forced prostitution. At least 2 million women are estimated to have been raped by Soviet soldiers in conquered eastern Germany in 1945. Mass rape has been a major feature of the recent ethnic wars in Bosnia, Rwanda, Darfur, and West Africa. In the armies of the Western democracies, although rape is severely punished, American and other Allied troops widely availed themselves of an abundant supply of low-cost prostitution in ruined Western Europe after World War II and, later, in desperately poor Vietnam.[103]

All in all, however, the much increased sexual opportunity within society has sharply decreased the incentives to enlist for war. Again, the modern transformation stood behind the sexual revolution: through much reduced housework and falling birth rates that prompted women's entry into the workforce outside the home; effective contraception; and the expansion of the liberal outlook to women's liberation. Men have been affected in many ways. Relevant to our subject, young men now are more reluctant to leave behind the pleasures of life for the rigours and chastity of the battlefield. 'Make love, not war' was the slogan of the powerful anti-war youth campaign of the 1960s, which not accidentally coincided with a far-reaching liberalization of sexual norms (Illustration 6.4). By comparison, consider young men's explosive militancy in the traditionalist and sexually ultra-conservative societies of the contemporary Arab Middle East, which have not embraced the sexual revolution. Barely registered at the level of national or foreign policy aims, the sexual revolution deeply affects national policy through the bulk of individual choice. There is no need to fully accept the reasoning

Illustration 6.4. Make love, not war

of Sigmund Freud, Wilhelm Reich, and Michel Foucault to appreciate the significance of this factor.

Gender roles, in relation to both men and women, have contributed to the Modernization Peace in other ways as well.

Aging Demographics

In addition to changes in the circumstances and attitudes of young males, the significant decline in their relative number is another factor that may have diminished enthusiasm for war in contemporary developed societies.[104] With the onset of industrialization, as child mortality fell sharply and birth rates followed only slowly, the number of young adults in a fast-growing population increased not only in absolute terms but also relative to the total adult population. A youth bulge emerged in the nineteenth-century West, as it did in the twentieth-century developing world. Young male adults were most conspicuous in the public enthusiasm for war in July to August 1914, as they were in all wars and revolutions. In today's developed societies, however, with birth rates falling below replacement levels and with increased longevity, young adults—including males—constitute a shrinking portion of an aging population. Before World War I, males aged 15 to 29 constituted 35 per cent of the adult male population in Britain, and 40 per cent in Germany; by 2000, their share had dropped to 24 per cent and 29 per cent, respectively. By comparison, young adult males of the same age cohort constituted 48 per cent of Iran's population in 2000.[105] As the fertility rate in Iran has been dropping like a stone, the median age of its population is rising sharply and is expected to be higher than Britain's and almost as high as Germany's by 2050. This dramatic change, like other changes in Iranian society, could have many effects over time, including a decrease in belligerency.[106]

Because young males have always been the most aggressive element in society while older men were traditionally associated with counsels of moderation and compromise, the youth bulge may have increased the enthusiasm for war in the earlier stages of modernization, while an aging population contributes to its decrease at a later stage. China's one child policy between the late 1970s and 2015 makes its demographics more similar to a developed society, a positive omen for the future, at least with respect to war propensity. In Islamic societies, booming population growth peaked more recently, and the relative share of young men is still at its height.[107]

Avoiding simplistic correlations, the restlessness of the cohorts of young adult males in the Islamic world should be understood in conjunction with the lack of economic (and sexual) opportunity in traditional, stagnant, and culturally defensive societies. At the height of the population growth in industrially booming Britain, around the middle of the nineteenth century, the share of young adult males was over 40 per cent of the adult male population, not unlike the proportion in Iran today, and yet this was the period of the *pax Britannica*.

Given the sharp decline in birth rates in developed societies, Edward Luttwak has suggested that the far smaller number of children per family may be the cause of these societies' decreased belligerency. According to this argument, when a typical present-day family only numbers one to two children, it is much more agonizing for parents to lose a child.[108] This reasoning, however, hardly stands up to scrutiny. Historically, only the period of demographic explosion during early industrialization saw families with many surviving children. Although birth rates had indeed been much higher in premodern societies, infant mortality was also higher, resulting in an overall demographic equilibrium. Women gave birth to many children, but few survived to adulthood, keeping average numbers at about the replacement rate. Thus, having raised their few surviving children to adulthood, parents in the past could no more easily 'afford' to lose them than can today's parents. In fact economically, parents then could less afford to lose their only support in old age. Certainly, mortality and other calamities were a more normal part of life in the past, and people necessarily resigned themselves to this. Furthermore, in traditional societies people were simply unable to oppose the dictates of faraway and alien authorities, who did not care about their wishes, or indeed about their life and death. Where the people themselves ruled, as in city-state republics, the expected rewards of war made the risks to life more acceptable. Both conditions have lost much of their validity in modern affluent societies, particularly in those of the liberal democratic sort.

Female Attitudes and Electorates

While young men have always been the most aggressive element in society, men in general have always been more aggressive and belligerent than women. Having won the right to vote in twentieth-century liberal democracies, women have been able to influence governments' policies by participating in electing the government. Studies in recent decades have shown a consistent gender gap in attitudes toward the use of military force.[109] Such differences might play a significant role in tilting the electoral balance against military ventures in modern affluent liberal democracies. Women's voting record has been suggested as one of the factors that accounts for why liberal democracies became more averse to war in the twentieth century than they had been in the nineteenth.[110]

It should be noted that women are not unconditionally pacifist. In some societies and conflicts, the attitudes of the sexes do not diverge significantly. For example, no such divergence has been evinced in studies of both sides of the Arab–Israeli conflict. The authors of these studies have suggested that their findings are most likely explained by the high 'salience' of the conflict, which generates high mobilization levels among members of both sexes.[111] Similarly, in the 2004 American presidential elections, the so-called 'security moms', who feared additional mega-terror attacks at home, cast more votes for the ostensibly tougher candidate George W. Bush than they did for his Democratic challenger. The effect was short-lived and was reversed in the 2008 elections, after the perceived military entanglements in both Afghanistan and Iraq. In Russia, mothers' voices that had been mute in the totalitarian system during the Soviets' failed Afghan campaign (1979–88) became dominant during the first Chechnyan War (1994–6), after Russia had become liberalized. Mothers took to the streets in public demonstrations, significantly contributing to the Russian decision to withdraw. However, the continuation of Chechen terror attacks on Russian soil after the Russian withdrawal legitimized Russian re-intervention in the eyes of Russian public opinion, which encompassed men and women alike.

Conclusion: The Modernization Peace—Kant's Tripod for Peace Must Stand on Something

The decrease in belligerency since 1815, progressively deepening with the process of modernization, has signalled a major shift in the relative balance between the violent and non-violent behavioural strategies for fulfilling human desires. It is not that war has become more costly in terms of life and wealth, or less profitable or unprofitable for other reasons, as is widely believed. Rather, it is peace that has become much more profitable and more attractive in comparison to the violent option.

The scholarly debate on whether democracy or trade/capitalism have been responsible for the decrease in war is somewhat off the mark, as both have been preconditioned by a broader and more fundamental factor: modernization, sparked by the process of industrialization from 1815 onwards. Industrialization brought about an exponential increase in the role and scope of trade, which together with rocketing wealth, rooted in internal growth, have tilted the preferences of people and states away from war and towards peace. This change was most acutely, though not exclusively, manifested in the choices made by democratic electorates. Other offshoots of the modernization process have deepened the trend. The factors of development, commerce, affluence, urbanism and urbanity, liberal democracy, sexual liberation, demographics, and gender are all interconnected and mutually affecting in the modern transformation and in the growth of the Modernization Peace. At the same time, they each exercise a distinct contributing effect that comes into play at different points in time, reinforcing the war aversion of the societies involved. Other factors in the modernization process, such as the globalization of mass culture or cultural convergence via the media and other forms of communication, can surely be added. Indeed, cultural convergence is so widely familiar as to make further discussion of it here redundant. Taken together, these factors help to account for the gaps and reconcile the discrepancies that close historical control reveals in theories such as the nuclear peace, the democratic peace, and the capitalist peace, now understood as part of a more comprehensive and unifying whole. There is no Ockham's razor here by which the causes of the modern peace can be reduced to any of its component parts. At best, each of them is a more or less adequate but still an imperfect proxy for a much broader development.

True, the effect of each of the above elements is sometimes difficult to isolate or measure, as sufficient variation among the relevant cases does not always exist. Affluent societies only emerged after World War II and practically all of them have been liberal democracies. Had non-democratic but capitalist Germany and Japan survived World War II and become affluent, the effect of prosperity could have been tested more effectively. The same applies to the metropolitan service society, and largely also to the sexual revolution, with the very limited test case offered by the later Soviet Union. The complexity of the causal web is demonstrated by the number of young males during the *pax Britannica*, which is similar to the number in today's Islamic world. All the same, the combination of the various elements of the Modernization Peace explains why war has all but died out—indeed, has become unthinkable—in the most developed parts of the world, has decreased dramatically in the developing parts, and mainly survives in or on the perimeters of the least developed parts. The aggregation of all wars in the world has its uses, but it averages a widely divergent range. Indeed, unless attention is given to how the wars are distributed on the map of modernization, aggregation may result in a failure to identify the crucial factor which accounts for the presence or absence of war. While the various parts of the world interact deeply, they still constitute different worlds.

The twenty-first century will offer further testing grounds for the Modernization Peace, possibly with greater variability in many of its contributing factors. In particular, the continued modernization of China is likely to test all of them, as will the development of presently poorly developed parts of the world, mostly in Asia and Africa. However, before we turn to examine potential future question marks with respect to the Modernization Peace, we have a monumental past challenge to explain. As noted at the beginning of this chapter, a comprehensive and coherent understanding of our subject needs to account for both the general decrease in belligerency since 1815 and the great exception to this trend: the two world wars. Both the past and future challenges to the Modernization Peace are the subject of our next and last chapter.

7

Challenges to the Modernization Peace

Past and Future

The literature on the decline of war has attracted much attention, including some very negative responses. Critics have been incredulous about the alleged decline (in whatever time frame), but have mostly been concerned about the future implications of this notion. Many of them regard war as an elementary force of one sort or another that will continue to play a major role in future reality, as it has throughout history. Many others fear a renewed addiction to old idealist illusions, most notably in liberal democratic societies. They are on guard against complacency and a decrease in vigilance in what is still—quite clearly—a very challenging, largely conflictual, and often dangerous international environment, where the use of force cannot be ruled out and is sometimes necessary.

I am sympathetic towards and partly share such concerns. But, precisely for this reason, a careful delineation of the processes involved—of both their scope *and* limitations, as well as of counter-processes, actual and potential—is called for, and should not be flattened into an ideological brawl. The processes of modernization that underlie the spread of peace have been real and deep. Indeed, they have been among the most sweeping in human history, and their effects have been nothing short of revolutionary. At the same time, reality is diverse, complex, and messy, and the future is largely open, and intrinsically so. Whether or not the world, and thus the future, is in principle predetermined—ruled by a strict 'mechanistic' chain of cause and effect—is a puzzle in physics and philosophy. But in practice we are limited to imaginative extrapolations from existing and expected trends and counter-trends. As nineteenth-century philosopher Søren Kierkegaard put it, our movement in the world resembles the backwards walk of the crab, as we advance towards the future while gazing upon the past. The human future-oriented modelling capacity is a very powerful tool, by far the most successful of its kind in nature, but it can only sketch a fuzzy range of probabilities. The exact playing out of forces, propensities, and events cannot be foreseen, and new developments and unexpected contingencies are bound to occur. With the slightest of changes, things can develop in substantially different and diverging directions. Thus, deep trends and towering structures *as well as* an infinite range of future unknowns need to be recognized. The scholarly literature on historical counterfactuals has become a growth industry for a very good reason, and its arguments hold with even greater force with respect to the future. The quip that predictions are just fine as long as they are not applied to the future expresses something profound, but it is only partly true, as not all future developments have the same probability. This is the source of our ability to steer our way through the world reasonably well on average. At the same time, to venture which known or unknown future options within an estimated range of higher and lower probabilities will eventually materialize, and exactly how they will interact, is a hopeless pretence. Not even an analysis after the event can fully resolve the question of which past prediction has turned out to be the 'right' one, because things may have taken a different course with the slightest of changes, including the idiosyncrasies and whims of individual leaders, and with each play of the game.

Thus, the aim of this chapter is not prediction, which has a notoriously dubious record, including in our subject.* Every future reader will be wiser than a present-day observer, knowing how the story eventually 'ended', in the same way that we know, for example, how things ultimately turned out

---

* A 2013 statistical study projecting the decline of intra-state conflict during the first half of the twenty-first century, with conclusions quite similar to mine, demonstrates the point, as it has already encountered problems with some of its most confident predictions: 'Our forecasts are most optimistic for the "Western Asia and North Africa" region, where the incidence of conflict is predicted to be reduced by almost two thirds, from over 27% in 2009 to 6.2% in 2050. The incidence of major conflict drops from 4.5% to 1.5%... Although we do model a strong conflict trap tendency, the conflict trap is not sufficiently strong to prevent this currently conflict-prone region from reducing the incidence of conflict to something closer to that observed in similar regions.' This was written just before Syria, Libya, and Yemen all imploded—joining Iraq in a murderous civil war—and before Egypt experienced an authoritarian military takeover that toppled an elected illiberal Islamist regime. Of course, all this may prove to be just a 'strong conflict trap', and reality in this region may change by 2050, as it did in Europe between 1910 and 1950. Or it may not. See Håvard Hegre, Joakim Karlsen, Håvard Mokleiv Nygård, Håvard Strand, and Henrik Urdal, 'Predicting Armed Conflict, 2010–2050', *International Studies Quarterly*, 57 (2013), 250–70, quotation from 261.

in the decade before 1914 or 1939. There will remain, however, as with 1914 or 1939, the inherently open question of how events could have unfolded had somewhat different trajectories materialized and other realistic options been followed. Furthermore, while anything resembling rigorous prediction is not possible, an attempt to identify some of the fundamental factors involved in the modern transformation and affecting the Modernization Peace is crucial for both retrospect and prospect, and at both the theoretical and practical levels. We begin with some cardinal past divergences from the Modernization Peace, with a view to both explaining major lingering puzzles and enriching our overall understanding of the forces involved, not least in order to see what these may augur for the future.

Why the Great Wars of the Nineteenth and Twentieth Centuries?

We have seen the changing rationale—prompted by the Industrial Revolution—that has vastly increased the attraction of the peaceful option for attaining human aims, while decreasing the attractiveness of the military option. The Long Peace phenomenon, comprising three consecutive periods of peace from 1815 onwards, strikingly coincides with the advent, spread, and deepening of industrial society and the sweeping processes associated with it, known as modernization. Thus, the reasons why strugglers in these processes, less affected by modernization, have continued to engage in wars during this period, and why they still do, should not be a mystery. However, during the nineteenth and first half of the twentieth century wars also broke out between countries that were among the leaders and most advanced along the path of modernization. Notably, since then the developed world has advanced much further down that path, which has made the Modernization Peace that much more entrenched. Still, what is to be made of the wars among the great powers that took place just after the middle of the nineteenth century, between the First and the Second Long Peace? And far more challenging, how can one explain the two cataclysmic world wars that crushingly broke the trend, interposed as they were between the Second and the Third Long Peace?

We begin with the great power wars that took place between 1854 and 1871 and disturbed the nineteenth century's relative peacefulness. These were the Crimean War (1854–6), the Franco-Austrian War (1859), which led to Italy's unification, the American Civil War (1861–5), and the Wars of German Unification (1864, 1866, 1870–1). What were these wars about? With the exception of the Crimean War, caused by traditional great power strategic considerations, it was above all issues of national unity, national independence, and national self-determination that constituted the deepest and most inflammatory motives for these major wars. The same held true for violent conflict in general throughout Europe. The hotspots of conflict were fuelled by aspirations for national unity and independence: conquered and partitioned Poland, fragmented and foreign-dominated Italy, disunited Germany, the territories of a future Belgium briefly stitched to Holland, oppressed Ireland, Habsburg-incorporated Hungary and southern Slav territories, Ottoman-held Balkans, and Alsace-Lorraine, annexed to Germany but retaining affinity for France. Whereas territory is documented to have been the main motive for war in early modern Europe, with trade as the second most common motive, ethno-national conflict is recorded to have been by far the primary cause of major war in the nineteenth century.[1] Thus, while the logic of the new economic realities worked against traditional material causes of war, sharply decreasing the occurrence of war, that logic was sometimes overridden by the rising tide of modern nationalism that engulfed Europe during the nineteenth century. As we have seen before, the survival, preservation, and growth of kin-culture communities is a major factor that intermeshes with economic considerations within the overall evolutionary rationale that underlies our system of desires.

During the past decades, ethno-national wars in the most developed parts of the world have all but disappeared. This is partly due to growing democracy, liberalism, and respect for minority rights, which helps to accommodate ethnic minority groups. However, the decline owes no less to the growing explicit or implicit acceptance of the right for national self-determination voted for by an aspiring national group as a legitimate justification for secession that would not be prevented by force, as in the past. Quebec, Scotland, Belgium, and Catalonia are some major recent cases in point.[2] This development is in itself part of the Modernization Peace, and it is also related to the particularly sharp decline in territorial disputes among advanced liberal democracies.[3] Indeed, the decline in ethno-national (cum territorial) disputes has had far less effect on the less developed parts of the world, where political and ethno-national boundaries often do not coincide, while peaceful secession is seldom allowed. Thus, ethno-national conflicts constitute the main cause of war in the developing parts of the world, as they did in nineteenth-century Europe.[4]

Nationalism was also a major contributing factor in the return of great power war during the first half of the twentieth century, as a significant shift had been taking place in the character of the emergent global industrial economy. From the middle of the nineteenth century onwards, British hegemony and the doctrine of free trade had gone hand in hand. However, by 1900 the great powers (except Britain) had resumed protectionist policies and were expanding them to the undeveloped parts of the world with the New Imperialism. The school of national economists, pioneered by Alexander Hamilton and Friedrich List, argued that nascent industries in newly industrializing countries needed the protection of tariff barriers in their home markets against the products of more established industrial economies, at least until they developed sufficiently to be able to compete successfully. With this in mind, the United States, Germany, France, Russia, and Japan all adopted strong protectionist policies against British manufacturing during their period of industrial take-off in the last decades of the nineteenth century. Steep tariffs did not prevent trade among the leading industrial nations from soaring to the highest levels ever, as a share of production, during the first global age around 1900, increasing economic interdependence. Nonetheless, the tariff barriers were the cause of growing concern for the future: in Britain vis-à-vis the rest of the industrial world by the late nineteenth century; in Germany mostly in relation to continental Europe from the early twentieth century; and in the United States and Japan by the 1930s, after Britain itself had abandoned free trade.

The unforeseen return of empire-building from the 1880s onwards was the corollary of national economic protectionism, and was perhaps the single most significant cause of the growing tensions among the great powers that led to the two world wars. The return of the quest for empire was and remains puzzling, because according to a maxim well recognized at the time 'imperialism does not pay'. Thus, in the middle of the nineteenth century, Britain's policy of choice—in Latin America, China, and the Ottoman realm—was the so-called 'informal imperialism' or 'imperialism of free trade'. Rather than extend direct rule over foreign lands and shoulder the expenses, responsibilities, and commitments involved, Britain only intervened, sometimes by force, to open them, and make sure they were kept open, to trade, investment, and other economic activities.[5] The imperialism of free trade differed from the older tributary imperialism (elements of which obviously lingered on) in that its underlying rationale was not extraction, but mutually beneficial trade. This was supposed to generate growing wealth and the whole range of attendant benefits—in principle, to everybody's advantage. Informal liberal imperialism constituted a radical departure from the past to the degree that the industrial take-off itself constituted a radical departure. To be sure, the process was anything but ideal. The Opium War (1839–42), which forced China to open up to the British export of that drug, is a glaring example of the many abuses involved. Still, in the final analysis, connecting others to the world economy—whether voluntarily, through pressure, or even through force—was their only road to sustained growth and away from the material deprivation, stagnation, zero-sum competition, and high mortality of the premodern world.

The unexpected resurrection of the race for colonies in the late nineteenth and early twentieth centuries is puzzling also because it centred on Africa, the least developed of continents, which accounted for only 1–2 per cent of the world's trade, then as a century later. Contrary to the famous thesis promoted by the British economist and publicist J. M. Hobson and adopted by Lenin, investment in Africa was not only negligible but also brought the lowest returns.[6] By far the lion's share of the world's wealth was derived from home-based production and trade within and among the developed countries, as it continues to be. In a telling confirmation of all of this, it was the British treasury that stood out in its objection to colonial expansion. The point is also illustrated by the fact that Britain and France— the leaders in the new colonial race and possessors of by far the largest empires—were the two powers that sharply declined in their relative share of the world's wealth and power between 1870 and 1914. At the same time, the two powers whose relative share increased spectacularly during that same period, rising to first and second/third place respectively, were the massively industrializing United States and Germany, whose participation in the colonial grab was much more limited.

So if imperialism did not pay, why did it return with such a vengeance? This question preoccupied thinkers at the time and has continued to do so ever since. I expanded on it in *War in Human Civilization*, and shall only repeat the main points here.[7] Obviously, many factors contributed to the New Imperialism, including strategic considerations of security; great improvements in armaments, medicine, and transportation, which made the penetration of Africa that much easier;[8] local initiatives by colonial officials and businessmen; a desire to bring Christianity and civilization to the natives; and, last but not least, the massive popular appeal of and prestige associated with colonial acquisitions. However, the main driving force for imperialism lay elsewhere.

The motives behind the scramble for Africa shifted as the process unfolded and escalated. It was triggered by the British landing in Egypt in 1882 to secure the Suez Canal from a popular revolution against the local government. This was followed by the French attempt to dislodge the British from Egypt by way of an eastward expansion across the Sahara towards the upper Nile. As Britain reacted pre-emptively by occupying the entire Nile basin, the imperial contest took a decisive turn and assumed a new meaning.[9] Because tariff barriers among the industrial countries had already been rising, the fear grew in the system that the emergent global economy might become closed rather than open as the world was being carved into large imperial blocs that would be barred to others. Indeed, by 1900 the erosion in British industrial competitiveness had brought Colonial Secretary Joseph Chamberlain and others to the view that Britain itself should abandon its traditional free trade policy and consolidate its empire into a protectionist trading zone. If this was the direction of the future, each power felt obligated to snap up as many of the territories that were up for grabs as it could, while it could.[10] It was this 'prisoner's dilemma' situation that drove the powers to press their claims in Africa.

A runaway, snowball process ensued. Although colonies in Africa were worthless at the time, they might become profitable in the more distant future, after they were developed by the imperial country as part of a large empire or commonwealth. The same logic made the partition of China look imminent by the last years of the nineteenth century. The 'open door', free trade approach to China came under stress as the building of the Trans-Siberian railroad made it possible for Russia to project military power onto East Asia. Thus, with partition taking place in Africa and looming over China, the British-dominated free trade system was being eroded by the reality and prospect of protectionism, which was a self-reinforcing process and self-fulfilling prophecy.

By the advent of the twentieth century, the Wilhelmine Germans widely felt that the trade barriers in Europe were a major constraint on the continued buoyant growth of German exports and industry. Only a United States of Europe free trade zone or a European common market, or at the very least an economically unified Central Europe (*Mitteleuropa*) would offer German industry sufficient scope to develop, comparable to the vast cross-continents spaces of the United States, the British Empire, and Russia. Furthermore, if the emerging global economy were to be geographically sliced among the powers rather than open to all, Germany, too, would require a large colonial empire, most likely in central Africa (*Mittelafrika*). As the territories in question were already occupied, this would require the transfer to Germany of the Belgian and Portuguese African colonies, hopefully with the consent of the other great powers. However, if Germany's vital policy aims were to prove impossible to achieve peacefully, the use of force might become necessary. Here was the main driving force behind the rising tensions and repeated crises among the powers in the decade before World War I, which eventually erupted into war.

The slide towards national economic protectionism accelerated with the Great Depression. In 1932, Britain abandoned free trade and adopted 'Imperial Preference'. The United States, which itself raised tariffs in the wake of the 1929 crash, would increasingly view the growth of protectionism as inhibiting its recovery. However, by far the most ominous consequences concerned Germany and Japan. For Adolf Hitler, the creation of an economically self-sufficient German Reich whose *Lebensraum* would bestride continental Europe was inseparable from his racist plans and vision of a perpetual global struggle. Much of this also held true for Japan. As it lacked raw materials and was heavily dependent on trade, the erection of protectionist barriers by the other great powers in the early 1930s hit Japan hard. It is therefore not surprising that Japan regarded the establishment of its own economically self-sufficient empire, or 'Greater East Asia Co-Prosperity Sphere', as essential to its survival. Correspondingly, the liberal parliamentary regime in Japan during the 1920s gave way to militarism and authoritarianism.

Thus, all the interconnected aspects of the liberal programme were replaced by their antitheses. In a partitioned global economy, economic power increased national strength, while national strength defended and increased economic power. The size of a nation made little difference in an open international economy, but it became the key to economic success in a closed, neo-mercantilist international economy dominated by power politics. It was again becoming necessary to politically own a territory in order to profit from it. Furthermore, the retreat from economic liberalism spurred, and in turn was spurred by, the rise to power of anti-liberal and anti-democratic political ideologies and regimes, incorporating a creed of violence: communism and fascism.

Is Alternative Modernity Viable? The Past

The question that these past experiences raise concerns the viability of alternative forms of modernization—different from the liberal democratic and capitalist—and their affinity with the Modernization Peace. The liberal political and economic order established in the nineteenth century by Britain, the first industrial nation and the global hegemon of the time, became the paradigm of development and modernization. But this standard would be challenged in different ways by later industrializers and new-comers to the modernization process. Some of the challenges were rela-tively mild, as was their effect on the Modernization Peace. Other challenges, often nourished by political and ideological traditions that were very different from the British, were more sweeping, and their effect on the Modernization Peace was in some cases devastating.

Let us look at the various challenges and their effects on peace in an ascending order. Lowest on the scale of challenges, the economic protec-tionism increasingly adopted by liberal democracies between 1870 and 1945 did not noticeably increase their belligerency vis-à-vis one another. As we have seen, the pacifying economic elements of industrialization encompass more than free trade, and these elements, together with the other—political, social, and normative—elements of the Modernization Peace held, and indeed continued to grow, in the democracies during that period. On the other hand, protectionism did increase the propensity of liberal democracies to get involved in (largely reactive) wars with industrializing non-democratic, non-liberal countries. Although the latter also exhibited a very marked decrease in belligerency compared to premodern times, their residual ten-dency to fight among themselves and against liberal democracies escalated when strong protectionist pressures pervaded the system and reinforced nationalistic tensions. Further up the scale, fascism, as a broad generic term—encompassing Nazism as its most extreme manifestation, as well as 1930s to 1945 Japan—constituted the most sweeping rejection of all aspects of the liberal political and economic model. It framed itself as a full-blown alternative route to modernity, retrospectively labelled 'reactionary mod-ernism'. Fascism's strong militant streak shattered the Modernization Peace. Finally, communism was another projected alternative route to modernity, competing in a three-way contest with capitalist democracy and fascism for which of them would inherit the future. The Soviet Union, at the head of the communist camp, felt itself weaker than the capitalist world, believed time was on its side, and, in addition, was self-sufficient in raw materials and therefore much less pressured than Germany or Japan to break the mould by taking direct military action. The Soviet bloc also shared in some aspects of the Modernization Peace, such as the premium given to internal industrial growth. Still, sharp ideological differences and commitment to armed revolution involved the Soviets in an intense cold war with the non-communist world, already before, and certainly after, World War II.

The last vestiges of autocratic rule in the industrially advanced world were defeated in World War I. The fascist challengers were almost literally pulverized in World War II, while the communist challengers were voluntarily dissolving themselves, in both China and the Soviet Union, by the 1980s. Thus, as the twentieth century drew to a close, the notion that there was ultimately only one successful road to modernity—the democratic capitalist one—was increasingly promoted as the verdict of History.[11] Capitalist liberal democracy was supposed to possess intrinsic selective advantages, which conferred an air of inevitability on the past as well as on the future. However, while capitalist democracy may still inherit the earth, this is far from being a foregone conclusion, 'proved' by past experience or the lessons of history. Famously, history is written by the victors. There is a strong tendency to read history backwards and view the final outcome—which may be strongly affected by contingent factors—as predetermined and, indeed, a vindication of the victors' path. Thus, what is called for is a careful scrutiny of the reasons for the triumph during the twentieth century of capitalist democracy over alternative and competing modernization projects. We shall then inquire what this past experience may teach us as we advance into the twenty-first century, with special attention to the Modernization Peace.

There are two main, interrelated, perspectives on the question of why the democracies won: that of great power politics and that of internal development. We begin with the former—with great power conflict and war. I argue that there were very different reasons for the defeat of the communist, as opposed to the capitalist non-democratic, challengers. The communist great powers, the Soviet Union and China, even though they were larger and therefore had the potential to be more powerful than the capitalist democracies, ultimately lost because they proved to be economically inefficient. It was their *system* that failed. Communism did not work, as both China and the Soviet Union separately recognized around 1980 and embarked on dismantling it, irrespective of their militarized conflict with the capitalist camp.

On the other hand, the capitalist non-democratic great powers were not defeated because of inefficiency. Economically and technologically, Germany was at least as advanced as its rivals in both world wars, and Japan exhibited the fastest growth rate of any country between 1913 and 1939. Their problem was that they happened to be too small. Both Germany and Japan were middle-sized countries with a limited resource and manpower base. Unable to contend with the giants, most notably the continent-sized US, they were crushed under the weight of the coalitions assembled against them. The reason for their fall was therefore largely contingent. Throughout the twentieth century, the United States' power consistently surpassed that of the next two strongest states combined (see the data below), and this decisively tilted the global balance of power in favour of the democracies. If any factor gave the liberal democracies their edge, it was above all the actual existence and continental size of the US rather than any inherent advantage of liberal democracy. The United States has been the butt of every criticism, some more justified than others. Yet it has not been fully recognized that only because the twentieth century was the American century, was it also the century of democratic victories.[12]

Put differently, if it were not for the existence of the United States, the liberal democracies would most likely have *lost* the great struggles of the twentieth century. For a start, Britain and France would probably have lost to Germany in either of the two world wars. This is a sobering thought, making the world created by the twentieth century's conflicts appear much more contingent—and tenuous—than unilinear theories of development and the view of history as Progress would have us believe. In a very real sense, we might have had a very different—and non-democratic—twentieth century, a very different world today, and a very different story to tell in the form of grand theories of development. If it were not for the 'US factor', the judgement of later generations on liberal democracy would probably have echoed the negative verdict on democracy's performance issued by the Greeks in the fourth century BC, in the wake of Sparta's defeat of Athens in the Peloponnesian War—a verdict reiterated by political philosophers down to the eighteenth century. We are inclined to rationalize backwards, but the lessons of history are a tricky thing.[†]

[†] I have recently read a similar view expressed by Nobel laureate Daniel Kahneman in his *Thinking, Fast and Slow* (2011). Based on the findings of experimental psychology, he concludes: 'we believe we understand the past, which implies that the future also should be knowable, but in fact we understand the past less than we believe we do' (p. 201). 'The idea that large historical

We now turn to the domestic development argument. It is widely held that after crossing a certain threshold in terms of development—wealth per capita, education, urbanization, and so forth—societies tend to democratize. This has been the case during the latter part of the twentieth century in East and Southeast Asia, southern Europe, and Latin America.[13] But again, I argue that this notion is an abstraction from a very particular set of circumstances that prevailed after 1945, with the result that the sample is skewed. This is so because all the post-1945 cases of development leading to democratization involved small countries, which after the defeat of the capitalist non-democratic great powers—Germany and Japan—could only choose between the communist and capitalist-democratic camps. If they chose the latter, they were invariably exposed to the massive pressures of the hegemonic liberal democratic centre, pressures that contributed decisively to their eventual democratization. Presently, Singapore is the only example of a truly developed economy that still maintains elements of a semi-authoritarian regime, and it too is unlikely to withstand the pressures from the hegemonic centre for long. But are Singapore-like great powers that prove resistant to the influence of the liberal order possible?

Is Alternative Modernity Viable? The Future

The supreme relevance of this question derives from the return to the international arena of capitalist non-democratic great powers, a category that has been absent from the system since 1945. Both China and Russia belong to this category, although very different from each other in some crucial respects. As this passage is written, Putin's Russia captures the headlines with its invasion and annexation of Crimea, militarized involvement in the Ukraine and Syria, and growing antagonism with the West. However, Russia's oligarchic and kleptocratic brand of authoritarian capitalism is shakily built on the 2000s bonanza in the price of oil and gas. Despite its

events are determined by luck is profoundly shocking, although it is demonstrably true. It is hard to think of the history of the twentieth century, including its large social movements, without bringing in the role of Hitler, Stalin, and Mao Zedong. But there was a moment in time, just before an egg was fertilized, when there was a fifty-fifty chance that the embryo that became Hitler could have been a female. Compounding the three events, there was a probability of one-eighth of a twentieth century without any of the three great villains and it is impossible to argue that history would have been roughly the same in their absence. The fertilization of these three eggs had momentous consequences, and it makes a joke of the idea that long-term developments are predictable' (p. 218).

renewed assertiveness, Russia remains a poor and, on the whole, weak country, and is unlikely to break through to the rank of the advanced economies
unless it is able to revive its manufacturing sector, building on its educated
workforce. China is far more important than Russia, and the greatest challenge for the future. Its population is nearly ten times larger than Russia's,
and its manufacturing and trade-driven growth has been spectacular. China
is the giant in the international system, formerly held far back by an inefficient communist economy, but, switching to capitalism while retaining an
authoritarian regime, it is fast realizing its huge potential. Although still only
around a quarter to a sixth as rich as the developed world in terms of GDP
per capita, China is fast narrowing the gap. Given its huge size, China has
already become the world's second most powerful country, and its power is
expected to continue to grow, as we shall later see. China thus presents a
new, historically unprecedented combination: a non-democratic superpower that is both big and capitalist. All extrapolations from past experience
are of limited value.

What effect China's rise will have on the international system, American
supremacy, the liberal hegemony, and the Modernization Peace may be the
most significant question of the twenty-first century. Whether or not China
will eventually undergo political liberalization and democratization is probably the most intriguing question, with a major bearing on all the above.
Furthermore, might China democratize along a different path, espousing a
populist-nationalist creed and becoming what has been dubbed an 'illiberal
democracy'?[14] Finally, even if the peaceful scenarios eventually materialize,
what major convulsions, including militarized confrontations, may shake
the world before the process runs its course? All these are open questions
that at present can only be regarded as thought experiments. I discussed the
reasons for democracy's past triumphs, the US' crucial role in securing them,
the return of the capitalist non-democratic great powers, and factors relevant to the future of China in an article and ensuing debate in *Foreign Affairs*,
and a subsequent book. Readers interested in the range of arguments on
these questions are referred there.[15] The following is a brief summary of
some of the questions concerning both the viability of an alternative capitalist non-democratic form of modernity and China's future trajectory.

With respect to the economy, it is widely argued that the more advanced
stages of the information age require an open and individualistic culture.
However, while evidence to the contrary from Imperial and Nazi Germany
and Imperial Japan may be regarded as outdated, semi-authoritarian Singapore

and Chinese-ruled Hong Kong both have highly successful information economies. It is also contended that, because of a lack of political account- ability and transparency, China will increasingly suffer from the ill effects of 'crony' favouritism and corruption, already much in evidence there today, as in most developing economies. However, as Alan Greenspan, the former chairman of the US Federal Reserve Bank, writes, Singapore is one of the *least* corrupt states in the world,[16] as indeed was Imperial Germany and its Prussian predecessor. For Max Weber, Prussian-German bureaucracy became paradigmatic, and it was, indeed, proverbial for its efficiency and clean hands. Whether or not China can put its house in order and enforce similar standards is an open question.

Hong Kong, where large-scale pro-democratic demonstrations erupted in 2014, brings us to the political arguments. It is widely held that economic and social development creates pressures for democratization that an authoritarian state structure will not be able to contain. It has been sug- gested, for example, that capitalism is based on the exercise of individual choice, and thus non-democratic capitalist regimes supposedly suffer from an internal contradiction that inclines them to implode.[17] This argument appears very convincing, until one remembers that capitalist democracy itself is a combination that has always been torn between the economic inequality generated by capitalism and democracy's overwhelming egalitar- ian drive.[18] This tension is so stark that socialists regarded it as an irreconcil- able contradiction that was certain to doom capitalist democracy, and that preordained socialism—economic democratization—as the wave of the future. Some of the tension has since been alleviated through the institution of the welfare state, but much of it remains. All the same, in real life, people regularly live with tensions and contradictions, and the question is which of them prove to be the more significant and irreconcilable.

Without ideological legitimacy and a guiding ethos no regime can stand for long. Unlike Russia, China is still ruled by a communist party, although in reality it is no longer communist. The Party's raison d'être and source of legitimacy since the beginning of market reforms in the late 1970s have been successful economic modernization and the maintenance of social sta- bility during that process. The Party is insecure, highly pragmatic, and ready to adopt any measure that would sustain its power and continue the process. Institutionally, the regime in China is trying to broaden its base, co-opt the business elite into the Party, and democratize the Party itself. It is experi- menting with various forms of popular participation, including village and some town elections, and public opinion surveys.[19] The internet is widely used in these experiments, as well as being heavily and quite effectively censored.[20] Analysts have dubbed these experiments 'deliberative dictatorship'. A possible ideology for China would emphasize Chinese traditions, incorporate Confucian values of meritocracy, hierarchy, public service, social order, and harmony, and be presented as a contrast to foreign liberal divisiveness and individual egotism. This has been dubbed mandarin rule without an emperor. In addition, nationalism is likely to be a powerful source of mobilization.

Critics argue that capitalist authoritarianism has no universal message to offer the world, nothing attractive to sell that people can aspire to, and hence no 'soft power' for winning hearts and minds. But there is a flip side to the universalist coin. Many around the world find liberal universalism dogmatic, intrusive, and oppressive. Resistance to a 'unipolar' world concerns not only American power but also the hegemony of human rights liberalism. There is a deep and widespread aversion in non-Western societies to being lectured by the West. Contrary to perception in the West, liberal democracy is not merely a neutral mechanism for choosing between values. It is itself an ideological choice, incorporating a whole set of values that many societies and cultures find to be deeply in conflict with other values they cherish more dearly. Throughout East and Southeast Asia, the world's fastest developing and most populous region, there is a widely voiced public sentiment in favour of traditional 'Asian values', promoted against Western cultural imperialism and emphasizing group values, social harmony, and hierarchy.[21] While cultures and social values are not immutable, nor are they inconsequential 'superstructures'.

A message need not necessarily be formulated in universalistic terms to have a broader appeal. Fascism during the 1920s and 1930s was a very particularistic creed: it was nationalistic, based on 'my country'. Still, it had a lot of devotees and people who imitated it outside Italy, Germany, and Japan. Everybody applied it to their own particular country and society. Indeed, East and Southeast Asia are not alone in their ambivalence towards Western liberalism and potential attraction to alternative models of modernity. Latin America, Central Asia, the Middle East, and Africa may also be particularly susceptible to the capitalist non-democratic model. In many of these regions Chinese economic involvement by way of trade, investment, and development has been booming, and it comes with no strings attached, no requests to reform the domestic system, and no humanitarian criteria to meet. In addition to a policy of non-interference, China offers a message of particularism, international ideological pluralism, state sovereignty, strong state involvement, and indigenous cultural development.[22]

In recent years, China has stepped up its rhetoric against and domestic repression of what it defines as the infiltration of Western values. Whether this will turn out to be a rearguard action in an ultimately futile struggle or something more ominous only the future will tell. All in all, loss of legitimacy because of failures, inertia, stagnation, and public weariness is perhaps the greatest future hazard for the regime. Democratic regimes may have a crucial inherent advantage in this respect, as they offer the option of a change of government while the system itself remains. However, whether or not this arguably general weakness of non-democracies will apply in a particular single case is impossible to predict. Indeed, China is a *huge* single case, which—as with the United States during the twentieth century, and today—makes its significance so exceptional and its trajectory crucial for shaping the rest of the world.

Russia, for its part, has a long tradition of deep ambivalence towards Western values, stretching as far back as the early modern period, if not earlier. Envy of and a sense of inferiority towards the Western model have coexisted and alternated with a strong sentiment of Russian and Slavic special identity and mission: religious, spiritual, and ideological. Perception of the West as advanced, civilized, and successful has always competed with its image as immoral, profane, and degenerate, celebrating individual egotism and hedonism, and practising false morals and double standards. Noble laureate author Aleksandr Solzhenitsyn expressed this outlook most typically during his exile in the West and in post-Soviet Russia. After what the Russians now feel was a disappointing and humiliating embrace of the West during the 1990s, a powerful backlash has taken place under Putin. There are good reasons to think that Russia's deep historical ambivalence towards all things Western might continue into the future. Will China and Russia ultimately converge into the liberal democratic range, or are they big enough to chart a different course and challenge the hegemonic model, creating a non-democratic but economically advanced and militarily powerful new Second World?

Before the outbreak of the Great Recession in 2007–8, when the capitalist-democratic model was still at the apex of its prestige, practically nobody suspected that triumphalism was soon to be replaced by a profound crisis and deep malaise. It was purely hypothetical on my part to suggest at the time that even in its current bastions in the West—in Europe and the United States—the liberal political and economic consensus may be vulnerable to the effects of a lingering economic recession. It was somewhat less speculative to suggest that liberal Europe may become vulnerable to a resurgence of ethnic strife and deeply concerned by non-integrating immigrant communities. I further suggested at the time that if the hegemonic core were to be shaken, the effect might be even greater in other parts of the world, where adherence to liberalism and democracy was either non-existent or more recent, incomplete, and insecure.

In the meantime, the world has experienced the worst economic crisis since the Great Depression. Indeed, analogies to the 1930s, when fascist and communist totalitarianism throve on the apparent failure of capitalist democracy, are inescapable. One hopes that the current economic crisis will not be nearly as catastrophic politically. And yet the hegemonic model's loss of much of its aura—as in the dramatic reversal in the image of the European Union within one decade, from the paradigm of the future to a deeply problematic and dysfunctional basket case—has left a strong impression. The recent election of Donald Trump as president of the United States has shocked many, and only time will tell to what extent their concerns are justified. Winston Churchill famously suggested that 'democracy is the worst form of government, except for all those other forms that have been tried from time to time'. Nonetheless, the more dysfunctional and crisis-ridden the liberal democratic countries appear, the greater the self-confidence and global allure of state-driven and nationalist capitalist authoritarianism might become. Illiberal popular parties that became marginal in Europe after 1945 are staging a comeback, both on the continent and around the world. The 'Third Wave' of democratic expansion since the 1970s has created an unprecedented situation whereby some 60 per cent of the world's countries hold more or less democratic elections and 40 per cent are classified as liberal. However, while not reversing, the trend has stalled since the beginning of the twenty-first century, and in some respects there has been a regression, prompting comments about an 'Authoritarian Resurgence'.[23]

Images and moods swing wildly from decade to decade (Japan was the envied model during the 1980s, before plunging into stagnation and structural crisis). Therefore, one should strive to ignore the hype and seek out the fundamentals. If before the outbreak of the Great Recession it was advisable to be cautious about the euphoria surrounding capitalist liberal democracy, the current gloom in many of the countries concerned is—despite very serious problems—probably just as exaggerated. By the same token, the massive challenges and obstacles that China faces and its structural weaknesses, as well as huge and yet unfulfilled potential, remain as clear at present as they were in 2007. As China gradually exhausts its reservoir of cheap rural labour with industrialization and increasing affluence, the country's hectic growth is slowing down. It is likely to remain lower than it was during the initial phase of China's economic take-off, despite the Chinese advance up the market towards technologically more sophisticated and high-value industries. With its low birth rate, which is unlikely to change much even after the lifting of the state-imposed one-child policy, China's population is aging fast. Unlike in earlier cases of modernization, it is predicted to grow old before it gets rich. The abilities of China's regime to fight corruption, retain domestic legitimacy when setbacks and crises inevitably occur after a long period of economic growth, and withstand pressures to embrace political liberalization and democratization remain open questions. Internationally, the more assertive China becomes vis-à-vis its neighbours, the more it might generate a backlash and actually lose influence over them. Indeed, in a replay of Germany's tragic course a century earlier, China might prompt a coalition to contain it, stretching all the way from Japan to India, with the backing of the United States. China's national traditions lack the militaristic streak of Prussia-Germany and the militant revolutionary revisionism of the former communist powers. At the same time, its historical self-perception as the centre of the world and its huge size suggest that the restraint it has shown since the beginning of its massive transformation may be hard to sustain. Furthermore, the combination of a regime that is insecure about its legitimacy, and resurgent nationalism does not augur well, as Imperial Germany and Putin's Russia suggest.

A comparison between the consequences of the 1929 and 2008 crises as concerns the United States is of particular importance. Having been the world's only superpower and a widely envied model of success during the 1920s, the United States was dealt a crushing blow by the Great Depression. It withdrew inwardly, leaving the scene open to the Axis' advance. At present, the United States has been experiencing isolationist pressures, fuelled by a number of costly and messy foreign entanglements. Simultaneously, American might, unrivalled during the brief unipolar moment in the 1990s, is widely expected to undergo relative decline.[24]

Here too, in view of the United States' pivotal role and the periodical sharp ups and downs in mood and image over the past hundred years concerning American power, both inside and outside the United States, an assessment of the fundamentals is called for. As the data in the tables below reveal, American economic-military potential was remarkably steady during the entire twentieth century, consistently comprising close to a third of the world's economic-military power (except for a brief spike after World War II, when Europe and Japan lay in ruins). Moreover, throughout the century, the United States was always more powerful than both the second and third most powerful countries combined. As noted earlier, American power preponderance was the most crucial political fact of the twentieth century, which decided the century's three great conflicts in favour of the democracies. However, the remarkable past resilience of America's share of world power does not guarantee that it will remain at the same level in the future. Indeed, with the expansion of industrialization and the market economy to other parts of the world, America's relative share of world power necessarily erodes. Moreover, giant and still developing China has four times the population of the United States and is capitalist—an unprecedented combination.

The Global Balance of Power

Economic capability and military power have been closely correlated since the beginning of the industrial-technological age, because the former translated into the ability to sustain war and win both the quantitative and qualitative race in the production of military hardware. In all the great powers' clashes of the industrial age the economically stronger side almost invariably won.[25] Tables 7.1 and 7.2 present measurements of economic power and the corresponding military potential for the major powers during the nineteenth and twentieth centuries (measured by GDP and GDP per capita). Originally appearing in my *War in Human Civilization*, they are followed by an update to the present and some projection into the future (Tables 7.3 and 7.4, and Diagrams 7.1 and 7.2).

Before proceeding to examine the statistics, the customary disclaimers are in order. What measurements best reflect economic power cum military potential is not an easy question (see extended note[26]). The data are inherently crude and inexact, especially with respect to undeveloped countries, today and in the past. Other data sets than those chosen here have somewhat different figures, and I had to make a choice which data set

Table 7.1. GDP (in PPP), world share, population (in millions), GDP/ca. (PPP), infrastructural power as percentage from the leader (1820–1913)

	1820	1870	1913
UK	$36,232m (5.2%) 21m♦ $1,707 (25–20%)	$100,179m (9.1%) 31m♦ $3,191 (100%)	$224,618m (8.3%) 45m♦ $4,921 (40%)
Germany	$26,349m (5.5%) 24m♦ $1,058 (15–12%)	$71,429m (6.5%) 39m♦ $1,821 (53–61%)	$237,332m (8.8%) 65m♦ $3,648 (37–40%)
France	$38,434m (5.5%) 31m♦ $1,230 (23–19%)	$72,100m (6.5%) 38m♦ $1,876 (55–62%)	$144,489m (5.3%) 41m♦ $3,485 (19–25%)
Italy	$22,535m (3.2%) 20m♦ $1,117 (13–10%)	$41,814m (3.8%) 27m♦ $1,499 (26–33%)	$95,487m (3.5%) 37m♦ $2,564 (12–15%)
Russia	$37,710m (5.4%) 54m♦ $689 (16–15%)	$83,646m (7.6%) 88m♦ $943 (44–60%)	$232,351m (8.6%) 156m♦ $1,488 (23–31%)
USA	$12,548m (1.8%) 10m♦ $1,257 (7–6%)	$98,374m (8.9%) 40m♦ $2,445 (85–90%)	$517,383m (19.1%) 97m♦ $5,301 (100%)
China	$229,237m (32.9%) 382m♦ $600 (100%)	$189,349m (17.2%) 357m♦ $530 (76–120%)	$241,084m (8.9%) 436m♦ $552 (14–26%)
India	$111,483m (16%) 209m♦ $533 (44%)		
Japan	$20,903m (3%) 31m♦ $669 (9–8%)	$25,319m (2.3%) 34m♦ $737 (10–17%)	$63,302m (2.3%) 45m♦ $1,387 (6–8%)

PPP—purchasing power parity; 1990 international USD[27]

seemed more reliable or made more sense. Furthermore, many factors other than economic strength played a role in determining war outcomes. Inter alia, these include political institutions and leadership, social cohesion, geography, economic self-sufficiency (especially in raw materials), investment in the armed forces, military effectiveness, and other material and non-material factors. That acknowledged, the data regarding the economic infrastructure of states' potential military power in the industrial-technological age are illuminating.

Table 7.2. GDP (in PPP), world share, population (in millions), GDP/ca. (PPP), infrastructural power as percentage from the leader (1938–1998)

	1938	1973	1998
USA	$800,300m 130m♦ $6,134 (100%)	$3,536,622m (22%) 212m♦ $16,689 (100%)	$7,394,598m (21.9%) 270m♦ $27,331 (100%)
Russia (USSR)	$359,000m 167m♦ $2,150 (26–34%)	$1,513,070m (9.4%) 250m♦ $6,058 (25–33%)	$664,495m (3.4%) 147m♦ $4,523 (3–5%)
Germany	$351,400m 68m♦ $5,126 (40–42%)	$944,755m (5.9%) 79m♦ $11,966 W&E (22–24%)	$1,460,069m (4.3%) 82m♦ $17,799 (15–17%)
UK	$284,200m 47m♦ $5,983 (35%)	$675,941m (4.2%) 56m♦ $12,022 (16–17%)	$1,108,568m (3.3%) 59m♦ $18,714 (12–13%)
France	$185,600m 42m♦ $4,424 (19–21%)	$683,965m (4.3%) 52m♦ $13,123 (17–18%)	$1,150,080m (3.4%) 58m♦ $19,558 (13–14%)
Italy	$140,800m (3.2%) 43m♦ $3,244 (13–15%)	$582,713m (3.6%) 54m♦ $10,643 (13–14%)	$1,022,776m (3%) 57m♦ $17,759 (11–12%)
Western Europe		$4,133,780m (25.7%) 358m♦ $11,534 (97–106%)	$6,960,616m (20.6%) 388m♦ $17,921 (76–84%)
China	$320,500m 411m♦ $778 (14–24%)	$736,588m (4.6%) 877m♦ $839 (4–10%)	$3,883,008m (11.5%) 1245m♦ $3,117 (21–30%)
India		$501,780m (3.1%) 588m♦ $853 (3–6%)	$1,688,264m (5%) 966m♦ $1746 (5–11%)
Japan	$169,400m 72m♦ $2,356 (13–17%)	$1,232,985m (7.7%) 107m♦ $11,439 (28–31%)	$2,582,000m (7.7%) 126m♦ $20,413 (30–32%)

PPP—purchasing power parity; 1990 international USD

While there are some GDP estimates for the various countries during the span of the twenty-first century, they involve many assumptions and are therefore too speculative. I produce here (Table 7.4) one short-term projection as an indication of very broad trends.

The past data and future projections suggest broadly familiar trends. The relative share of the developed countries in the world's economy is

Table 7.3. Distribution of world power, 2014[28]

Country	GDP in PPP billions of USD and world share	Population in millions in	GDP per/ca. PPP USD	Infrastructural power as percentage from the leader
USA	17,460 (16.2%)	320	52,800	100%
European Union (28)	17,610 (16.4%)	506	34,500	79–91%
China	17,630 (16.4%)	1,369	9,800	42–66%
Japan	4,807 (4.5%)	126	37,100	22–25%
India	7,277 (6.8%)	1,279	4,000	11–22%
Russia	3,568 (3.3%)	146	18,000	12–15%

shrinking, but not in equal measure among the various countries concerned. Thus, the decrease in the United States' share of world power is more moderate than that of other developed countries. It is expected to decrease from close to a third of the world's economic-military potential during the twentieth century to perhaps a quarter to a fifth by 2030. However, two main factors moderate this relative decrease. First, as an immigrant country, the United States is a demographic pump whose population continues to grow steadily, whereas all the other centres of world power experience an aging and ultimately shrinking population.[29] Having crossed the 100 million mark in population just after World War I, and the 200 million mark in the 1960s, the United States reached 300 million in the 2000s and is predicted to reach 400 million around the middle of the twenty-first century. It still has only around a quarter of the population density of Europe or China, and a tenth that of Japan or India. Second, due to its strong entrepreneurial spirit and the enduring fact that 'the business of America is business', American economic adaptability and agility remain superior.[30]

Japan is expected to show the most dramatic erosion of economic power and military potential, owing to a shrinking and aging population (coupled with a particularly restrictive immigration policy) and a stagnant economy. The European Union may be entering a similar trajectory, albeit less steeply, due to demographic and economic problems. At the same time, Europe is expected to keep its place as the second largest concentration of economic power, after the United States, until the 2030s,

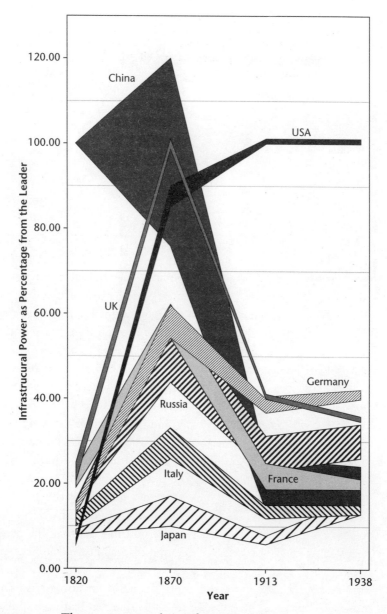

Diagram 7.1. The great powers: their infrastructural power as percentage from the leader (nineteenth to early twentieth centuries)

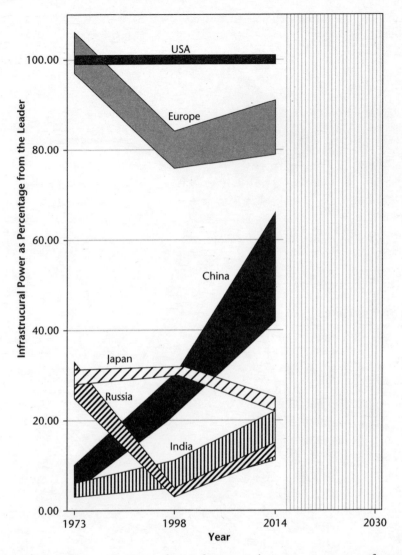

Diagram 7.2. The great powers: their infrastructural power as percentage from the leader (twentieth century into the future)

although probably not later. Europe's low rate of military investment compared to other powers (as a share of GDP), which has been described as free-riding on American might extending back to the Cold War era, has crystallized into an entrenched cultural norm. That, as well as the European Union's loose political organization, has prevented Europe

Table 7.4. The balance of power: GDP (nominal) and world share, GDP/ca. (nominal)—projection[31]

	2000	2013	2030
USA	12,713 (26%) 45,013	15,902 (22.8%) 50,249	24,821 (20.2%) 69,878
European Union (28 states)	14,235 (29.2%) 29,069	16,560 (23.8%) 32,450	22,601 (20.2%) 43,516
China	2,188 (4.5%) 1,732	7,513 (10.8%) 5,567	22,165 (18%) 15,930
Japan	5,090 (10.4%) 40,150	5,631 (8.1%) 44,257	6,417 (5.2%) 53,144
India	821 (1.7%) 817	1,988 (2.9%) 1,629	6,593 (5.4%) 4,514
Russia	951 (1.9%) 6,471	1,666 (2.4%) 11,693	2,433 (2.0%) 17,610

Table 7.5. The great powers: manufacturing output (and world share)—historical[32]

	1830	1860–80	1913	1938	1973
UK	17.5 (9.5%)	45–73 (19.9–22.9%)	127 (13.6%)	181 (10.7%)	462 (4.9%)
France	9.5 (5.2%)	18–25 (7.9–7.8%)	57 (6.1%)	74 (4.4%)	328 (3.3%)
Germany	6.5 (3.5%)	11–27 (4.9–8.5%)	137 (14.8%)	214 (12.7%)	550 (5.9%)
Austria	5.8 (3.2%)	9.5–14 (4.2–4.4%)	40 (4.4%)		
Italy	4.6 (2.4%)	5.7–8.0 (2.5–2.5%)	22 (2.4%)	46 (2.8%)	258 (2.9%)
Russia	10.3 (5.6%)	16–24 (7.0–7.6%)	76 (8.2%)	152 (9%)	1,345 (14.4%)
USA	4.6 (2.4%)	16–47 (7.2–14.7%)	298 (32%)	528 (31.4%)	3,089 (33%)
China	54.9 (29.8%)	44–40 (19.7–12.5%)	33 (3.6%)	52 (3.1%)	369 (3.9%)
India	32.5 (17.6%)				194 (2.1%)
Japan	5.2 (2.8%)	5.8–7.6 (2.6–2.4%)	25 (2.7%)	88 (5.2%)	819 (8.8%)

UK in 1900=100

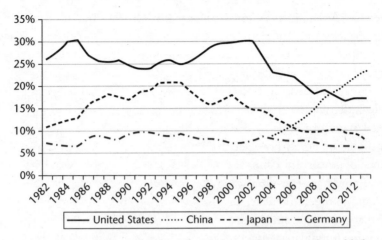

Diagram 7.3. Select countries' share of manufacturing value added

from becoming a military giant in its own right, almost equal to the United States. Russia stands on feet of clay as far as the economic foundations of military power are concerned, even more than during the days of the Soviet Union. The country's poor standing is partly concealed and offset under Putin by its assertive policy, high level of investment in the armed forces, dangling of the nuclear card, and the surge in oil and gas prices during the 2000s.

The most significant advances are registered by China, followed by India, by far the world's most populous countries, which have vastly accelerated their economic growth since their embrace of the market. China, which was still very weak in terms of infrastructural power in the 1970s, grew to become around half as powerful as the United States by 2013. Furthermore, China's power potential is poised to match that of the United States in the foreseeable future, perhaps as early as the 2030s. This may create a situation of power parity at the top, unprecedented since the onset of the twentieth century, and much greater bi-polarity than existed during the Cold War, when the Soviet Union maintained huge conventional and nuclear forces but was greatly inferior to the United States in economic size. Moreover, when reaching parity, China will still have only a half to a third the per capita wealth of the developed world. Thus, without making assumptions of 'present trends continuing' regarding its specific future growth rates (evidently slowing down), while at the same time remembering the steep trajectory of economic growth and high levels of modernization achieved by earlier East Asian 'tigers', China's potential will be far from exhausted at the point of parity. In combination with its huge size, this suggests that its power may surpass that of the United States towards the middle of the twenty-first century (even if it would still lag behind in GDP per capita). India's growth, although for a long time slower than China's, is nonetheless impressive. While India is projected to be in a very different league from either the United States or China by the 2030s, it is likely to become a major power.

It should be noted, however, that despite the erosion of America's preponderance of power and China's steep rise, the change in the overall global balance of power may be significantly less dramatic. In a world that the United States did so much to create, it is the pivot of a democratic and capitalist alliance that comprises, among the world's greatest concentrations of power, the European Union, Japan, other major East Asian and Pacific allies, and, increasingly it would seem, India. Taken together, this bloc's share of the world's economic-military potential is, and may remain, as preponderant as that of any of the American-centred coalitions of the twentieth century. Although the democratic-capitalist alignment is far from being cohesive around the United States, and military cooperation between the countries concerned in case of a great power conflict presupposes very extreme circumstances indeed, this alignment still comprises more than half of the world's military potential. This is roughly on a par with the Allies' economic-military might that crushed the Axis powers in World War II. The current distribution of power is roughly mirrored by the major countries' share of global military expenditure. As of 2013, the United States' share of that expenditure was a staggering 37 per cent, with China second at 11 per cent. China is rapidly increasing its defence budget; it is likely to narrow the gap as its wealth grows, and may close it by the 2030s. However, after Russia (5 per cent) and Saudi Arabia (3.8 per cent), the big spenders as a share of the world's military expenditure include France (3.5 per cent), Britain (3.3 per cent), Germany (2.8 per cent), Japan (2.8 per cent), India (2.7 per cent), South Korea (1.9 per cent), Italy (1.9 per cent), and Australia (1.4 per cent).[33] All of these are liberal democracies and American allies (India informally). One hopes that China's leaders, rumoured to be obsessed with measurements of countries' power, do not fail to consider this aspect of the global balance of power.

There is much truth in the claim that the United States cannot play the 'world's policeman' in every corner of the world and exhaust itself with unlimited military commitments abroad. Rather than the world's policeman, the United States' crucial role is as the *system*'s policeman. The United

States remains the 'indispensable nation' in the twenty-first century as it was in the twentieth century for the cause of a world order which is both politically and economically liberal—the most peaceful brand of the Modernization Peace. It is possible that as the twenty-first century progresses the United States will be less able to serve effectively as the insurer of last resort that it was during the twentieth century, guaranteeing the victory of liberal democracy even after the catastrophic disasters and setbacks in the two world wars. All the same, if not guaranteeing the victory of the liberal order, the United States remains the main buttress against its decline or even destruction. It is primarily in this crucial sense that American 'exceptionalism' is more exceptional than that of other countries.

I do not profess to know whether or not a capitalist non-democratic 'alternative modernity' is here to stay. My only claim is that those who do purport to know that it is not base their claims on an interpretation of twentieth-century history that may be skewed in some crucial ways. The future is open, even if it is not *wide* open, as what may presently be judged to be lower-probability events and developments could materialize. It may well be that because the United States-centred coalition (with the decisive contribution of the Soviet Union) was able to defeat the democracies' most pernicious enemies in 1945, crushing both the popular Nazi dictatorship and deeply entrenched traditions of Imperial Japan and forcefully democratizing these countries, a tipping point has been reached. Inter alia, its victory in 1945 may have earned liberal democracy the opportunity to demonstrate its merits and win the popularity and legitimacy contest. Liberal democracy was then able to further extend its hegemony with the collapse of communism, the Soviet Union, and the Soviet bloc. This could mean that not even a giant like China, in combination with Russia, would be able to withstand or reverse the global wave at this stage. If so, a highly favourable causal chain or developmental path during the twentieth century may prove decisive in shaping the twenty-first century. Or it may prove less decisive than that, as only time will tell.

Political liberalization and democratization in China, if they occur (and if they go hand in hand), may become the final major step towards a global ascendency of the Modernization Peace. But as we have seen, while liberal democracy is a strong contributing factor to the Modernization Peace, this peace is a broad phenomenon that also encompasses non-democratic (and non-capitalist) countries which share elements of it other than democracy. Thus, peace may prevail even if China does not democratize, or takes a very

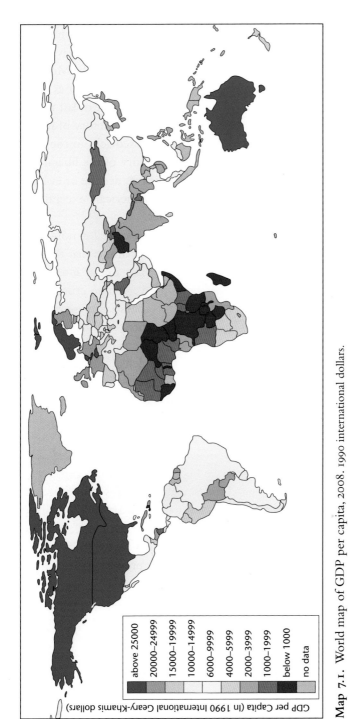

Map 7.1. World map of GDP per capita, 2008. 1990 international dollars.

Wealthy, developed regions, marked by the blueish colours, are the most peaceful (oil producers are a partial exception), while the poorest, least developed regions, marked by the brownish shades, have the greatest potential for war.

GDP per Capita (in 1990 International Geary-Khamis dollars)

- above 25000
- 20000–24999
- 15000–19999
- 10000–14999
- 6000–9999
- 4000–5999
- 2000–3999
- 1000–1999
- below 1000
- no data

long time to do so. Just how warm that peace might be is anybody's guess. The entire spectrum is possible: from more or less cordial economic and political cooperation, to heightened ideological rivalry and arms races fuelled by the security dilemma, to cold war and limited wars—with fluctuations between all of these. Ultimately, only nuclear deterrence may prevent a repeat of what Bismarck called 'some damn foolish thing in the Balkans' from materializing in the South or East China Seas, or around Taiwan, and setting off a major war. It was quite plain during the initial period of China's market reforms that the country's leadership was very conscious of the fact that China was going to become much more powerful with every decade that passed, and that it was best for it to lie low in the international arena until this happened. It was equally easy to predict that China would become more assertive as its power grew—as indeed has been the case. In addition, the regime's insecurity and Chinese nationalism are a potentially combustive blend. Rather than try to predict the future, what follows seeks to sketch out a broad spectrum within which each of the various elements of the Modernization Peace other than democratization might play out, with special reference to the capitalist non-democratic great powers.

Who Fights?

Table 7.6 contains a list of countries that saw inter- or intra-state armed conflicts (at least 1,000 dead) taking place on their territory during the post-Cold War era. They are tabulated according to both region and wealth, measured by nominal GDP per capita (global ranking/2013 dollar value; oil producing countries marked with an asterisk).[34]

Some major features of these armed conflicts stand out. The world's 'zone of war' is located in the poorer parts of the globe (see Map 7.1), mostly in countries with GDP per capita in the lowest 50 per cent of countries (less than 4,000 in 2013 USD). Wealthier countries that experience war on their territory are mostly major oil producers (marked by an asterisk), whose wealth derives largely or mainly from this resource. The reason for this may not necessarily be that oil encourages war, but that the income from it gives a false picture of these countries' level of modernization.[35] Poor countries in general are particularly exposed to intra-state conflict, by far the most common type of armed conflict in today's world, in its two main forms: ethnic strife; and violence conducted by non-state armed

Table 7.6. Scenes of intra- or inter-state war in the post–Cold War era

By region	By wealth
Sub-Saharan Africa:	**From the 10th decile (8 countries)**
Burundi (global ranking: 193; GDP per capita: $229)	Burundi (193/229)
Democratic Republic of Congo (192/286)	Democratic Republic of Congo (192/286)
Ethiopia (191/354)	Ethiopia (191/354)
Liberia (189/356)	Liberia (189/356)
Eritrea (185/507)	Eritrea (185/507)
Mozambique (181/579)	Mozambique (181/579)
Somalia (177/600)	Somalia (177/600)
Rwanda (176/620)	Rwanda (176/620)
Sierra Leone (169/725)	
Chad (167/818)	**From the 9th decile (7 countries)**
South Sudan (161/1,045)	Afghanistan (173/683)
Sudan (151/1,438)	Sierra Leone (169/725)
Nigeria (129/2,966*)	Chad (167/818)
Angola (98/5,668*)	Tajikistan (162/1,036)
	South Sudan (161/1,045)
Middle East (including North Africa):	Burma-Myanmar (158/1,183)
	Pakistan (157/1,238)
Yemen (152/1,422)	
Syria (147/1,606)	**From the 8th decile (4 countries)**
Palestine (131/2,908) (conflicts with Israel 29/37,704)	Yemen (152/1,422)
	Sudan (151/1,438)
Algeria (100/5,325*)	India (149/1,548)
Iraq (97/5,790*) (American & allies involvement)	Syria (147/1,606)
Lebanon (73/9,793) (Israeli and American involvements)	**From the 7th decile (7 countries)**
	Philippines (134/2,765)
Turkey (66/10,972)	Palestine (131/2,908)
Libya (63/12,029*) (NATO involvement)	Nigeria (129/2,966*)
	Sri Lanka (125/3,159)
Kuwait (14/52,198*) (Invaded by Iraq 97/5,790)	Guatemala (122/3,478)
	Armenia (121/3,504)
	Georgia (118/3,715) (conflict with Russia 55/14,680)
South and Southeast Asia:	**From the 6th decile (4 countries)**
Afghanistan (173/683) (American & allies involvement)	El Salvador (115/3,826)
	Ukraine (113/4,024) (involving Russia 55/14,680)
Burma-Myanmar (158/1,183)	East Timor (107/4,362) (conflict with Indonesia 123/3,475)
Pakistan (157/1,238)	
India (149/1,548)	Algeria (100/5,325*)
Sri Lanka (125/3,159)	
Philippines (134/2,765)	

East Timor (107/4,362) (conflict with Indonesia 123/3475★)

Latin America:
Guatemala (122/3,478)
El Salvador (115/3,826)
Peru (90/6,593)
Colombia (79/7,826)
Mexico (69/10,293)

Former Soviet Union and Soviet bloc
Tajikistan (162/1,036)
Armenia (121/3,504)—Azerbaijan (80/7,814★)
Georgia (118/3,715) (conflict with Russia 55/14,680)
Ukraine (113/4,024) (involving Russia 55/14,680)
Former Yugoslavia (Serbia 93/6,313; Kosovo 128/2,972)

From the 5th decile (5 countries)
Angola (98/5,668★)
Iraq (97/5,790★)
Former Yugoslavia (Serbia 93/6,313; Kosovo 128/2,972)
Peru (90/6,593)
Azerbaijan (80/7,814★)

From the 4th decile (5 countries)
Colombia (79/7,826)
Lebanon (73/9,793)
Mexico (69/10,293)
Turkey (66/10,972)
Libya (63/12,029★)

From the 3rd decile
Israel (29/37,704) (conflicts with Palestine 131/2,908, and Lebanon 73/9,793)

From the 1st decile
Kuwait (14/52,198★) (invaded by Iraq 97/5,790★)
USA (12/52,392) (9/11 attack)

---

forces, such as guerrilla terrorist organizations, private armies or local militias, and criminal-mafia groups, primarily in the drug business.[36] These non-state armed forces thrive where state structure is weak and productive economic opportunity is lacking—again, both a function of relatively low levels of modernization. The so-called 'new wars' are pretty much a reincarnation of an old, premodern mould.[37]

Moreover, the patterns of internal armed conflict belie the possible claim that wars take place in the poor parts of the world because the rich countries, most notably the United States and its allies, are powerful enough to take them there and avoid war on their own territory. Although this claim is valid in a limited sense, it is grossly misleading overall, as most armed conflicts take place either within or between the less developed countries themselves, whereas no such conflict takes place either within or between the top 30 per cent wealthiest countries (roughly above 13,500 GDP per capita in 2013 USD). This reality indicates a strong correlation between modernization and peace, and suggests that the armed conflicts that developed countries have with less developed rivals are a function of factors relating to the latter's poor record of development. Extending the survey of death in wars and conflicts further back, to the period since 1945, reveals a remarkably similar geographical/wealth-related distribution.[38] As mentioned in Chapter 6, the fact that the democracies tend to wage their wars against weaker opponents mainly reflects the same reality, rather than superior powers of discrimination. As all the developed countries today are democracies, and developed affluent democracies do not fight each other, they fight only weaker rivals almost by definition.

Elements of the Modernization Peace: Trends, Counter-Trends, and Potential Trajectories

These data on the distribution of armed conflicts reflect several interrelated elements of the Modernization Peace. One is the **internal development or growth of production element**. As we have seen, the quantum leap in the rate of growth in the industrial-technological age has made home-based economic performance the main avenue to wealth. *Ipso facto* this has decreased the attractiveness of the alternative military path and its diversion of resources away from economic growth. To a large degree, this logic has also applied to non–democratic or non–capitalist countries in the industrial-technological age, reducing their war-making activity in comparison to premodern times. It exercises its powerful effect on whoever embarks on the road to industrialization or economic modernization, as Moltke noted with respect to Prussia as early as 1841.

At present, this logic extends most notably to China and the countries of East, Southeast, and South Asia, but also to aspiring countries in other undeveloped parts of the world that have yet to succeed in getting the process going in earnest. Sub-Saharan Africa, one of the world's least developed areas, has registered steep growth rates in recent years. On the less encouraging side, most of the continent's countries have a complex ethnic mosaic, and many of them are beset by ethnic conflicts, with more potentially in store. The Arab Middle East, which so far has failed to kick-start economic (and other aspects of) modernization, has been one of the world's regions most afflicted by both inter- and intra-state conflict. And Russia, a failing industrial developer whose economy relies heavily on the extraction of oil and gas, is a problematic case. Globally, as more and more countries and regions are drawn into the process of industrial development, there are good prospects for the spread of the Modernization Peace to proceed and deepen.

Commercialism is the twin of industrial-technological development, as mass production and global markets are two sides of the same coin. Free trade lessens the incentives to engage in war, by maximizing mutual economic interdependence and mutual prosperity; by increasing vulnerability to economic punishment through political action or through the free operation of the mercantile and financial markets; and by disassociating political control over territories from the economic benefits that can be gained from them.

With the bitter lessons of the 1930s in mind, the architects of the post-1945 period in the West worked to decrease trade barriers globally. Through the General Agreement on Trade and Tariffs (GATT), established in 1947 (replaced by the World Trade Organization in 1995) and expanding over time to include most of the world's countries, average tariffs on manufactures were reduced from 40 to only a few per cent.[39] As during the nineteenth century, the volume of international trade in the aftermath of World War II grew twice as fast as the explosive rise in GDP, fuelling the latter. With the collapse of communism and the massive advances in communication technology, globalization was further boosted. Trade in goods tripled between 1985 and 2000, while trade in capital increased sixfold.[40] As of 2012, '35 percent of goods cross borders, up from 20 percent in 1990. More than a third of all financial investments in the world are international transactions, and a fifth of Internet traffic is cross-border'. While the developed countries are the most connected in terms of the cross-border flow of trade, finance, and communication, the developing countries have fast narrowed the gap, increasing their share of the world's foreign direct investments, for example, from 17 per cent in 1990 to 58 per cent in 2012.[41] This is a striking demonstration of the growing benefits that both modernized and modernizing countries derive from the system, with the potential positive effect that these benefits have on the growth of the Modernization Peace.

China is the most important test case for the future. During its meteoric industrial take-off from 1979 onwards, that averaged an annual growth rate of nearly 10 per cent in GDP over three decades, China's foreign trade increased at double that rate. Thus, China's international trade volume as a share of its GDP has increased from less than 20 per cent in the early 1980s to just above 50 per cent. In absolute terms, China's foreign trade now equals that of the United States, whose trade volume is about 30 per cent of its GDP. China's massive transformation was made possible by the favourable reaction of the United States and its liberal democratic allies to Beijing's opening to the world and embrace of the markets. They opened their own markets to Chinese imports and flocked to invest in China, thereby fuelling its meteoric growth. They did not condition this policy on political liberalization in China, believing that eventually everybody stood to gain from cheap goods, global growth, and the expansion of purchasing power; that political liberalization would in any case arrive in China in the wake of economic liberalization and development; and that China's integration into the world economy is, either way, the best guarantee for world peace. Whether these assumptions will materialize or whether, instead, a non-liberal China will turn out to be a formidable political and military rival as its wealth and power grow remains an open question that mirrors Britain's nineteenth-century dilemmas referred to in Chapter 6.[42]

As of 2013, China's main trading partners are, in descending order: the European Union, the United States, Japan, South Korea, and indeed China's bête noire, Taiwan. All of these are liberal democracies and are politically and militarily allied. Similarly, China is the United States' second largest trading partner, after Canada, and the European Union's second largest trading partner after the United States. Financially, China (including Hong Kong) is on a par with the United States as the largest destination of foreign direct investment, as well as being the largest holder of US treasury bonds. Thus, China's economy is symbiotically intertwined with the global economy, in which the countries of the free world dominate. Indeed, while China accounts for 15 per cent of American trade and 13 per cent of the European Union's trade, trade with the major liberal democratic countries amounts to about half of China's trade.[43] These are facts of major significance that highlight China's vital dependency on the system, and its great vulnerability if the system were to be disrupted. As we have seen, the twentieth century's particular historical sequence or developmental path that has shaped the system into what it is has become an objective reality that is bound to exercise a great effect on China's behaviour. Still, shadows of 1914 and 1939–41 linger on.

The first global age, before 1914, saw very high volumes of trade among the leading powers—similar to today's—and very high levels of interdependency. However, unlike today, all the powers, with the exception of Britain, maintained high tariff walls, and with the New Imperialism the prospect of worldwide protectionism loomed. Furthermore, Germany, the main player in the drama, planned a short and decisive war that would spare it economic strangulation. In the aftermath of the 1929 Wall Street crash, protectionism increased and 'imperial preference' became a reality. With international trade collapsing, the result was both economic stagnation and political disaster, as both Germany and Japan moved to swiftly secure for themselves large-scale autarkic imperial domains. The memory of these past catastrophes persists. In the wake of the 2008 Wall Street crash, the world's leading economic powers stressed the importance of avoiding a return to protectionism. They were mainly concerned about the economic consequences of such a trend, but the potential political effects were just as grave, because protectionism is likely to encourage a grab for markets and raw materials. For all that, international trade in goods, services, and finance shrank from above 50 per cent of global GDP in 2007 to just over 35 per cent in 2012, and has not recovered since. Whereas the growth of international trade was twice as fast as the growth of global production before 2008, it now barely keeps pace.[44]

While decreasing consumption and credit problems have been partly responsible for the stagnation and relative decline of international trade, the trend has also been affected by increasing protectionist pressures and 'currency wars' between the major countries, each trying to devalue its currency in order to boost its exports. More strikingly, it remains to be seen if and how the Brexit vote in Britain is going to affect the freedom of trade in Europe and to what extent President Trump's protectionist campaign slogans will be translated into policy. If so, we may cross a historical watershed. Irrespective of these political developments, some observers are concerned that the second global age may have peaked. Certainly, the growth of international trade as share of global GDP must reach a plateau at some point. Furthermore, as the gap between the developed and developing countries narrows and labour costs in the latter rise, there may be decreased incentives for the movement of production away from home. As the first global age was experiencing increasing strains, Keynes in the 1920s began to wonder if the levelling of economic conditions between countries had not decreased the advantages of international trade. In the twenty-first century, robots and three-dimensional printing are expected to take the automation of production to a new level, further lessening the incentives for offshoring.

While the economic equilibrium point that the level of international trade finds is one thing, protectionist political actions that affect the openness of the system are quite another. As both the economic and political benefits of free trade are clearer today than they were either before 1914 or in the 1930s, and the harsh lessons of the two world wars are also clear, there are very strong incentives for the open trade system and its peaceful effects to persist. China, for example, acutely dependent on the importation of raw materials—from oil to metals to foodstuffs—needs to export in order to pay for them. Thus, if denied easy access to the world's markets, China's policy on the oil resources of the South and East China Seas, for example, already alarming, might become overtly aggressive. In addition, China's reliance on the importation of raw materials from Russia, and the political association between these two non-democratic powers, might deepen.

Notably, however, the openness of the world economy does not depend exclusively on the democracies and the domestic currents against free trade they are presently experiencing. China has profited enormously from the current system. Yet further on in the twenty-first century, as China grows wealthier, its labour costs rise, and its current competitive edge diminishes, China itself might face the temptation to become more protectionist. As a huge market, it may choose to go on its own or in cooperation with regional neighbours. Such reversals have occurred in the past, engulfing, not least, the paragon of free trade and the system's long-time hegemon, Britain, in 1932. They cannot be entirely ruled out when considering the future. Political scientist John Ikenberry has insisted that the open trade, rule-based system that the United States created is best for the world and best for China, irrespective of the United States, and that China has no better option than to integrate into it. (He has reserved all his concerns to the United States' unilateral and allegedly irresponsible military actions under G. W. Bush.[45]) His view with respect to China may very well be true in the abstract, and it is not an implausible scenario for the future. But it is not the only scenario, as countries, like individuals, do not always follow the optimal course or prefer the calculus of economic benefit to other national or governmental goals and priorities. Moreover, giants like China are as likely to want to change the global system in their own image and to suit their needs as to passively integrate into it.

Recent years have seen a rise in anti-Western rhetoric in China. Indeed, according to one assessment:

The People's Republic of China...has begun to flex its muscles as a major power. Setting aside Deng Xiaoping's mantra of 'hide our light and nurture our strength' and Jiang Zemin's policy of 'increase trust, reduce trouble, develop cooperation, and do not seek confrontation,' Beijing today actively challenges its neighbors. It also confronts U.S. interests in the South and East China Seas, [and] builds up its navy and missile forces to oppose a U.S. intervention should an armed clash erupt over Taiwan...There is growing worry among Western analysts about the extent to which China, as its power grows, will seek to remake the world in its authoritarian image.[46]

China has intensified its efforts to create alternative institutions to the International Monetary Fund and World Bank, which it and other large developing countries regard as being overly dominated by the United States. In 2014, Brazil, Russia, India, China, and South Africa (the BRICS countries) signed a deal to create a development bank and emergency reserve fund. In early 2015, despite the United States' outright objection, its closest allies—including Britain, Germany, France, Italy, Holland, Denmark, Australia, and South Korea—joined the Chinese-led Asian Infrastructure Investment Bank, which ultimately comprised fifty-seven founding states. The United States and Japan were the only major economies that did not join. American officials claim that the new institution will not be committed to the same standards of governance and transparency currently upheld by other organizations. But they are obviously even more concerned about the erosion of American hegemony and the gravitation of power towards China.

China may be content with an adjustment of international organizations in a way that would reflect its growing power, most notably vis-à-vis the United States—or it may not. Nobody knows which of many possible paths the future will take.[47] It is a coin toss. Inter alia, 'some damn foolish thing' in the South or East China Seas (see Map 7.2), around Taiwan, or elsewhere, may arouse nationalist passions that would trump commercial gain. The rising tensions between Russia and the West over the former's military involvement in the Ukraine (and in Syria) are a recent reminder of this ominous potential, as well as of the intricacies of trade relations and armed conflict.

Unlike China, early twenty-first-century Russia is a failing—more than an alternative—modernizer. The communist failure was followed in the post-Soviet period by problematic and painful privatization, by an erosion of Russia's industrial base, and by increasing reliance on the export of natural resources in Putin's rentier state. By 2014, the share of oil, natural gas, and minerals had grown to more than two-thirds of Russia's exports, close to a

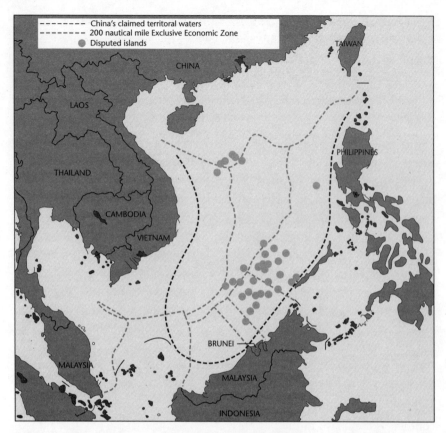

Map 7.2. The world's most dangerous hotspot? Tensions over the East and South China Seas

third of its GDP, and more than half of the state's revenues. The overwhelming share of Russia's trade is with the European Union, the destination of about half of Russia's exports in 2013. By comparison, China, Russia's second largest trade partner, consumed only 7 per cent of Russia's exports, while Russia ranked only in ninth to tenth place among China's trading partners. Russian–American trade is negligible. In terms of the volume of trade, Europe's dependency on trade with Russia is less than Russia's dependency on trade with Europe. In 2013, Russia was the European Union's third largest trading partner, and trade with Russia comprised less than a tenth of the EU's trade. However, importing close to 40 per cent of its gas and nearly a third of its oil from Russia, Europe's dependency on Russia is as critical as Russia's dependency on trade with Europe. While Europe could find substitutes for

Russian oil, European demand for Russian natural gas is rigid, and a replacement of that import is unfeasible in the short term and expensive overall. On
the other side, nor does Russia have real alternative destinations for its gas, as
China's demand is far more limited, for both economic and political reasons.[48]
Thus, both Russia and the European Union are critically dependant on their
mutual trade.

In 2014, Russia's occupation and annexation of Crimea and military
intervention in the Ukraine sparked the most severe international crisis
between the powers since the end of the Cold War. It again raised the
spectre of a major armed confrontation in Europe, which had been believed
to be a thing of the past. The United States and the European Union have
adopted a policy of limited economic sanctions, hoping to tame Russia
without escalating the crisis. Europe's dependency on energy imports from
Russia has in any case ruled out the possibility of harsher sanctions. Mutual
trade dependency has proved to be a double-edged sword, inhibiting not
only war, but also the alternative policy of economic coercion. Meanwhile,
the fall in the price of oil, for reasons unconnected with the crisis, is
expected to bring about a great deterioration in Russia's already weak
economy. Nobody can tell how events will unfold, and, in any regard, this
book is not about current affairs. The Ukrainian crisis serves here merely as
an illustration of how nationalist sentiments on the one hand, and the
rationale of economic growth and trade dependency on the other, may
conflict, as they have in the past, heightening security concerns, accentuat-
ing the security dilemma, and threatening the Modernization Peace.

Russia's claims are not without merit. Since the break-up of the Soviet
Union tens of millions of ethnic Russians have found themselves placed
outside Russia and adjacent to its borders: mainly in the Ukraine, the Baltic
countries, and the former Soviet republics of Central Asia. In some of these
places (the Baltics), they have cause for complaint about state discrimination against them. This would be a major concern to any country.
Furthermore, Russia's supreme historical connection to territories such as
Crimea, which is also populated by ethnic Russians, is unquestionable.
With the dissolution of the Soviet Union, Russia was made to accept the
proclaimed international norm that no changes could be made to the borders between the former republics. Russia was therefore incensed by what
it regarded as a violation of this principle and double standards in the
break-up of Yugoslavia, most notably with respect to Western military
interventions and recognition of the secession of Kosovo. All these are

inherently problematic and ambiguous questions with no clear-cut solutions. One could argue that Hitler's claim to the German-populated
Sudetenland in Czechoslovakia in 1938 was also not without merit. While
Putin is not Hitler, political gains achieved by force for his regime could
bear very negative consequences for the future.

More broadly, the ethno-national question reinforces the negative attitude in both China and Russia towards the liberal creed. There is a strong
suspicion in both countries that the further advancement of liberal norms
may well lead to the loss of significant parts of national territory on the
principle of self-determination. This applies to some of the non-Russian
autonomous republics in the Russian Federation, as well as to Tibet, Sinkiang,
Taiwan, and perhaps even Hong Kong in China. The old tensions that dominated nineteenth-century Europe, between the changing economic rationale and ethno-national aspirations, still endure. Africa, as well as South and
Southeast Asia, may be particularly susceptible to these tensions.

Returning to the political implications of trade, while the reasons for
Russia's military action in the Ukraine are multifarious, economic considerations are not absent among them. To all appearances, Russia is a lesser participant in the development peace and a greater one in the commercial
peace, due to its energy and minerals exports. However, in reality, Russia's
condition as a failing modernizer extends from production to trade. Because
of the failure of its industrial sector to compete in the world markets, Russia
is inclined to resort to political pressure in its trade relations with close
neighbours and previous members of the Soviet imperial system, who have
their eyes fixed on the much more attractive economic connection with the
European Union.[49] Thus, at present, Russia does not view the open trade
system as advantageous as far as its own manufacturing sector is concerned.
Indeed, the system is viewed as a threat. Russia's imperial traditions with
respect to its small neighbours and historical satellites are in any case strong.
US Secretary of State John Kerry condemned the Russian invasion of
Crimea and military involvement in the Ukraine, indignantly stating that
'you just don't in the 21st century behave in 19th century fashion'. However,
what the twenty-first century will be like remains to be seen.

We have dwelt at some length on the democratization, economic development, and commercial elements of the Modernization Peace—and the
challenges to them—as these elements are among the major pillars of this
peace. We now proceed to review some of the other elements of the
Modernization Peace more briefly. We specified **affluence and comfort** in

developed societies as distinct from rates of economic growth and commercial openness, or indeed from democracy (see Map 7.3). In conditions of abundance, people become more risk-averse. As we have seen, the top 30 per cent most affluent countries—roughly above 13,500 GDP per capita in 2013 USD—do not fight among themselves, nor experience intra-state armed conflict (with oil countries, again, somewhat diverging from the general trend). Returning to the most vital case with respect to the future of the international system, China's wealth per capita as of 2015 is around $7,000 (in rate of exchange terms), a fifth to a sixth that of the developed countries (or a quarter to a fifth in Purchasing Power Parity). China's affluence rates are more or less in the same range as those of the most advanced societies during the world wars era, which exhibited considerable enthusiasm for the war in 1914 and a marked lack of enthusiasm for war twenty-five years later. As China's wealth doubles, supposedly by the 2030s, and its comfort levels rise, the Chinese people's willingness to endure the risks and hardship of war (not high today) may enter much safer territory. On the other hand, China's power, international clout, and potentially more assertive political claims may increase in proportion to its growing wealth. Thus, conflicting processes and effects may be at work here, and it remains to be seen how they will unfold and interact.

Urbanism and urbanity partly correlate with affluence and comfort, inter alia because affluence levels in cities tend to be higher than in the less developed countryside. The world in general has recently crossed the 50 per cent urbanism rate, an average that bridges a broad spectrum between the developed and developing countries. In the former, at least two-thirds of the population live in urban centres.[50] China crossed the 50 per cent point in the 2000s, as Germany did around 1900, and Britain around 1850. Wealth per capita in China's industrial cities is two to three times the national average, and indulgence in the good life is very noticeable there. Urbanization rates in each country are most instructively viewed in connection with the structure of occupations. While villagers and industrial workers have historically been the most suitable recruits for war, office workers have been markedly less so. As of 2008–10, China's labour force was divided almost equally between the agricultural, industrial, and service sectors. By comparison, in most developed countries the service sector accounted for close to four-fifths of the economy and the agricultural sector comprised only a few per cent (less than 1 per cent in the US).[51] Over time, China's urban-urbane features are likely to deepen.

Iran is another pertinent case. Its GDP per capita was just over 6,000 USD in 2013 (ninety-first out of 193 countries), much of it derived from oil. Its urbanization rate is around 70 per cent. Among the urban more affluent classes, indulgence in the good life, liberalizing norms, opposition to the Islamist regime, and aversion to the prospect of war are increasingly noticeable. However, all of the above apply much less to the peasants and urban poor, who together comprise the great majority of the population. All in all, it is not surprising that the more reformist faction in the Islamic regime, scoring victory against the hardliners in the Iranian elections of 2016, did spectacularly well in Tehran, where its candidates won twenty-nine out of the thirty seats reserved to the capital in the national parliament.

Expanding **sexual freedom** is part of the 'good life' indulged in by much of the world today, and it constitutes an important element of the Modernization Peace. It is prevalent in both China and Russia. Sub-Saharan Africa displays both sides of the coin. Societies there generally exhibit fairly relaxed sexual mores, but in quite a few of them there are also incentives to join sectarian, tribal, and private armies that regularly engage in mass rape. In the Arab world, which falls behind in all the elements of modernization, highly restrictive sexual norms are a major factor driving young men's belligerency. Indeed, virgins are on offer to jihadists not only in paradise, but sadly also as spoils of war in this world.

The relationship between young men's sexual opportunities, the youth bulge, **aging demographics**, and peace is most intriguing with respect to Iran. To the alarm of the mullah regime, the fertility rate in Iran has plummeted from six to seven children per woman in the 1980s to less than two. In consequence, as mentioned in Chapter 6, the share of young males aged 15 to 29 in the population, traditionally the most militant element of society, which constituted 48 per cent of all males in Iran in 2000, is fast dropping and is expected to halve by 2050.[52] Fertility rates in some Arab countries have also been dropping sharply (though less radically than in Iran), while in others, as well as in Islamic countries of Central Asia, including Afghanistan and Pakistan, the decrease has been much slower. This means that these parts of the world still have a huge youth bulge, strongly contributing to their deep deficit in everything relating to the Modernization Peace. At the same time, long-term prospects are improving, at least by this measurement. Fertility rates in Sub-Saharan Africa, although also decreasing, are still by far the world's highest, with a corresponding youth bulge.

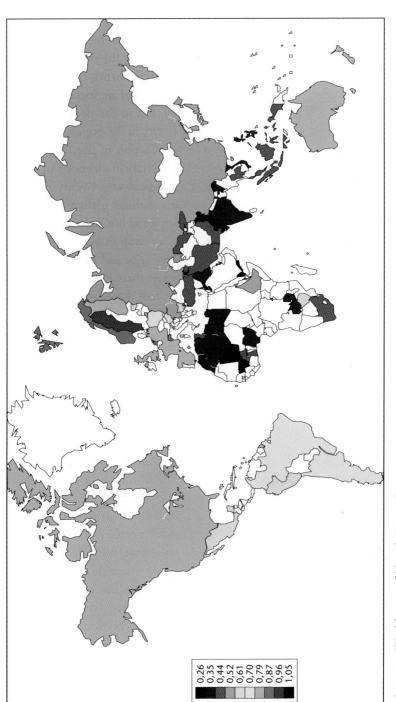

Map 7.3. World map of liberal civic culture

The map reflects social attitudes concerning a civic culture of tolerance, gender equality, secularization, and non-violence (declining from blueish to brownish; white—no data). Note the remarkable similarity with the world's affluence map (7.1: GDP per capita) and the strong correlation with the world's zones of peace and war.

0,26	
0,35	
0,44	
0,52	
0,61	
0,70	
0,79	
0,87	
0,96	
1,05	

By contrast, in many developed countries, such as Japan, South Korea, Taiwan, Italy, Spain, and Germany, but also in less developed or developing countries such as China and Russia, fertility has fallen far below the replacement rate, and the population is fast aging.[53] According to UN projections, by 2050 China will have 500 million people over the age of 60 out of a total population of some 1.35 billion—a staggering statistic.[54] This is probably the most serious economic shadow hanging over China's future, but it also might well be the most pacifying aspect of its development. Indeed, whatever other problems global aging brings, the pacifying aspects of an older social age structure and something like a youth deficit seem to be quite straightforward over time.

Women are generally less militant than men, and this is widely documented in their voting patterns. Thus, **growing female involvement** in society and politics tends to contribute to the Modernization Peace. The two most populous state societies in the world send warning signals with respect to this element of the Modernization Peace. Because of a state-enforced onechild policy and preference for a male child, the people of China have been practising female abortion and infanticide. As a result, China holds the world's most extreme sex ratio, with 116 boys to 100 girls under the age of 14. Similar preferences and practices in India make that country almost as extreme a case, with 113 boys to 100 girls under the age of 14.[55] The female deficit also results in greater restlessness among young males, as sexual prospects for many of them are bleak. How much weight this factor will carry within the plurality of elements that comprise the Modernization Peace is difficult to say.

The **globalization of mass culture and cultural convergence** are such widely discussed elements of modernization that we have found it unnecessary to expand on them in the previous chapter. Shared cultural themes disseminated by the media, the entertainment industry, and more recently and dramatically by the internet and social media, decrease the difference in outlook and values between societies worldwide, and make them appear more familiar and less alien. The limitations of this powerful trend have also been recognized. The 'Lexus and the olive tree' has been one metaphor for the tension between the universal and the particular, modernity and tradition. Local cultures remain deeply entrenched, and indeed may sometimes react to the pressures from 'global culture' with self-assertiveness, hostility, and even violence. Alternative and failed modernizers have reacted most strongly, and have been using the internet and social media most effectively to spread their message. While the globalization of trade and finance has stalled since the outbreak of the Great Recession in 2008, the flow of information across borders via the internet has continued to grow. At the same time, the internet has also spurred a massive expansion of indigenous cultural expression.[56]

Finally, there is the **nuclear** element of the Modernization Peace, with nuclear deterrence working as the means of last resort against war and the escalation of conflict. This factor, which was missing before 1945, has greatly contributed to the peace among the powers ever since, and is likely to continue to do so. However, the nuclear factor cuts both ways. Its unparalleled destructive potential, and, perhaps even more so, the destructive potential of more accessible weapons of mass destruction, might hugely empower non-state actors, against which deterrence is far less effective.

Having so far concentrated on the challenge of 'alternative modernizers', we now turn our attention to the challenge to the Modernization Peace posed by failed modernizers and anti-modernizers.

Anti-Modernity, Failed Modernity, and Unconventional Terror

The 9/11 mega-terror attacks in the United States were a historical landmark not only because of their direct and indirect consequences, but also because they have drawn attention to an ominous potential that had been building for some time and has yet to be realized. This is the threat of unconventional terror employing weapons of mass destruction (WMD)—nuclear, biological, and chemical—to which cyberterrorism has recently been added.

Neither terrorism nor weapons of mass destruction are new. Similarly, failed modernizers and anti-modernizers—the two are often connected—are as old as the process of modernization itself. However, rather than a significant cause of death and destruction, terror has been above all a spectacle intended to capture the headlines and influence public opinion; failed modernizers have been almost by definition weak; and states that possessed unconventional weapons could be effectively deterred by the threat of retaliation in kind. It is the joining of all these elements, the possibility that small groups or even individuals—often motivated by fanatical anti-modernist ideology and willing to die in pursuit of their cause—will resort to weapons of mass destruction, that creates the new and alarming potential for the future.

The so-called weapons of mass destruction are an assortment of technologies that vary widely in both their potency and accessibility to terrorists. The potential use of chemical weapons by terrorists is predicated on the element of surprise, catching concentrated masses of people unprotected and therefore highly vulnerable. The production of these weapons is relatively easy and can be mastered by non-state organizations. Still, chemical weapons pose the least serious threat of the WMDs, because of the large volume of chemical agents needed and the problem of spreading them effectively using the means that terrorists might possess. A highly successful chemical terror attack is estimated to have a potential casualty rate in the thousands.

Nuclear weapons stand on the opposite end of the scale in terms of lethality and accessibility. While there is no defence that is even remotely commensurate with their destructiveness, terrorists cannot produce the fissile material necessary for a bomb, at least for the foreseeable future. However, scientists have advised the American authorities that a primitive nuclear device could conceivably be built from parts available on the open market, with fissile material that is either bought or stolen. The nuclear weapons themselves might be stolen or bought on the black market. Abdul Qadeer Khan, the Pakistani nuclear scientist who headed his country's programme to manufacture an atomic bomb, sold nuclear secrets to perhaps a dozen countries—from Southeast Asia to the Middle East, including North Korea, Iran, and Libya—reportedly for as little as millions or tens of millions of dollars. The extent to which the Pakistani government was involved in or had knowledge of this trade has yet to be clarified.

The greatest potential threat of nuclear technology leakage presented itself during the 1990s, when the disintegration of the Soviet Union left in the debris of its advanced military infrastructure, spread throughout its various former republics, an array of unemployed nuclear scientists, production facilities, unaccounted for and poorly guarded nuclear materials, and the weapons themselves. The United States invested a lot of effort in the attempt to remove the materials, safeguard the facilities, and keep the scientists busy. As a result, the threat has greatly subsided, though disturbing news of thwarted attempts to smuggle nuclear materials out of the former Soviet sphere occasionally reach the headlines. Short of nuclear weapons, terrorists can use stolen or purchased radioactive materials to create a 'dirty bomb', which while not coming anywhere close to a nuclear weapon in destructiveness, could contaminate entire city blocks with radioactivity that is exceedingly difficult to remove.

A number of scholars have argued that the spread of nuclear weapons would actually be a good thing, because it would expand to other regions of the world the same deterrence against war that prevailed between the blocs during the Cold War. Proponents of this view dismiss suggestions of differences in political behaviour between developed and undeveloped or developing countries, and argue that the logic of mutual assured destruction (MAD) is so overwhelming that even the most militant state authorities in the world's less developed areas are unlikely to initiate the use of nuclear weapons. Nor, they argue, are these states likely to compromise their control and hand over such weapons to terrorists. Critics of this view doubt that the logic of MAD is entirely foolproof as nuclear weapons spread into a growing number of hands in the less developed parts of the world.[57] Either way, the greatest threat of nuclear proliferation may lie elsewhere—in the increased danger of leakage. Not only, as in the Pakistani case, may people and organizations with access to nuclear facilities sell or otherwise transfer nuclear materials, expertise, and even weapons to terrorists, with greater or lesser awareness by weak and segmented states; states in the less developed and more unstable parts of the world are also in danger of disintegration and anarchy, a danger which has all but disappeared in the developed world. Again, nuclear Pakistan is a case in point, where the threat of a Taliban takeover or general anarchy has been the cause of much concern. When state authority collapses and anarchy takes hold, who will guarantee the security of a country's nuclear arsenal? The collapsed Soviet Union rather than the former nuclear superpower may be the model for future threats.

Biological weapons are perhaps the most dangerous potential threat, as the revolutionary breakthroughs in decoding the genome, biotechnology, and genetic engineering during recent decades have made such weapons both much more lethal and more accessible. Strains of bacteria and viruses regarded as particularly potent in terms of lethality, resistance to medication, and persistence in the environment include anthrax, plague, tularemia, typhoid fever, cholera, typhus, Q fever, smallpox, and Ebola. Toxins such as botulinum and ricin also carry the potential for mass killing. Moreover, a virulent laboratory-cultivated strain of bacteria or virus, let alone a specially engineered 'superbug' with no immunological or medical antidote,[58] could make biological weapons as lethal as nuclear attacks, and result in anywhere from thousands to millions of fatalities. Worse still, biological weapons are more easily available to terrorists than nuclear weapons and are likely to become yet easier to acquire, as the biotechnological revolution is one of the spearheads of the current technological advance. It has been estimated that there are tens of thousands of labs in the world where one or a few individuals could synthesize highly potent viruses.[59] Acquiring materials, equipment, and know-how online, often for ostensibly benign civilian purposes, has become much easier than ever before.

The root of the problem lies in the technologies and materials of WMD trickling down to below the state level. For much of history, non-state players such as tribal and armed gang leaders challenged states successfully. With modernity, states' dominance increased as they controlled the heavy infrastructure underlying power. Although states still dominate despite encroachments from various directions, the encapsulation of destructive power in WMD, particularly nuclear and biological, recreates a situation in which a player no longer has to be big to deliver a devastating punch. World-threatening individuals and organizations, previously the preserve of James Bond-style fiction, have suddenly become real (Illustration 7.1).

Herein lies the bewildering problem of unconventional terror: deterrence is infinitely less effective against terrorist groups than it is against states. Not only are such groups more likely to consist of extremist zealots willing to sacrifice their own lives and even positively desiring a general apocalypse; they are also too elusive to offer a clear enough target for retaliation, on which the whole concept of deterrence is based. States have far superior access to weapons of mass destruction. However, because deterrence based on mutual assured destruction does not apply to terrorists, they are more likely than states are to use the ultimate weapons. In contrast to the habits of mind that have dominated since the onset of the nuclear age, unconventional capability acquired by terrorists is *useable*. If only because

Illustration 7.1. James Bond genre mega-terrorist

of the technical problems involved, unconventional terror may be used in relatively few cases. Yet, once the potential is available, it is difficult to see what will stop it from being realized by someone, somewhere. The Clinton, Bush, and Obama administrations alike have shared this working assumption. Similarly, the threat of cyberterrorism has been rapidly becoming a major concern, prompting action by governments and the private sector worldwide.

In the wake of 9/11, some have argued that it is wrong to define terror as the enemy, because terror is only a tactic, whereas the enemy is militant Islam. True, radical Islam stands behind most terrorist attacks in today's world, and dealing with it is an intricate and complex problem. Yet, although this new challenge is sometimes labelled as fascist, the Arab and Muslim societies from which it arises are generally poor and stagnant. They do not represent an alternative model for the future. Nor do they pose a military threat to the developed liberal democratic world, as did the fascist great powers, which were among the world's strongest and most advanced societies, or as the new capitalist non-democratic great powers may do. Only the potential use of WMD makes the threat of militant Islam significant.

Furthermore, even if the problem of militant Islam were overcome, other causes and 'super-empowered angry men' (as *New York Times* columnist Thomas Friedman has called them) would always be present and, in contrast to the past, could now assert themselves with horrific consequences. Pioneers of unconventional terror such as the Japanese Aum Shinrikyo cult and American anthrax scientist Bruce Ivins, or for that matter the perpetrators of the massive conventional bombings in Oklahoma City (1995) and the Atlanta Olympics (1996), were not Muslim. While societies in general tend to become more pacific as they modernize, there will always be individuals or small groups who will embrace massive violence for some cause. Thus, unconventional terror *is* the problem.

To be sure, the practical difficulties facing terrorist groups that wish to follow the unconventional path are still enormous. In 1990–5, the Aum Shinrikyo cult in Japan was the first non-state group to build production facilities for biological and chemical weapons. It struggled with acute production and safety problems, the biological materials it produced proved ineffective, and it lacked a dissemination mechanism for the chemical agents. Its sarin attack in the Tokyo subway in 1995 killed only twelve, as the gas was primitively carried in plastic bags pierced by umbrellas. However, when the police closed in on the cult and its facilities following the attack, the group was working on manufacturing more effective spraying mechanisms and synthesizing 70 tonnes of sarin, while also building a large biological laboratory.[60]

Similarly, the long-unresolved anthrax attack in the United States in the wake of 9/11, eventually traced to a scientist in the US biological warfare laboratory who committed suicide in 2008, involved stolen military-quality anthrax delivered in envelopes sent through the US postal service. The attack killed five people, created panic, contaminated entire buildings, and shut down facilities. While the scientist, Bruce Ivins, seems to have been mentally disturbed and his motives remain unclear, he probably did not want to cause mass death. However, according to a Congressional assessment made as early as 1993, aerosolized anthrax sprayed over a major city by a light plane (and now drones), could cause a disaster of an entirely different order of magnitude, kill millions, and contaminate large urban areas. 'Dark Winter', an exercise simulating a covert terrorist smallpox attack on the United States, was carried out in June 2001, again before the 9/11 attacks, at the Johns Hopkins Center for Civilian Biodefense Strategies, in collaboration with other bodies. The worst case scenarios projected 3 million people infected and one million dead within two months.[61] The exercise's assumptions, particularly with respect to contagiousness, have been criticized as vastly exaggerated and unrealistic by some experts, and later exercises have lowered them considerably. In addition, the ability to produce, handle, and effectively disperse military-quality pathogens presents massive obstacles that no terror organization has as yet succeeded in mastering.[62] That said, and given the ongoing spectacular advances in biotechnology, there is much reason for concern.

Critics, most notably John Mueller, argue that the threat of terror is massively overrated and that the American response has been hysterical to the point of irrationality, extremely costly, and far more harmful than the problem itself.[63] Mueller and others also emphasize the major difficulties surrounding the acquisition and successful use of unconventional weapons by terrorists, the tiny number of terror casualties so far compared to other sources of mortality as trivial as road accidents or people drowning in their bathtubs, and, indeed, to the number of the dead in the 'war on terror' itself. Mueller highlights people's completely unrealistic assessment of the (minuscule) odds of dying in a terror attack. Indeed, coolness of mind in judging the risks and a measured response are always recommended. The critics are right to ask what the rational priorities in allocating resources should be.

The disproportion between the terrorists' investment and that required of states to fight them is mind-boggling. The wars in Afghanistan and Iraq cost trillions of dollars. At home, between 2001 and 2008, the United States spent $57 billion on bioterrorism defence alone, including developing and stocking drugs, preparing hospitals, and surrounding thirty-five major cities with detection stations.[64] In view of all of this, and although Mueller concedes that some (unspecified) international policing is necessary, he suggests that the United States should drop most of its expensive offensive and defensive countermeasures (including airport security) and take its chances with the occasional terror attack, including unconventional terror, whose prospects he considers to be remote.‡

However, while demonstrating the limited killing potential of a chemical terror attack and the enormous difficulties surrounding nuclear terror,[65] Mueller has little to say about the threat of bioterror, which he himself admits 'could, indeed, if thus far only in theory, kill hundreds of thousands, perhaps even millions of people'.[66] Not only might a successful biological attack result in casualties on a par with the US' greatest wars, it is likely to target the country's main population centres and economic hubs. While there is a danger of worst case scenarios becoming self-fulfilling prophesies, they cannot be dismissed either. The critics argue that, even if the worst comes to the worst, the US will 'survive' the loss of Manhattan, or hundreds of thousands dead across the country from a bioterror attack. Still, the consequences of such a national disaster are untold. Furthermore, people seem to be evolutionarily programmed to react to attacks with a hostile intent with much greater alarm than to the prospects of 'natural' or accidental calamities. Consider the record of dead in World War I as compared to that of the great influenza epidemic that followed the war, or Hiroshima compared to the 2004 tsunami.

Terrorist groups may work from within their target countries, smuggling in or even manufacturing unconventional weapons undetected by the

---

‡ While Mueller's work is a thought-provoking correction on many significant points, one cannot help noting that some of his suggestions do not inspire confidence in his policy recommendations. For example, he argues that the US' involvement in both World War II and the Cold War were as unnecessary as the 'War on Terror'. The US should not have gone to war after Pearl Harbor but merely stuck to economic sanctions and containment that would have brought down Japan (how, after the latter had conquered East and Southeast Asia, thereby becoming economically self-sufficient, is unclear). In turn, he suggests that containing the Soviet Union was unnecessary and the United States should not have opposed Soviet expansion, because the failed Soviet system was in any case doomed.

authorities. The Aum Shinrikyo cult built its facilities for the manufacture of biological and chemical agents undetected in one of the world's most advanced countries, Japan. The perpetrators of the 9/11 conventional mega-terror attacks trained in the United States and other Western countries. The notion of 'a bomb in the basement', originally conceived in relation to states' undeclared development of nuclear weapons, has acquired a chilling new meaning, most notably, it would seem, with respect to biological weapons.

The problem is even greater as concerns countries in the developing world. Not only can terrorists find a safe haven for their activities in militant or failed states; these countries are also a source of dangerous materials and weapons, because of their low security standards, high levels of corruption, and the salience of organized crime. Indeed, failed states may constitute as great as or even greater a problem than militant ones. Although some militant regimes, most notably the Taliban, have demonstrated little concern for the massive retaliation that would follow acts of mega-terror originating from their territory, others are likely to be more susceptible to deterrence. By contrast, weak or failed states simply do not exercise effective control over their territories and cannot be held accountable. Recent years have seen the collapse of state authority in a number of countries in the developing world, most notably Syria and Iraq, Yemen, Libya, Somalia, and north Nigeria. In all of them, militant Islamist organizations thrive. In vast and largely inaccessible tracts of the globe inhabited by fragmented and unruly societies, monitoring and cracking down on the activity of terrorist groups may be harder than finding a needle in a haystack.

Rolf Mowatt-Larssen, the US Energy Department's director of intelligence, reported that al-Qaeda had been showing interest in weapons of mass destruction for nearly a decade before 9/11. According to his briefing, Osama bin Laden offered $1.5 million to buy uranium for a nuclear device. In August 2001, just before the attack on the US, bin Laden and his deputy, Ayman al-Zawahiri, met with Pakistani scientists to discuss how al-Qaeda could build such a device. Al-Qaeda also had an aggressive anthrax programme that was discovered in December 2001, after the organization was driven out of Afghanistan. In 2003, Saudi operatives of al-Qaeda tried to buy three Russian nuclear bombs. Around the same time, Zawahiri decided to cancel a cyanide attack in the New York subway system, telling the plotters to stand down because 'we have something better in mind'.[67] Clearly, al-Qaeda's interests and efforts in the field of unconventional weapons were still rudimentary. But even more than with Aum Shinrikyo, the price of al-Qaeda's successful terror attack on 9/11 may have been to nip its far more dangerous plans in the bud.

The failure of al-Qaeda to initiate further terrorist acts on US soil after 9/11 (pointed out by those who believe that the danger has been exaggerated) is largely attributable to the loss of its Afghan safe haven. As with other offensive and defensive countermeasures, the problem of the 'dog that didn't bark', as Sherlock Holmes put it—actions prevented and therefore remaining uncounted—may distort our perspective, and is a warning against complacency. Hence the alarm raised as jihadist Islamist organizations win control over large territories. I have long suggested that unconventional terror is a serious potential threat that requires great attention and vigilance to forestall. New events brought this threat to the headlines. The rapid expansion of the Islamic State group in Iraq and Syria and beyond in 2014–15, coupled with the organization's virulent anti-modernist ideology and hideous practices, have attracted great attention. The Islamic State, its affiliates, and other non-state militias have captured stocks of chemical weapons and possibly biological facilities in crumbling Syria and Libya. The organization has allegedly used chemical weapons against the Kurds in Syria, and is flirting with the broader use of WMD.[68] Its abilities in this respect are probably very rudimentary. Still, in response to a question, the American ambassador to the United Nations, Samantha Power, confirmed American concern about the possibility of Syria's chemical weapons falling into the organization's hands.[69] Similarly, British Home Secretary (and later Prime Minister) Theresa May expressed concern that the Islamic State 'will acquire chemical, biological or even nuclear weapons to attack us'.[70]

The Islamic State's November 2015 terror attacks in Paris were followed by repeated warnings from French President François Hollande and in Brussels regarding threats of chemical and biological terror. In the wake of the Islamic State's March 2016 suicide bombing in Brussels, it has been reported that in August 2014 the Doel-4 nuclear reactor in Belgium may have been intentionally sabotaged. In November 2015, Belgian police discovered that the perpetrators of the Paris attacks used a secret video camera to monitor an official at nuclear research sites with a wide range of nuclear and radiological materials. In early 2016, raiding American Special Forces reportedly targeted and captured the head of the Islamic State's chemical weapons development.

While the details and significance of this information have yet to be clarified, they have been considered ominous enough by US President Barak Obama. Obama shares the view that the threat of terrorism is greatly inflated and that it distracts attention and resources from other, more important security and non-security needs. Thus, it is all the more significant that he is well aware of the crucial difference between traditional conventional terrorism and the potential and growing danger of non-conventional terror. In his speech on 1 April 2016 at the international Nuclear Security Summit in Washington, Obama urged the more than fifty world leaders present to do more to safeguard vulnerable nuclear facilities. He said the world faced a persistent and evolving threat of nuclear terrorism, which he called 'one of the greatest threats to global security' in the twenty-first century. He pointed out that no group had succeeded in obtaining bomb materials, but confirmed that al-Qaeda had long sought them, and argued that the presence of Islamic State militants raised similar concerns. 'There is no doubt that if these madmen ever got their hands on a nuclear bomb or nuclear material, they would certainly use it to kill as many innocent people as possible.' Obama warned that such an attack 'would change our world' and that 'we cannot be complacent'.

The problem of unconventional terror is baffling and does not lend itself to easy or clear solutions. The most feasible measure against the threat is a coordinated global crackdown, which includes tightened security measures, tougher controls on the materials and facilities for the production of weapons of mass destruction, and the relentless pursuit of terrorists.[71] Although disputes and conflicting national interests are sure to arise, such concerted action is not wholly utopian, for no state is immune to the threat. International norms and international law are likely to change in response to the new challenges, most notably perhaps with respect to the question of sovereignty.

In the wake of 9/11, American interventionism has proved inherently messy. It has become the subject of a heated debate in the liberal democracies, to say nothing of reactions in the rest of the world. The normative and legal aspects of the democracies' defensive measures are just as problematic. The expansion of the state's authority in such spheres as the detention of suspects by means of extraordinary legal procedures, debriefing methods, surveillance of people and communication, and other infringements of privacy, are fervently debated in the liberal democracies. The threat of cyberterrorism has reinforced the debate. As with respect to the foreign policy options, this legal and public debate assumes a bitterly ideological and righteous character. Indeed, all the measures concerned are deeply problematic for advanced liberal democratic societies. And yet, as encapsulated technologies of mass destruction proliferate and become available to non-state organizations and individuals, the potential threat is genuine, will not go away any time soon, and has no simple solutions.

Conclusion

The Modernization Peace is very real, and has been spreading and deepening in conjunction with the process of modernization itself since the onset of the industrial age in the early nineteenth century. This historical transformation accounts for the Long Peace phenomenon, occurring three consecutive times and for ever longer periods from 1815 onwards. Indeed, the Long Peace phenomenon encompasses both the nineteenth century's well-recognized pacificity and the post-1945 decline of war within a comprehensive explanatory framework.

By its very nature, the Modernization Peace does not affect all parts of the world to the same degree. Modernization is least consequential in reducing belligerency in undeveloped countries, but it has significantly reduced belligerency in developing countries, while turning the most developed countries into a zone of peace. Aggregate measurements of global belligerency often fail to present the full extent of the steep drop in belligerency within the developed world, better reflected by the democratic and capitalist peace as aspects of the Modernization Peace. More importantly, they leave unspecified the underlying factor responsible for the entire trend.

Some dominant international relations concepts and approaches fall short on similar grounds. Attempts to find cyclical patterns of war occurrence (all unsuccessful) and 'realist' theorizing both assume an unchanging reality and fail to grasp how fundamental the modern transformation has been. This sometimes results in comic predictions of the 'Back to the Future' genre—the claim that everything stays basically the same even in the most modernized and most deeply pacified parts of today's world, such as Western Europe and North America. In these parts, the security dilemma itself, that most elementary phenomenon of international relations throughout history, has remarkably disappeared—indeed, in an astonishing reversal, it is war itself that has become unthinkable—an entirely unprecedented occurrence. 'Realists' have never been able to explain why Holland and Belgium no longer have the slightest concern regarding the possibility of a German military invasion, or what exactly defends Canada from conquest by the United States and accounts for its total complacency in the face of such a prospect.

This is not to say that regressions and relapses in the modernization processes and, as a result, also in the Modernization Peace, could not occur. Such relapses have happened at an earlier stage of modernization—during the world wars period—and an unravelling of the process is not inconceivable even at a much more advanced stage. Although both the modernization process and the Modernization Peace are powerful and deeply entrenched trends, there is no 'guarantee' that they will persist. The point is different: the Modernization Peace represents as radical a change from earlier history as the modern transformation itself; and for it to fail requires a breakdown of modernization itself or serious setbacks in its major aspects as they are currently known.

While liberal theorists have been fundamentally correct in analysing the transformative nature of the changes that have occurred since the beginning of the nineteenth century, there is always the peril of being carried away by ideological preconceptions and underplaying the considerable limitations and constraints of the process. 'Realism' retains credence and value as a warning against idealist illusions with respect to rivals that do not conform to the full spectrum of the Modernization Peace: above all, today, China and Russia. This, however, does not mean that great power relations remain basically the same, as 'realists' presage. Rather, what it means is that the validity of the Modernization Peace depends on the level and scope of modernization. What so conspicuously applies to North America, Western Europe, and Japan (as well as to the second generation 'tigers' and by now highly developed societies of East Asia, such as South Korea and Taiwan), the most advanced modernizers and the most liberal and democratic countries, may not apply or may apply less effectively to China and Russia. Not only are these countries still far behind on the road to modernization; it also remains to be seen how sustainable their professed alternative models of modernization will be, with their resistance to democratization and liberalization, both highly potent elements of the Modernization Peace.

In the peaceful core of the world, the most developed countries, which at present happen also to be the most liberal democratic, aversion to war has become a sweeping cultural phenomenon of overwhelming significance. War is felt to be entirely irrational—understandably, given the changing logic of modernity—and almost completely lacking in legitimacy, unless as the very last resort. Given this basic reality, but as the world is not yet an entirely safe place, the United States, the guarantor of the global order and insurer of last resort for the cause of liberal democracy, periodically swings between war aversion and military assertiveness. These swings have occurred with almost predictable regularity ever since the days of President Carter, if not Wilson. Each of these pendulum swings is accompanied in its turn by partisan ideological rhetoric and semi-religious conviction that tend to ignore the complexity and conflicting currents of reality. The dilemma of whether or not to initiate humanitarian military intervention to stop disastrous wars and massacres further complicates the picture. The United States seems to be able to do nothing right, blamed as it is for either intervening or not intervening. In Europe, long habituated to depending on America's hegemonic role for its security while criticizing its excesses— real and imagined—pacifism among the public has become even more deeply entrenched. While governments in Europe have been obligated to heed to their voters' wishes, some observers, such as former French President Nicolas Sarkozy, suspect a dangerous disconnect from reality. As he put it: 'Does Europe want to be left in peace or does Europe want peace? We know what becomes of continents and countries whose sole ambition is to be left in peace: one day, they see the return of war.'[72]

US President Barak Obama's speech on receiving the Nobel Peace Prize in 2009 is exemplary in its historical and theoretical sweep and its balancing of the conflicting pressures and deep ambivalence that modern liberal societies experience with respect to the phenomenon of war.[73] This is all the more remarkable as Obama is closely identified with one side of the political-ideological map, and attitudes towards him and his policies are polarized. Indeed, I refer purely to the content of his speech, putting aside both the problematic ideological gesture of the award to a president at the beginning of his tenure in office, and the very serious and highly contentious question of how much Obama's subsequent presidency succeeded in living up to his programmatic speech and escaping the pendulum swing between too much and too little exercise of force.

Obama started by stating correctly that 'War, in one form or another, appeared with the first man.' Addressing modern developments, he said: 'Commerce has stitched much of the world together. Billions have been lifted from poverty. The ideals of liberty, self-determination, equality and the rule of law have haltingly advanced.' Turning to the twenty-first century, he cautioned: 'The world may no longer shudder at the prospect of war between two nuclear superpowers, but proliferation may increase the risk of catastrophe. Terrorism has long been a tactic, but modern technology allows a few small men with outsized rage to murder innocents on a horrific scale.' Obama further emphasized the two faces of globalization:

> As the world grows smaller, you might think it would be easier for human beings to recognize how similar we are...And yet, given the dizzying pace of globalization, and the cultural leveling of modernity, it should come as no surprise that people fear the loss of what they cherish about their particular identities—their race, their tribe, and perhaps most powerfully their religion. In some places, this fear has led to conflict.

In dealing with countries that do not accept the norms of a peaceful international system, Obama stated: 'we must develop alternatives to violence that are tough enough to change behavior'. At the same time, he stressed:

> We must begin by acknowledging the hard truth that we will not eradicate violent conflict in our lifetimes...A non-violent movement could not have halted Hitler's armies. Negotiations cannot convince al Qaeda's leaders to lay down their arms...I raise this point because in many countries there is a deep ambivalence about military action today, no matter the cause. At times, this is joined by a reflexive suspicion of America, the world's sole military superpower...Yet...whatever mistakes we have made, the plain fact is this: the United States of America has helped underwrite global security for more than six decades.

Obama continued: 'I understand why war is not popular. But I also know this: the belief that peace is desirable is rarely enough to achieve it.' At the same time, he emphasized America's need for support from its allies and its obligation to work within the norms and institutions of international legitimacy. Rejecting what he described as a tension between 'realists' and 'idealists' in America, he asserted the US commitment to human rights—in itself, and as an American enlightened self-interest. On the other hand, he emphasized the need to work with regimes that fail to comply with liberal norms and standards: 'There is no simple formula here. But we must try as best we can to balance isolation and engagement; pressure and incentives.'

The attempt to defuse tensions by offering the other side a combination of compromises, concessions, and rewards has been the natural inclination of liberal affluent societies, as it is indeed the most sensible option for all the parties involved in the modern transformation. But as the 1930s demonstrated, this policy may signal weakness and embolden an opponent who does not share the same assumptions. This is the dilemma that affluent liberal societies have constantly been forced to grapple with. The new Trump administration in the United States will need to steer its own course between the horns of this dilemma. In policy terms, ever since the beginning of the twentieth century, the liberal democracies have tended to move cautiously up the scale of belligerency: from appeasement, to containment and cold war, to limited war, and only most reluctantly to full-scale war.

Overall, there is room for cautious long-term optimism. Modernization is an extremely powerful trend and it would require extraordinary forces to derail it. We are clearly experiencing the most peaceful times in history by far, a strikingly blissful and deeply grounded trend. At the same time, alternative routes to modernity are back on offer and competing in the world arena, with significant policy implications. And both anti-modernism and failed modernism are still evident, sometimes assuming fanatical and gruesome expressions. Ethno-national tensions are another deep source of potential armed conflict, especially, though not solely, in the less developed parts of the world and where political and ethnic borders do not coincide. Indeed, the developed West is also experiencing rocky times, a compound of the economic and immigration crises, accompanied by a general loss of confidence. Furthermore, the observation that at least since 1945 this is also the most dangerous world ever, with mankind for the first time possessing the ability to destroy itself completely, and even individuals and small groups gaining the ability to cause mass death, is far from a cliché. While the modern transformation decreases the likelihood of war between states, the democratization and individualization of mass death, destruction, and disruption may become a real and disconcerting prospect.

Conclusion

The Logic of War and Peace

The phenomenon of war has always evoked distress and puzzlement because of the killing, misery, and overall net loss it involves in terms of destruction and wasted resources. This has led to war being widely seen (even if not necessarily clearly conceptualized) as a 'prisoner's dilemma' situation, in which everybody loses. Equally, however, the glory and heroism of war have been celebrated throughout the ages—from oral epics to movies—with the activity of fighting serving as a source of excitement and exhilaration, above all for young men. Relatedly, the prizes to be won or defended by the high-stakes enterprise of war were often very great. Only with modernity did war begin to be regarded, most notably in liberal societies, as something utterly repugnant and futile, indeed incomprehensible to the point of absurdity.

As we have seen, there have been good reasons for this attitude in the wake of the Industrial Revolution and in the context of an increasingly affluent world, in which the Malthusian trap was broken. Abundance based on production and exchange has been increasing at a staggering pace, and the balance of benefits between war and peace has radically altered as interdependent growth in real wealth has replaced the zero-sum game. However, what may be true for the modern affluent world, most notably (though not exclusively) for its liberal democratic parts, is not necessarily so with respect to the reality that preceded it, or, indeed, that may presently prevail in parts of the world that have not yet successfully embarked on the process of modernization. A map of the world's 'zones of war' strikingly reveals the correlation, and suggests the causal relationship, between modernization and peace. Still, since people tend to generalize from their own circumstances, the occurrence of war has increasingly been perceived in modern liberal societies as a disturbing puzzle, a true enigma—in relation to the past as well as to the present. The view that took hold during the height of Rousseauism in the 1960s—that widespread intraspecific killing and war are something uniquely human, or that they are a late cultural invention—only underscored the puzzle.

In reality, there is nothing special about deadly human violence and war. Fundamentally, the solution to the 'enigma of war' is that no such enigma exists. Violent competition, alias conflict—including intraspecific conflict—is the rule throughout nature, as organisms vie among themselves to survive and reproduce under ever-prevalent conditions of scarcity, which are accentuated by the organisms' own process of propagation. Within this fundamental reality organisms can resort to cooperation, competition, or conflict—behavioural strategies which they mix to different degrees, depending on each strategy's utility in a given situation and in relation to each organism's particular configuration along its evolutionary path. Evolution-shaped mechanisms embedded in organisms, from the most primitive to the highest forms, regulate the choice and combination of these behavioural strategies. Since conflict always exists as an option, organisms' structural and behavioural traits (the two are obviously interlinked) are funnelled to succeed in it, variably offensively and defensively. Only a few need to adopt this option to radically affect the behaviour of all the others in a perpetual chain reaction. We are 'hardwired' and possess the heavy biological machinery necessary for violent action—as for the other behavioural options—*and* we choose between these options opportunistically. The solemn 'Seville Statement on Violence' got only half of the picture right. *Both* nature and social-historical conditions factor in heavily.

Contrary to the Rousseauian imagination, the evidence of historically observed hunter-gatherers and, more dimly but increasingly, the archaeology of pre-state, pre-agricultural, and nomadic Palaeolithic societies shows that humans have been fighting among themselves throughout the history of our species and genus. Fighting was widespread and very lethal in the human 'evolutionary state of nature', at the individual, familial, and group levels alike. The rate of violent death among adult males in pre-state societies appears to have been about 25 per cent, 15 per cent among the adult population in general, with the rest of the men covered with scars and society as a whole overshadowed by the ever-present prospect of conflict. Although there was some variation between societies, the prevalence of deadly conflict seems to have taken the form of a bell curve, with a few cases of relatively peaceful and extremely belligerent societies at each end. Recent last-ditch attempts to dispute this picture are refuted in Chapter 1. Pre-state violent mortality rates were much higher than those registered by state societies and are only approximated by the most destructive state wars; yet they correspond to normal rates of intraspecific killing among animals in nature.

Indeed, group fighting exists among many social animals—there is nothing uniquely human about it. That 'war' is customarily defined as large-scale organized violence is merely a reflection of the fact that our species' social groups were always larger, more complex, and more cooperative, and, particularly, that societies have grown exponentially and become more organized since the transition to agriculture and statehood. Thus, to insist that 'true war' only emerged with the state and state politics is to substitute conceptual artefacts for the living process of human history. Furthermore, while the size of the societies that engaged in fighting, and consequently also their armed forces, increased spectacularly under the state, the death toll of human fighting actually decreased. Lawrence Keeley pioneered this insight, further established, among others, by my own work, by Steven Pinker, and by Ian Morris. Non-state violence within the state's realm has been outlawed and more or less successfully suppressed by the state's coercive authority. As suggested by Hobbes, even low-quality services provided by the Leviathan tended to promise greater security than its collapse, as civil war and anarchy regularly resulted in greater destructiveness and death than inter-state wars. Foreign inter-state war, too, despite its grand scale in absolute terms, has involved a lower death toll per population than pre-state fighting in all but the most severe wars. As explained in Chapter 3, the reason for this is that larger societies, and hence larger territories and greater distances, translated into a lower social participation rate in war for the men, as well as into lesser exposure of the civilian rear.

Furthermore, created and maintained above all by the force of arms, state societies were probably the most significant 'spin-off' of warfare, which in turn created the necessary preconditions for a relatively peaceful civilian existence, dense and complex orderly societies, integrated economies of scale with a developed division of labour, and literate civilizations. Ultimately, this would create the infrastructure for industrialization and its pacifying effects. Morris's *War: What is It Good For?* has brilliantly developed this point. Sociologist Charles Tilly influentially argued that 'War made the state, and the state made war.' But as Morris corrects: war made the state, and the state made peace, first domestically and then increasingly internationally.

Certainly, the emergence of large-scale, stratified state societies also created a differential balance of benefits and costs in war, as in all other social dealings. The benefits from war often went disproportionately to the rulers and the elite, while sharply decreasing down the social ladder, with much of the population receiving very little to compensate for their losses of life, efforts, and property. The glaring inequality in the distribution of the benefits and costs of war was largely responsible for the Enlightenment's belief that war should be blamed on autocratic and aristocratic interests. Yet this reasoning is far from exhausting the logic of war. As in all other social activities, inequality did not necessarily mean a negative cost–benefit balance for the populace in a war. Even under inequality, the populace very often had considerable stakes in the war, whether to protect their own against invaders—including life, family, and property, but also their people in general and their communal independence—or to gain from the enemy. Furthermore, contrary to the Enlightenment's view, it was the more egalitarian-participatory societies in history that proved the most formidable in mobilizing for and sustaining war, as both egalitarian tribal societies and imperial democratic-republican city-states, such as ancient Athens and Rome, demonstrate.

As this book has argued, wars have been fought for the attainment of the same objects of human desire that underlie the human motivational system in general—*only by violent means*, through the use of force. Rather than dealing with some special kind of objectives, elevated 'reasons of state', politics—domestic and foreign—is the activity intended to achieve these evolution-shaped human desires at the intra- and inter-state levels. International relations theory has increasingly lost sight of human desires as the engine of conflict and war, focusing almost exclusively on 'enabling conditions' such as international anarchy (which in any case ceased to be conducive to war among countries participating in a modern liberal order). On the other hand, human quests, for instance for dominance or ideology, are no more 'demons' than the desire for love and sex. They can all just as well be counted on the side of the 'angels' when pursued by peaceful means and for peaceful ends. On this I take issue with Pinker, with whom I otherwise much agree. The 'problem' of war is not these or other human desires—desires that make us what we are, that are the stuff of life. Fundamentally, violence and war occur when the conflictual behavioural strategy is judged to be more promising than peaceful competition and cooperation for achieving any object of human desire. Both our basic desires and the conditions that channel the efforts to fulfil them towards the conflictual path are necessary for understanding why war occurs. Thus, human desires constitute the motives for war, and are therefore the fundamental causes of war. At the same time, other factors, such as the expected utility of the violent option and prisoner's dilemma situations of insecurity and escalation arising from the potential for conflict, complete the causal array that lead to war.

The desire and struggle for scarce resources—wealth of all sorts—have always been regarded as a prime aim of 'politics' and an obvious motive for war. They seem to require little further elaboration. By contrast, reproduction appears not to figure as a direct motive for war in large-scale societies. Appearance is often deceptive, however, for somatic and reproductive motives are two sides of the same coin. Indirectly, the material means gained or protected by war enhanced reproductive success in societies—again differentially, down the social ladder—for they affected people's ability to provide for their families, while also feeding the social competition among men for more and 'better' women, as for all the other 'good things' in life. Furthermore, like looting, sexual adventure remained central to *individual* motivation in going to war, even if it usually failed to be registered at the level of 'state politics'. This may be demonstrated by the effects of the sexual revolution since the 1960s, which, by lessening the attraction of foreign adventure for recruits, may have contributed to advanced societies' growing aversion to war. Honour, status, glory, and dominance—both individual and collective—enhanced access to somatic and reproductive success and were thus hotly pursued and defended, even by force. The 'security dilemma' sprang from this state of actual and potential competition, in turn adding fuel to the fire. Power has been the universal currency through which all of the above could be obtained and/or defended, and has been sought as such, often in an escalating spiral.

Kinship, real or perceived—expanding from family and tribe to peoples—has always exerted overwhelming influence in determining one's loyalty and willingness to sacrifice in the defence and promotion of a common good. Contrary to widely held views, it has always been paramount in shaping political boundaries, as well as relations within multi-ethnic polities. Shared culture is a major attribute of ethnic communities, and people can be invested in its defence as heavily as in the community's political independence and overall prosperity. Finally, religious and secular ideologies have been capable of stirring up enormous zeal and violence, as grand questions of cosmic and socio-political order have been perceived as possessing paramount *practical* significance for securing and promoting life on earth and/or, indeed, the afterlife. In the human problem-solving menus, ideologies have functioned as the most general blueprints.

Rather than separate items, a 'laundry list' of causes for war—all of the above—partake in the interconnected human motivational system, *originally* shaped by the calculus of survival and reproduction, as the great majority of people struggled through a precarious existence until quite recently. People have been willing to risk and even sacrifice their lives when this calculus suggested that by the use of violence they might gain greater rewards or defend against greater losses for them and their kin. This logic continues to guide human behaviour, mostly through its legacy of innate proximate mechanisms: human desires. This remains so even where the original link between these proximate mechanisms and the original somatic and reproductive aims they evolved to serve may have loosened or even been severed under altered conditions, as humans have developed monumental cultural edifices that have taken them a dazzling distance from their original state of nature. Thus, more wealth is desired even though above a certain level it has ceased to translate into greater reproduction; with effective contraception much the same applies to sexual success; power, status, honour, and fame—connected to the first two—are still hotly pursued even though their reproductive significance has become as ambivalent. It is the evolutionarily-shaped proximate mechanisms—the web of desire—that dominate human behaviour, even when much of their original adaptive rationale has weakened.

All in all, to the extent that modernization sparked by the industrial-technological revolution, most notably its liberal path, has fundamentally reduced the prevalence of war—indeed, totally eliminated it in the most developed parts of the world—the reason for this change is that the violent option for fulfilling human desires has become much less promising than the peaceful option of competitive cooperation. Furthermore, the more affluent and satiated the society and the more lavishly people's most pressing needs are met—with all the attractions available for them to indulge in, all the way up the 'hierarchy of needs'—the less their incentive to take risks that might involve the loss of life and limb. People in affluent liberal societies have sensed this change very well, even when they could not always clearly conceptualize it, increasingly shrinking away from the violent option and resorting to more peaceful strategies. The advent of nuclear weapons has reinforced the military arm of this pincer effect between nuclear states, but the process had already manifested itself before the nuclear age, and it is strongly evident also where mutual nuclear deterrence does not exist. While people in developed societies continue to fiercely compete over objects of desire, the violent option in the human behavioural 'toolkit' has become less practical for them, while the more peaceful tools have been increasing in significance. At the same time, much of humanity is still going through the process of modernization, and is affected by its pacifying aspects, while struggling to catch up and charting various cultural and national paths, some of which are and may remain illiberal and undemocratic. Finally, some parts of the world have so far failed in their efforts to modernize, yet experience many of the frustrations and discontents of that process. How these developments will unfold and interact, affecting the use of wide-scale violence, especially in the presence of immensely destructive ultimate weapons whose use is only variably constrained—only the future will tell.

Notes

PREFACE

1. Geoffrey Blainey, *The Causes of War*, New York: The Free Press, 1973, and Stephen van Evera, *Causes of War: Power and the Roots of Conflict*, Ithaca, NY: Cornell UP, 1999, are concerned with various conditions that affect the likelihood and frequency of war. They deal with enabling circumstances rather than with the actual causes, about which they have very little to say. Dale Copeland's *The Origins of Major War*, Ithaca, NY: Cornell UP, 2000, is very narrow, while David Sobek, *The Causes of War*, Cambridge: Polity, 2009, is broader and intelligent. Hidemi Suganami, *On the Causes of War*, Oxford: Oxford UP, 1996, is a first-class analytical critique, with a less interesting positive contribution. Greg Cashman, *What Causes War? An Introduction to Theories of International Conflict*, Lanham, MD: Lexington, 1993, and Jack Levy and William Thompson, *Causes of War*, Chichester: Wiley-Blackwell, 2010, are two fairly comprehensive literature surveys. John Stoessinger, *Why Nations Go to War*, New York: St Martin, 1993, is superficial. John Vasquez, *The War Puzzle*, Cambridge: Cambridge UP, 1993, scarcely resolves the puzzle. A collective effort by historians and political scientists, R. Rotberg and T. Rabb (eds.), *The Origins and Prevention of Major Wars*, Cambridge: Cambridge UP, 1989, mainly reveals perplexity. Richard Ned Lebow, *Why Nations Fight*, Cambridge: Cambridge UP, 2010, is a step in the right direction, referred to in Chapter 5 (and Chapter 7). Recently published, Gary Goertz, Paul Diehl, and Alexandru Balas, *The Puzzle of Peace: The Evolution of Peace in the International System*, Oxford: Oxford UP, 2016, approaches the topics of this book from a very narrow angle (see footnote in 'Liberal Democracy' section in Chapter 6).
2. Jack Levy, 'The Causes of War: A Review of Theories and Evidence', in P. Tetlock et al. (eds.), *Behavior, Society and Nuclear War*, New York: Oxford UP, 1989, i. 209–333, especially 210, also 295.
3. I condensed part of my argument in that book into journal articles intended, respectively, for students of anthropology and international relations: Azar Gat, 'The Human Motivational Complex: Evolutionary Theory and the Causes of Hunter-Gatherer Fighting', *Anthropological Quarterly*, 73:1/2 (2000), 20–34, 74–88; Gat, 'So Why Do People Fight: Evolutionary Theory and the Causes of War', *European Journal of International Relations*, 15 (2009), 571–99.

CHAPTER I

1. Konrad Lorenz, *On Aggression*, London: Methuen, 1966.
2. J. D. Bygott, 'Cannibalism among Wild Chimpanzees', *Nature*, 238 (1972), 410–11; G. Teleki, *The Predatory Behavior of Wild Chimpanzees*, Lewisburg: Bucknell UP, 1973; Jane Goodall, *The Chimpanzees of Gombe*, Cambridge, MA: Belknap, 1986; J. Itani, 'Intraspecific Killing among Non-human Primates', *Journal of Social and Biological Structure*, 5 (1982), 361–8; Frans de Waal, *Good Natured: The Origins of Right and Wrong in Humans and Other Animals*, Cambridge, MA: Harvard UP, 1996; Richard Wrangham and Dale Peterson, *Demonic Males: Apes and the Origins of Human Violence*, London: Bloomsbury, 1997.
3. Edward Wilson, *On Human Nature*, Cambridge, MA: Harvard UP, 1978, 103–5; George Williams, cited in Daniel Dennet, *Darwin's Dangerous Idea*, New York: Simon & Schuster, 1995, 478.
4. R. L. Sussman (ed.), *The Pygmy Chimpanzee*, New York: Plenum, 1984; T. Kano, *The Last Ape: Pygmy Chimpanzee Behavior and Ecology*, Stanford: Stanford UP, 1992; Wrangham and Peterson, *Demonic Males*; Frans de Waal, *Bonobo: The Forgotten Ape*, Berkeley: U. of California, 1997; Amy Parish, Frans de Waal, and David Haig, 'The Other "Closest Living Relative": How Bonobos (*Pan paniscus*) Challenge Traditional Assumptions about Females, Dominance, Intra- and Intersexual Interactions, and Hominid Evolution', *Annals of the New York Academy of Sciences*, 907 (April 2000), 97–113.
5. E. N. Wilmsen and J. R. Denbow, 'The Paradigmatic History of San-Speaking Peoples and Current Attempts at Revision', *Current Anthropology*, 31 (1990), 489–525.
6. Elizabeth Thomas, *The Harmless People*, New York: Knopf, 1959.
7. Richard Lee, *The !Kung San*, New York: Cambridge UP, 1979, 398; Lee, 'Politics, Sexual and Non-Sexual, in Egalitarian Society', in R. Lee and E. Leacock (eds.), *Politics and History in Band Societies*, New York: Cambridge UP, 1982, 44; also Marshall Sahlins, 'The Original Affluent Society', in R. Lee and I. DeVore (eds.), *Man the Hunter*, Chicago: Aldine, 1968.
8. Jean Briggs, *Never in Anger*, Cambridge, MA: Harvard UP, 1970; Briggs, '"Why Don't You Kill Your Baby Brother?" The Dynamics of Peace in Canadian Inuit Camps', in L. Sponsel and T. Gregor (eds.), *The Anthropology of Peace and Nonviolence*, London: Lynne Rienner, 1994, 156; Donald Symons, *The Evolution of Human Sexuality*, New York: Oxford UP, 1979, 145; J. Darwent and M. Christyann, 'Scales of Violence across the North American Arctic', in M. Allen and T. Jones (eds.), *Violence and Warfare among Hunter-Gatherers*, Walnut Creek, CA: Left Coast Press, 2014, 182–203.
9. Morton Fried, *The Notion of the Tribe*, Mento Park, CA: Cummings, 1975, following on his 'On the Concepts of "Tribe" and "Tribal Society"', in J. Helm (ed.), *Essays on the Problem of the Tribe*, Seattle: American Ethnological Society, 1968, 3–20.

10. R. Brian Ferguson, 'A Reexamination of the Causes of Northwest Coast Warfare', in R. B. Ferguson (ed.), *Warfare, Culture and Environment*, Orlando, FL: Academic Press, 1984, 267–328; Ferguson, 'A Savage Encounter: Western Contact and the Yanomami War Complex', in R. B. Ferguson and N. Whitehead (eds.), *War in the Tribal Zone*, Santa Fe, NM: School of American Research, 1992, 199–227; Ferguson, *Yanomami Warfare*, Santa Fe, NM: School of American Research, 1995; Jeffrey Blick, 'Genocidal Warfare in Tribal Societies as a Result of European-Induced Culture Conflict', *Man*, 23 (1988), 654–70; Neil Whitehead, 'The Snake Warriors—Sons of the Tiger's Teeth: A Descriptive Analysis of Carib Warfare, ca. 1500–1820', in J. Haas (ed.), *The Anthropology of War*, New York: Cambridge UP, 1990, 146–70.

11. Ferguson, 'A Savage Encounter', 225; Ferguson, *Yanomami Warfare*, 14; Whitehead, 'The Snake Warriors', 160. Blick, 'Genocidal Warfare' is the exception in postulating a pacific pre-contact past.

12. Ferguson, 'A Reexamination of the Causes of Northwest Coast Warfare', 271, 272–4, 278, 285, 298, 312; relying on George MacDonald, *Kitwanga Fort National Historic Site, Skeena River, British Columbia: Historical Research and Analysis of Structural Remains*, Ottawa: National Museum of Man, 1979, and other unpublished research by MacDonald. The thousands of years old antiquity of complex hunter-gatherers and warfare in southern Alaska and other areas of the Northwest Coast is similarly pointed out by David Yesner in his 'Seasonality and Resource "Stress" among Hunter-Gatherers: Archaeological Signatures', in E. Burch and L. Ellanna (eds.), *Key Issues in Hunter-Gatherer Research*, Oxford: Berg, 1994, 161–2; Brian Hayden, 'Competition, Labor, and Complex Hunter-Gatherers', ibid., 237; Ernest Burch and T. Correll, 'Alliance and Conflict: Inter-Regional Relations in North Alaska', in L. Guemple (ed.), *Alliance in Eskimo Society*, Seattle: U. of Washington, 1972, 24; Ernest Burch, 'Eskimo Warfare in Northwest Alaska', *Anthropological Papers of the University of Alaska*, 16 (1974), 1; Leland Donald, *Aboriginal Slavery on the Northwest Coast of North America*, Berkeley: U. of California, 1997, 27, 205–9.

13. Erna Gunther, *Indian Life on the Northwest Coast of North America, as Seen by the Early Explorers and Fur Traders during the Last Decades of the Eighteenth Century*, Chicago: U. of Chicago, 1972, 14, 43, 114, 133, 159, 187. For armour and shields among the Eskimo of the Alaskan coast see E. Nelson, *The Eskimo about Bering Strait*, Washington, DC: Smithsonian, 1983 [1899], 330; Robert Spencer, *The North Alaskan Eskimo*, Washington, DC: Smithsonian, 1959, 72; Wendel Oswalt, *Alaskan Eskimos*, San Francisco: Chandler, 1967, 186, 188; Burch, 'Eskimo Warfare', 5; Ernest Burch, *Alliance and Conflict: The World System of the Inupiaq Eskimos*, Lincoln: U. of Nebraska, 2005. For the Plains Indians see, e.g., Frank Secoy, 'Changing Military Patterns on the Great Plains', *American Ethnological Monographs*, 21 (1953); John Ewers, 'Intertribal Warfare as the Precursor of Indian–White Warfare on the Northern Great Plains', *The Western Historical Quarterly*, 6 (1975), 390, 401.

14. Lawrence Keeley, *War Before Civilization: The Myth of the Peaceful Savage*, Oxford: Oxford UP, 1996; Keeley, 'Frontier Warfare in the Early Neolithic', in D. Martin and D. Frayer (eds.), *Troubled Times: Violence and Warfare in the Past*, Amsterdam: Gordon and Breach, 1997, 303–19; J. Carman and A. Harding (eds.), *Ancient Warfare: Archaeological Perspectives*, Phoenix Mill: Sutton, 1999. Even Brian Ferguson, in 'The Prehistory of War and Peace in Europe and the Near East', in D. Fry (ed.), *War, Peace, and Human Nature: The Convergence of Evolutionary and Cultural Views*, Oxford: Oxford UP, 2013, 191–241, cannot but admit this for Neolithic Europe.

15. See Azar Gat, *War in Human Civilization*, Oxford: Oxford UP, 2006, chap. 9.

16. Azar Gat, 'The Pattern of Fighting in Simple, Small Scale, Pre-State Societies', *Journal of Anthropological Research*, 55 (1999), 563–83 and 'The Human Motivational Complex: Evolutionary Theory and the Causes of Hunter-Gatherer Fighting', *Anthropological Quarterly*, 73:1–2 (2000), 20–34, 74–88 (both incorporated into my *War in Human Civilization*); Steven LeBlanc with Katherine Register, *Constant Battles: The Myth of the Peaceful Noble Savage*, New York: St Martin's, 2003; also J. Guilaine and J. Zammit, *The Origins of War: Violence in Prehistory*, Malden, MA: Blackwell, 2005.

17. Gat, 'The Pattern of Fighting in Simple, Small Scale, Pre-State Societies'; Gat, *War in Human Civilization*, chap. 6.

18. Kim Hill, A. Hurtado, and R. Walker, 'High Adult Mortality among Hiwi Hunter-Gatherers: Implications for Human Evolution', *Journal of Human Evolution*, 52 (2007) 443–54, esp. 449, 451.

19. For the sources see Gat, *War in Human Civilization*, 129–32.

20. Patrick Kirch, *The Evolution of the Polynesian Chiefdoms*, Cambridge: Cambridge UP, 1984, quotation from 195; also Irving Goldman, *Ancient Polynesian Society*, Chicago: University of Chicago Press, 1970; Timothy Earle, *How Chiefs Come to Power: The Political Economy in Prehistory*, Stanford: Stanford UP, 1997.

21. Summarized in Michael Wilson, 'Chimpanzees, Warfare, and the Invention of Peace', in Fry, *War, Peace, and Human Nature*, 370–1.

22. Richard Wrangham, Michael Wilson, and Martin Muller, 'Comparative Rates of Violence in Chimpanzees and Humans', *Primates*, 47 (2006), 14–26. The suggestion that the factor that drove chimpanzees to violent killing is the expansion of human settlement (the chimpanzee equivalent of the 'tribal zone' theory) has been persuasively refuted: Michael Wilson et al., 'Lethal Aggression in *Pan* is Better Explained by Adaptive Strategies than Human Impacts', *Nature*, 513 (18 Sept. 2014), 414–17.

23. Philip Walker, 'A Bioarchaeological Perspective on the History of Violence', *Annual Review of Anthropology*, 30 (2001), 573–96; Patricia Lambert, 'The Archaeology of War: a North American Perspective', *Journal of Archaeological Research*, 10:3 (2002), 207–41.

24. Patricia Lambert, 'Patterns of Violence in Prehistoric Hunter-Gatherer Societies of Coastal Southern California', in Martin and Frayer, *Troubled Times*, 45–75.

25. M. Pilloud, A. Schwitalla, and T. Jones, 'The Bioarchaeological Record of Craniofacial Trauma in Central California', in Allen and Jones, *Violence and Warfare among Hunter-Gatherers*, 257–72, esp. 265; A. Schwitalla et al., 'Archaic Violence in Western North America: The Bioarchaeological Record of Dismemberment, Human Bone Artifacts, and Trophy Skulls from Central California', ibid., 273–95, esp. 290–1.

26. Jerome Cybulski, 'Culture Change, Demographic History, and Health and Disease on the Northwest Coast', in C. Larsen and G. Milner (eds.), *In the Wake of Contact: Biological Responses to Conquest*, New York: Wiley-Liss, 1994, 75–85.

27. Lambert, 'The Archaeology of War', 215; Cybulski, 'Culture Change'.

28. Walker, 'A Bioarchaeological Perspective on the History of Violence', 584, 591.

29. Ibid., 588–9.

30. Ibid., 590.

31. J. C. Chatters, 'Wild-Type Colonizers and High Levels of Violence among Paleoamericans', in Allen and Jones, *Violence and Warfare among Hunter-Gatherers*, 70–96, esp. 79–81, 91–2.

32. Elizabeth Arkush and Tiffiny Tung, 'Patterns of War in the Andes from the Archaic to the Late Horizon: Insights from Settlement Patterns and Cranial Trauma', *Journal of Archaeological Research*, 21 (2013), 307–69.

33. V. Eshed, A. Gopher, R. Pinhasi, and I. Hershkovitz, 'Paleopathology and the Origin of Agriculture in the Levant', *American Journal of Physical Anthropology*, 143:1 (2010), 121–33.

34. R. Brian Ferguson, 'Violence and War in Prehistory', in Martin and Frayer, *Troubled Times*, 321–55, quotation from 321.

35. Ferguson, 'The Prehistory of War and Peace in Europe and the Near East'. For my rebuttal and a more detailed elaboration of some of the themes discussed in this chapter see Gat, 'Proving Communal Warfare among Hunter-Gatherers: The Quasi-Rousseauan Error', *Evolutionary Anthropology*, 24 (2015), 111–26, esp. 113–14.

36. See Ferguson's propositions in his 'Violence and War in Prehistory', 322, which he would repeat in his later works.

37. Raymond Kelly, *Warless Societies and the Origin of War*, Ann Arbor: U. of Michigan, 2000, 18–21.

38. Douglas Fry, *The Human Potential for Peace*, Oxford: Oxford UP, 2006; Fry (ed.), *War, Peace, and Human Nature*; Fry and Patrik Söderberg, 'Lethal Aggression in Mobile Forager Bands and Implications for the Origins of War', *Science*, 341 (2013), 270–3.

39. Carol Ember, 'Myths about Hunter-Gatherers', *Ethnology*, 17 (1978), 439–48; Marc Ross, 'Political Decision Making and Conflict: Additional Cross-Cultural Codes and Scales', *Ethnology*, 22 (1983), 169–92.

40. See also Allen and Jones, *Violence and Warfare among Hunter-Gatherers*, 20, 27, 232.

41. http://www.iep.utm.edu/war/

42. Franz Boas, *Kwakiutl Ethnography*, Chicago: U. of Chicago, 1966, 108; also Donald, *Aboriginal Slavery on the Northwest Coast of North America*, 104.

43. Marilyn Roper, 'Evidence of Warfare in the Near East from 10,000–4,300 BC', in M. Nettleship et al. (eds.), *War: Its Causes and Correlates*, The Hague: Mouton, 1975, 304–9, quotation from 299.

44. Quoted in E. Arkush and M. Allen (eds.), *The Archaeology of War: Prehistories of Raiding and Conquest*, Gainesville: U. of Florida, 2006, 253.

45. Kelly, *Warless Societies*, 3–7.

46. Margaret Mead, 'Warfare is Only an Invention—Not a Biological Necessity', *Asia*, 15 (1940), 402–5; reprinted in L. Bramson and G. Goethals (eds.), *War: Studies from Psychology, Sociology and Anthropology*, New York: Basic Books, 1968, 269–74.

47. Samuel Bowles, 'Did Warfare Among Ancestral Hunter-Gatherers Affect the Evolution of Human Social Behaviours?', *Science*, 324 (5 June 2009), 1293–8.

48. Cf. Allen and Jones, *Violence and Warfare among Hunter-Gatherers*, 20, 106, 232. Kim Hill et al., 'Co-Residence Patterns in Hunter-Gatherer Societies Show Unique Human Social Structure', *Science*, 331 (2011), 1286–9, find that a quarter of the band's members were kin, and another roughly 50 per cent were about equally divided between marriage affiliates and marriage affiliates of the marriage affiliates. It should be noted that the logic of marriage alliances is also kinship, with the kin in question being the resulting offspring. Furthermore, humans are unique in investing lifetimes in raising and caring for their offspring, an effort that is shared by both sides of the marriage alliance and involves several generations. Finally, preference for distant kin is mostly evident in a conflict with an alien group.

49. Fry, who in his 2006 book *The Human Potential for Peace* did not share this position, now champions it, supposedly on the strength of his sample of simple hunter-gatherer societies: Fry and Söderberg, 'Lethal Aggression in Mobile Forager Bands'.

50. Christopher Boehm, 'The Biocultural Evolution of Conflict Resolution Between Groups', in Fry, *War, Peace, and Human Nature*, 315–40, esp. 329–30, 334.

51. Wilson et al., 'Lethal Aggression in *Pan*'.

52. Marilyn Roper's 'A Survey of the Evidence for Intrahuman Killing in the Pleistocene', *Current Anthropology*, 10:4 (1969), 427–59, is largely outdated. But see, for example, Erik Trinkaus and Jiří Svoboda, *Early Modern Human Evolution in Central Europe: The People of Dolní Věstonice and Pavlov*, Oxford: Oxford UP, 2006; Virginia Estabrook, 'Violence and Warfare in the European Mesolithic and Paleolithic', in Allen and Jones, *Violence and Warfare among Hunter-Gatherers*, 49–69.

53. See note 16.

54. Mark Allen, 'Hunter-Gatherer Violence and Warfare in Australia', and Colin Pardoe, 'Conflict and Territoriality in Aboriginal Australia: Evidence from Biology and Ethnography', both in Allen and Jones, *Violence and Warfare among Hunter-Gatherers*, 97–111 and 112–33.

55. J. Morgan, *The Life and Adventures of William Buckley: Thirty-Two Years a Wanderer among the Aborigines of the Unexplored Country Round Port Philip*, Canberra: Australian National UP, 1980 [1852], 39, 65–6.

56. Ibid., 72.

57. Ibid., 40–2.

58. Ibid., 49–51.

59. Ibid., 68–72.

60. Ibid., 81–3.

61. Ibid., 108, 190, also 73, 97.

62. Ibid., 189.

63. Lorimer Fison and A. Howitt, 'The Kurnai Tribe: Their Customs in Peace and War', in L. Fison and A. Howitt, *Kamilaroi and Kurnai*, Oosterhout, The Netherlands: Anthropological Publications, 1967 [1880], 213–14.

64. Ibid., 214–15, 223–4.

65. Ibid., 215–16.

66. Ibid., 219.

67. Ibid., 218–20.

68. Ibid., 220–1.

69. Gerald Wheeler, *The Tribe, and Intertribal Relations in Australia*, London: John Murray, 1910, 128–47.

70. Ibid., 148–9; my emphasis.

71. Ibid., 151; my emphasis.

72. Ibid., 152.

73. Ibid., 152–3; my emphasis.

74. Lloyd Warner, *A Black Civilization: A Social Study of an Australian Tribe*, n.p.: Harper, 1958 [1937], 155.

75. Ibid., 457–8.

76. Arnold Pilling, 'Discussion Comments', in Lee and DeVore, *Man the Hunter*, 158.

77. T. G. H. Strehlow, 'Geography and the Totemic Landscape in Central Australia', in R. Berndt (ed.), *Australian Aboriginal Anthropology*, Nedlands: U. of Western Australia, 1970, 92–140, quotation from 124–5.

78. Wilbur Chaseling, *Yulengor: Nomads of Arnhem Land*, London: Epworth, 1957, 79; my emphasis.

79. R. G. Kimber, 'Hunter-Gatherer Demography: The Recent Past in Central Australia', in B. Meehan and N. White (eds.), *Hunter-Gatherer Demography: Past and Present*, Sydney: U. of Sydney, 1990, 160–75, quotations from 163.

80. Mervin Meggitt, *Desert People: A Study of the Walbiri Aborigines of Central Australia*, Chicago: U. of Chicago Press, 1962, 38.

81. Ibid., 42.

82. N. Plomley (ed.), *Friendly Mission: The Tasmanian Journals and Papers of George Augustus Robinson 1829–1834*, Kingsgrove: Tasmanian Historical Research Association, 1966, 968–9; H. Ling Roth, *The Aborigines of Tasmania*, Halifax: King, 1899, 14–15, 82; Rhys Jones, 'Tasmanian Tribes', in Norman Tindale,

Aboriginal Tribes of Australia, Berkeley: U. of California, 1974, 328; Lyndall Ryan, *The Aboriginal Tasmanians*, Vancouver: U. of British Columbia, 1981, 13–14.

83. Again, for similar conclusions see Allen, 'Hunter-Gatherer Violence and Warfare in Australia', and Pardoe, 'Conflict and Territoriality in Aboriginal Australia', 129.

84. Warner, *A Black Civilization*, 157–8.

85. Brian Ferguson, 'Pinker's List: Exaggerating Prehistoric War Mortality', in Fry, *War, Peace, and Human Nature*, 112–50.

86. Graham Knuckey, 'Patterns of Fractures upon Aboriginal Crania from the Recent Past', *Proceedings of the Australian Society for Human Biology*, 5 (1992), 47–58.

87. Stephen Webb, *Palaeopathology of Aboriginal Australians: Health and Disease across a Hunter-Gatherer Continent*. Cambridge: Cambridge UP, 1995, 203–8, also 88.

88. Cf. Napoleon Chagnon's seminal study, *Yanomamo: The Fierce People*, 2nd edn, New York: Holt, 1977.

89. While furnishing evidence for very high levels of violence in some of the earliest and sparsest North American populations, Lambert, in 'The Archaeology of War: A North American Perspective', tended to believe that violence increased with denser and more settled habitation. She was also inclined to the opinion that most of the early violence took the form of homicide and feuds, rather than inter-group warfare, a view shared by Chatters, 'Wild-Type Colonizers and High Levels of Violence among Paleoamericans', 82. However, this is a theoretical presupposition rather than an empirical finding. For example, David Dye's *War Paths, Peace Paths: An Archaeology of Cooperation and Conflict in Native Eastern North America*, Lanham, MD: Altamira, 2009, 31, relies specifically on Kelly and Fry in making the same assumption, so what we have is a (false) theory guiding the empirical investigation.

90. W. W. Newcomb, 'A Re-Examination of the Causes of Plains Warfare', *American Anthropologist*, 52 (1950), 317–30, see 325; Thomas Biolsi, 'Ecological and Cultural Factors in Plain Indian Warfare', in Ferguson, *Warfare, Culture, and Environment*, 148–50.

91. Marian Smith, 'The War Complex of the Plains Indians', *Proceedings of the American Philosophical Society*, 78 (1938), 425–64, see 436, 431.

92. Ewers, 'Intertribal Warfare as the Precursor of Indian–White Warfare on the Northern Great Plains', 397–410, see 401.

93. Frank Secoy, *Changing Military Patterns of the Great Plains Indians*, New York: Augustin, 1953, 34–5.

94. Gat, 'Proving Communal Warfare among Hunter-Gatherers', esp. 119–22. See also Steven LeBlanc, 'Warfare and Human Nature', in T. Shackelford and R. Hansen (eds.), *The Evolution of Violence*, New York: Springer, 2013, 73–97, see 83–6; Allen and Jones, *Violence and Warfare among Hunter-Gatherers*, 357, 363.

95. Fry, *The Human Potential for Peace*, chap. 3.

96. Unfortunately, the latter position seems to have been at least implied recently by a leading evolutionary biologist: E. O. Wilson, 'Is War Inevitable?', *Discover*, 12 June 2012; excerpted from his *The Social Conquest of Earth*, New York: Norton, 2012.

97. See note 46.

98. Georg Simmel, *Conflict: The Web of Group Affiliations*, Glencoe, IL: Free Press, 1955.

99. 'The Seville Statement', UNESCO; emphasis in the original (on the UNESCO website).

100. Walker, 'A Bioarchaeological Perspective on the History of Violence', quotation from 590.

101. Burch, *Alliance and Conflict*.

102. Robert Kelly, 'From the Peaceful to the Warlike: Ethnographic and Archaeological Insights into Hunter-Gatherer Warfare and Homicide', in Fry, *War, Peace, and Human Nature*, 151–67, quotation from 158.

103. Ibid., 165.

104. Boehm, 'The Biocultural Evolution of Conflict Resolution between Groups', quotation from 333.

105. Ibid., 334; also 327, 333.

106. Ibid., 327.

107. Ibid., 330.

108. Ember, 'Myths about Hunter-Gatherers', 443.

CHAPTER 2

1. See, for example, Abraham Maslow, *Motivation and Personality*, New York: Harper, 1970 [1954]; John Burton (ed.), *Conflict: Human Needs Theory*, London: Macmillan, 1990.

2. Robert Ardrey, *The Territorial Imperative*, New York: Atheneum, 1966; Konrad Lorenz, *On Aggression*, London: Methuen, 1966; Niko Tinbergen, 'On War and Peace in Animals and Man', *Science*, 160 (1968), 1411–18.

3. William Durham, 'Resource Competition and Human Aggression. Part I: A Review of Primitive War', *Quarterly Review of Biology*, 51 (1976), 385–415; R. Dyson-Hudson and E. Alden Smith, 'Human Territoriality: An Ecological Reassessment', *American Anthropologist*, 80 (1978), 21–41; Felicity Huntingford and Angela Turner, *Animal Conflict*, London: Chapman, 1987, 229–30, 233–7; Charles Mueller, 'Environmental Stressors and Aggressive Behavior', in R. G. Geen and E. I. Donnerstein (eds.), *Aggression*, New York: Academic Press, 1983, ii. 63–6; Frans de Waal, *Good Natured: The Origins of Right and Wrong in Humans and Other Animals*, Cambridge, MA: Harvard UP, 1996, 194–6.

4. See again Marvin Meggitt, *Desert People*, Chicago: U. of Chicago, 1965, 42. For the expectation of stress as a strong promoter of war and anticipatory action, see M. Ember and C. R. Ember, 'Resource Unpredictability, Mistrust, and War:

A Cross-Cultural Study', *Journal of Conflict Resolution*, 36 (1992), 242–62; also W. D. Hamilton, 'Innate Social Aptitudes of Man: An Approach from Evolutionary Genetics', in R. Fox (ed.), *Biosocial Anthropology*, New York: John Wiley, 1975, 146.

5. E. W. Nelson, *The Eskimo about Bering Strait*, Washington, DC: Smithsonian, 1983 [1899], 327; also Ernest Burch, *Alliance and Conflict: The World System of the Inupiaq Eskimos*, Lincoln: U. of Nebraska, 2005.

6. See e.g. Donald Symons, *The Evolution of Human Sexuality*, New York: Oxford UP, 1979; Martin Daly and Margo Wilson, *Sex, Evolution, and Behavior*, Boston: Willard Grant, 1983; Matt Ridley, *The Red Queen: Sex and the Evolution of Human Nature*, New York: Macmillan, 1994; D. Buss and N. Malamuth (eds.), *Sex, Power, Conflict: Evolutionary and Feminist Perspectives*, New York: Oxford UP, 1996.

7. John Morgan, *The Life and Adventures of William Buckley: Thirty-Two Years a Wanderer among the Aborigines of the Unexplored Country Round Port Philip*, Canberra: Australian National UP, 1980 [1852], citations from 41, 68; see also 42, 59, 70, 74, 76, 81, 96.

8. Rhys Jones, 'Tasmanian Tribes', in Norman Tindale, *Aboriginal Tribes of Australia*, Berkeley: U. of California, 1974, 328.

9. Mildred Dickemann, 'Female Infanticide, Reproductive Strategies, and Social Stratification: A Preliminary Model', in N. Chagnon and W. Irons (eds.), *Evolutionary Biology and Human Social Behavior*, North Scituate, MA: Duxbury, 1979, 363; Symons, *The Evolution of Human Sexuality*, 152; Martin Daly and Margo Wilson, *Homicide*, New York: Aldine, 1988, 222 (quotation), citing A. Balikci, *The Netsilik Eskimo*, Garden City, NY: Natural History, 1970, 182; C. Irwin, 'The Inuit and the Evolution of Limited Group Conflict', in J. van der Dennen and V. Falger (eds.), *Sociobiology and Conflict*, London: Chapman, 1990, 201–2; Nelson, *The Eskimo about Bering Strait*, 292, 327–9; Wendel Oswalt, *Alaskan Eskimos*, San Francisco: Chandler, 1967, 178, 180, 182, 185, 187, 204; Ernest Burch and T. Correll, 'Alliance and Conflict: Inter-Regional Relations in North Alaska', in L. Guemple (ed.), *Alliance in Eskimo Society*, Seattle: U. of Washington, 1972, 33.

10. Cited in Laura Betzig, 'Comment', *Current Anthropology*, 32 (1991), 410.

11. Brian Ferguson, *Yanomami Warfare*, Santa Fe, NM: School of American Research, 1995, 355–8 and *passim*.

12. Napoleon Chagnon, 'Is Reproductive Success Equal in Egalitarian Societies', in Chagnon and Irons, *Evolutionary Biology and Human Social Behavior*, 385–401; I. Keen, 'How Some Murngin Men Marry Ten Wives', *Man*, 17 (1982), 620–42.

13. Daly and Wilson, *Sex, Evolution, and Behavior*, 88–9, 332–3; Symons, *The Evolution of Human Sexuality*, 143; Chagnon, 'Is Reproductive Success Equal in Egalitarian Societies', 380.

14. William Divale and Marvin Harris, 'Population, Warfare and the Male Supremacist Complex', *American Anthropologist*, 78 (1976), 521–38; Dickemann, 'Female Infanticide', 363–4.

15. Steve Jones, *The Language of the Genes*, New York: Anchor, 1993, 92; Daly and Wilson, *Sex, Evolution, and Behavior*, 92–7, 297–301.

16. Daly and Wilson, *Homicide*, 145–9.

17. Charles Darwin, *The Descent of Man*, Ch. iii, in *The Origin of the Species and the Descent of Man*, New York: Modern Library, n.d., 467–8; Dobbi Low, 'Sexual Selection and Human Ornamentation', in Chagnon and Irons, *Evolutionary Biology and Human Social Behavior*, 462–87; Jared Diamond, *The Rise and Fall of the Third Chimpanzee*, London: Vintage, 1992, chap. 9.

18. W. D. Hamilton and Robert Axelrod, *The Evolution of Cooperation*, New York: Basic Books, 1984; in effect anticipated by J. Maynard Smith and G. R. Price, 'The Logic of Animal Conflicts', *Nature*, 246 (1973), 15–18. For 'adjusting' mechanisms to prevent tit-for-tat from becoming a self-perpetuating process see: Robert Axelrod, *The Complexity of Cooperation*, Princeton: Princeton UP, 1997, 30–9; also the review in Matt Ridley, *The Origins of Virtue: Human Instincts and the Evolution of Cooperation*, New York: Viking, 1996, 67–84.

19. John Herz, 'Idealist Internationalism and the Security Dilemma', *World Politics*, 2 (1950), 157–80; Robert Jervis, 'Cooperation under the Security Dilemma', *World Politics*, 30 (1978), 167–214.

20. R. Dawkins and J. R. Krebs, 'Arms Races between and within Species', *Proceedings of the Royal Society of London Bulletin*, 205 (1979), 489–511.

21. Richard Dawkins, *The Selfish Gene*, Oxford: Oxford UP, 1989, 189–201, 329–31; Dawkins, *The God Delusion*, Boston: Houghton Mifflin, 2006; Pascal Boyer, *Religion Explained: The Evolutionary Origins of Religious Thought*, New York: Basic Books, 2001; also John Bowker, *Is God a Virus: Genes, Culture and Religion*, London: SPCK, 1995.

22. Dawkins, *The Selfish Gene*, 331; Brian Heiden, *A Prehistory of Religion: Shamanism, Sorcerers and Saints*, Washington, DC: Smithsonian, 2003; David Wilson, *Darwin's Cathedral: Evolution, Religion, and the Nature of Society*, Chicago: U. of Chicago, 2002.

23. See e.g. Johan Huizinga, *Homo Ludens*, Boston: Beacon, 1955, *passim*, and, with respect to war, 89–104.

24. Robert Fagan, *Animal Play Behavior*, New York: Oxford UP, 1981; also P. Smith (ed.), *Play in Animals and Humans*, Oxford: Blackwell, 1984; Huntingford and Turner, *Animal Conflict*, 198–200.

25. Gilbert Lewis, 'Payback and Ritual in War; New Guinea', in R. A. Hinde and H. E. Watson (eds.), *War: A Cruel Necessity?*, London: Tauris, 1995, 34–5; Walter Goldschmidt, 'Inducement to Military Participation in Tribal Societies', in R. Rubinstein and M. Foster (eds.), *The Social Dynamics of Peace and Conflict*, Boulder, CO: Westview, 1988, 51–2.

26. Mancur Olson, *The Logic of Collective Action: Public Goods and the Theory of Groups*, Cambridge, MA: Harvard UP, 1965.

27. First suggested by Darwin, R. A. Fisher, and J. B. S. Haldane, this idea has become the cornerstone of modern evolutionary theory with W. D. Hamilton, 'The

Genetical Evolution of Social Behaviour', *Journal of Theoretical Biology*, 7 (1964), 1–16, 17–52. For Darwin see *The Origin of the Species*, chap. viii, and *The Descent of Man*, chap. v, in *The Origin of the Species and the Descent of Man*, 203–5, 498.

28. See Chapter 1, note 48.

29. Again this has been pointed out by Hamilton, 'The Genetical Evolution of Social Behavior', 16, and developed by Robert L. Trivers, 'Parent–Offspring Conflict', *American Zoologist*, 14 (1974), 249–64.

30. Darwin, *The Descent of Man*, chap. v, 499–500; Robert L. Trivers, 'The Evolution of Reciprocal Altruism', *Quarterly Review of Biology*, 46 (1971), 35–57; Richard Alexander, *The Biology of Moral Systems*, New York: Aldine, 1987, 77, 85, 93–4, 99–110, 117–126, and *passim*.

31. Robert Frank, *Passions within Reason: The Strategic Role of the Emotions*, New York: Norton, 1988; Ridley, *The Origins of Virtue*; Marc Hauser, *Moral Minds: The Nature of Right and Wrong*, New York: HarperCollins, 2006; Jonathan Haidt, *The Righteous Mind: Why Good People are Divided by Politics and Religion*, New York: Pantheon, 2012.

32. Azar Gat, with Alexander Yakobson, *Nations: The Long History and Deep Roots of Political Ethnicity and Nationalism*, Cambridge: Cambridge UP, 2013.

33. This has been the subject of the most intense debate, but the balance of opinion clearly moves in this direction. Both of the pioneers of kin altruism, W. D. Hamilton and E. O. Wilson, have later come to endorse group selection: Hamilton, 'Innate Social Aptitudes of Man: An Approach from Evolutionary Genetics'; W. D. Hamilton, *Narrow Roads of Gene Land*, Oxford: Freeman, 1996; David S. Wilson and E. Sober, *Unto Others: The Evolution and Psychology of Unselfish Behavior*, Cambridge, MA: Harvard UP, 1998; David S. Wilson and E. O. Wilson, 'Rethinking the Theoretical Foundations of Sociobiology', *Quarterly Review of Biology*, 82 (2007), 327–48; Martin Nowak, Corina Tarnita, and Edward O. Wilson, 'The Evolution of Eusociality', *Nature*, 466 (26 Aug. 2010), 1057–62; Samuel Bowles, 'Group Competition, Reproductive Leveling, and the Evolution of Human Altruism', *Science*, 314 (2006), 1569–72; Bowles, 'Did Warfare among Ancestral Hunter-Gatherers Affect the Evolution of Human Social Behaviors', *Science*, 324 (2009), 1293–8; Samuel Bowles and Herbert Gintis, *A Cooperative Species: Human Reciprocity and its Evolution*, Princeton: Princeton UP, 2011, highlighting the significance of group sanctions against defectors and free-riders; Oleg Smirnov, Holly Arrow, Douglas Kennett, and John Orbell, 'Ancestral War and the Evolutionary Origins of "Heroism"', *The Journal of Politics*, 69 (2007), 927–40. Darwin suggested the idea in *The Descent of Man*, chap. v, 496–500.

34. C. J. Lumsden and E. O. Wilson, *Genes, Mind and Culture*, Cambridge, MA: Harvard UP, 1981; L. L. Cavalli-Sforza and M. W. Feldman, *Cultural Transmission and Evolution*, Princeton: Princeton UP, 1981; Robert Boyd and P. J. Richerson, *Culture and the Evolutionary Process*, Chicago: U. of Chicago, 1985; Boyd and Richerson, *Not by Genes Alone: How Culture Transformed Human Evolution*,

Chicago: U. of Chicago, 2005; W. H. Durham, *Coevolution: Genes, Culture, and Human Diversity*, Stanford: Stanford UP, 1991.

CHAPTER 3

1. Cf. Michael Mann, *The Sources of Social Power*, i, Cambridge: Cambridge UP, 1986, 130, 142–61.
2. Max Weber, *Economy and Society*, New York: Bedminster, 1968, 54, 904.
3. The argument regarding which sphere holds 'primacy' goes back to nineteenth-century Germany. For a summary see Eckart Kehr, *Economic Interest, Militarism, and Foreign Policy*, Berkeley: U. of California, 1977. For more recent theorizing see: Robert Putnam, 'Diplomacy and Domestic Politics: The Logic of Two-Level Games', *International Organization*, 42 (1988), 427–60; Jeffrey Knopf, 'Beyond Two-Level Games: Domestic–International Interaction in the Intermediate-Range Nuclear Forces Negotiations', *International Organization*, 47 (1993), 599–628.
4. For Clausewitz's limited historical horizons in this respect, see: Azar Gat, *The Origins of Military Thought from the Enlightenment to Clausewitz*, Oxford: Oxford UP, 1989, incorporated in Gat, *A History of Military Thought*, Oxford: Oxford UP, 2001; Martin van Creveld, *The Transformation of War*, New York: Free Press, 1991; John Keegan, *A History of Warfare*, New York: Knopf, 1994.
5. Cf. Mancur Olson, *Power and Prosperity: Outgrowing Communist and Capitalist Dictatorships*, New York: Basic Books, 2000.
6. Jack Levy and William Thompson, *The Arc of War: Origins, Escalation, and Transformation*, Chicago: U. of Chicago Press, 2011, suggesting that violent mortality increased with the emergence of the state, combine several errors. First, they take little account of the recent studies on the tremendous lethality of the pre-state condition. Second, they measure lethality by battle casualties, whereas the main tribal fighting modes were not the battle but the raid and the ambush—taking the enemy by surprise and often annihilating entire sleeping camps: men, women, and children. Third, death toll in battle is an indication of the absolute size of states and their armies—obviously big—rather than of relative mortality rate in war.
7. Charles Tilly, 'War Making and State Making as Organized Crime', in P. Evans, D. Rueschemeyer, and T. Skocpol (eds.), *Bringing the State Back In*, Cambridge: Cambridge UP, 1985, 169–91.
8. Rome is the best documented case: Tenney Frank, *An Economic Survey of Ancient Rome*, Baltimore, MD: Johns Hopkins UP, 1933, i. 146, 228, and *passim.*; v. 4–7, and *passim.*; Keith Hopkins, 'Taxes and Trade in the Roman Empire (200 BC–AD 400)', *Journal of Roman Studies*, 70 (1980), 101–25. More broadly, see Raymond Goldsmith, *Premodern Financial Systems: A Historical Comparative Study*, Cambridge: Cambridge UP, 1987, 18, 31–2 (Athens), 48 (Rome), 107, 121 (Moghal India), 142 (Tokugawa Japan).

9. Carl von Clausewitz, *On War*, Princeton, NJ: Princeton UP, 1976, viii, 6B, pp. 606–7. One does not have to be a Marxist to agree with Lenin's criticism of this view; see Gat, *The Origins of Military Thought from the Enlightenment to Clausewitz*, 236–50; Gat, *The Development of Military Thought: The Nineteenth Century*, Oxford: Oxford UP, 1992, 237–8; both incorporated in Gat, *A History of Military Thought*, 238–52, 505–6.

10. For summaries see R. Cohen and E. Service (eds.), *Origins of the State*, Philadelphia: Institute for the Study of Human Issues, 1978; Jonathan Haas, *The Evolution of the Prehistoric State*, New York: Columbia UP, 1982.

11. Cf. Michael Mann, 'States, Ancient and Modern', in his *State, War and Capitalism*, Oxford: Blackwell, 1988, 64–5.

12. Even Bradley Thayer, *Darwin and International Relations: On the Evolutionary Origins of War and Ethnic Conflict*, Lexington: U. of Kentucky, 2004, generally shies away from sexuality in his evolutionary account of war. There have been, of course, attempts to connect sexuality with politics, most famously, in Freud's footsteps, those by Wilhelm Reich and Michel Foucault.

13. Randy Thornhill and Craig Palmer, *A Natural History of Rape: Biological Bases of Sexual Coercion*, Cambridge, MA: MIT, 2000, is a sound, evolution-informed study of this distressing subject; also, D. Buss and N. Malamuth (eds.), *Sex, Power, Conflict: Evolutionary and Feminist Perspectives*, New York: Oxford UP, 1996. Susan Brownmiller's pioneering *Against Our Will: Men, Women and Rape*, London: Penguin, 1976, 31–113, represents much of the prevailing confusion on the subject while cursorily incorporating some historical evidence. The view that rape is an act of domination and humiliation rather than of sex finds expression even in Joshua Goldstein, *War and Gender: How the Gender Shapes the War System and Vice Versa*, New York: Cambridge UP, 2001, 362–9; Martin van Creveld, *Men, Women and War*, London: Cassell, 2001, 33.

14. Chiara Batini, Pille Hallast, Daniel Zadik, et al., 'Large-Scale Recent Expansion of European Patrilineages Shown by Population Resequencing', *Nature Communications*, 2015, DOI: 10.1038/ncomms8152; also David Poznik, Yali Xue, Fernando Mendez, et al., 'Punctuated Bursts in Human Male Demography Inferred from 1,244 Worldwide Y-Chromosome Sequences', *Nature Genetics*, 2016, DOI: 10.1038/ng.3559.

15. Tatiana Zerjal, Yali Xue, Giorgio Bertorelle, et al., 'The Genetic Legacy of the Mongols', *The American Journal of Human Genetics*, 72 (2003), 717–21.

16. E.g. Jack Goody, *The Oriental, the Ancient and the Primitive: Systems of Marriage and the Family in the Pre-Industrial Societies of Eurasia*, Cambridge: Cambridge UP, 1990.

17. J. Cook, in I. Gershevitch (ed.), *The Cambridge History of Iran*, Cambridge UP, 1985, ii. 226–7; Cook, *The Persian Empire*, London: Dent, 1983, 136–7.

18. Hans Bielenstein, *The Bureaucracy of the Han Times*, Cambridge: Cambridge UP, 1980, 73–4.

19. Elizabeth Perry, *Rebels and Revolutionaries in North China, 1845–1945*, Stanford: Stanford UP, 1980, 51–2; Matthew Sommer, *Sex, Law, and Society in Late Imperial China*, Stanford: Stanford UP, 2000, 12–15, 93–101.

20. Leslie Peirce, *The Imperial Harem: Women and Sovereignty in the Ottoman Empire*, New York: Oxford UP, 1993, 122–4.
21. Ibn Khaldun, *The Muqaddimah: An Introduction to History*, New York: Pantheon, 1958, chap. 3.1.
22. Cicero, *Tusculan Disputations* 5.20–1.
23. Cook, in *The Cambridge History of Iran*, ii. 227, 331.
24. For the data on the late Empire, when usurpation was particularly frequent, see Pat Southern and Karen Dixon, *The Late Roman Army*, London: Batsford, 1996, x–xii.
25. S. E. Finer, *The History of Government From the Earliest Times*, Oxford: Oxford UP, 1997, 702.
26. Richard Abels, *Lordship and Military Obligation in Anglo-Saxon England*, Berkeley: U. of California, 1988, 12.
27. Paddy Griffith, *The Viking Art of War*, London: Greenhill, 1995, 26.
28. Peirce, *The Imperial Harem*, 21, 44, 99–103.
29. Laura Betzig, *Despotism and Differential Reproduction: A Darwinian View of History*, New York: Aldine, 1986, overlooks both the 'downside' of power politics in terms of ultimate reproductive success and the dominance of the proximate mechanisms in determining behaviour in conditions that may have substantially diverged from those of the evolutionary state of nature, where these mechanisms had proved adaptive.
30. Two works on the subject are: Jonathan Mercer, *Reputation and International Politics*, Ithaca, NY: Cornell UP, 1996, which unpersuasively rejects the significance of that factor in crisis; Barry O'Neill, *Honor, Symbols and War*, Ann Arbor: U. of Michigan, 1999.
31. Cited in Michael Prawdin, *The Mongol Empire*, London: George Allen, 1961, 60.
32. Long towering over the field, L. Luca Cavalli-Sforza, Paolo Menozzi, and Alberto Piazza, *The History and Geography of Human Genes*, Princeton: Princeton UP, 1994, and, more popularly, Cavalli-Sforza, *The Great Human Diasporas*, Reading, MA: Addison, 1995, are still instructive but are fast being rendered obsolete by modern genetic techniques.
33. See Azar Gat, with Alexander Yakobson, *Nations: The Long History and Deep Roots of Political Ethnicity and Nationalism*, Cambridge: Cambridge UP, 2013.
34. Cf. Pascal Boyer, *Religion Explained: The Evolutionary Origins of Religious Thought*, New York: Basic Books, 2001, 135–42.
35. See, for example, Marcel Gauchet, *The Disenchantment of the World: A Political History of Religion*, Princeton: Princeton UP, 1997.
36. For example, by John Keegan in *A History of Warfare*, 106–14.
37. Barry Isaac, 'Aztec Warfare: Goals and Battlefield Comportment', *Ethnology*, 22 (1983), 121–31.
38. See, similarly: Stark, *The Rise of Christianity*, Princeton: Princeton UP, 1996, chap. 8: 'The Martyrs: Sacrifice as Rational Choice'; David S. Wilson, *Darwin's Cathedral: Evolution, Religion, and the Nature of Society*, Chicago: U. of Chicago, 2002. Both works overlook the military aspect.

39. Richard Dawkins, *The Selfish Gene*, Oxford: Oxford UP, 1989, 331.
40. See Regina Schwartz, *The Curse of Cain: The Violent Legacy of Monotheism*, Chicago: U. of Chicago, 1997. Historically naïve, this book overstates a good case, overlooking the fact that pagans too fought for common, partly religious identity, sacred land, and the glory of the gods, as well as relying on heavenly support. Daniel Martin, *Does Christianity Cause War?*, Oxford: Oxford UP, 1997, while idiosyncratic and apologetic, rightly claims that religion was merely one interacting element within a complex array of factors. Rodney Stark, *One God: Historical Consequences of Monotheism*, Princeton: Princeton UP, 2001, chap. 3, is the closest to the approach presented here.
41. 'Pyrrhus', xxvi, in *Plutarch's Lives*, Cambridge, MA: Loeb, 1959, vol. ix.
42. Ibid., xiv.
43. Norbert Elias, *The Civilizing Process*, Oxford: Blackwell, 1994.

CHAPTER 4

1. Franz Boas, *Kuakiutl Ethnography*, Chicago: U. of Chicago, 1966, 105–19.
2. Derek Freeman, *Margaret Mead and Samoa: The Making and Unmaking of an Athropological Myth*, Cambridge, MA: Harvard UP, 1983; Freeman, *The Fateful Hoaxing of Margaret Mead*, Boulder, CO: Westview, 1999. For balance see: Martin Orans, *Not Even Wrong: Margaret Mead, Derek Freeman, and the Samoans*, Novato, CA: Chandler and Sharp, 1996; Paul Shenkman, *The Trashing of Margaret Mead*, Madison: Wisconsin UP, 2009.
3. Margaret Mead, *Coming of Age in Samoa*, New York: Blue Ribbon, 1928, 198. For fighting in her other works on Samoa, see Freeman, *Margaret Mead and Samoa*, 89–90.
4. See the wealth of data in Freeman, *Margaret Mead and Samoa*, chap. 11.
5. Margaret Mead, 'Warfare is Only an Invention—Not a Biological Necessity', *Asia*, 15 (1940), 402–5, reprinted in L. Bramson and G. Goethals (eds.), *War: Studies from Psychology, Sociology and Anthropology*, New York: Basic Books, 1968, 269–74.
6. Overviews of interpretations can be found in Brian Ferguson, 'A Reexamination of the Causes of Northwest Coast Warfare', in Ferguson (ed.), *Warfare, Culture and Environment*, Orlando, FL: Academic Press, 1984; J. van der Dennen and V. Falger (eds.), *Sociobiology and Conflict*, London: Chapman, 1990.
7. C. R. Hallpike, *The Principles of Social Evolution*, Oxford: Oxford UP, 1986, 113, also 372.
8. Robert Kelly, 'From the Peaceful to the Warlike: Ethnographic and Archaeological Insights into Hunter-Gatherer Warfare and Homicide', in D. Fry (ed.), *War, Peace, and Human Nature: The Convergence of Evolutionary and Cultural Views*, Oxford: Oxford UP, 2013, 151–67, quotation from 154; also 151, 160.
9. David Dye, 'Trends in Cooperation and Conflict in Native Eastern North America', in Fry, *War, Peace, and Human Nature*, 132–50, quotation from 137.

10. V. Gordon Childe, *Social Evolution*, Cleveland: Meridian, 1951; Leslie White, *The Science of Culture*, New York: Grove, 1949; White, *The Evolution of Culture*, New York: McGraw-Hill, 1959; J. H. Steward, *Theory of Cultural Change*, Urbana: U. of Illinois, 1955; Marshall Sahlins and Elman Service (eds.), *Evolution and Culture*, Ann Arbor: U. of Michigan, 1960; Elman Service, *Primitive Social Organization: An Evolutionary Perspective*, New York: Random House, 1962; Service, *Origins of the State and Civilization: The Process of Cultural Evolution*, New York: Norton, 1975; Morton Fried, *The Evolution of Political Society*, New York: Random House, 1967; Marvin Harris, *The Rise of Anthropological Theory*, New York: Crowell, 1968; R. L. Carneiro, 'Foreword' to K. Otterbein, *The Evolution of War*, New Haven: HRAF, 1970; Carneiro, 'The Four Faces of Evolution: Unilinear, Universal, Multilinear and Differential', in J. Honigmann (ed.), *Handbook of Social and Cultural Anthropology*, Chicago: Rand, 1973, 89–110; A. W. Johnson and T. Earle, *The Evolution of Human Societies: From Foraging Group to Agrarian State*, Stanford: Stanford UP, 1987; Tim Ingold, *Evolution and Social Life*, Cambridge: Cambridge UP, 1986; David Rindos, 'The Evolution of the Capacity for Culture: Sociobiology, Structuralism, and Cultural Selectionism', *Current Anthropology*, 27 (1986), 315–32; Stephen Sanderson, *Social Evolutionism*, Oxford: Blackwell, 1990; Sanderson, *Social Transformations*, Oxford: Blackwell, 1995.

11. Richard Dawkins, *The Selfish Gene*, Oxford: Oxford UP, 2nd edn, 1989, chap. 11; Daniel Dennet, *Darwin's Dangerous Idea*, New York: Simon & Schuster, 1995; Dan Sperber, *Explaining Culture: A Naturalistic Approach*, Oxford: Blackwell, 1996; J. M. Balkin, *Cultural Software*, New Haven, CT: Yale UP, 1998.

12. See Jack Cohen and Jan Stewart, *Figments of Reality: The Evolution of the Curious Mind*, Cambridge: Cambridge UP, 1997, and their earlier *The Collapse of Chaos: Discovering Simplicity in a Complex World*, New York: Viking, 1994; also John Bonner, *The Evolution of Complexity by Means of Natural Selection*, Princeton: Princeton UP, 1988, and Simon Morris, *Life's Solution: Inevitable Humans in a Lonely Universe*, Cambridge: Cambridge UP, 2003. These are more than ample rebuttals of Stephen J. Gould's overdrawn celebration of evolution as contingency in *Wonderful Life*, New York: Norton, 1989.

13. In addition to the references in note 12, see esp. Stuart Kaufman, *The Origins of Order: Self-Organization and Selection in Evolution*, New York: Oxford UP, 1993. An overview is offered by M. Mitchell Waldrop, *Complexity: The Emerging Science at the Edge of Order and Chaos*, New York: Simon & Schuster, 1992. See also Richard Dawkins, *The Blind Watchmaker*, London: Longman, 1986; John Holland, *Hidden Order: How Adaptation Builds Complexity*, Reading, MA: Helix, 1995; Matt Ridley, *The Origins of Virtue*, New York: Viking, 1996; Philip Ball, *The Self-Made Tapestry: Pattern Formation in Nature*, Oxford: Oxford UP, 1999; Peter Corning, *Nature's Magic: Synergy in Evolution and the Fate of Humankind*, Cambridge: Cambridge UP, 2003.

14. Noam Chomsky, *Cartesian Linguistics*, New York: Harper & Row, 1966; Steven Pinker, *The Language Instinct*, New York: Morrow, 1994; Pinker, *The Blank Slate:*

The Modern Denial of Human Nature, New York:Viking, 2002;Terrence Deacon, *The Symbolic Species:The Co-Evolution of Language and the Human Brain*, London: Penguin, 1997.

15. A seminal, and probably still the best, discussion of this point is John Tooby and Leda Cosmides, 'The Psychological Foundations of Culture', in L. Cosmides, J. Tooby, and J. Barkow (eds.), *The Adapted Mind: Evolutionary Psychology and the Generation of Culture*, New York: Oxford UP, 1992.

16. See Chapter 2, note 34.

17. Marvin Harris, *Cultural Materialism:The Struggle for a Science of Culture*, Walnut Creek, CA: Altamira, 2001 [1979].

18. Ibid., 119–40.

19. All of these strikingly manifest themselves in Harris's multi-edition textbooks: Marvin Harris, *Cultural Anthropology*, New York: Harper Collins, 4th edn, 1995; Harris, *Culture, People, Nature:An Introduction to General Anthropology*, New York: Longman, 1997.

20. A survey and bibliography of the protracted 'protein controversy' by one of the chief protagonists is Marvin Harris, 'A Cultural Materialist Theory of Band and Village Warfare: The Yanomamo Test', in Ferguson, *Warfare, Culture and Environment*, 111–40. Also on the frustrations of the ecological/materialist approach by one of its chief proponents and an authority on Highland New Guinea warfare: Andrew Vayda, *War in Ecological Perspective*, New York: Plenum, 1976, 1–7.

21. Napoleon Chagnon, 'Male Competition, Favoring Close Kin, and Village Fissioning Among the Yanomamo Indians', in N. Chagnon and W. Irons (eds.), *Evolutionary Biology and Human Social Behavior*, North Scituate, MA: Duxbury, 1979, 86–132; Chagnon, 'Is Reproductive Success Equal in Egalitarian Societies?', ibid., 374–401; Chagnon, 'Life Histories, Blood Revenge and Warfare in a Tribal Population', *Science*, 239 (1988), 985–92.

22. See eminent anthropologist Marshall Sahlins's *The Use and Abuse of Biology:An Anthropological Critique of Sociobiology*, Ann Arbor: U. of Michigan, 1976; and Dawkins's devastating rebuttal: *The Selfish Gene*, 291–2. Sahlins has restated his all-culture view in his *The Western Illusion of Human Nature*, Chicago: Prickly Paradigm, 2008; see most notably 104. Sahlins's *What Kinship Is—And Is Not*, Chicago, U. of Chicago, 2013, is a striking demonstration of a common failure to realize that human fundamentals tend to be *both* biologically grounded *and* socially construed.

23. Clark McCauley, 'Conference Overview', in J. Haas (ed.), *The Anthropology of War*, New York: Cambridge UP, 1990, 3.

24. Ibid.; Brian Ferguson, *Yanomami Warfare*, Santa Fe, NM: School of American Research, 1995, 358–9.

25. Again see a survey and bibliography in Harris, 'A Cultural Materialist Theory of Band and Village Warfare'; Napoleon Chagnon, *Yanomamo:The Fierce People*, 2nd edn, New York: Holt, 1977, 33. Chagnon himself admits that humans, like

other animals, fill up new ecological niches, rapidly approaching these niches' carrying capacity of life-sustaining material resources; in contradiction to his general argument, he concedes that somatic conflict is then the norm: 'Reproductive and Somatic Conflicts of Interest in the Genesis of Violence and Warfare among Tribesmen', in Haas, *The Anthropology of War*, 87–9.

26. This point was brought home to Chagnon by Richard Alexander, *The Biology of Moral Systems*, New York: Aldine, 1987. See Chagnon, 'Life Histories, Blood Revenge and Warfare'; Chagnon, 'Reproductive and Somatic Conflicts', 77–104.

27. Brian Ferguson, 'Introduction', in his *Warfare, Culture and the Environment*, 38–41; Ferguson, 'Northwest Coast Warfare', ibid., 269–71, 308–10, and *passim*; Ferguson, 'Explaining War', in Haas, *The Anthropology of War*, 26–55; Ferguson, *Yanomami*, xii, 8–13, and *passim*.

28. Ferguson, 'Explaining War', 54–5; Ferguson, *Yanomami*, 8.

29. William Divale and Marvin Harris, 'Population, Warfare and the Male Supremacist Complex', *American Anthropologist*, 78 (1976), 521–38.

30. Ferguson, *Yanomami*, 355–8 and *passim*. For my exchange with Ferguson see his 'The Causes and Origins of "Primitive Warfare": On Evolved Motivations for War', and my 'Reply', both in *Anthropological Quarterly*, 73 (2000), 159–64, 165–8.

31. Chagnon, 'Reproductive and Somatic Conflicts', 77–104.

32. Andrew Vayda, 'Hypotheses about Functions of War', in M. Fried, M. Harris, and R. Murphy (eds.), *War: The Anthropology of Armed Conflict and Aggression*, New York: The Natural History Press, 1968, 85–91.

33. William Graham Sumner, 'War', reprinted from his *War and Other Essays* (1911) in Bramson and Goethals, *War*, 212; Sumner, *Folkways*, New York: Mentor, 1960 [1906], para. 22; followed by Maurice Davie, *The Evolution of War*, New Haven: Yale UP, 1929, 65. See also Walter Goldschmidt, 'Inducement to Military Participation in Tribal Societies', in R. Rubinstein and M. Foster (eds.), *The Social Dynamics of Peace and Conflict*, Boulder CO: Westview, 1988, 47–65.

CHAPTER 5

1. Hans Morgenthau, *Politics among Nations*, New York: Knopf, 1967, 4–5, 25–36, 109–12, and chaps. 5–8.

2. Ibid., 48; emphasis added.

3. Ibid., 5.

4. Cf. Robert Keohane, *After Hegemony: Cooperation and Discord in the World Political Economy*, Princeton: Princeton UP, 2005 [1984], 21–5.

5. Reinhold Niebuhr, *Moral Man and Immoral Society: A Study in Ethics and Politics*, New York: Scribner, 1953 [1932], 16, also 16–17.

6. Ibid., 18.

7. Ibid., 42.

8. Ibid., 26.

9. Ibid., 42.

10. Ibid., 26.

11. Arnold Wolfers, *Discord and Collaboration: Essays on International Politics*, Baltimore, MD: Johns Hopkins UP, 1962, 5–6.

12. Ibid., 12.

13. Ibid., 13; also 70.

14. Ibid., 15.

15. Ibid., 72.

16. Ibid., 89.

17. Ibid., 152–8.

18. Ibid., 153.

19. Ibid., 67.

20. Robert Gilpin, *War and Change in World Politics*, New York: Cambridge UP, 1981, 10; also, somewhat differently, 50.

21. Ibid., 22; also 23.

22. Ibid., 19–23.

23. Stephen Krasner, *Defending the National Interest: Raw Materials Investments and US Foreign Policy*, Princeton: Princeton UP, 1978, 13.

24. Ibid., 41.

25. Ibid., 13–14. Still, somewhat inconsistently Krasner in the end distinguishes between interests and ideology: 334–42.

26. Ibid., 38–9.

27. Kenneth Waltz, *Theory of International Politics*, Reading, MA: Addison, 1979, especially 72–3, 88–93, 102, III–14, 122, 126.

28. Waltz, *Theory of International Politics*, 186–7, mentions the dilemma only cursorily. But the point has been brought out by Charles Glaser, 'The Necessary and Natural Evolution of Structural Realism', in J. Vasquez and C. Elman (eds.), *Realism and the Balancing of Power*, Upper Saddle River, NJ: Prentice Hall, 2003, 266–79; see 268.

29. Waltz, *Theory of International Politics*, chaps. 2–3.

30. Wolfers, *Discord and Collaboration*, 67; emphasis added.

31. Alexander Wendt, 'Anarchy is What States Make of it: The Social Construction of Power Politics', *International Organization*, 46:2 (1992), 391–425, esp. 394–5; Wendt, *Social Theory of International Politics*, Cambridge: Cambridge UP, 1999; and, citing Wolfers, Hidemi Suganami, *On the Causes of War*, Oxford: Oxford UP, 1996, esp. 25, 50–1, 153.

32. Randall Schweller, 'Neorealism's Status-Quo Bias: What Security Dilemma?', *Security Studies*, 5:3 (1996), 90–121, quotations from 91–2; see also Schweller, 'Bandwagoning for Profit: Bringing the Revisionist State Back In', *International Security*, 19:1 (1994), 72–107.

33. Waltz, *Theory of International Politics*, 108–9, 137; implicitly in Stephen Walt, *The Origins of Alliances*, Ithaca, NY: Cornell UP, 1987; and most strongly, Jack Snyder, *Myths of Empire*, Ithaca, NY: Cornell UP, 1991. Snyder's defensive bias has been

criticized by Fareed Zakaria, 'Realism and Domestic Politics', *International Security*, 17:1 (1992), 177–98.

34. W. Wohlforth, R. Little, S. Kaufman, et al., 'Testing Balance-Of-Power Theory in World History', *European Journal of International Relations*, 13 (2007), 155–85.

35. John Mearsheimer, *The Tragedy of Great Power Politics*, New York: Norton, 2001, 20.

36. Ibid., esp. 2–3, 18–21, 53–4.

37. Glenn Snyder, 'Mearsheimer's World: Offensive Realism and the Struggle for Security', *International Security*, 27:1 (2002), 157.

38. Schweller, 'Bandwagoning for Profit'; Schweller, 'Neorealism's Status-Quo Bias', 115.

39. William Wohlworth, *The Elusive Balance: Power and Perceptions during the Cold War*, Ithaca, NY: Cornell UP, 1993; Gideon Rose, 'Neoclassical Realism and Theories of Foreign Policy', *World Politics*, 51 (October 1998), 144–72; Fareed Zakaria, *From Wealth to Power: The Unusual Origins of America's World Role*, Princeton: Princeton UP, 1998; S. Lobell, N. Ripsman, and J. Taliaferro (eds.), *Neoclassical Realism, the State, and Foreign Policy*, Cambridge: Cambridge UP, 2009. For a different evolution-informed criticism see Dominic Johnson and Dominic Tierney, *Failing to Win: Perceptions of Victory and Defeat in International Politics*, Cambridge, MA: Harvard UP, 2006, 28–9.

40. Schweller, 'Bandwagoning for Profit'.

41. Andrew Kydd, 'Sheep in Sheep's Clothing: Why Security Seekers Do Not Fight Each Other', *Security Studies*, 7:1 (1997), 114–54.

42. Exhibiting this ambiguity between power and other aims and between wealth as a coveted objective and as a source of power: Randall Schweller, 'The Progressiveness of Neoclassical Realism', in C. Elman and M. Elman (eds.), *Progress in International Relations Theory*, Cambridge, MA: MIT, 2003, 311–47, esp. 326–9; Schweller, 'New Realist Research on Alliances: Refining, Not Refuting, Waltz's Balancing Proposition', in Vasquez and Elman, *Realism and the Balancing of Power*, 74–9. By comparison, Schweller, *Unanswered Threats: Political Constraints on the Balance of Power*, Princeton: Princeton UP, 2006, 103, 106, 109, and *passim*, is one-dimensional and its thesis is flimsy.

43. Charles Glaser, *Rational Theory of International Politics: The Logic of Competition and Cooperation*, Princeton: Princeton UP, 2010. A few other scholars have made similar points. Stephen Brooks, 'Dueling Realisms', *International Organization*, 51:3 (1997), 445–77, stresses the connection and trade-off between the economy and security. However, by referring to the former as 'economic capacity', he might create the impression that wealth is sought mainly as an investment in security, rather than also—if not primarily—for consumption. Glenn Palmer and Clifton Morgan, in *A Theory of Foreign Policy*, Princeton: Princeton UP, 2006, argue that there is an infinite number of possible aims in the foreign policy 'portfolio', which they classify under the two categories of 'change' and 'maintenance'. As with Brooks, this is basically a restatement of a position held by the pioneers of classical realism.

44. Schweller, too, conflates offensive realism and offensive structural realism: Schweller, 'Neoclassical Realism and State Mobilization: Expansionist Ideology in the Age of Mass Politics', in Lobell, Ripsman, and Taliaferro, *Neoclassical Realism, the State, and Foreign Policy*, 227–50, see 227; also, Schweller, 'The Progressiveness of Neoclassical Realism', 328.

45. Schweller, 'Neorealism's Status-Quo Bias', 93.

46. Wolfers, *Discord and Collaboration*, 5–6.

47. Glaser, *Rational Theory of International Politics*, 3.

48. This lacuna has also been stressed in Jack Donnelly's comprehensive critique of realism, *Realism and International Relations*, Cambridge: Cambridge UP, 2000, 51, 56, 62–3; Richard Ned Lebow, *Why Nations Fight*, Cambridge: Cambridge UP, 2010.

49. E.g. John Keegan, *History of Warfare*, New York: Knopf, 1993.

50. Bradley Thayer, *Darwin and International Relations: On the Evolutionary Origins of War and Ethnic Conflict*, Lexington: U. of Kentucky, 2004, 178–9.

51. Cf. Bradley Thayer, 'Bringing in Darwin: Evolutionary Theory, Realism, and International Politics', *International Security*, 25:2 (2000), 126, 137–8, 140; Thayer, *Darwin and International Relations*, 11–12, 93.

52. Donnelly, *Realism and International Relations*, 43. Annette Freyberg-Inan, *What Moves Man: The Realist Theory of International Relations and its Judgment of Human Nature*, Albany, NY: SUNY, 2004, is an intelligent and comprehensive critique of the realist view of human nature and its theoretical and practical implications.

53. Lebow, *Why Nations Fight*, particularly chap. 3; based on his *A Cultural Theory of International Relations*, Cambridge: Cambridge UP, 2008. Although Lebow points out that motives are mixed, he overlooks the intrinsic connection between them. For this reason, most notably as he fails to see the close connection between 'spirit' and 'appetite', his analysis of causes for war during consecutive historical eras and in modern times tends, in my opinion, to be lopsided in one direction or the other. See Chapter 7, note 2 in this volume.

54. Two works in that tradition that are relevant to our subject are: Bruce Bueno de Mesquita, *The War Trap*, New Haven, CT: Yale UP, 1981, stressing the actors' expected utility in going to war; James Fearon, 'Rationalist Expectations for War', *International Organization*, 49:3 (1995), 379–414, refining the uncertainty and shortage of information problems that surround the sides' decisions on war.

55. Waltz, *Theory of International Politics*, chap. 1; Waltz, 'Foreword: Thoughts about Assaying Theories', in Elman and Elman, *Progress in International Relations Theory*, vii–xii.

56. For the literature, see Preface, note 1. In addition, many of the specific factors cited have little practical bearing on the occurrence of war, while other factors

that have a decisive effect are left out in some of these books. The most important of the factors that discourage wars are, as we shall see, modern liberal democracy and economic development. True to his realist convictions, Stephen van Evera, for example, in his *Causes of War: Power and the Roots of Conflict*, Ithaca, NY: Cornell UP, 1999, does not even mention them among his list of variables. However, both David Sobek, *The Causes of War*, Cambridge: Polity, 2009, and Suganami, *On the Causes of War*, do so very well.

57. Wendt, 'Anarchy is What States Make of it'; Wendt, *Social Theory of International Politics*, 18, 20, and chap. 6.

58. Unfortunately, Jack Donnelly, the author of an excellent book critiquing realism, has subscribed to the myth that in the aboriginal state of anarchy foragers knew no inter-group fighting: 'The Elements of the Structures of International Systems', *International Organization*, 66 (2012), 609–43.

59. From the more recent literature see most notably: R. Keohane (ed.), *Neorealism and its Critics*, New York: Columbia UP, 1986; Barry Buzan, Charles Jones, and Richard Little, *The Logic of Anarchy*, New York: Columbia UP, 1993; Wendt, *Social Theory of International Politics*. Shiping Tang, 'Social Evolution of International Politics: From Mearsheimer to Jervis', *European Journal of International Relations*, 16:1 (2010), 31–55, sensibly suggests that social evolution has transformed the world and the nature of international relations. However, he remains tied to realist perceptions in claiming that the change has been from offensive to defensive realism. Furthermore, his deductive schema of how that change has occurred is no less ahistorical and contrived than those of the realists he faults.

60. Kenneth Waltz, 'A Response to My Critics', in Keohane, *Neorealism and its Critics*, 340, 344.

61. Waltz, *Theory of International Politics*, chap. 7.

62. Gilpin, *War and Change in World Politics*, chap. 6 and Epilogue.

63. A. F. K. Organski, *World Politics*, 2nd edn, New York: Knopf, 1968; A. F. K. Organski and Jacek Kugler, *The War Ledger*, Chicago: U. of Chicago, 1980; Dale Copeland, *The Origins of Major War*, Ithaca, NY: Cornell UP, 2000.

64. Robert Keohane and Joseph Nye, *Power and Interdependence: World Politics in Transition*, Boston: Little and Brown, 1977; Keohane, *After Hegemony: Cooperation and Discord in the World Political Economy*; John Gerard Ruggie, 'What Makes the World Hang Together? Neo-utilitarianism and the Social Constructivist Challenge', *International Organization*, 52:4 (1998), 855–85, see 883–5.

65. Wendt, *Social Theory of International Politics*, 241–2.

66. This situation and sense of impasse have recently been the subject of a special issue of the *European Journal of International Relations*, 19:3 (2013), titled 'The End of International Relations Theory?'

67. Robert Jervis, 'The Future of World Politics: Will it Resemble the Past?', *International Security*, 16 (winter 1991–2), 39–73.

CHAPTER 6

1. John Gaddis, *The Long Peace: Inquiries Into the History of the Cold War*, Oxford: Oxford UP, 1989.
2. Paul Schroeder, in 'The Life and Death of a Long Peace, 1763–1914', in Raimo Väyrynen, *The Waning of Major War: Theories and Debates*, London: Routledge, 2006, 33–63, senses something but draws none of the conclusions suggested here. Similarly, in passing, Charles Kegley, 'Explaining Great-Power Peace: The Sources of Prolonged Postwar Stability', in Kegley (ed.), *The Long Postwar Peace: Contending Explanations and Projections*, New York: HarperCollins, 1991, 3–22, reference to p. 3.
3. Pitirim Sorokin's pioneering *Social and Cultural Dynamics*, vol. 3, *Fluctuation of Social Relationships, War, and Revolution*, New York: Bedminster Press, 1962 [1937], goes back to ancient Greece and Rome, and then covers late medieval and modern Europe. Quincy Wright, *A Study of War*, Chicago: U. of Chicago, 1965, while attempting a global, long-term perspective, concentrates on modern Europe. Jack Levy, *War in the Modern Great Power System, 1495–1975*, Louisville: U. of Kentucky, 1983, covers modern Europe, as do basically also Evan Luard, *War in International Society*, London: Tauris, 1986, and Kalevi Holsti, *Peace and War: Armed Conflicts and International Order 1648–1989*, Cambridge: Cambridge UP, 1991. Jack Levy and William Thompson, *The Arc of War: Origins, Escalation, and Transformation*, Chicago: U. of Chicago Press, 2011, is mostly an unsuccessful attempt to assume a fully global perspective from prehistory onwards; see note 21 to this chapter, and more comprehensively Azar Gat, 'Is War Declining— And Why?', *Journal of Peace Research*, 50:2 (2013), 149–57.
4. Levy, *War in the Modern Great Power System*, 113.
5. See the data in Wright's *A Study of War*, 653, which is skewed against colonial powers, such as Britain and France, by the inclusion of the European powers' 'small wars' against minor rivals abroad. Also see the data in Luard, *War in International Society*, chap. 2, especially pp. 24–5, 35, 45, 53, and appendices 1–4, which is careful to distinguish between the two types of war.
6. See, for example, Levy and Thompson, *The Arc of War*, 15, 144–5.
7. Levy, *War in the Modern Great Power System*.
8. Ibid., 110. At most, he finds that such an inverse relationship is weak.
9. Sorokin, *Social and Cultural Dynamics*, 3:297, 341–2; Melvin Small and David Singer, *Resort to Arms: International and Civil Wars, 1816–1980*, Beverly Hills: SAGE, 1982, 146, 150 (comparing to the twentieth century); Levy, *War in the Modern Great Power System*, 138–44; Luard, *War in International Society*, chap. 2, especially pp. 24–5, 35, 45, 53, and appendices 1–4; Holsti, *Peace and War*, 142.
10. Sorokin, *Social and Cultural Dynamics*, 347, 361–2; Levy, *War in the Modern Great Power System*, 144; followed by Luard, *War in International Society*, 76–7, 79–80. Also, for a much shorter time span: Small and Singer, *Resort to Arms*, 141, 156–7, 198–201, 275. Levy has now changed his views and detects a recent decline in war: Levy and Thompson, *The Arc of War*, 15, 144–5.

11. Levy, *War in the Modern Great Power System*, 144.

12. Sorokin, *Social and Cultural Dynamics*, 297, 341–2; Levy, *War in the Modern Great Power System*, 138–44, quotation from 142.

13. Levy, *War in the Modern Great Power System*, 144.

14. Sorokin, *Social and Cultural Dynamics*, 3:265–83; Levy, *War in the Modern Great Power System*, 84–6; Steven Pinker, *The Better Angels of Our Nature: Why Violence has Declined*, New York: Penguin, 2011, 193–200.

15. Victor Hanson, *A War Like No Other: How the Athenians and Spartans Fought the Peloponnesian War*, New York: Random House, 2005, 10–11, 79–80, 82, 264, 296.

16. See, for example, Stewart Flory's review of Hanson's book in *Bryn Mawr Classical Review* (2006), 03:40.

17. Peter Brunt, *Italian Manpower 225 B.C.–A.D. 14*, Oxford: Oxford UP, 1971.

18. Frederick Mote, 'Chinese Society under Mongol Rule', in H. Franke and D. Twitchett (eds.), *The Cambridge History of China: Alien Regimes and Border States, 907–1368*, Cambridge: Cambridge UP, 1994, 618–22.

19. See also the general statistical collection by Matthew White, *Atrocitology: Humanity's 100 Deadliest Achievements*, London: Canongate, 2011, summary on p. 529.

20. Peter Wilson, *The Thirty Years War: Europe's Tragedy*, Cambridge, MA: Harvard UP, 2009, 786–8.

21. The attempt by Levy and Thompson, in *The Arc of War*, 5–6, to assess the lethality of war throughout history is way off the mark. Among other things, they extrapolate from the size of a few, arbitrarily selected, historical battles and their death tolls, and fail to calibrate for the size of the populations involved.

22. Levy, *War in the Modern Great Power System*, 83, makes that assumption. For an overall critique see Pinker, *The Better Angels of Our Nature*, 317–20.

23. In this respect, the decision by Lewis Richardson, in *Statistics of Deadly Quarrels*, Pacific Grove, CA: Boxwood, 1960, to include civilian dead is more helpful than that by Small and Singer and by Levy not to do so. For the confusion in the COW data, see: Bethany Lacina, Nils Petter Gleditsch, and Bruce Russett, 'The Declining Risk of Death in Battle', *International Studies Quarterly*, 50:3 (2006), 673–80.

24. Richard Bonney (ed.), *Economic Systems and State Finance*, Oxford: Oxford UP, 1995; Bonney, *The Rise of the Fiscal State in Europe, c. 1200–1815*, Oxford: Oxford UP, 1999; Azar Gat, *War in Human Civilization*, Oxford: Oxford UP, 2006, 371 (and n. 92), 412, 472–6, 484–90. For more see Chapter 3, note 8 in this volume.

25. Recently see, for example, John Horgan, *The End of War*, San Francisco: McSweeney, 2012.

26. John Mueller, *Retreat from Doomsday: The Obsolescence of Major War*, New York: Basic Books, 1989; Mueller, 'Accounting for the Waning of Major War', in Väyrynen, *The Waning of Major War*, 64–79.

27. Carl Kaysen, 'Is War Obsolete?: A Review Essay of Retreat from Doomsday: The Obsolescence of Major War', *International Security*, 14:4 (1990), 42–64,

remains the most penetrating critique. On Mueller's claims see also later in this chapter and note 45.

28. See, for example, Kaysen, 'Is War Obsolete?', with which I am on most other points in much agreement. Similarly, Joseph Schumpeter, 'The Sociology of Imperialism', in his *The Economics and Sociology of Capitalism*, Princeton: Princeton UP, 1991, ed. R. Swedberg, 141–219, argued, erroneously, that foreign expansion had generally been caused by atavistic drives rather than by economic logic, and had been perpetuated by elites to preserve their social dominance.

29. Jean-Jacques Rousseau, 'Abstract and Judgement of Saint Pierre's Project for Perpetual Peace' (1756), in S. Hoffmann and D. Fidler (eds.), *Rousseau on International Relations*, Oxford: Oxford UP, 1991, 53–100.

30. In Thomas Paine, *Rights of Man, Common Sense, and Other Political Writings*, Oxford: Oxford UP, 1995, 212.

31. Ibid., 195–6, 321.

32. Immanuel Kant, 'Perpetual Peace: A Philosophical Sketch', in H. Reiss (ed.), *Kant's Political Writings*, Cambridge: Cambridge UP, 1991, 93–130.

33. Plutarch, 'Life of Pericles', section 12.

34. Thucydides, *History of the Peloponnesian War*, London: Loeb, 1958, II.62–4.

35. For the major initial statements of the thesis see: Dean Babst, 'A Force for Peace', *Industrial Research*, 14 (April 1972), 55–8; Melvin Small and David Singer, 'The War-Proneness of Democratic Regimes, 1816–1965', *Jerusalem Journal of International Relations*, 1:4 (1976), 50–69; R. J. Rummel, 'Libertarianism and International Violence', *Journal of Conflict Resolution*, 27 (1983), 27–71; Michael Doyle, 'Kant, Liberal Legacies, and Foreign Affairs', *Philosophy and Public Affairs*, 12 (1983), 205–35, 323–53; Steve Chan, 'Mirror, Mirror on the Wall: Are the Free Countries More Pacific?', *Journal of Conflict Resolution*, 28 (1984), 617–48; William Domke, *War and the Changing Global System*, New Haven, CT: Yale UP, 1988; Zeev Maoz and Nasrin Abdolali, 'Regime Type and International Conflict 1816–1976', *Journal of Conflict Resolution*, 33 (1989), 3–35; Zeev Maoz and Bruce Russett, 'Normative and Structural Causes of Democratic Peace 1946–1986', *American Political Science Review*, 87 (1993), 624–38; Bruce Russett, *Grasping the Democratic Peace*, Princeton, Princeton UP, 1993; John Owen, *Liberal Peace, Liberal War*, Ithaca, NY: Cornell UP, 1997; Michael Mousseau, 'Democracy and Compromise in Militarized Interstate Conflicts, 1816–1992', *Journal of Conflict Resolution*, 42 (1998), 210–30; Bruce Russett and John Oneal, *Triangulating Peace: Democracy, Interdependence and International Organizations*, New York: Norton, 2001.

36. Bruce Russett and William Antholis, 'The Imperfect Democratic Peace of Ancient Greece', reprinted in Russett, *Grasping the Democratic Peace*, chap. 3.

37. Thucydides, *History of the Peloponnesian War*, VII.55.

38. Spencer Weart, *Never at War: Why Democracies Will not Fight One Another*, New Haven, CT: Yale UP, 1998. This highly problematic work was criticized by Eric Robinson, a leading expert on early Greek democracies: 'Reading and Misreading the Ancient Evidence for Democratic Peace', *Journal of Peace*

Research, 38 (2001), 593–608. A short exchange resulted: Weart, ibid., 609–13; Robinson, ibid., 615–17. See also the criticism by the leading authority on the Greek polis and fourth-century BC Athenian democracy: Mogens Hansen and Thomas Nielsen, *An Inventory of Archaic and Classical Poleis*, Oxford: Oxford UP, 2004, 84–5.

39. Weart, *Never at War*, 246, postpones any mention of the first Athenian Empire to as late in his book as possible, and then summarily disposes of this inconvenience. The problem was better acknowledged by: Russett and Antholis, 'The Imperfect Democratic Peace of Ancient Greece'; Tobias Bachteler, 'Explaining the Democratic Peace: The Evidence from Ancient Greece Reviewed', *Journal of Peace Research*, 34 (1997), 315–23; and is addressed in Lorem Samons, *What's Wrong with Democracy? From Athenian Practice to American Worship*, Berkeley: U. of California, 2004.

40. Alexander Yakobson, *Elections and Electioneering in Rome*, Stuttgart: Steiner, 1999.

41. Polybius, *The Histories*, VI.11–18.

42. Livy, XXIII.ii–vii, XXIV.xiii.

43. Polybius, VI.5; Aristotle, *The Politics*, II.11 and IV.8–9. Weart, *Never at War*, mentions Rome only once in his appendix of problematic cases (p. 297), where he lamely excuses himself from discussing it on the grounds that we lack information about Carthage.

44. Doyle, 'Kant, Liberal Legacies, and Foreign Affairs'.

45. Ibid.; Michael Doyle, *Ways of War and Peace: Realism, Liberalism, and Socialism*, New York: Norton, 1997; Russett and Oneal, *Triangulating Peace*. Contrary to John Mueller's world of random ideas, serfdom and slavery were phased out because they were replaced by mobile capitalist wage labour.

46. Montesquieu, *The Spirit of the Laws*, Cambridge: Cambridge UP, 1989 [1748], trans. A. Cohler, B. Miller, and H. Stone, Bk. 20, chap. 2.

47. Paine, *Rights of Man, Common Sense, and Other Political Writings*, 265–6; also see 128–31, 227; Michael Howard, *War and the Liberal Conscience*, Oxford: Oxford UP, 1981, 29; Thomas Walker, 'The Forgotten Prophet: Tom Paine's Cosmopolitanism and International Relations', *International Studies Quarterly*, 44 (2000), 51–72.

48. Kant, 'Perpetual Peace', 114.

49. For some of the most important works, supportive, sceptical, or qualifying, see: Richard Rosecrance, *The Rise of the Trading State: Commerce and Conquest in the Modern World*, New York: Basic Books, 1986; Edward Mansfield, *Power, Trade, and War*, Princeton: Princeton UP, 1994; Erich Weede, 'Economic Policy and International Security: Rent-Seeking, Free Trade and Democratic Peace', *European Journal of International Relations* 1:4 (1995), 519–37; Katherine Barbieri, 'Economic Interdependence: A Path to Peace or a Source of Interstate Conflict?', *Journal of Peace Research*, 33 (1996), 29–49; Katherine Barbieri and Gerald Schneider, 'Globalization and Peace: Assessing New Directions in the Study of Trade and Conflict', *Journal of Peace Research*, 36 (1999), 387–404;

Solomon Polachek, 'Why Democracies Cooperate More and Fight Less: The Relationship between Trade and International Cooperation', *Review of International Economics*, 5 (1997), 295–309; Edward Mansfield and Brian Pollins (eds.), *Economic Interdependence and International Conflict*, Ann Arbor: U. of Michigan, 2003; G. Schneider, K. Barbieri, and N. Gleditsch (eds.), *Globalization and Armed Conflict*, Lanham, MD: Rowman & Littlefield, 2003; Russett and Oneal, *Triangulating Peace*, 125–55; Omar Keshk, Brian Pollins, and Rafael Reuveny, 'Trade still Follows the Flag: The Primacy of Politics in a Simultaneous Model of Interdependence and Armed Conflict', *Journal of Politics*, 66:4 (2004), 1155–79; Jun Xiang, Xu Xiaohan, and George Keteku, 'Power: The Missing Link in the Trade–Conflict Relationship', *Journal of Conflict Resolution*, 51:4 (2007), 646–63; Zeev Maoz, 'The Effects of Strategic and Economic Interdependence on International Conflict across Levels of Analysis', *American Journal of Political Science*, 53:1 (2009), 223–40; Han Dorussen and Hugh Ward, 'Trade networks and the Kantian peace', *Journal of Peace Research*, 47:1 (2010), 29–42; Håvard Hegre, John Oneal, and Bruce Russett, 'Trade Does Promote Peace: New Simultaneous Estimation of the Reciprocal Effects of Trade and Conflict', *Journal of Peace Research*, 47:6 (2010), 763–74.

50. Erik Gartzke, 'The Capitalist Peace', *American Journal of Political Science*, 51:1 (2007), 166–91; also, Erik Gartzke and J. J. Hewitt, 'International Crises and the Capitalist Peace', *International Interactions*, 36 (2010), 115–45.

51. Bruce Russett, 'Capitalism or Democracy? Not So Fast', *International Interactions*, 36:2 (2010), 198–205; Allan Dafoe, 'Statistical Critiques of the Democratic Peace: Caveat Emptor', *American Journal of Political Science*, 55:2 (2011), 247–62; Allan Dafoe, John Oneal, and Bruce Russett, 'The Democratic Peace: Weighing the Evidence and Cautious Inference', *International Studies Quarterly*, 57 (2013), 201–14. Christopher Gelpi and Joseph Grieco, 'Democracy, Interdependence, and the Sources of the Liberal Peace', *Journal of Peace Research*, 45:1 (2008), 17–36, arrive at contrasting conclusions to Gartzke's for the period 1950–92. They find that trade interdependence mainly constrains war among democracies, which are in any case unlikely to fight each other irrespective of trade.

52. B. Mitchell, *European Historical Statistics 1750–1970*, London: Macmillan, 1975, 526, 573. This was emphasized by Kenneth Waltz in his *Theory of International Politics*, Reading, MA: Addison, 1979, 212–15, as a refutation of the trade interdependence peace, and has become a standard realist argument. See, for example: Norrin Ripsman and Jean-Marc Blanchard, 'Commercial Liberalism under Fire: Evidence from 1914 and 1936', *Security Studies*, 6:2 (1996/97), 4–50.

53. Patrick McDonald, *The Invisible Hand of Peace: Capitalism, the War Machine, and International Relations Theory*, Cambridge: Cambridge UP, 2009; Patrick McDonald and Kevin Sweeney, 'The Achilles' Heel of Liberal IR Theory? Globalization and Conflict in the Pre-World War I Era', *World Politics*, 59:3 (2007), 370–403.

54. Dale Copeland, 'Economic Interdependence and War: A Theory of Trade Expectations', *International Security*, 20:4 (1996), 5–41; Erich Weede, 'Globalization: Creative Destruction and the Prospect of a Capitalist Peace', in Schneider, Barbieri, and Gleditsch, *Globalization and Armed Conflict*, 311–23; Weede, *Balance of Power, Globalization and the Capitalist Peace*, Potsdam: Liberal Institute, 2005; Gat, *War in Human Civilization*, 2006, 554–7, 585; Erik Gartzke and Lupu Yonatan, 'Trading on Preconceptions: Why World War I was Not a Failure of Economic Interdependence', *International Security*, 36:4 (2012), 115–50.

55. See Stephen Walt, *The Origins of Alliances*, Ithaca, NY: Cornell UP, 1987, 33–4; Michael Simon and Erik Gartzke, 'Political System Similarity and the Choice of Allies', *Journal of Conflict Resolution*, 40 (1996), 617–35; Brian Lai and Dan Reiter, 'Democracy, Political Similarity, and International Alliances, 1812–1992', *Journal of Conflict Resolution*, 44 (2000), 203–27; and Brett Leeds, Jeffrey Ritter, Sara Mitchell, and Andrew Long, 'Alliance Treaty Obligations and Provisions, 1815–1944', *International Interactions*, 28:3 (2002), 237–60.

56. Ripsman and Blanchard, in their 'Commercial Liberalism under Fire: Evidence from 1914 and 1936', address Britain and France versus Germany in the 1936 Rhineland crisis, but not the inter-democratic peace of the 1930s.

57. Michael Mousseau, 'The Social Market Roots of Democratic Peace', *International Security*, 33:4 (2009), 52–86; Mousseau, 'The Democratic Peace Unraveled: It's the Economy', *International Studies Quarterly*, 57:1 (2012), 186–97; Mousseau et al., 'Capitalism and Peace: It's Keynes, not Hayek', in G. Schneider and N. Gleditsch (eds.), *Assessing the Capitalist Peace*, London: Routledge, 2013, 80–109.

58. For the critics see: Allan Dafoe and Bruce Russett, 'Does Capitalism Account for the Democratic Peace? The Evidence Still Says No', in Schneider and Gleditsch, *Assessing the Capitalist Peace*, 110–26. For more on the subject: Erich Weede, suggesting a mutually reinforcing relationship between capitalism, prosperity, democracy, and peace in his 'Economic Policy and International Security: Rent-Seeking, Free Trade and Democratic Peace', has begun to wonder if capitalism is not the most decisive factor: Weede, 'Globalization: Creative Destruction and the Prospect of a Capitalist Peace', 311–23. Håvard Hegre, 'Democracy and Armed Conflict', *Journal of Peace Research*, 51 (2014), 159–72, insists on the strong contributory effect of democracy.

59. Russett and Oneal, in *Triangulating Peace: Democracy, Interdependence and International Organizations*, suggest a distinct but mutually reinforcing (rather than independent) effect to all three factors, which would seem to be the right answer for the industrial age, the period covered by their study. Similarly, see: Domke, *War and the Changing Global System*; Doyle, *Ways of War and Peace*, 284, 286–7.

60. Kaysen, 'Is War Obsolete?', is practically alone in pointing to the Industrial Revolution and the socio-economic changes it brought in its wake as the

process behind the decline of war. For capitalism, enhanced by the Industrial Revolution, as a force for peace see Schumpeter, 'The Sociology of Imperialism'.

61. These are my rough calculations based on the estimated data. The most comprehensive and up-to-date estimates are Angus Maddison, *The World Economy: A Millennial Perspective*, Paris: OECD, 2001, 28, 90, 126, 183–6, 264–5. See also Paul Bairoch, 'Europe's Gross National Product: 1800–1975', *Journal of European Economic History*, 5 (1976), 301; and Bairoch, 'International Industrialization Levels from 1750 to 1980', *Journal of European Economic History*, 11 (1982), especially 275, 284, 286; W. W. Rostow, *The World Economy: History & Prospect*, Austin: U. of Texas, 1978, 4–7, 48–9.

62. Auguste Comte, 'Plan of the Scientific Operations Necessary for Reorganizing Society' (1822), and 'Course de Philosophie Positive' (1832–42), in G. Lenzer (ed.), *Auguste Comte and Positivism: The Essential Writings*, Chicago: U. of Chicago, 1975, 37, 293–7.

63. Helmuth von Moltke, *Essays, Speeches and Memoirs*, New York: Harper, 1893, i. 276–7.

64. Adam Smith, *The Wealth of Nations*, V.I.i.

65. Erik Gartzke and Alex Weisiger suggest something along these lines in 'Under Construction: Development, Democracy, and Difference as Determinants of Systemic Liberal Peace', *International Studies Quarterly*, 58 (2014), 130–45. However, they make little sense in claiming that the developed countries themselves are hypocritical in that they continue to fight, whereas in actuality they practically ceased to fight among themselves.

66. Max Singer and Aaron Wildavsky, *The Real World Order: Zones of Peace, Zones of Turmoil*, Chatham, NJ: Chatham House, 1993; James Goldgeier and Michael McFaul, 'A Tale of Two Worlds: Core and Periphery in the Post-Cold War Era', *International Organization*, 46 (1992), 467–91; Paul Collier et al., *Breaking the Conflict Trap: Civil War and Development Policy*, Washington, DC: The World Bank and Oxford UP, 2003; Paul Collier, *The Bottom Billion: Why the Poorest Countries are Failing and What can be Done About it*, Oxford: Oxford UP, 2007; B. Lacina and N. P. Gleditsch, 'Monitoring Trends in Global Combat: A New Dataset of Battle Deaths', *European Journal of Population*, 21 (2005), 145–66. John Mueller, in *The Remnants of War*, Ithaca, NY: Cornell UP, 2007, stresses the sharp difference between the developed and undeveloped world, but fails to draw the obvious conclusion regarding the key factor involved: economic development.

67. Joshua Goldstein, *Winning the War on War: The Decline of Armed Conflict Worldwide*, New York: Penguin, 2011. Andrew Mack, 'Global Political Violence: Explaining the Post-Cold War Decline', in M. Fischer and V. Rittberger (eds.), *Strategies for Peace*, Leverkusen: Barbara Budrich, 2008, 75–106, focuses on the effect of peacekeeping forces on the decline of belligerency after 1990, which has indeed occurred mainly in the developing world.

68. Meredith Sarkees, Frank Wayman, and David Singer, 'Inter-State, Intra-State, and Extra-State Wars: A Comprehensive Look at their Distribution over Time, 1816–1997', *International Studies Quarterly*, 47:1 (2003), 49–70, re-evaluating the

COW data, find little change in the overall occurrence of war during the entire period. However, while noting the decrease of war in nineteenth-century Europe and in today's developed world, they overlook the fact that most wars today, whether external or internal, are concentrated in the developing world. They thus compare apples with pears, and miss the key factor involved. David Singer was actually more discriminate in his 'Peace in the Global System: Displacement, Interregnum, or Transformation?', in Kegley, *The Long Postwar Peace*, 56–84, where he noted that wars between major powers as well as between 'advanced industrial nations' had decreased sharply. He wrote that war had changed both form and neighbourhood (p. 59), but here, indeed, lies the key to the entire process. One of the advantages of using only the great powers' wars among themselves for measuring the long-term changes in belligerency, before and after 1815, is that modern great powers are almost by definition economically developed, whereas many if not most of the other states in the system are not. (Gigantic and nuclear China, before its adoption of capitalism, is the exception.) Thus the modernization factor comes out very sharply.

69. Mary Kaldor, *New and Old Wars*, 2nd edn, Cambridge: Polity, 2006.
70. Michael Mousseau, 'Market Prosperity, Democratic Consolidation, and Democratic Peace', *Journal of Conflict Resolution*, 44 (2000), 472–507; Mousseau, 'The Nexus of Market Society, Liberal Preferences, and Democratic Peace', *International Studies Quarterly*, 47 (2003), 483–510; Mousseau, 'Comparing New Theory with Prior Beliefs: Market Civilization and the Democratic Peace', *Conflict Management and Peace Science*, 22 (2005), 63–77; Håvard Hegre, 'Development and the Liberal Peace: What Does it Take to be a Trading State?', *Journal of Peace Research*, 37 (2000), 5–30; Michael Mousseau, Håvard Hegre, and John Oneal, 'How the Wealth of Nations Conditions the Liberal Peace', *European Journal of International Relations*, 9 (2003), 277–314 (the only study among those mentioned here that extends to the period before World War II); Timothy Besley and Torsten Persson, *Pillars of Prosperity: The Political Economics of Development Clusters*, Princeton: Princeton UP, 2011, quotation from p. xi. See also Azar Gat, 'The Democratic Peace Theory Reframed: The Impact of Modernity', *World Politics*, 58:1 (2005), 73–100.
71. The effects of both democracy and wealth in reducing belligerency during the entire period were first observed by Stuart Bremer, 'Dangerous Dyads: Conditions Affecting the Likelihood of Interstate War, 1816–1965', *Journal of Conflict Resolution*, 36 (1992), 309–41.
72. Produced as part of his research by Meir Moalem, a doctoral student at Tel Aviv University. Sources and definitions—several databases have been combined for different time periods and extra validation:

   • **Democracy**: Polity IV, 1946–1990, scores range from -10 to +10 (a state with a score higher than 0 has been defined as a democracy); Freedom House database of Individual Country Ratings and Status, 1973–2015, scores range from 1 to 7 (a state with a score lower than 4 has been defined as a democracy); The Economist Democracy Index 2012 (and earlier versions), where states are ranked on a 1–10 scale (a state with a score higher than 6 has been defined as a democracy).

- **Capitalism** (major role to the market): Economic Freedom of the World (EFW) database, 1970–2014, scores range from 1 to 10 (a state with a score higher than 6 has been defined as capitalist); Heritage Economic Freedom provides graphic data for 1995–2016 (a state with a score higher than the world's average has been defined as capitalist). In addition, for purposes of validation and for years earlier than 1970, the following databases were used: World Bank database on R&D; Heritage Foundation combined world data; multiple UN databases; Gartzke, The Capitalist Peace database.
- Indexes of **modernization** are not common. Several parameters have been integrated, including GDP per capita compared to the global average (excluding oil states); technology level; transportation and communication level. Multiple sources include: The Maddison Project database (a state with GDP higher than the global average (excluding oil states) has been defined as modern); World Bank (WB) database on R&D, including parameters such as GDP per capita, high-tech export, number of scientists per capita, etc.; modernization indexes for 2008 at http://www.s3school.org/soc_index/mi.php; http://www.modernization.com.cn/ms201101.pdf; multiple UN databases.

From the total number of 324 deadly MIDs during the period 1946–2010, the following is a list of those registered between **democratic** states. In no case are both democracies categorized as modernized at the time of the conflict, and in the great majority of cases neither democracy is categorized as modernized (the numbers are the values for dem, mod, and cap, respectively):

1976 Botswana 1 0 0	Zimbabwe 1 0 0
1981 Ecuador 1 0 0	Peru 1 0 0
1984 Ecuador 1 0 0	Peru 1 0 0
1986 Greece 1 0 1	Turkey 1 0 0
1988 Cyprus 1 1 1	Turkey 1 0 0
1989 El Salvador 1 0 0	Honduras 1 0 1
1993 India 1 0 0	Pakistan 1 0 0
1996 Cyprus 1 1 1	Turkey 1 0 1
2002 Bangladesh 1 0 0	India 1 0 0
2008 India 1 0 0	Pakistan 1 0 0

From the total number of 324 deadly MIDs during the period 1946–2010, the following is a list of those registered between **capitalist** states. In no case are both states categorized as modernized at the time of the conflict, and in the great majority of cases neither of the capitalist states involved are categorized as modernized (the numbers are the values for dem, mod, and cap, respectively):

1948 Lebanon 0 0 1	Israel 1 0 1
1949 Israel 1 0 1	Jordan 0 0 1
1950 Israel 1 0 1	Jordan 0 0 1

1955 Israel 1 0 1	Jordan 0 0 1
1957 Israel 1 0 1	Jordan 0 0 1
1959 Israel 1 0 1	Jordan 0 0 1
1962 Israel 1 0 1	Jordan 0 0 1
1963 Israel 1 0 1	Jordan 0 0 1
1964 Israel 1 0 1	Jordan 0 0 1
1967 Israel 1 0 1	Jordan 0 0 1
1967 Israel 1 0 1	Jordan 0 0 1
1971 Israel 1 1 1	Jordan 0 0 1
1973 Saudi Arabia 0 0 1	Israel 1 1 1
1980 Israel 1 1 1	Lebanon 0 0 1
1993 Israel 1 1 1	Lebanon 0 0 1
1995 Ecuador 1 0 1	Peru 0 0 1
1996 Cyprus 1 1 1	Turkey 1 0 1
2006 Israel 1 1 1	Lebanon 0 0 1

73. Although correct on the principle, Rosecrance, *The Rise of the Trading State*, misses the radical change brought about by the Industrial Revolution as the crucial element that tilted the balance towards the rationale of free trade. See also Richard Rosecrance, *The Rise of the Virtual State: Wealth and Power in the Coming Century*, New York: Basic Books, 1999.

74. Calculated on the basis of the data in B. R. Mitchell, *International Historical Statistics, Europe 1750–1988*, New York: Stockton, 1992, 553–62; Maddison, *The World Economy*, 126, 127, 184; Simon Kuznets, *Modern Economic Growth*, New Haven, CT: Yale UP, 1966, 306–7, 312–14.

75. Rosecrance, *The Rise of the Virtual State*, 37.

76. John Stuart Mill, *Principles of Political Economy*, New York: Kelley, 1961, bk. III, chap. xvil, sect. 5, p. 582.

77. Recently see Douglas Gibler and Steven Miller, 'Quick Victories? Territory, Democracies, and Their Disputes', *Journal of Conflict Resolution*, 57:2 (2013), 258–84, and the bibliography cited. See also Chapter 6, note 4 in this volume.

78. Smith, *The Wealth of Nations*, IV.ii.23.

79. Mitchell, *European Historical Statistics 1750–1970*, pp. B6 and B7.

80. Ronald Inglehart and Christian Welzel, *Modernization, Cultural Change and Democracy: The Human Development Sequence*, New York: Cambridge UP, 2005; Ronald Inglehart, B. Puranen, and Christian Welzel, 'Declining Willingness to Fight for One's Country: The Individual-Level Basis of the Long Peace', *Journal of Peace Research*, 52:4 (2015), 418–34.

81. Thomas Friedman, *The New York Times*, 8 Dec. 1996.

82. For the statistics, see Friedrich von Bernhardi, *Germany and the Next War*, New York: Longmans, 1914, 243–4.

83. Bill Bishop, 'Who Goes to War', *Washington Post*, 16 November 2003; Ann Scott Tyson, 'Youths in Rural U.S. Are Drawn to Military', *Washington Post*, 10 November 2005. The second article emphasizes the recruits' poor economic background but not their rural roots.

84. Rosecrance, *The Rise of the Virtual State*, p. xii, also p. 26 for the other major industrial countries; Robert Gilpin, *The Challenge of Global Capitalism*, Princeton, NJ: Princeton UP, 2000, 33.

85. This helps to explain some of the (limited) findings in Mark Peceny, Caroline Beer, and Shannon Sanchez-Terry, 'Dictatorial Peace?', *The American Political Science Review*, 96:1 (2002), 15–26. Also, for the long-term decrease in the belligerency of non-democratic countries: Lars-Erik Cederman, 'Back to Kant', *American Political Science Review*, 93:4 (2001), 791–808.

86. For the correlation between the level of liberalism and peace, see Rummel, 'Libertarianism and International Violence'; Rummel, *Power Kills: Democracy as a Method of Nonviolence*, New Brunswick, NJ: Transaction, 1997, p. 5 and chap. 3. For historical gradualism, see Bruce Russet and Zeev Maoz, incorporated in Russet, *Grasping the Democratic Peace*, 72–3; this is more fully developed in Zeev Maoz, 'The Controversy over the Democratic Peace: Rearguard Action or Cracks in the Wall?', *International Security*, 22:1 (1997), 162–98; and integral in Russett and Oneal, *Triangulating Peace*, 111–14.

87. Russet and Maoz, in Russet, *Grasping the Democratic Peace*, 86. Generally regarding today's developing world: Edward Friedman, 'The Painful Gradualness of Democratization: Proceduralism as a Necessary Discontinuous Revolution', in H. Handelman and M. Tessler (eds.), *Democracy and its Limits: Lessons from Asia, Latin America, and the Middle East*, Notre Dame: U. of Notre Dame, 1999, 321–40.

88. The idea goes back to the nineteenth century, but the modern argument was seminally made by Seymour Lipset in his *Political Man*, New York: Anchor, 1963. More recently see: Samuel Huntington, *The Third Wave: Democratization in the Late Twentieth Century*, Norman, OK: U. of Oklahoma, 1991; Francis Fukuyama, *The End of History and the Last Man*, New York: Free Press, 1992; Larry Diamond, *Developing Democracy*, Baltimore, MD: Johns Hopkins UP, 1999, especially 34–60, 279–80; Adam Przeworski, Michael Alvarez, Jose Cheibub, and Fernando Limongi, *Democracy and Development*, Cambridge: Cambridge UP, 2000; Michael Mandelbaum, *The Ideas that Conquered the World: Peace, Democracy, and Free Markets in the Twenty-First Century*, New York: Public Affairs, 2002; Mandelbaum, *Democracy's Good Name: The Rise and Risks of the World's Most Popular Form of Government*, New York: Public Affairs, 2007.

89. Mueller, *Retreat from Doomsday*.

90. Contra Mueller, *Retreat from Doomsday*, 53–68.

91. This is the Achilles' heel of Bruce Bueno de Mesquita, James Morrow, Randolph Siverson, and Alastair Smith, 'An Institutional Explanation of the Democratic Peace', *The American Political Science Review*, 93:4 (1999), 791–807.

92. Azar Gat, 'Isolationism, Appeasement, Containment, Limited War: Western Strategic Policy from the Modern to the "Post-Modern" Era', in Zeev Maoz and Azar Gat (eds.), *War in a Changing World*, Ann Arbor: U. of Michigan Press, 2001, 77–91; Azar Gat, *Victorious and Vulnerable: Why Democracy Won in the 20th Century and How it is Still Imperiled*, Stanford: Hoover/Rowman & Littlefield, 2010, chap. 6.

93. Rummel, *Power Kills*; Mathew Krain and Marrissa Myers, 'Democracy and Civil War: A Note on the Democratic Peace Proposition', *International Interaction*, 23 (1997), 109–18, which fails to distinguish between advanced and less advanced democracies; Tanja Ellingson, 'Colorful Community or Ethnic Witches-Brew? Multiethnicity and Domestic Conflict during and after the Cold War', *Journal of Conflict Resolution*, 44 (2000): 228–49; Errol Henderson and David Singer, 'Civil War in the Post-Colonial World, 1946–92', *Journal of Peace Research*, 37 (2000), 275–99; Errol Henderson, *Democracy and War: The End of an Illusion*, Boulder, CO: Lynne Rienner, 2002, chap. 5; Håvard Hegre, Tanja Ellingsen, Scott Gates, and Nils Petter Gleditsch, 'Toward a Democratic Civil Peace? Democracy, Political Change, and Civil War, 1816–1992', *American Political Science Review*, 95:1 (2001), 33–48; James Fearon and David Laitin, 'Ethnicity, Insurgency, and Civil War', *American Political Science Review*, 97:1 (2003), 75–90; Kristine Eck and Lisa Hultman, 'One-sided violence against civilians in war', *Journal of Peace Research*, 44:2 (2007), 233–46; Christian Davenport, *State Repression and the Domestic Democratic Peace*, Cambridge: Cambridge UP, 2007; Nils Petter Gleditsch, Håvard Hegre, and Håvard Strand, 'Democracy and Civil War', in M. Manus (ed.), *Handbook of War Studies III*, Ann Arbor: U. of Michigan, 2009, 155–92; Besley and Persson, *Pillars of Prosperity*.

94. The pioneering study is again Rummel, *Power Kills*.

95. While both Small and Singer, 'The War-Proneness of Democratic Regimes', and Chan, 'Mirror, Mirror on the Wall', note the difference between the democracies' participation in inter-state and extra-systemic wars, they hold that democracies initiated wars nearly as often as non-democracies. But see Nils Gleditsch and Håvard Hegre, 'Peace and Democracy: Three Levels of Analysis', *Journal of Conflict Resolution*, 41:2 (1997), 283–310. Rummel's claim in 'Libertarianism and International Violence' and *Power Kills*—that liberal countries are more peaceful in general—is corroborated by Domke, *War and the Changing Global System*; Bremer, 'Dangerous Dyads: Conditions Affecting the Likelihood of Interstate War, 1816–1965'; Kenneth Benoit, 'Democracies Really are More Pacific (in General)', *Journal of Conflict Resolution*, 40 (1996), 636–57; David Rousseau, Christopher Gelpi, Dan Reiter, and Paul Huth, 'Assessing the Dyadic Nature of the Democratic Peace, 1918–1988', *American Political Science Review*, 90 (1996), 512–33; David Rousseau, *Democracy and War*, Stanford: Stanford UP, 2005; Jean-Sebastien Rioux, 'A Crisis-Based Evaluation of the Democratic Peace Proposition', *Canadian Journal of Political Science*, 31 (1998), 263–83; Russett, altering his initial position, in Russett and Oneal, *Triangulating Peace*, 49–50.

96. Gil Merom, *How Democracies Lose Small Wars*, Cambridge: Cambridge UP, 2003; Azar Gat and Gil Merom, 'Why Counterinsurgency Fails', in Gat, *Victorious and Vulnerable*, chap. 7.

97. This is the main idea of Ian Morris's brilliant *War: What is it Good For?*, New York: Farrar, Straus, & Giroux, 2014.

98. Cf. Francis Fukuyama, *State Building: Governance and World Order in the 21st Century*, Ithaca, NY: Cornell UP, 2004, 38–9, 92–3.

99. Azar Gat, 'The Democratic Peace Theory Reframed: The Impact of Modernity', quotation from 99. See also Azar Gat, 'The Arabs' 1848', *The National Interest*, 20 April 2014.

100. Noted by Small and Singer, 'The War-Proneness of Democratic Regimes', 63–4; and developed by Rummel, *Power Kills*.

101. Rousseau, *Democracy and War*.

102. Edward Mansfield and Jon Pevehouse, 'Trade Blocs, Trade Flows, and International Conflict', *International Organization*, 54:4 (2000), 775–808; Russett and Oneal, *Triangulating Peace*; Charles Boehmer, Erik Gartzke, and Timothy Nordstrom, 'Do Intergovernmental Organizations Promote Peace?', *World Politics*, 57:1 (2004), 1–38; Jon Pevehouse and Bruce Russett, 'Democratic International Governmental Organizations Promote Peace', *International Organization*, 60:4 (2006), 969–1000; Yoram Haftel, 'Designing for Peace: Regional Integration Arrangements, Institutional Variation, and Militarized Interstates Disputes', *International Organization*, 61:1 (2007), 213–37.

103. For the Soviets, see Anthony Beevor, *The Fall of Berlin 1945*, New York: Penguin, 2003, 410. For the Americans and Japanese in World War II, see Joshua Goldstein, *War and Gender: How Gender Shapes the War System and Vice Versa*, New York: Cambridge UP, 337, 346, respectively.

104. Herbert Moller, 'Youth as a Force in the Modern World', *Comparative Studies in Society and History*, 10 (1967/8), 237–60; Christian Mesquida and Neil Wiener, 'Human Collective Aggression: A Behavioral Ecology Perspective', *Ethology and Sociobiology*, 17 (1996), 247–62; Henrik Urdal, 'A Clash of Generations? Youth Bulges and Political Violence', *International Studies Quarterly*, 50 (2006), 607–29.

105. Mitchell, *European Historical Statistics*, section B2, especially pp. 37 and 52; United Nations, *World Population Prospects: The 2000 Revision*, New York: UN, 2001.

106. United Nations, *World Population Prospects: The 2012 Revision*, New York: UN, 2013, Table S.8.

107. Samuel Huntington, *The Clash of Civilizations and the Remaking of World Order*, New York: Simon & Schuster, 1997, 116–20.

108. Edward Luttwak, 'Blood and Computers: The Crisis of Classical Military Power in Advanced Postindustrialist Societies', in Z. Maoz and A. Gat (eds.), *War in a Changing World*, Ann Arbor, U. of Michigan, 2001, 49–75.

109. Lisa Brandes, 'Public Opinion, International Security and Gender: The United States and Great Britain since 1945', unpublished doctoral dissertation, Yale University, 1994.

110. Bruce Russet, 'The Democratic Peace—And Yet it Moves', in M. Brown, S. Lynn-Jones, and S. Miller (eds.), *Debating the Democratic Peace*, Cambridge,

MA: MIT Press, 1996, 340; Michael W. Doyle, 'Michael Doyle on the Democratic Peace—Again', ibid., 372.

III. Mark Tessler and Ira Warriner, 'Gender, Feminism, and Attitudes towards International Conflict', *World Politics*, 49 (1997), 250–81; Mark Tessler, Jodi Nachtwey, and Audra Grant, 'Further Tests of the Women and Peace Hypothesis: Evidence from Cross-National Survey Research in the Middle East', *International Studies Quarterly*, 43 (1999), 519–31.

CHAPTER 7

1. Kalevi Holsti, *Peace and War: Armed Conflict and International Order 1648–1989*, Cambridge: Cambridge UP, 1991, 139–45. Richard Ned Lebow, *Why Nations Fight*, Cambridge: Cambridge UP, 2010, also documents the decline of territory and profit as motives for war after the eighteenth century. However, by coding the overwhelming majority of later wars under what he calls the 'standing' or 'spirit' motive, Lebow misses their actual, concrete motive: ethno-national aspirations.

2. Azar Gat, with Alexander Yakobson, *Nations: The Long History and Deep Roots of Political Ethnicity and Nationalism*, Cambridge: Cambridge UP, 2013, chap. 6.

3. Douglas Gibler and Steven Miller, 'Quick Victories? Territory, Democracies, and Their Disputes', *Journal of Conflict Resolution*, 57:2 (2013), 258–84, find that fewer territorial disputes is the cause of reduced belligerency in general, and particularly among democracies. However, they do not convincingly explain *why* democracies have fewer territorial disputes or relate the decrease to either open trade or level of democracy and liberalism.

4. Gat, *Nations*, chap. 6; Benjamin Miller, *States, Nations and Great Powers: The Sources of Regional War and Peace*, Cambridge: Cambridge UP, 2007.

5. John Gallagher and Ronald Robinson, 'The Imperialism of Free Trade', *Economic History Review*, 4 (1953), 1–15.

6. Lance Davis and Robert Huttenback, in *Mammon and the Pursuit of Empire: The Political Economy of British Imperialism, 1860–1912*, Cambridge: Cambridge UP, 1986, invalidate J. M. A. Hobson, *Imperialism: A Study*, Ann Arbor: U. of Michigan, 1965 [1902], and V. I. Lenin, *Imperialism: The Highest Stage of Capitalism*, New York: International Publishers, 1939. See also D. K. Fieldhouse, *Economics and Empire 1830–1914*, Ithaca, NY: Cornell UP, 1973; and on France, Henri Brunschwig, *French Colonialism 1871–1914: Myths and Realities*, New York: Praeger, 1966, 90–1, 96.

7. Azar Gat, *War in Human Civilization*, Oxford: Oxford UP, 2006, 542–57.

8. Daniel Headrick, *The Tools of Empire: Technology and European Imperialism in the Nineteenth Century*, New York: Oxford UP, 1981.

9. Ronald Robinson and John Gallagher, *Africa and the Victorians: The Climax of Imperialism*, Garden City, NY: Doubleday, 1968.

10. Cf. Dale Copeland, 'Economic Interdependence and War: A Theory of Trade Expectations', *International Security*, 20:4 (1996), 5–41.

11. Seymour Lipset, *Political Man*, New York: Anchor, 1963; Francis Fukuyama, *The End of History and the Last Man*, New York: Free Press, 1992; Michael Mandelbaum, *The Ideas that Conquered the World: Peace, Democracy, and Free Markets in the Twenty-First Century*, New York: Public Affairs, 2002; Mandelbaum, *Democracy's Good Name: The Rise and Risks of the World's Most Popular Form of Government*, New York: Public Affairs, 2007.

12. For example, this factor is not mentioned in Robert Dahl, *On Democracy*, New Haven, CT: Yale UP, 1998, 163–5, though his *Polyarchy*, New Haven, CT: Yale UP, 1971, does recognize foreign occupation and influence as a possible cause of democracy. Nor is the US factor mentioned in Niall Ferguson, *The Cash Nexus: Money and Power in the Modern World, 1700–2000*, New York: Basic Books, 2001, chap. 12, despite the chapter's title: 'The American Wave: Democracy's Flow and Ebb'. Also, implicitly, Michael Doyle, *Ways of War and Peace: Realism, Liberalism, and Socialism*, New York: Norton, 1997, 269–70, 277. Above all see Mandelbaum, *The Ideas that Conquered the World*, 87–95; Mandelbaum, *Democracy's Good Name*, 66ff.; Walter Russell Mead, *God and Gold: Britain, America, and the Making of the Modern World*, New York: Knopf, 2007, which is very good on the unique sources of British and American power but has little to say about the twentieth century; Robert Kagan, *The World America Made*, New York: Knopf, 2012. Fukuyama, *The End of History*, 16–17, 127–9, writes that fascism was defeated because it clashed with the international system, but he fails to mention the reason why that 'system' was stronger; after all, there were two opposing coalitions. Dan Reiter and Allan Stam, *Democracies at War*, Princeton: Princeton UP, 2002, 136, recognize that it was the United States' participation that tilted the scales in both Europe and the Pacific, but reject this as an explanation for the democracies' military success with the comment that one should not generalize from a single case—apparently not even if this case involves by far the greatest global power, whose participation decided the twentieth century's mightiest military conflicts and the fate of democracy. Samuel Huntington, in *The Third Wave: Democratization in the Late Twentieth Century*, Norman, OK: U. of Oklahoma, 1991, is well aware of the international context, including the victories in the two world wars, though he does not discuss the reasons for the democracies' victories in these wars. And see Tony Smith, *America's Mission: The United States and the Worldwide Struggle for Democracy in the Twentieth Century*, Princeton: Princeton UP, 1994, 10–12, 147.

13. Lipset, *Political Man*; Dahl, *Polyarchy*; Larry Diamond, 'Economic Development and Democracy Reconsidered', in G. Marks and L. Diamond (eds.), *Reexamining Democracy*, Newbury Park: Sage, 1992, 93–139; Axel Hadenius, *Democracy and Development*, Cambridge: Cambridge UP, 1992; Robert Barro, 'Determinants of Economic Growth: A Cross-Country Empirical Study', *National Bureau of Economic Research Working Paper*, 5698 (1996); Amartya Sen, *Development and*

Freedom, New York: Knopf, 1999, which offers little historical perspective. Theoretically, see Mancur Olson, *Power and Prosperity: Outgrowing Communist and Capitalist Dictatorships*, New York: Basic Books, 2000. Ferguson, *The Cash Nexus*, 348–9, 363–9, is a good summary and analysis; also, Fukuyama, *The End of History*, 123. Two comprehensive studies—Adam Przeworski, Michael Alvarez, Jose Cheibub, and Fernando Limongi, *Democracy and Development*, Cambridge: Cambridge UP, 2000, which is excellent, and the more limited book by Morton Halperin, Josef Siegle, and Michael Weinstein, *The Democracy Advantage: How Democracies Promote Prosperity and Peace*, New York: Routledge, 2005—both fail to distinguish between capitalist and non-capitalist (including communist!) dictatorships, or to account for the staggering performance of the East Asian capitalist non-democratic economies.

14. Fareed Zakaria, *The Future of Freedom: Illiberal Democracy at Home and Abroad*, New York: Norton, 2003.

15. Azar Gat, 'The Return of Authoritarian Great Powers', *Foreign Affairs*, 86:4 (2007), 59–69; Gat, 'Which Way is History Marching: Debating the Authoritarian Revival', *Foreign Affairs*, 88:4 (2009), 150–5; Gat, *Victorious and Vulnerable: Why Democracy Won in the 20th Century and How it is Still Imperiled*, Stanford: Hoover/Rowman & Littlefield, 2010. Making many similar points with greater breadth, and highly readable, is Martin Jacques' inadequately titled *When China Rules the World: The End of the Western World and the Birth of a New Global Order*, 2nd edn, New York: Penguin, 2012.

16. Alan Greenspan, *The Age of Turbulence*, New York: Penguin, 2007, 275.

17. Mandelbaum, *Democracy's Good Name*, 114–18.

18. Ibid., 96–100; Fukuyama, *The End of History*, chap. 27; Dahl, *On Democracy*, 173–9.

19. Merle Goldman, *From Comrade to Citizen: The Struggle for Political Rights in China*, Cambridge, MA: Harvard UP, 2005; Susan Shirk, *China: Fragile Superpower*, Oxford: Oxford UP, 2007; John Thornton, 'Long Time Coming: The Prospects for Democracy in China', *Foreign Affairs*, Jan.–Feb. 2008; James Mann, *The China Fantasy: Why Capitalism Will not Bring Democracy to China*, New York: Penguin, 2006, many arguments in which are similar to mine. A broad survey of relevant aspects can be found in Cheng Li (ed.), *China's Changing Political Landscape: Prospects for Democracy*, Washington, DC: Brookings, 2008; Jacques, *When China Rules the World*; Mark Leonard, *What Does China Think*, London: HarperCollins, 2008.

20. J. Damm and S. Thomas (eds.), *Chinese Cyberspaces: Technological Changes and Political Effects*, New York: Routledge, 2006; Johan Lagerkvist, 'Internet Ideotainment in PRC: National Responses to Cultural Globalization', *Journal of Contemporary China*, 17 (2008), 121–40; Fareed Zakaria, *The Post-American World*, New York: Norton, 2008, 83.

21. Books on the subject are now legion. See: Robert Taylor (ed.), *The Idea of Freedom in Asia and Africa*, Stanford: Stanford UP, 2002; Daniel Bell, *Beyond*

Liberal Democracy: Political Thinking for an East Asian Context, Princeton: Princeton UP, 2006; Randall Peerenboom, *China Modernizes: Threats to the West or Model for the Rest?*, Oxford: Oxford UP, 2007.

22. See, for example, Joshua Kurlantzick, *Charm Offensive: How China's Soft Power is Transforming the World*, New Haven, CT: Yale UP, 2007.

23. Freedom House, 'Freedom in the World 2015: Discarding Democracy: Return to the Iron Fist' (online); see also, Larry Diamond, 'Facing Up to the Democratic Recession', *Journal of Democracy*, 26:1 (2015), 141–55, and the other contributions to that issue.

24. Zakaria, *The Post-American World*.

25. Paul Kennedy, *The Rise and Fall of the Great Powers: Economic Change and Military Conflict from 1500 to 2000*, New York: Random House, 1987. Some significant variations in interpretation can be found in Ferguson, *The Cash Nexus*; and my own *War in Human Civilization*, 515–24.

26. No method for assessing economic power and military potential is without drawbacks. For example, GDP alone has turned out to be an inadequate measurement of power when comparing pre-industrial, agricultural societies with industrial-technological ones. Most notably, nineteenth-century China and, to a lesser degree, Russia remained giants in terms of total GNP even when their pre-industrial economies' backwardness was starkly exposed, and, with it, their military weakness and plummeting status as great powers. By contrast, GDP seems to offer a pretty good measurement of military potential with respect to players that have firmly embarked on the process of modernization. Manufacturing production was probably the most reflective of a country's military potential during the age of mass industry in the nineteenth and twentieth centuries. However, as manufacturing has gravitated to developing or second-tier developed societies, whereas both wealth and the most advanced high-technology largely remain concentrated in the top developed countries, this measurement seems to have become less representative. I offer a select variety of major measurements, partly because of these problems and partly because of different sources of data.

      Paul Bairoch, 'Europe's Gross National Product: 1800–1975', *Journal of European Economic History*, 5 (1976), 273–340; and Bairoch, 'International Industrialization Levels from 1750 to 1980', *Journal of European Economic History*, 11 (1982), 269–333, provided a seminal set of comparative historical economic statistics. He focused on the value size of countries' manufacturing output, which reflected the leading, more advanced, element of the economy during the classical industrial age. Adopted by Kennedy, *The Rise and Fall of the Great Powers*, this measurement proved to be no less remarkably representative of the great powers' relative war-waging potential during that period.

      Angus Maddison, *The World Economy: A Millennial Perspective*, Paris: OECD, 2001, has produced the most comprehensive estimates to date of historical GDP and GDP per capita. He has used purchasing power parity (PPP) to level the data. However, as Fareed Zakaria correctly notes in *The Post-American World*, nominal, rate of exchange, GDP figures seem to give a pretty straightforward picture of countries' military potential, whereas PPP values do not. As Maddison's historical estimates are invaluable, and indeed, irreplaceable, I have adjusted the PPP values by compounding a country's total GDP and GDP per capita, the latter being the most obvious and generalized indicator of economic advance. The formula multiplies a country's GDP with the square or cubic root of its GDP per capita (all for PPP figures). There might be various reasons why a root value should be used, but the fact is that it seems to best fit historical experience with respect to relative power. The range between the square and cubic root values for potential power mainly correlates with the technological intensity of the type of warfare engaged in; for example, naval and air warfare have tended to be more technologically intensive and therefore more dependent on level of development (thus tending towards the square root value) than land warfare (tending towards the cubic root value).

There are several other indexes of power, including the National Material Capabilities statistical set of the Correlates of War Project (online). This is a composite index that gives equal weight to six indicators: two industrial—iron/steel production and energy consumption; two relating to population size—general and urban; and two military—number of military personnel and military expenditure. The inclusion of the two military indicators means that the index is better at assessing existing military power and readiness at a given moment than potential power. For example, it systematically undervalues the United States during most of the past two centuries, whose actual levels of peacetime military mobilization and expenditure tended to be low compared to its rivals, while its potential mobilized power was overwhelming. In addition, the index's chosen indicators for technological advance create serious distortions outside the 'classical' industrial period (*c.*1870–1970). Energy consumption rose meteorically when steam power was introduced, much faster than the rise in military power. Thereafter it continued to grow at a far slower rate, slower than technological and military advance in general. Moreover, since the 1973 oil crisis and during the information age, the growth in energy consumption has slowed further and has even become negative in some of the most developed countries, owing to greater efficiency. A similar trajectory applies to iron and steel production, long a central indicator for a country's economic power. As with manufacturing production in general, iron and steel production has been declining in developed countries during the information age and has become a mark of developing, second-rank economies. Level of urbanization, too, reaches a plateau after industrialization and ceases to grow any further. In conclusion, the National Material Capabilities index is not generalized enough to take account of changing historical conditions and is highly distorting in many cases.

A. Organski and Jacek Kugler, in *The War Ledger*, Chicago: U. of Chicago, 1980, have devised a measurement that combines GNP with the government's extraction share. On the whole, this is a good rough measurement, because both economic surplus and the state extraction capability increase with modernization.

27. My calculations of infrastructural power are based on the data in Maddison, *The World Economy*, except for 1938 (unavailable in Maddison), where the data are derived from Mark Harrison (ed.), *The Economies of World War II: Six Great Powers in International Comparison*, Cambridge: Cambridge UP, 1998, 3, 7.

28. Based on the data in the *CIA World Factbook* (online).

29. See, for example, Nicholas Eberstadt, 'The Demographic Future', *Foreign Affairs*, 89:6 (Nov. 2010), 54–64.

30. Cf. Michael Beckley, 'China's Century? Why America's Edge Will Endure', *International Security*, 36:3 (2011–12), 41–78, and Kagan, *The World America Made*, 105–7. Both are very intelligently argued, but perhaps not sufficiently appreciative of the significance of future trends. See also Joseph Nye, 'The Future of American Power', *Foreign Affairs*, 89:6 (Nov. 2010), 2–12.

31. United States Department of Agriculture, Economic Research Service, 'Real GDP (2010 dollars) Projections', and 'Real Per Capita GDP (2010 dollars) Projections' (online).

32. Bairoch, 'International Industrialization Levels'.

33. Sam Perlo-Freeman and Carina Solmirano, 'Trends in World Military Expenditure, 2013', Solna, Sweden: The Stockholm International Peace Research Institute (SIPRI), April 2014, 2. The International Institute for Strategic Studies, London's *Military Balance 2015*, 'Top 15 Defence Budgets 2014', basically portrays the same picture, with slight variations.

34. Data on conflicts from: Uppsala University's Battle-Related Deaths data set; 'List of Ongoing Armed Conflicts', Wikipedia; 'Modern Conflicts Table', Political Economy Research Institute, University of Amherst; Joshua Goldstein, 'Wars in Progress', July 2014, International Relations.com (all online). GDP per capita (nominal) from the United Nations, Statistics Division, 'National Accounts, Main Aggregates Database' (online).

35. For similar and other explanations see: Håvard Hegre, Joakim Karlsen, Håvard Mokleiv Nygård, Håvard Strand, and Henrik Urdal, 'Predicting Armed Conflict, 2010–2050', *International Studies Quarterly*, 57 (2013), 250–70; James Fearon and David Laitin, 'Ethnicity, Insurgency, and Civil War', *The American Political Science Review*, 97:1 (Feb. 2003), 75–90; Nicolas Berman, Mathieu Couttenier, Dominic Rohner, and Mathias Thoenig, 'This Mine is Mine! How Minerals Fuel Conflicts in Africa', Oxford Centre for the Analysis of Resource Rich Economies, Research Paper 141 (online).

36. John Mueller, *The Remnants of War*, Ithaca, NY: Cornell UP, 2007.

37. See Chapter 6, note 68 and adjacent text.

38. Milton Leitenberg, *Death in Wars and Conflicts in the 20th Century*, Cornell University Peace Studies Program, Occasional Paper 29, 2006, 70–6; Timothy Besley and Torsten Persson, *Pillars of Prosperity: The Political Economics of Development Clusters*, Princeton: Princeton UP, 2011.

39. John Jackson, *The World Trading System*, Cambridge, MA: MIT, 1997, 74.

40. Richard Rosecrance, *The Rise of the Virtual State*, New York: Basic Books, 1999, 37; Robert Gilpin with Jean Gilpin, *The Challenge of Global Capitalism: The World Economy in the 21st Century*, Princeton: Princeton UP, 2000, 20–3.

41. McKinsey Global Institute, 'Global Flows in a Digital Age: How Trade, Finance, People, and Data Connect the World Economy', 2014, 4–5, 88 (online).

42. Cf. Thomas Christensen, 'Fostering Stability or Creating a Monster? The Rise of China and US Policy toward East Asia', *International Security*, 31:1 (2006), 81–126.

43. Data collected and compiled from the following sources (all online): US Census Bureau, 'US Trade: Top Trading Partners—Total Trade, Exports, Imports', Dec. 2012; The European Commission, Directorate General for Trade, 'Top Trading Partners 2013'; World Trade Organization, 'Trade Profiles by Country'; *The CIA World Factbook 2013*, Country Comparison: Stock of Direct Foreign Investment.

44. McKinsey, 'Global Flows in a Digital Age', 4–5; World Trade Organization, 'Modest Trade Recovery to Continue in 2015 and 2016 Following Three Years of Weak Expansion', Press release, 14 April 2015 (online).

45. John Ikenberry, 'The Future of the Liberal World Order: Internationalism After America', *Foreign Affairs* (May–June 2011); Ikenberry, *Liberal Leviathan: The Origins, Crisis, and Transformation of the American World Order*, Princeton: Princeton UP, 2011.

46. Andrew Nathan, 'China's Challenge', *Journal of Democracy*, 26:1 (2015), 156–70, quotation from 156.

47. Sketching possible scenarios and stressing that it is impossible to know which of them will eventually materialize are: Aaron Friedberg, 'The Future of U.S.–China Relations: Is Conflict Inevitable?', *International Security*, 30:2 (2005), 7–45; Friedberg, *The Contest for Supremacy: China, America, and the Struggle for Supremacy in Asia*, New York: Norton, 2011 (the most comprehensive and balanced review to date); Legro Jeffrey, 'What China Will Want: The Future Intentions of a Rising Power', *Perspective on Politics*, 5:3 (2007), 515–34; Randall Schweller and Xiaoyo Pu, 'After Unipolarity: China's Visions of International Order in an Era of U.S. Decline', *International Security*, 36:1 (2011), 41–72; Henry Kissinger, *On China*, New York: Penguin, 2011. Scholar and media commentator Fareed Zakaria, who initially cited Ikenberry with approval: 'Obama Needs to Lead with Feeling', *The Washington Post*, 8 May 2014, has become more aware of the other side of the coin: 'China's Growing Clout', *The Washington Post*, 13 Nov. 2014, and 'With an Absent United States China Marches On', *The Washington Post*, 2 July 2015. Edward Steinfeld, *Playing Our Game: Why China's Economic Rise Doesn't Threaten the West*, Oxford: Oxford UP, 2010, is generally optimistic, though the sensationalist title poorly reflects the book's actual content. Yong Deng, *China's Struggle for Status: The Realignment of International Relations*, Cambridge: Cambridge UP, 2008, and David Shambaugh, *China Goes Global: The Partial Power*, Oxford: Oxford UP, 2013, are useful surveys.

48. World Trade Organization, 'Trade Profiles by Country'; US Census Bureau, 'Top Trading Partners—December 2013'; European Commission, Directorate-General for Energy, 'Registration of Crude Oil Imports and Deliveries in the European Union, 1-12/2013'; European Commission, 'Quarterly Reports on European Gas Markets' (2014); Ralf Dickel et al., 'Reducing European Dependence on Russian Gas', Oxford Institute for Energy Studies (2014); all online.

49. A recent exposition of this subject is Lilia Shevtsova, 'Forward to the Past in Russia', *Journal of Democracy*, 26:2 (2015), 22–36.

50. The World Bank, 'Urban Population (% of Total)'; Wikipedia, 'Urbanization by Country' (both online).

51. The CIA, 'A Look at International Labor and Unemployment' (online).

52. United Nations, *World Population Prospects: The 2000 Revision*, New York: UN, 2001; United Nations, *The 2012 Revision*, New York: UN, 2013, Table S.8.

53. The World Bank, 'Fertility Rates, Total (Births per Woman)' (online); A. Korotayev et al., 'A Trap at the Escape from the Trap? Demographic-Structural Factors of Political Instability in Modern Africa and West Asia', *Cliodynamics*, 2:2 (2011), 1–28.

54. Cited by *The Economist*, 15 Aug. 2015, 49.

55. The CIA, 'The World Factbook: Sex Ratio' (online).

56. McKinsey, 'Global Flows in a Digital Age'; Zakaria, *The Post-American World*, 83.

57. Scott D. Sagan (against) and Kenneth N. Waltz (for), *The Spread of Nuclear Weapons*, New York: Norton, 1999; references to the terrorist nuclear threat have been added in the second edition (2003), 126–30, 159–66. In a series of articles in *The Wall Street Journal* since 2007, George Shultz, William Perry, Henry Kissinger, and Sam Nunn have underlined the dangers of increased pro-liferation, the differences from the Cold War, and the threat of unconventional terrorism. Also, a good, balanced treatment is Devin Hagertly, *The Consequences of Nuclear Proliferation*, Cambridge, MA: MIT Press, 1998.

58. Philip Cohen, 'A Terrifying Power', *New Scientist*, 30 Jan. 1999, 10; Rachel Nowak, 'Disaster in the Making', *New Scientist*, 13 Jan. 2001, 4–5; Carina Dennis, 'The Bugs of War', *Nature*, 17 May 2001, 232–5; S. Drell, A. Sofaer, and G. Wilson (eds.), *The New Terror: Facing the Threat of Biological and Chemical Weapons*, Stanford: Hoover Institution, 1999. Note that all of these and many of the other works cited in this chapter were written before, and were unaffected by, the 'scare' of 9/11.

59. Nadine Gurr and Benjamin Cole, *The New Face of Terrorism: Threats from Weapons of Mass Destruction*, London: Tauris, 2000; anonymous scientist cited by Anne Applebaum, 'The Next Plague', *The Washington Post*, 18 Feb. 2004; Spencer Hsu, 'Modest Gains against Ever-Present Bioterrorism Threat', *The Washington Post*, 3 Aug. 2008.

60. David Kaplan, 'Aum Shinrikyo', in J. Tucker (ed.), *Toxic Terror: Assessing Terrorist Use of Chemical and Biological Weapons*, Cambridge, MA: MIT Press, 2000, chap. 12; Gurr and Cole, *New Face of Terrorism*, 51.

61. Tara O'Toole, Mair Michael, and Thomas Inglesby, 'Shining Light on "Dark Winter"', *Clinical Infectious Diseases*, 34:7 (2002), 972–83.

62. A thorough critique is offered by Milton Leitenberg, in *Assessing the Biological Weapons and Bioterrorism Threat*, Carlisle, PA: The US Army War College Strategic Studies Institute, 2005; Leitenberg, 'Assessing the Threat of Bioterrorism', in Benjamin H. Friedman et al. (eds.), *Terrorizing Ourselves*, Washington, DC: CATO Institute, 2010, 161–83.

63. John Mueller, *Overblown: How Politicians and the Terrorism Industry Inflate National Security Threats, and Why We Believe Them*, New York: Free Press, 2006; also Mueller, *Atomic Obsession: Nuclear Alarmism from Hiroshima to Al-Qaeda*, New York: Oxford UP, 2010.

64. Hsu, 'Modest Gains'.

65. See also John Parachini's 'Putting WMD Terror into Perspective', *Washington Quarterly*, 26:4 (2003), 37–50. More worrisome is Michael Levi's comprehensive and balanced *On Nuclear Terror*, Cambridge, MA: Harvard UP, 2007.

66. Mueller, *Overblown*, 20. A well-informed critique of the threat of bioterror is Leitenberg, *Assessing the Biological Weapons and Bioterrorism Threat*; and Leitenberg, 'Assessing the Threat of Bioterrorism'.

67. David Ignatius, 'Portents of a Nuclear Al-Qaeda', *The Washington Post*, 18 Oct. 2007.

68. For example, a computer captured in Syria and belonging to a Tunisian chemistry student who had joined the organization revealed, among a large collection of terrorist instruction material, also a manual for how to use bubonic plague as a weapon. Also in the computer was a religious fatwa authorizing the use of WMD against infidels: *Foreign Policy*, 28 Aug. 2014.

69. United States Mission to the United Nations, 4 Sept. 2014 (online).

70. *The Spectator*, 30 Sept. 2014.

71. Graham Allison, *Nuclear Terrorism: The Ultimate Preventable Catastrophe*, New York: Times Books, 2004; Levi, *On Nuclear Terror*; and more generally Philip Bobbitt, *Terror and Consent: The Wars for the Twenty-First Century*, New York: Knopf, 2008.

72. *The Independent*, 16 March 2009.

73. Obama's Nobel Peace Prize Speech, 10 Dec. 2009 (online).

Illustration Credits

140	Bundesarchiv Bild 183-B21845. Photo: Wahner
141	David Turnley/Corbis/VCG/Getty Images
159	Max Roser, OurWorldInData.org (based on data from Angus Maddison)
160–161	Meir Moalem
181	THE AGE/Fairfax Media/Getty Images
212	United Nations Accounts Main Aggregates Database, value added by economic activity, at current prices—US dollars.
Between 214 and 215	Max Roser, OurWorldInData.org (based on data from Clio Infra)
Between 228 and 229	Arno Tausch, based on Ronald Inglehart's World Values Survey
233 left	Photofest/United Artists
233 right	Getty/Stringer

The publisher and author apologize for any errors or omissions in the above list. If contacted they will be pleased to rectify these at the earliest opportunity.

Index